ALSO BY WILLIAM J. CROTTY

Political Reform and the American Experiment

DECISION FOR THE DEMOCRATS

Reforming the Party Structure

WILLIAM J. CROTTY

THE JOHNS HOPKINS UNIVERSITY PRESS

BALTIMORE AND LONDON

The Johns Hopkins University Press, Baltimore, Maryland 21218
The Johns Hopkins Press Ltd., London

Library of Congress Catalog Card Number 77–16725
ISBN 0–8018–2050–2
Library of Congress Cataloging in Publication data will be found on the last printed
page of this book.

CONTENTS

BEGINNING WITH the fateful Democratic National Convention of 1968 and ending, at least in its initial phase, with the McGovern candidacy in 1972 and the backlash that followed, the Democratic party underwent an experimentation with reform unequaled in this nation's history.

This book is about that enormously creative time in American politics. It narrates the reform movement and its generative forces, its contributions, and its problems. The focus is primarily on the serious attempts at major institutional change put forward by the two reform committees instituted by the Democrats: the Commission on Party Structure and Delegate Selection (the McGovern-Fraser Commission) and its less well known companion, the Commission on Rules (the O'Hara Commission). The McGovern-Fraser Commission revolutionized the presidential nomination system by introducing previously unheard-of due process guarantees backed by the authority of national party law and attempting to force an equitable representation of minority groups in party affairs. The O'Hara Commission directed its energies to modernizing a shopworn but still highly essential institution, the national nominating convention. The extent to which these reform bodies succeeded and the difficulties they encountered speaks to the nature of political institutions and their contributions to a functioning democratic society in the last third of the twentieth century.

A book of this nature is difficult to write. Fortunately there were a number of factors working in my favor. I was awarded an American Political Science Association Fellowship, which permitted a stay in Washington and first-hand experience with the reform movement. I appreciate the courtesies extended me by Dr. Evron Kirkpatrick, Executive Director of the American Political Science Association, and members of the national headquarters staff: Earl Baker, Walter Beach, and Thomas Mann. Many people gave of their time and knowledge. I cannot name them all, but I can thank some of those who were most consistently helpful: Andrew J. Valuchek, Sheila Hixson, William Welsh, Ken Bode, Carol Casey, Monica Borkowski,

Joseph Brady, and, of course, Robert W. Nelson, Staff Director of the McGovern-Fraser Commission, whose talents and skills made a singularly distinctive contribution to the reform movement. I am grateful to the two national chairmen of the Democratic party whom I had the opportunity to observe in office, then-Senator Fred R. Harris and long-time party leader Lawrence F. O'Brien—two men quite different in temperament and approach to their job, but without whom meaningful party improvements would not have been possible.

I appreciate the help of all those at The Johns Hopkins University Press who contributed so ably to the publication of this book. I am particularly thankful to Henry Y. K. Tom, the Press' Social Sciences Editor, for his expert advice and assistance and to Jacqueline Wehmueller, Barbara Kraft, and Julie Zignego, who skillfully edited the final text.

Finally, I should add a note on my own views, which are reflected in this book and in my desire to become involved in what I believe to have been a uniquely significant enterprise. I had the good fortune to serve as a consultant to both the McGovern-Fraser Commission and the O'Hara Commission (and also, as it turned out, to the Charter—or Sanford—Commission, an outgrowth of the original two and treated in passing in this book). I tend to place a high priority on openness, participation, and democratic procedural guarantees in all forms of public business. My natural inclinations, then, are to favor those who give these objectives their highest priority.

DECISION FOR THE DEMOCRATS

ONE

Prelude
to Reform

THE PRESIDENTIAL election year of 1968 turned out to be a bad year. The aura of "Camelot" that began the decade had become in its later years a memory, as remote in its own way as the legendary times of King Arthur. As the years passed the excitement and high hopes of the early sixties gave way to a spiritual exhaustion that fed the bitterness and, all too often, the blind violence that was characteristic of the later years.

Symbolic of this period was a man whose acrimonious career extended back to 1946, encompassing the whole of the postwar era; a man who had been the losing candidate in a contest for the presidency in the decade's very first year; a man whose conduct while in office established a new low for a public stewardship. For those alarmed by the governmental suppression evident during the second half of the sixties, the next decade's early years were to prove even more upsetting.

Bleak as things were, some good did emerge from the rubble. Even the chaos that was the Chicago convention of 1968 yielded some benefits. The honest effort to reevaluate and then democratically open leadership selection processes—the "reform movement" as it was called—was the biggest plus, one with enormous significance for the conduct of American politics in the future.

It is important to place the events of 1968 in perspective, to understand what happened and why. It is equally important to recognize the intensity of feelings unleashed by the reform movement. The emotions generated led, on the one hand, to a determination by a loose coalition of reformers to reshape the entire nature of a political party. Particular attention was given to the recasting of the party's presidential nominating procedures, easily the party's most important concern. On the other hand, an opposition that included the elements that controlled the party until 1968—party regulars, elective officeholders, big-city machines, organized labor, and a profusion of other groups and individuals with a fixed investment in the status quo—reacted belatedly, but stormily, to reform. The political war

1

that followed shook the party to its roots. Eventually the reformers prevailed; it is difficult to say what the consequences will be for the future of the Democratic party, the two-party system, and for American democratic institutions, although some considerations can be put forth.

A national political party was transformed. The reforms were carried out under the direct supervision of the party and were enforced with whatever muscle it could command. Such occurrences are rare. During the reforms the party's institutional processes for leadership selection and for representation of social groups were transformed. A new political party was engineered.

The impact of the events of 1968 and the years following has been, by any calculation, enormous. It has also been unique. The rest of this book tells the story of the Democratic experience with reform that found birth in the Chicago convention of 1968.

A Stormy Background to Reform

The stage was set in Chicago for a major series of confrontations whose scope and intensity was impossible to imagine. The shock impact on the average citizen of what was to come was difficult to calculate, although the issues of the convention were to continue as an underlying force in American politics for years.

The events that were ignited at the Chicago convention had smoldered for some time. The listless fifties surrendered to an era of change and expansion best captured, unfortunately, in the divisiveness of the tumultuous years beginning in 1963. The catchwords of the period tell its story: the cities that burned—Detroit, Newark, Washington; the leaders who evoked the strongest reactions—John and Robert Kennedy, Martin Luther King, Barry Goldwater, George Wallace, Ronald Reagan; the student rebellions and campus uprisings at Columbia, Berkeley, Wisconsin, and their tragic culmination at Kent State and Jackson State; Viet Nam, perhaps the force unloosing all others; the shock of assassinations—the Kennedys, King, Evers, and the others; Salisbury, Maryland; the Kerner and Warren commissions; Black Power; Catonsville; the Berrigans; Stokely Carmichael; Eugene McCarthy. The government appeared unresponsive to demands, unable to deal effectively with a constantly volatile and continually trying internal situation, and, worst of all, seemed to think of itself as unaccountable to the people it presumed to serve. The results were predictable: disappointment became intense anger for many and cultivated apathy for others. Loss of faith in political institutions and leaders abounded. Cynicism and alienation seemed to characterize a country and a people that had lost their way. The Chicago convention of 1968 represented a vivid climax to a highly troubled era.

The election year of 1968 did an unsettled decade proud. Eugene Mc-

Carthy fired the opening guns of the presidential campaign a full year before the November vote. McCarthy's task—unseating an incumbent president by denying him his own party's nomination—was universally agreed to be suicidal. It simply was not how things worked. Should an incumbent desire it, a political party, virtually disregarding the circumstances, will reward him with renomination. Not doing so passes judgment on the party's own record during the previous four years. The classic example is Herbert Hoover. Although he was widely regarded by the public as the architect of the Great Depression, his party dutifully put him forward for reelection. Disaster ensued. The political patterns forged during the 1932 election determined both parties' coalitions for the next generation.

The merits of an incumbent president do not completely explain his party's willingness to renominate him. A president can reward or punish in an incredible variety of ways; courting his ill will can be extremely costly. A president controls the national party machinery, such as it is. A president has virtually unchallenged power to manage a convention's proceedings, as Richard Nixon vividly and repeatedly illustrated in 1972. His appointed representative, the national chairman, runs the convention and makes (in concert with a submissive national committee) its most sensitive decisions, such as location, size, and principal officers. State and local political figures of consequence in selecting, as well as leading delegations, are indebted to a reigning president for several reasons, not least among which is that he was probably their choice four years earlier. Challenge is frowned upon. More than this, the "old politics" placed a heavy stress on "loyalty" to the individual; questioning an incumbent's qualities or policies represented the height of ingratitude and ignorance as to how the "game is played."

If these facts were not troublesome enough, McCarthy, a quiet senator from Minnesota, was further handicapped by commanding no national following and choosing to challenge Johnson on the basis of the conduct of a little-understood war in far-off southeast Asia. Wars bring out an ingrained sense of patriotism. The challenge was not only impolitic, to some it was treasonous, a point they (and, less directly, the administration) repeatedly attempted to make. Successful challenges have better chances if based on domestic economic duress, not something as exotic as an Indo-China war. Nonetheless, 1968 was the year of the unexpected, and for McCarthy the unimaginable occurred early.

The early-bird New Hampshire primary established McCarthy, quite unexpectedly, as a credible candidate. It did more. It demonstrated a fundamental disaffection with Lyndon Johnson's leadership. Opposition was no longer hopeless. Within days Robert Kennedy entered the contest for the Democratic nomination, and just prior to his humiliating defeat in the Wisconsin primary, President Johnson declined to seek renomination.

The president's emotional withdrawal from the race preceded another of the decade's recurring horrors: assassination. This time the victim was the Reverend Martin Luther King, Jr., the nation's leading black civil-rights advocate. King was killed in Memphis by a white racist, James Earl Ray. Riots ensued in an estimated one hundred cities, and major outbreaks stunned Washington, D.C., Chicago, and Baltimore (the latter helped establish nationally one Spiro Agnew, the little-known governor of Maryland, as a hard-liner on race and law and order, campaign issues-to-be). The new racial turmoil and the police's hard-nosed reaction to the upheaval (characterized by Chicago's Mayor Daley's "shoot to kill" order) were grafted onto an electorate already torn by more conventional racial splits, pro- and anti-Wallace sentiments, and an unpopular war; the life-style divisions were characterized by the "hard-hat" (laborers) and student confrontations and by the elements supporting and condemning the rash of demonstrations against authority that had marked the previous several years. The bizarre search for Ray and the totally unsatisfactory trial that resulted added other dimensions to an already overly troubled national psyche.

On 27 April, a full twenty-eight days after Johnson's declaration of noncandidacy, Vice President Hubert Humphrey, the heir apparent, announced his intention of seeking the presidency. The timing of Humphrey's entrance was carefully calculated to avoid the filing dates for most of the primaries. His intent was to rely on the party pros and the union leaders, the "old politics" as they came to be called, to deliver the nomination to him; this was a strategy that, while successful, gave (correctly) the appearance that Humphrey was ignoring the opportunity to take his case to the people through the primaries. This action added to the public's mounting frustration with politics and political procedures.

Robert Kennedy gradually emerged as the most promising candidate of the insurgents, capturing major victories in Indiana and Nebraska. After suffering defeat in Oregon, Kennedy and McCarthy, with a stand-in Humphrey slate led by the state's attorney general thrown in for good measure, squared off in the crucial winner-take-all California primary, the last and most important of encounters. Kennedy won, but before he could begin to organize the nonprimary delegations and plan his convention strategy, in fact before the precise dimensions of his success could settle in, Robert Kennedy, the most formidable of the challengers, was assassinated. A twenty-year-old Jordanian immigrant, Sirhan Sirhan, added another tragedy to a year that claimed more than its share.

The unpredictable McCarthy proved unable to convert the old-line party leadership, and the entrance of Senator George McGovern into the race a meager three weeks before the convention opened amounted to little more than a gesture. Humphrey won the nomination handily on the first ballot with a whopping 1,761¾ votes to McCarthy's 601 and McGovern's

146½ (with another 99¾ scattered among six minor candidates). The victory came in a badly shaken and thoroughly aroused convention.

The general election campaign proved anticlimactic. Richard Nixon, crowning a six-year comeback effort from the depths of 1960 and 1962, easily claimed the Republican party's nomination, overwhelming muted and inept opposition from an assortment of challengers (Romney, Reagan, Rockefeller). Nixon ran a bland campaign. Identifying with a series of supply-your-own-meaning slogans ("bringing people together," "winning the peace," "law and order"), he intended to offend no potential voter and to take advantage of the Democrats' disarray. He succeeded, but barely.

Typically, Humphrey's campaign was poorly organized. It lacked a clear focus, especially on the decisive Viet Nam question, until the Salt Lake City speech in late September, which redefined his position as more flexible than that of the current administration. Democrats only belatedly responded to the cues. The damage had been done. The weight of the convention, the deep split within the party, and an unpopular president and administration, in conjunction with a well-financed and trouble-free opposition, proved to be too much to overcome. Rallying, Humphrey came close in the popular vote, a remarkable achievement that was not fully believed until the election became history. Ultimately, however, the Democratic candidate did not have the time (squandered foolishly during the summer months), the personal decisiveness, or the financial resources to swing the electoral college outcome his way. George Wallace, running as the third-party candidate of his own American Independent party, faded as election day drew near, but he still captured a respectable 13 percent of the vote. Each of these events came to bear on the reform effort that followed.

The year 1968 seemed predestined for sorrow. It suffered from the accumulated grievances of the preceding years, which were exacerbated by two assassinations, riots, and an administration hellbent on pursuing a major war while denying that this was its intent. It experienced a government out-of-touch with its public and neglectful, to the point of being scornful, of any and all dissent from its policies, and it witnessed a frustration born of attempting a challenge through conventional means destined to be mocked by a system unresponsive at best, closed at worst, to its pressures. The result was the explosions that shook the nation during the Chicago convention.

The "why" of Chicago is relatively easy to document. Far more difficult is tracing and evaluating the response of the political parties. The reaction of the parties, and especially the Democratic party, to the upheavals was unprecedented by any standard: it resulted in nothing less than an attempt to reshape fundamental structural mechanisms to better accommodate a diversity of views, to provide a fully representative and "open" convention, and to modernize, in line with democratic principles, procedures notoriously unreceptive to change. Whether these ambitious goals were achieved, and at what price, is another story. It is possible, though, that the reforms emanating from the convention are of far greater substantive importance than anything to emerge from that fateful election year.

The attempt of the Democratic party to become more representative of and accountable to its constituency represents the balance of this book. The reform grew from the pain of the 1968 convention. In order to begin to understand the extraordinary developments that took place, it is first necessary to know something of the sorrow as well as the achievements of those four days in August.

The Democratic Convention

"When a convention is convened, we are living in another country,"[1] or so contends former Senator Eugene McCarthy with particular reference to the Chicago convention of 1968. It would have been more agreeable and more understandable if the events that took place in Chicago in August 1968 had occurred in some other country. Unfortunately this was not the case; the soul-searching and rationalizations that followed the convention never totally erased the images transmitted to millions of Americans during these four fateful days.

The convention can be viewed on two levels. First, there were the internal dynamics of the convention itself, consisting of the normal give-and-take of political exchange combined with several factors of consequence (the oppressive security, the pummeling of individual newsmen, the arrogance and ineptitude of major convention leaders, and the near-hysteria that characterized some of the sessions). Secondly, and of far greater significance, there were the street demonstrations and the police responses, carried by the media to every home with a television set, which gave a bizarre, otherworldly twist to what the Democrats were attempting to accomplish inside the convention hall. In reality, the two worlds seldom overlapped. When they did, it was in the general mood of intolerance and anger that pervaded the entire convention period. The repressiveness of official actions was evident in the streets and in the convention itself; the anger of participants was seen in the several highly dramatic incidents of direct consequence to the proceedings of the convention. Most notable was Senator Abraham Ribicoff's speech nominating George McGovern for the presidency. In this speech he made explicit reference to the "Gestapo" tactics outside, evoking in return (for television watchers everywhere) profane utterances from Mayor Daley and his entourage, which was sitting immediately in front of the speaker's rostrum.

The convention was held in Chicago as a tribute to Daley and his position of eminence within party councils. The convention did not honor the mayor, as intended, but it did illustrate his enormous power. The mayor seemed to be everywhere, directing everything: frantic screams were showered on friend and foe alike, and were dutifully recorded by the ubiquitous television cameras; Speaker Carl Albert (chairman of the convention) refused to allow Wisconsin delegate Donald Peterson's motion for adjournment during one uproarious session until notified by Daley (again, captured by television) to curtail the proceedings; Daley's forlorn-looking patronage workers jammed into the visitor's galleries with their signs and chants of "We Love Dick Daley," appearing "spontaneously" when the good mayor seemed to be taking a particularly ferocious buffeting from the press; the heavy-handed use of police and Andy Frain ushers to maintain "order" was also, inevitably, Daley's doing. Daley's hand appeared even in the rides in chartered buses delegates took to the convention hall (walking to the hall was prohibited by the police for fear it would lead to demonstrations). The mayor had his city workers clean the streets designated for access to the Chicago Amphitheatre and erect gaily painted fences in slum areas to hide the filth, and he did all this in the interest of improving the Windy City's image. The absurd and the frightening mixed with regularity, overshadowing the normal business of politics and transforming Daley, in the minds of many, into the symbol of all that was bad with a party, a political process, and a nation. The association was personalized, and thus conveniently and all too simply came to stand for the real ills underlying a party and a social order under stress. Nonetheless, it also came to effect the reform effort that followed.

The Streets

Alexander Pope's view that politics is the madness of many for the gain of a few was shared by large numbers of people involved in the events of Chicago during convention week. The pressures that culminated there had been building for a long time. Many party supporters believed they had been frozen out of the Democratic party's representational and decision-making processes. The claim that what had transpired in 1968 was no different from the events of any other election year hardly alleviated their anger. They came to Chicago determined to do whatever necessary to influence the party, and the country, to see things from their perspective. The convention witnessed the culmination of their outrage. The police and city authorities unwittingly did their best to whip up the frenzy.

The weeks preceding the convention were filled with rumors of things to come. Chicago was to be invaded by an army of hippies, yippies, dissenters against the war, student malcontents, pacifists, free-lovers, leftists of all descriptions; in short, Abbie Hoffman writ large. A "festival of life" was planned for the public park, including (according to whisperings) hard drugs, fornication, rock music, and the other staples of the "counterculture." Schemes reported ranged from a "Yippie Olympics" and an "unbirthday party" for Lyndon Johnson to attacks designed to disrupt the convention and a plan to place LSD in the city's drinking water supply.

The city braced itself for the worst. The city fathers chose to believe the most extreme of the rumors, and they pledged themselves to meet any possible disruptions with as much force as needed. The authorities in Chicago would "show who was boss." City officials took a hard line with representatives of the incoming hordes, refusing to relax city ordinances as to the use of the parks, failing to provide adequate alternative sites for rallies, closing the streets to marchers (including delegates attending the convention), and enforcing the letter of the law, regardless of the risks to civil order and human well-being. To complicate matters, the city experienced extraordinarily hot and humid weather as well as the inconveniences posed by the many concurrent strikes in progress. The mood was ugly. The police department, a department constantly riddled by accusations of corruption and brutality, was unprepared psychologically or professionally for what it was to face. As the week wore on, its restraint snapped. Violence was inevitable, and it came with a vengeance.

About five thousand uninvited people did arrive in the city, considerably fewer than anticipated. They did seek to use the parks along Lake Michigan for living purposes; they did nominate a live pig for president; they did frequent the parks "after hours"; they did verbally abuse the police; they did say provocative and disrespectful things; they did tear down the American flag; they did conduct incessant rallies and rock performances; and they did follow their peculiar life-styles—all of which the city and its officials found infuriating.

On the Saturday preceding Monday's convention opening, the police cleared everyone from Lincoln Park, an area used to coordinate dissident activities and practice the highly publicized "washoi," a Japanese human-wave tactic employed in demonstrations. People spilled over into the streets, police cars were stoned, and eleven arrests were made. Sunday's incidents took on an even uglier tone, a harbinger of things to come. Some people were clubbed and several were arrested in a small afternoon confrontation; a pocket of policemen was surrounded and taunted by a crowd and, after receiving reinforcements and removing their identification tags, the patrolmen rushed and beat those around them, severely injuring some. A full contingent of policemen cleared the park in the evening, utilizing batons and tear gas indiscriminately. In the actions that followed, both within the parks and in the streets leading away from them, reporters and cameramen were also beaten, establishing a pattern for later developments. Monday saw many incidents of police-demonstrator confrontations on the streets and in the parks, with the now-familiar rocks, clubs, epithets, and tear gas in full display. The increasingly violent battles continued Tuesday, when the National Guard was called in to supplement the police.

Wednesday witnessed the culmination of the violence. In addition to the now-expected skirmishes, a major showdown took place between three hundred policemen and an estimated forty-five hundred demonstrators in front of the Conrad Hilton Hotel on Michigan Avenue. Clubbings, macings, arrests, rocks, screams, tear gas, and blood filled the night, products of a police attempt to clear the intersection. Once the main body of protestors was dispersed, the police charged down side streets, through the parks, and even into the lobby and the bar of the Hilton, pushing, kicking, and clubbing as they went. The violence continued throughout the night. The mad scene was captured by mobile television units despite Daley's attempts to restrict their movement. The ugly scenes of violent confrontations in a major American city appeared on the nation's home screens just as Humphrey neared victory in the presidential roll call.

On Thursday the first of many reactions set in.[2] The media in particular were incensed. Mayor Daley and the police went on the defensive. Still aggressive, an aroused Daley appeared unexpectedly in the Columbia Broadcasting System television booth immediately prior to the opening of the last session of the convention and told a CBS audience, and an unnerved Walter Cronkite, that the mob violence had been caused by "outsiders." The mayor went on to laud the police actions as heroic; to recount the vile acts (real or imagined) of the protestors; and to reveal for the first time that his own life (allegedly) had even been threatened. In the years that followed, Daley never changed either his arguments or his views. Serenaded by Chicago's patronage workers in the convention galleries, the sullen and exhausted delegates concluded their business by listening to the acceptance speeches of their duly chosen presidential and vice-presidential nominees.

Unfortunately, the violence was not yet over. One more major incident was to take place. Early Friday morning (five o'clock) the police, believing themselves to be harassed by people from a suite of rooms on the fifth floor of the Hilton, cleared the area, which was reserved for McCarthy workers. The result was again screams, beatings, and hysteria, a ritual that did not end until McCarthy, aroused from his sleep, came to the hotel lobby and demanded to see the police official in charge. When none appeared, he sent the campaign workers back to their rooms. On this note, the remaining conventioneers straggled home.

Overall the events of Chicago, in both the streets and the convention hall, went well beyond one party, one city, or one election. To those concerned with the operations of democratic institutions, the entire affair represented an odious display of unbridled power. For many others (the majority, it would seem) the actions in the streets and halls demonstrated how alienated from basic American values the demonstrators and their supporters had become, and represented an implicit threat to a stable

political order. Either way the Democratic party stood to reap an unwanted harvest in the months to come.

The Convention Responds

Eugene McCarthy's observation rings true: Conventions are a world
unto themselves, removed in perspective and operations from the world
around them. Throughout the sixties, those who contemplated participation in demonstrations or who resisted government policy were exhorted to
"give the system a chance." When prospective dissidents did "work within
the system," they found the system unresponsive. Worse, many discovered
it to be basically undemocratic, invulnerable, they felt, to every effort to
effect basic change. Containing no ground rules, few entry points, and no
procedural guarantees, the "system," many came to believe, constituted a
sham, a convenient front understood by few, and put forward by those in
positions of influence to preserve their control.

Such charges were not without foundation. The encounters with party
operations represented a particularly bitter lesson to the suburban housewives, young lawyers, independent businessmen, college youths, and
blacks drawn to the party as the arena in which to fight out their controversies, and, they hoped, through which they could change the course of
national policy. Despite the problems, the commitments made by these
groups had led them to Chicago and a potentially receptive hearing of their
complaints by the assembled national party. The emphasis was on procedural adjudication of seemingly remote institutional concerns that had,
nevertheless, broad representational dimensions. The specific focus centered on the Credentials Committee of the convention, the body charged
with resolving any delegate selection controversies.

Since 1948 the Credentials Committee of the Democratic party had
become the focal point for debating the question of black representation in
party politics. The problem had been resolved through a little-publicized
side action of the 1964 convention. As part of the compromise forced by
the Mississippi Freedom Democratic party, a Special Equal Rights Committee under Governor David Lawrence of Pennsylvania (and later, on
Lawrence's death, Governor Richard Hughes of New Jersey) was established to resolve the difficulty by the time of the next convention. The
Hughes Commission, as it was called, promulgated a series of "six basic
elements" that were strikingly similar to the more elaborate McGovern-
Fraser guidelines that followed. For the moment, though, the antidiscrimination rules clarified the situation: the burden was placed on the state
delegations challenged to show that their procedures were open to all,
regardless of race. Race per se was to be removed as a central point of
contention in delegate selection controversies. The party's position was
unusually straightforward, and the selection of Richard Hughes as creden-

tials chairman should have removed any doubts that might have remained that the new antidiscrimination guidelines would be strictly enforced.

Given the tough rules and the new firmness in applying them, it could be expected that the South would be well represented among the challenged delegations. And it was. Mississippi, Texas, Georgia, Alabama, North Carolina, and Tennessee were challenged in whole or in part on the basis of racial discrimination. What made the 1968 Credentials Committee hearings unusual, however, were the unprecedented number of challenges (seventeen involving fifteen states), the appearance of many nonsouthern states among those questioned, and the scope of the indictments leveled against the contested delegations. Delegate selection practices in such northern strongholds as Pennsylvania, Michigan, Connecticut, New York, Washington, Indiana, Minnesota, and Wisconsin came under attack. The questions raised were engulfing. In place of race came challenges on: the permissibility of including in delegations appointive ex officio delegates; the intrastate apportionment of delegate strength in response to the Supreme Court's "one man, one vote" edict; the fairness of methods for selecting national committee members; proportionate representation of candidate preferences within delegations and among at-large selections; the justification for the unit rule; the desirability of party loyalty oaths as tests for seating delegates (McCarthy's and Wallace's); the representativeness of procedures employed in caucuses, state conventions, and state committees in choosing delegations; and the standards for ascertaining the validity of bodies active in delegate selection.

The Credentials Committee floundered. Such questions are not answered lightly. The adjudication of racial controversies, though difficult, did not prepare committee members for the broader assault they had begun to experience. No rules or party traditions existed that could be adopted to the novelty of challenging major northern states on fundamental questions of procedural equity.

The usual approach when a Credentials Committee blundered into an unknown area was to deemphasize the significance of the conflict and to delay, trusting in part that some outside force would assert itself to alleviate the pressure. More often than not, as it had so frequently in the past with racial pressures, the tactic worked. Apathy, a compromise at the state level, a change in the principals, or a clear-cut victory by one faction over the other removed the question from the agenda. When pressed, the credentials chairman, usually in concert with other convention leaders, played a comfortably political role, acting as broker among the competing forces and attempting to pacify all with short-run, ad hoc détentes.

But the new challenges were different, not amenable to the panaceas of the past. The appeals being made were to abstract principles of procedural due process, and rules for deciding such appeals were not contained in the party's code of behavior. And the applicants were deadly serious. The new breed of challenges had been brought by relative newcomers to the national scene who had been drawn into politics by a candidacy (McCarthy or Robert Kennedy) or a cause (the Viet Nam War). They found compromise with the system and with the political professionals, for a variety of personal and psychological reasons, odious. Politically inspired compromises in credentials fights worked well when the combatants were basically political regulars whose livelihoods and long-run interests were identified with political accommodation. As the party base widened, however, the values, loyalties, and priorities of the groups invoked in the challenges changed markedly.

A tortuous resolution of the conflicts followed. The fundamental logic underlying the compromises was murky. Predictably, the outcomes satisfied no one. The entire insurgent delegation won seats in Mississippi; the Georgia delegation was divided, half to the regulars and half to the challengers; and in Alabama one of the insurgent factions was permitted to replace any delegate of the regulars that failed to sign a loyalty oath or any alternate that had replaced such a delegate. Another insurgent faction, which had contested 130 local offices (certainly some sign of vitality), unlike its sister challengers, received no accommodation whatsoever.

A liberal Texas delegation of one hundred, led by United States Senator Ralph Yarborough, sued the regulars, who were led by former Governor (and, later, Secretary of Commerce in the Nixon administration and a Republican presidential contender) John Connally, representative of the convention's absentee landlord, Lyndon Johnson. Yarborough's group argued that they had been denied any of the delegate votes that would normally accrue to a sizeable minority faction through the arbitrary imposition of a unit rule from the precinct to the state levels. The Credentials Committee (and later the convention) outlawed the unit rule, but while it damned the principle, it still treated the Yarborough liberals shabbily. The contingent was awarded no seats, and in fact, except for Yarborough's gallery (but not floor) pass, none was even allowed within the convention hall.

Assorted challenges in North Carolina, Tennessee, Louisiana, Washington, Pennsylvania, Minnesota, Connecticut, Wisconsin, Michigan, and Indiana were denied outright. Even if it wanted to, the committee could not resolve questions that centered on standards of adequate representation or procedural fair play. Although the precise resolution was unpredictable, the committee felt qualified to settle challenges based on racial bias. The convention call and the work of the Special Equal Rights Committee and the 1964 convention provided guidelines. It had taken one hundred years, but the convention's will had become clear on racial questions. Neither precedent nor a sense of the party's position applied to controversies over the performance of state parties in meeting abstract standards of democratic process.

Another complication arose from the association of the insurgents with the McCarthy candidacy. The adjudication struggle became one more extension of an already bitter (even by Democratic standards) encounter. The consistent failure to provide relief to the insurgents strengthened their distaste for the entire proceedings; the effort to seek redress of what the insurgents considered just grievances was perceived by the regulars as a political ploy, designed to embarrass the front runner (Humphrey) and his supporters and further divide a demoralized party. Within such an atmosphere, and with nothing beyond instinct to guide them, any reasonable compromising of the difficulties remained impossible.

The deliberations of the Credentials Committee painfully illustrated to all involved the need for more general standards by which to guide their judgments and against which to assess state party performances. The exasperated Credentials Committee chairman, Richard Hughes, drove the point home in his address to the convention. After laboriously guiding the convention through the complicated delegation challenges (the balance of the first two days' activities), Hughes requested permission to pass on some "further thoughts" to the assembled delegates. His committee, Hughes informed the convention, would like to "encourage appropriate revisions in the delegate selection process to assure the fullest possible participation and to make the Democratic party completely representative of grass root sentiment."[3] Hughes recommended that the convention establish a "special committee," not unlike the Special Equal Rights Committee he had headed, to: study the delegate recruitment process and its diversity of traditions and needs; "recommend to the Democratic National Committee" means to provide broader participation in delegate selection; and aid the state parties in working toward the needed modifications in party rules and state law, which were to be made "available" to the 1972 convention and its committees. As to substantive concerns, Hughes tactfully pointed out that his party had not "in the past expressed itself clearly and directly" on a number of questions. Among these, and proposed for consideration on the new group's agenda, were the problems of "timeliness," (beginning the delegate selection process "prior to the calendar year" of the national convention); "grass roots participation" (more appropriately, the question of open procedures in which large numbers of qualified party supporters can take part, rather than the contemporary practices, which ranged from direct primaries to the appointment of an entire delegation by two men); and the unit rule and its attendant suppression of minority views and representation. The resolution proposed by the Credentials Committee specified that all Democrats have "meaningful and timely opportunities to participate fully" in delegate selection and that the "special committee" aid the state parties "in fully meeting the responsibilities and assurances thus required for inclusion in the call for [the] 1972 Democratic national convention."[4]

Given the controversies that were to follow, the language is important. At the time, there was no minority report and *no debate* of the proposal. A disinterested convention perfunctorily passed the resolution by voice vote. Hughes took the opportunity to remind the delegates that they had placed "the mandate of the convention . . . four square behind the principle of full voter participation in the affairs of our party [and] behind the broadening of democratic processes."[5] No one seemed to care much. (A few years later, though, their feelings would be quite evident.) The presiding officer of the convention dutifully thanked Hughes, entertained a smattering of applause for the departing Credentials Committee chairman, and called for the final vote of the New York delegation on the Alabama challenge, a decision that had been interrupted for the proposals creating a reform committee. Wedged between the resolution of challenges to fifteen states, the commotion caused by security men roughing up newsmen and delegates, and the committee reports that were to follow, the resolution for investigating and codifying delegate recruitment procedures excited little interest.

Other Roots of Reform

THE AD HOC COMMISSION

As the nomination season rolled on, some began to feel that the upcoming convention's Credentials Committee would offer no relief for the problems they had encountered. They looked forward to committee deliberations little different from those of earlier years. By midsummer they had decided that either unusually well-grounded presentations would have to accompany the challenges placed before the Credentials Committee or, and perhaps preferably, some other convention committee would have to be used as an outlet for their concerns. A number of these people expected little or nothing to emerge from the nomination fights of 1968 that would be of interest to them. Their hope was to capitalize on their unhappy experiences in the preconvention battles to provide a basis for long-run changes. Such a stand at that time took a mixture of vision, determination, and faith. Their efforts came to focus, first, on an ad hoc committee chaired by Governor Harold Hughes of Iowa during the summer months, and later, on the convention's Committee on Rules and Order of Business, presided over by a party regular, Governor Sam Shapiro of Illinois.

Normally the Rules Committee (as it is called) consists of delegates whose main concern is in settling on an agenda for the convention (not too difficult a task since the agenda is usually provided by the national chairman). The committee traditionally has been responsive to the wishes of the convention managers, obediently reflecting their perception of political needs. While the rules that guide convention sessions and the priorities given agenda items constitute critical decisions for any deliberative body (witness the role of the Rules Committee in the House of Representatives), the convention's Rules Committee has seldom been the focus of controversy, ranking generally after platform and credentials and above permanent organization in importance in delegate and public recognition. Because of the leadership provided by some of the committee members and the implicit power of the group, however, the Rules Committee became a significant focal point for the reformers.

First was the Ad Hoc Commission. The thinking, tentative at first, behind the institution of the extraparty committee is clarified in a letter of one of the principals, Anne Wexler, to a kindred spirit in Iowa during July 1968. Wexler, at the time the disillusioned vice-chairman of the Connecticut McCarthy for President Committee, found that the arbitrary methods of delegate selection and the deep feelings of anger they provoked were common to other states than her own. She joined with others in calling for an impartial, broad-based study group, staffed principally by lawyers, to prepare a report to instruct and inform the members of a credentials and rules committee of the convention. The purpose of the new group was explained as follows: "Because delegates are selected in at least twenty different ways and the method of deciding how they should vote [unit rule or no] may be both illegal and unconstitutional, the [Ad Hoc] Commission will provide us [the members of the convention's relevant committees] with material sufficient . . . to make a more intelligent appraisal of the questions we will be asked to consider. . . . If it evolves that the Democratic Party begins to standardize requirements on how delegates may be selected and abolishes the unit rule, we will accomplish a great deal."[6] The group came to achieve these goals and more.

The formation of the Ad Hoc Commission was announced on 4 August by Governor (and later United States Senator) Harold Hughes of Iowa, who had agreed to serve as chairman. In his statement, Hughes called attention to the difficulties facing the committees of the convention and said it was his group's intention to "greatly alleviate" their burden by providing a "comprehensive, factual, up-to-date reference work" on delegate selection practices nationwide (incredible as it may seem, a work of such a nature did not exist). Hughes noted that his commission would also consider and make recommendations on the problems likely to appear before the convention and, in addition, would supply ". . . some guidelines of a somewhat permanent nature that could be used for organizing future national conventions and for selecting delegates in future years."[7] This last objective is by far the most ambitious and, like the others, directly anticipated the work of the McGovern-Fraser Commission.

In late July the commission staff began intensive work out of New York under the direction of Thomas Alder and Geoffrey Cowen. An early policy decision to deal with issues divorced from the candidacy of any one presidential contender contributed to a lowering of group tensions. The commission members themselves were intentionally selected to represent all the major contenders as well as to reflect views basically in line with the group's orientation. Such an approach gave the task force's final report added legitimacy. One other aspect of their work is of interest. The staff researchers drew heavily on the work of Richard Hughes's Special Equal Rights Committee, particularly its prophetic emphasis on "full, timely and meaningful" participation in political processes, a standard reiterated in the commission report, by the convention, and in the later efforts of the McGovern-Fraser Commission.

Immediately prior to the opening of the convention, the Ad Hoc Commission released its report, *The Democratic Choice*.[8] The document was an impressive, forward-looking publication, quite unlike anything that had been produced for earlier conventions. The effort was broadly conceived and, in retrospect, if anything, was too inclusive. It explored in one way or another virtually the entire political process as it in any way related to the Democratic party. Its pages included discussions of the evolution of the convention system; the influence of the primaries, radio, television, public opinion polls, and the "new electorate" (registered blacks and an affluent, issue-oriented white middle class) on presidential nominations; state delegate selection procedures, including evaluations of state convention, party appointment, primary election, and presidential preference poll methods; the authority of the national convention; the problems facing convention delegates, from the handling of credentials challenges to the right to be heard on the convention floor; profiles of the socioeconomic characteristics of delegates, from income to race; and, of course, recommendations for change. The presentation proved to be influential.

The Democratic Choice opens with this warning: "This Convention is on trial." After briefly touching the magnitude of the problems facing the meeting, it goes on to "question the integrity of the convention system" itself as a representative device. Its basic conclusion is equally stark: "State systems for selecting delegates to the National Convention and the procedures of the Convention itself, display considerably less fidelity to basic democratic principles than a nation which claims to govern itself can safely tolerate."[9] This represents a fair statement of the anxiety entertained by many at the time, and is an indication of the implicit standards underlying the recommendations that flowed from a variety of reform groups over the next several years.

While sweeping in their challenges, the actual recommendations of the study group were limited to immediate problems and were practical, in light of the situation. They were put forth with "compassion" (as the commission said), with an appreciation of the magnitude of the job that lay ahead, and with the realization that they did not constitute the only possible remedies to the difficulties. An air of compromise and, in my view, professionalism marked the approach made to the party.

The most significant of the recommendations can be divided into three parts: those directed to the 1968 national convention; those applying to future conventions; and those intended to be general rules for guiding party deliberations. Concerning immediate and future convention behavior, the task force recommended:

1. Strong action against racial discrimination. It advised: the adoption of the "six basic elements" of the Special Equal Rights Commission and the inclusion of these in the call to the convention; the creation of a "specific formula" to insure racial representativeness; that an "affirmative obligation" be placed on state parties to encourage "full and meaningful" black participation; that the burden of proof in racial challenges before the Credentials Committee be placed on state parties; and that the percentage of minority group members in a state delegation approximate that found in the state's population.
2. The abolition of the unit rule (the practice whereby all members of a delegation, regardless of individual preference, are bound to vote the choice of the majority).
3. The convention seat only national committee members elected in that presidential year (rather than those chosen four years previously, then the practice).
4. That a state's delegation enjoy the same proportionate vote in convention committees that they had on the floor (rather than the automatic two committee votes regardless of delegation size).
5. That procedures be introduced for an early resolution of credentials challenges; that a delegation not be allowed to vote on convention business until its challenge had been resolved.
6. That the balloting be temporarily suspended any time a delegation was deliberately kept from caucusing or communicating within itself (an indication of the procedures expected to be encountered in Chicago).

As to the standards in delegate selection future national conventions should abide by, the study group recommended:

1. The replacement of a system allowing state party officials to appoint delegates with one offering "meaningful popular participation."
2. The incorporation of five basic guidelines in all state conventions and primary election delegate selection systems. These were:
   a. Meaningful access to the process by the public.
   b. Clarity of purpose, defined as the opportunity to vote independently for delegates who have declared their candidate preferences and national policy stands without having delegate selection combined with elections for other party offices (e.g., state or national committeemen or state convention delegates).
   c. Timely selection, meaning that no delegate to the convention be chosen by a process begun more than six months prior to the convention.

d. Fair apportionment, meaning the allocation of convention votes to electoral units on the basis of "one man, one vote."

e. Fair representation of voter preferences, so that minority candidate support is reflected at all stages of the delegate selection process.[10]

Further, the commission called for either

1. The upcoming convention to direct the National Committee to include these basic standards in the 1972 call, thus requiring all state parties to honor them.

Or

2. The national convention to order the National Committee to establish a special commission, similar to the Special Equal Rights Committee of Richard Hughes, to investigate state systems and recommend that similar principles be included in the 1972 call.

The Ad Hoc Commission report did not emerge to universal acclaim. It was overshadowed by the rush of events in the convention city, and its inclusiveness diluted its impact. Three weeks allowed for neither intensive exploration of any one problem nor studied decisions on a number of corollary issues, a difficulty accentuated by the lack of a solid core of information to build on. The commission, of course, did not claim infallibility.

The Democratic Choice did catalogue an extensive amount of factual information of direct consequence to convention procedures and of use, as intended, to members of the Rules and Credentials committees. Some of the data was elementary, such as the brief sketches of the nominating procedures in each of the states and of the financial status of delegates and the racial composition of state delegations. Yet it constituted vital, and to this point unavailable, background materials for the people most concerned with making the decisions that affected convention deliberations, as well as, of course, providing a basis for recommending change. The wonder is that no such systematic fact book had been previously made available to convention or committee participants, an omission that speaks as clearly as any to the unstructured nature of convention procedures and the transiency of the entire operation. The convention was the supreme organ of the party—in theory. The influence it allowed the continuing bodies concerned with party affairs (in particular the National Committee and its chairman) was exercised virtually without check. The sad state of delegate preparation for the quadrennial meeting of the governing body of the party constituted one further acknowledgment of the de facto low status of that meeting.

Many party leaders met the Ad Hoc Commission's recommendations with *pro forma* announcements that certain proposals required more careful study. Other reactions (such as they were) to the report were not so bland. Rather, the political implications of the suggestions sparked immediate controversy, which is not surprising, given the nature of the convention and the events that preceded it. The report was seen by many as a plot of the insurgents (McCarthy and Kennedy supporters) to win during the convention what they had failed to gain in the states. These dissenters pointed out that the balance of commissioners supported anti-establishment candidates, and that many of the staff had worked in the campaigns of one of the two senators who had challenged Johnson. The party regulars, who controlled the convention, resented such impertinence. They also perceived the report (not incorrectly) as a fundamental attack on prerogatives that they had long enjoyed by virtue of their official party positions. The remedies put forward by the Ad Hoc Commission argued for a more open party structure than they cared to accept. These proposals also pointed toward a delegate selection process freed from other party encumbrances and the control of party officers, geared singularly to providing an election choice among the party's presidential nominees. Logical as it may seem to us, this emphasis constituted another unwelcome intrusion into a restricted domain of party affairs, one that had not before, curiously, been afforded extensive thought.

In reviewing the recommendations, it is striking to see the extent to which they foreshadowed those adopted, after far more extensive inquiry, by the later reform commissions. The commission's deliberations also anticipated the areas of greatest controversy for succeeding reform groups. The authors of the report were sympathetic to the political parties and the distinctive contribution they made to American democracy. Without reform, they argued, without the ability to embrace "new interests and sentiments," the two-party system would become a relic of the past. If the two-party system were supplanted, they contended, "a powerful force for stability [would] disappear from the fabric of American politics."[11] Their forebodings were shared by many. The ultimate objective of the Ad Hoc Commission centered on preserving a vital two-party system through strengthening it; an approach, it should be noted, of polarity to that of most earlier reformers, whose efforts, in effect, were attempts to dismantle the parties under the guise of making them more democratic. This love affair with the contemporary party system proved a hallmark of the reform movement that followed, one that was not reflected in the at times excessive criticisms of its protagonists.

THE RULES COMMITTEE

Ignored at birth, deficient in some aspects, the Ad Hoc Commission report nevertheless survived to serve as a cornerstone of the emerging reform emphasis, and was the principal contributor to this movement at the Chicago convention.

The Rules Committee, soon to emerge as a reluctant hero in the drive for change, began its deliberations inauspiciously. Conforming to tradition, the committee did not hold its organizational meeting until four days before the convention opening. In the initial business of the group, the chairman, Governor Sam Shapiro of Illinois, a Daley loyalist, permitted the Mississippi regulars to both participate in and vote on Rules Committee matters, despite the 1964 convention ruling on the Mississippi party's discriminatory practices and a challenge pending before the Credentials Committee. When disputed, Shapiro's ruling was sustained forty-five to thirty-four, establishing that the balance of power in the committee rested with the party regulars and the southerners. The inability (or refusal) of the chairman to find larger quarters for conducting the committee hearings, which effectively limited the number of press and public representatives present,[12] argued for another routine series of meetings firmly controlled by the party orthodoxy.

Initial appearances proved to be deceptive. Matters were not as well in hand as the early maneuvering indicated, and the sessions, even more surprisingly, were anything but dull. Taking advantage of the committee rule that permitted anyone to address the group who requested time (few availed themselves of this opportunity in earlier conventions), Harold Hughes appeared and reviewed his commission's proposals. Hughes initially cast his appeal broadly, arguing that the integrity of the Democratic party "as well as the continuity of the two-party system" necessitated general reform. He ended, however, by focusing on the immediate changes possible, emphasizing the dictatorial qualities of the unit rule as then enforced.

The committee was quiet no longer. Any hope it had held for an expeditious handling of routine matters had vanished.[13] Stephen Mitchell, a Democratic national chairman during the fifties and a McCarthy supporter, continued the assault on the unit rule by claiming it was designed "to control minorities and to stifle dissent." A sharp debate ensued in the afternoon session. The unit rule idea (like all the proposed reforms) employs a concept of majority rule that raises theoretical and practical questions concerning democratic procedures. The committee members were quick to bring these out. Basically the reformers hoped to attack the practice whereby the majority of a delegation could bind the entire group to voting for its candidate or policy position, potentially negating the will of up to 49 percent of the members. Some states (Texas, for example) applied the practice with vengeance, enforcing it down to the precinct level. In effect, a delegation bound by this rule could easily give a highly distorted view of the state party's views. The rule did retain the virtue, as party regulars viewed it, of keeping the delegation comfortably under the control of its leaders. A good argument could be made for outlawing the practice on principle. The problem lay in determining where to stop. Some committee members felt that the prohibition should be extended to all delegates bound by state conventions (thus hurting Humphrey); others thought it should apply to those bound by primary election (thus eliminating most of McCarthy's support). The plea was that the delegate should be able to exercise his own free conscience in deciding issues. In truth, the last two proposals moved well beyond the unit rule and what the reformers had intended, raising questions as to the delegate's role and where his true responsibility lay. Those who opted for a broad interpretation took the position that to be bound by a plurality vote in a primary or state convention could be considered no more commendable than being directed by the majority will of a delegation. Few wanted to go this far. The debate illustrated the complex probings each of the reform proposals invited and foreshadowed the soul-searching that was to face the reform commissions.

The oratorical battle over principle, of course, had a practical aspect of great consequence, another indication of events to come. Other than the state delegations (Texas, Missouri, Illinois) that applied it, few actually supported the unit rule in merit. Nevertheless, the states that did were heavyweights, carrying, in Mayor Daley's term, "clout" with the national party and its professionals. Any change in the rules under which the Texas delegation operated would in addition be construed as an insult directed against the absent national party leader, President and de facto delegation head, Lyndon Johnson. This slap was more than Texans could tolerate. They made their position clear. The spokesman for John Connally's Texas delegation was Frank C. Erwin, a wealthy and influential figure in the state, and its national committeeman. While admitting the rule might be modified for future conventions, Erwin thundered his "keen sense of disapproval" of giving any thought to changing it in that convention. He went so far as to threaten that if the unit rule was abandoned, Texas would withdraw Connally's name from nomination as a favorite son candidate for the presidential nomination and submit that of "another great Texan who now holds the highest office in the land [Johnson, not present at the convention]."[14] Taking it from there, Governor Connally (who later switched parties) continued to feed press speculations.

Passions ran high. A Johnson nomination would represent the final blow (as if it were needed) to a thoroughly disorganized convention. In reality, however, the ploy was directed against the Humphrey supporters. They occupied the middle ground on reform questions, and many supported individual changes such as the abolition of unit voting. The threat was that an active Johnson candidacy would remove Humphrey's chances for nomination, the implications being that the party's endorsement was Johnson's to bestow. The price, then, for support of the reform effort, for most of the professionals, was high. Humphrey occupied this middle position with no particular grace, straddling issues, failing to organize and emphasize his own substantial strength, and attempting to keep uncommitted to but on speaking terms with as many factions as possible. Many Humphrey delegates, as events made clear, nonetheless chose to support the efforts for a change.

At the end of the second day of meetings Rules Committee Chairman Shapiro emerged from lengthy closed-door sessions to announce that the drafting subcommittee (with representatives from only Texas, South Carolina, and Tennessee of its twenty-one opposing members) and, in turn, the full committee, had adopted a "freedom of conscience" proposal. It provided that the convention would not enforce a voting obligation on a delegate, whether it arose from a state law, convention, committee, primary, or, lastly, the vote of a state delegation (the unit rule practice). The delegate was to look inward for guidance.[15] The focus was broader than the reformers wanted or intended it to be, and did in fact negate rank-and-file control over delegates once they reached the convention, a *sine qua non* of the later reform litany.

Further into the evening Shapiro announced the completion of the committee's work. The most significant of the recommendations to be made to the full convention called for the national chairman

. . . to appoint a Commission to be called the Rules Commission, and consisting of members knowledgeable in matters of parliamentary procedure and familiar with Convention procedure of the Democratic Party [which is substantially different from that of the Republican party], and that said Commission be charged with the duty of studying and evaluating and codifying the rules of past Democratic National Conventions, and investigating the advisability of rules changes, and that *the Commission report its findings to the Democratic National Committee in a timely manner in order that the Democratic National Committee may submit said findings to the Rules Committee of the 1972 Convention for acceptance, rejection or modification or amendment*.[16] (Italics added.)

The Rules Committee charged the new group with establishing permanent rules for the convention and its committees and exploring "other matters that may be appropriate." This resolution, as it was endorsed by the convention, resulted in the creation of the O'Hara Commission.

The gains for the reformers were substantial. Still, they were not completely satisfied. Shapiro had emphasized in his press conference that the new commission would report (indirectly, it turned out) to the Rules Committee of the next convention, which had (with full convention support) the power to accept or reject its recommendations. The point was an extremely important one, and it spoke to both the new group's powers of enforcement and its independence from other party agencies in its deliberations. Shapiro failed to mention that his committee had only narrowly rejected (by a forty-four to forty vote) a proposal to allow the new commission to force inclusion of their recommendations in the call for the next convention, which would have given them the power of party law. He did hint at what was a certainty: a minority report more closely reflecting the reformers' position as to what should be included in the call to the convention four years hence would accompany the Rules Committee report to the convention.

The Reform Movement on the Floor of the Convention

Those who look for the delegates assembled in convention to be an example of mass democracy are doomed to disappointment. The spectacle itself, however, never fails to impress. The 1968 Democratic convention was no exception. The convention opened with the usual eminently forgettable formalities: the invocation, welcoming addresses by local dignitaries, a crush of resolutions honoring party functionaries, and assorted calls to battle by the party leaders. Such as it was, perhaps the high point of the initial sessions was Mayor Daley's speech, though Daley was never known for his rhetorical skills. Chicago hosted the convention because Lyndon Johnson had insisted on holding it there despite grumblings from some local party chieftains and outright opposition from others, who sensed what might happen. Johnson persisted despite the plague of strikes by communications workers (among others), a very real question as to whether the convention hall itself could be readied in time, the ugly mood prevalent in the city, and a foreshadowing of Daley's approach to civil dissent, which had been demonstrated in the violent crushing of a protest meeting early in the spring. Daley, without smiling, obligingly thanked the delegates for their "show of faith" in holding the convention in Chicago (and in a hastily touched up slum area at that). The mayor went on to tell his listeners that "law and order" would prevail (should they have had any doubts), but that they themselves would be selecting a president, not a chief of police, which was nothing if not illogical. Reassured, the delegates progressed with the business at hand. For those obsessed with logic, a few other matters are of interest. The assemblage suffered through a reading of the call to the convention and then endorsed it, thus giving the document full sanction at the exact moment it was no longer relevant. They also voice voted the authorization for the various committees of the convention, which of course had already completed their work and were waiting to present their reports.

Little more than two hours into the ceremonies, Rules Chairman Shapiro appeared at the podium to present for discussion and adoption the convention's temporary rules (really his committee's report, although the final action on the recommendations was to be delayed until the next session). As expected, the provision abolishing the unit rule created the most controversy. An uninspired but determined debate ensued, overshadowed by the incessant commotion on the floor. The debate was punctuated by the temporary chairman's persistent calls for order and intermittent jeers and applause from listeners. The restless anger, unfocused energy, periodic outbursts of hostility, and overwhelming confusion witnessed this first night came to characterize each of the sessions.

The minority committee position favoring the unit rule was perfunctorily defeated by a voice vote, although the issue was not yet dead. The Credentials Committee report began immediately after Shapiro's initial appearance, but was interrupted at 2:45 A.M. by an exhausted convention.

The second day broke to newspaper and television reports of violence in the parks and streets of the city. Sixty were known injured, including seventeen media representatives. The mood was ugly. Criticism focused on police actions, including one incident in which policemen attacked demonstrators who were chanting in unison, "Kill, kill, kill." On the surface the convention seemed unaffected. Anita Bryant, at Mayor Daley's request, opened the ceremonies singing "Happy Birthday" to the absent Lyndon Johnson. This quaint interlude preceded a resumption of the Credentials Committee report and Chairman Richard Hughes's call for a "special commission" to review delegate selection procedures in the states.

Hughes's presentation left it unclear whether his proposal called for two committees—one to examine the substantive issues involved in reform and the other to implement the regulations—or just one. Several years later the national chairman chose to interpret this as authorization to appoint an "implementation" committee chosen from the National Committee membership to assist both the McGovern-Fraser and O'Hara commissions, a move both groups resented. The Credentials Committee recommendation also did something that proved to be critical to the later enforcement responsibilities of the McGovern-Fraser Commission. It introduced the power to implement the proposals of a reform commission through an implicit threat not to seat in the next convention state delegations that failed to meet the standards proposed.[17]

The McGovern-Fraser Commission was quick to assume the power of enforcement as one of its prerogatives. The Credentials Committee motion left the new commission's relationship to the National Committee unclear, although the national body did retain an implicit role, at least in its power to appoint the reform group and to pass on the substance of the next convention's call. The limits on the new group remained unclear; its area of investigation was potentially quite broad. The convention was in no mood to quibble. The resolution was passed by voice vote *without debate of any kind*. In this way the seeds of reform were sown.

The delegates underwent a few more formalities (including the wholly unnecessary report of the Committee on Permanent Organization) before the Rules Committee chairman was reintroduced to place his group's report before the convention for final adoption. One of the two other minority reports was presented to the convention by Joseph Crangle (later an O'Hara Commission member and New York State and Erie County

Democratic chairman) on behalf of thirty-three delegates on the Rules Committee, the nucleus of reform. It was quite brief:

Be it resolved, that the Call to the 1972 National Democratic Convention shall contain the following language:

It is understood that a State Democratic Party in selecting and certifying delegates to the National Convention thereby undertakes to assure that such delegates have been selected through a process in which all Democratic voters have a full and timely opportunity to participate.

In determining whether a state party has complied with this mandate, the Convention shall require that:

(1) the unit rule not be used in any stage of the delegate selection process, and

(2) all feasible efforts have been made to assure that delegates are elected through party primary, convention or committee procedures, open to public participation within the calendar year of the National Convention.[18]

The proposal repeats in several places, especially in the first substantive paragraph, points made in other reform authorizations. The unit rule, by this stage, was being beaten to death, although the wording does clarify that it is outlawed at all stages of the delegate selection process. Crangle's minority report did serve two functions. It specified in rather demanding language ("all feasible efforts") the nature of the requirement that the state parties and their delegation would have to meet to gain access to the quadrennial convention. Secondly, "full . . . opportunity" meant that a state party had to make a determined attempt to include blacks, other minorities, and youths in its deliberations. The wording was indirect, but the door had been opened. This particular interpretation of the meaning was stressed in the remarks of those supporting the proposal, particularly in the statement made by Congressman Brock Adams of Washington.

It appeared that the reformers, buttressed by the recommendations of the Special Equal Rights Committee that were now party law,[19] at least knew what they intended. To anyone who followed the presentation carefully, the general contours (although in no sense the specific formula) for a more inclusive party were certainly apparent. Even so, a number of significant questions were left unanswered. Governor Shapiro touched on some of the more important of these in his rejoinder opposing the minority amendment. The committee chairman was not blind to the implications of the requirement. The motion, with all its difficulties, had been debated by the full Rules Committee. Would some state arbitrarily be harshly punished under a hastily concocted formula? If legislation were required to achieve "full participation," what could the Democratic party do in a state with a Republican-controlled legislature? Shapiro urged that such questions be left to the new study group to answer. Precipitate action was to be avoided. The Rules Committee chairman suggested in passing that the entire Ad Hoc Commission report was an appropriate agenda for the new commission.

The brief statements of the sponsors completed (this was the only review the proposal received), the delegates voted. In this most disrupted of conventions, the lengthy and rambling roll call was interrupted by "unanimous consent," an action the presiding officer (Carl Albert, Speaker of the House of Representatives) said should never be allowed right before he advanced it,[20] to permit arguments on the second minority report. This was a traditional appeal, not related to the reform effort, to permit Young Democrats and state chairmen to sit on the National Committee. The speeches on this topic complete, the roll call on the Crangle motion resumed; the motion was carried by a slim margin of 144 votes: 1,350 to 1,206.

At no point did the convention *in any way* actively debate or intensively review the major issues associated with commencing a reform initiative, the rationale for creating reform commissions, the reality of the need for reform commissions, the jurisdiction of reform commissions, or the obligations and potential consequences of the actions of reform commissions. Both majority reports of the Credentials and Rules committees establishing the new study groups were passed uncritically by voice vote. The minority report demanding a tightening of standards of delegate selection did receive some brief adversary examination, although this report was less important. While the report gave impetus to a serious test of existing institutions, Governor Shapiro was correct in predicting the questions raised therein would need more extensive review by the upcoming reform commission. The vote, while confused, was mostly symbolic. The delegates themselves remained silent partners during the birth of the reform movement, content to follow their leaders' recommendations for fulfilling what must have been (given the limited information available) hazy conceptions of the party's needs. Such naive complacency this time around benefited the more highly aroused reformers. It is fair to say that the delegates held little appreciation of what they were voting on behalf of, or why.

Many problems were left unresolved by the actions of the convention. Party regulars were later astounded at the precociousness of the agencies they only imperfectly remembered endorsing. Little specific guidance was given in the remarks introducing the resolutions creating the commissions. The absence of a critical debate (except in the perfunctory comments associated with the Crangle motion) did not help. The overlap in sentiment and phraseology in the several reports adopted compounded the difficulties of the National Committee in attempting to sort out exactly what the convention "mandated," how it could be implemented, and what precise form it should assume. A formidable set of difficulties remained to be worked out in the operations of the groups, many on an ad hoc, emergency basis. Some questions continued to be in contention until the eve of the next convention. One point soon became clear. The leeway in the wording of the various proposals provided the reformers, once they had begun, a basis for extending their jurisdiction and for arguing for the immediate, and full, application of their standards. A large reward would go to the boldest, most daring of those associated with the reform commissions, those who could visualize the commissions' preferred objectives, convince others of the rightness of their stand, and then persist until the goals were realized. The opportunity was there. Still, it is a safe bet that the reformers' broad application to their work, their accomplishments, and their impact far exceeded even the most visionary dreams of the delegates who created the agencies.

In this uncertain way, reform was launched. It was potentially the most significant—and undoubtedly the least understood and most underpublicized—event of an unusual convention. All that remained was for the incoming national chairman to appoint the members of the proposed groups and for them to begin their work. Amid the violence, the hatred, and the recriminations that marked those unhappy days in Chicago, the actions recorded here were among the least noticed. Yet they were among the most important.

TWO

The McGovern-Fraser Commission: The Early Phases

PARTY REFORM took second place to a lackluster general election campaign in the fall. The Humphrey campaign meandered, spiritually and organizationally, toward a November decision. The Nixon drive concentrated on packaged media presentations, carefully worded slogans designed to reassure an anxious electorate, and the presentation of a low political profile engineered to take advantage of the divisiveness within the Democratic ranks and the schisms in a tired electorate. The voters did not appear inclined to award any of the contenders with a decisive plurality. Everyone appeared relieved when the unhappiest of election years finally drew to its inevitable close.[1]

While the victorious Republican candidate readied himself for his oath of office, another inauguration of sorts was being prepared for January, though this one received considerably less press and public attention. The efforts of a broken and dispirited party to reexamine its unhappy immediate past and to remedy its ways to insure, in the words of George McGovern, that the events of 1968, and particularly the gross abuses that occurred at the Chicago convention, would never happen again, do not constitute an especially interesting story. Yet defeat—especially after an election year so debilitating for a party—can lead to a period of profound change and, in time, to a spiritual regenesis. This had happened to the Republicans after a bitter defeat in 1912, and, on a more superficial level, after their loss in 1964. In a different manner, a defeat was about to trigger a profound transformation of Democratic party procedures, one without precedent in the history of the American two-party experience.

The lethargic semiannual meeting of the Democratic National Committee in January took the first tentative steps. Democrats are political animals, and the National Committee gathering presented them with an opportunity to partially revive their lagging spirits through the give-and-take they cherish.

The main event in the agenda—buried among the statements of homage

28

and thanks to the party spear-carriers and the burden of minor committee business—was the choice of a new national chairman. Lawrence O'Brien, the incumbent for the campaign, had announced his intention to step down and, after more than two decades of politics, to turn to the private sector to make his fortune. (He would be back.) Meanwhile, the selection of a new party leader faced the national committeemen. Humphrey, the party's titular head and the man whose choice would undoubtedly be followed, willed that the mantle fall on an eager, youngish senator from Oklahoma, Fred R. Harris. The new nominee was an interesting choice. A personal friend of Robert Kennedy, he had nonetheless cochaired the preconvention Humphrey campaign. His cochairman, Senator Edmund Muskie, had received the vice presidential nod; Harris was awarded the less prizeworthy national chairmanship.

The new chairman was something of a phenomenon. He was a populist liberal from a conservative state, and he had a remarkable record.[2] Literally "dirt poor," he had excelled in college and law school. His intelligence and wit, deliberately hidden behind a country-boy openness, came to startle the many who underestimated him over the next several years. An indefatigable worker who appeared not to require sleep, he had risen through the state legislature to become speaker and then, in a people-to-people, underfinanced "walking" campaign (before these became the rage), had won nomination and then election over far better known contenders to fill the United States Senate seat of the legendary force in the upper chamber, the late Robert Kerr. Two years into his first term, he was chosen to lead his national party.

A formidable task faced Humphrey, Harris, and the other Democrats. The traditional call to action took on an urgency not often found in such party meetings. Humphrey, at his best before party gatherings, placed himself in the forefront of the drive for change. The standard-bearer of the party's center repeatedly cautioned the assembled regulars that the party must be opened ("the winds of change are strong . . . they will not be denied") to the young, new groups, creative ideas, and modifications forced upon them by time.[3]

Humphrey saw a party in transition, a party in need of reform. The national committee members responded by passing unanimously several resolutions authorizing the new national chairman to appoint the required commissions. The discussion surrounding the voice vote was a model of confusion. Former Nevada Governor Grant Sawyer had the unenviable job of presenting the resolutions establishing the reform groups and tracing their antecedents.[4] Sawyer did his best, but as he noted, three different actions of the national convention appeared to underlie the reform. Incredibly little discussion followed, given the import of the matter before the members. In fact, two scrambled questions by an antagonist (and, later, highly vocal critic of reform) from Louisiana constituted the only inquiry into the pending actions.[5] The motions passed routinely. Its work done, the National Committee disbanded, resolving to regroup again at an indeterminate future date.

Harris Creates the New Commissions

The burden now fell on the new national chairman. His appointments (cleared, of course, with party leaders),[6] the official or unofficial guidelines he established, and the nature of the support (in the initial stages, the critical question of funding, especially) that would be forthcoming from the national party headquarters would set the tone of the reform emphasis over the tenure of Harris's stewardship and would constitute a significant influence over the entire working life of the reform groups. The national chairman's role remained a sensitive one throughout. Much of what the reform groups could hope to accomplish depended on the constancy of the chairman's (that of Harris and of his immediate successor, O'Brien, who returned for another term) support,[7] his political interests, the objectives he visualized for the party, and, most vital of all, his political acumen in implementing his and the reformers' goals.

Harris's own thinking at this point bears brief comment. While in the process of forming the McGovern-Fraser and O'Hara commissions and providing the movement for change with its initial thrust, Harris was also deeply immersed in revitalizing the dormant National Committee. National party operations under Presidents Kennedy and Johnson came to little more than formalities. Harris visualized the national party headquarters as the location of the spearhead of the attempt to reunite warring party factions. The reunion would be accomplished on the basis of, as he put it, an "interest in the issues" (anathema to the "old politics") and by providing a modernized, service-oriented central office. Harris devoted his considerable energies toward these ends. He began by rebuilding the depleted staff, calling on younger men of experience and obvious talent to carry the initial load.[8]

The ideal and the reality of the time made sharp contrasts. Harris's ambitions for the party had to be reconciled with a national party deficit thought to be in the vicinity of $6 million (actually, it later was found to be $9.3 million), swollen by the assumption of all the presidential candidates' debts (only McCarthy insisted on covering his own) of the election year by the outgoing party treasurer.[9] The annual operating costs of the National Committee were in the vicinity of one and one-half million dollars. A party out of power holds little hope of raising substantial funds. Harris persisted nonetheless. His intention was to remake the committee, and, with it—through the party's reform commissions and other task forces, and, preferentially, in concert with the Republicans (a level of cooperation never approached)[10]—much of the archaic American electoral structure. He planned to achieve these minor miracles by calling in, as he said, "a bunch of young guys around the country who have both money and social consciences . . . guys [who] really care about the social problems."[11]

The appointment of the personnel of the two commissions constituted the first giant step. Harris stated that the new movement's goal was "an open party, encouraging the widest possible participation in all its decision-making."[12] He remained faithful to his commitment despite the vicissitudes the party encountered in the months ahead and a drastic reversal of his own political fortunes, which included a falling out with Humphrey and his being replaced as national chairman.

Harris presented three criteria for appointment to either of the new groups. First, that the nominee believe the mandate of the convention, an indication that the national chairman expected something of substance from both bodies' deliberations. Second, that the appointee work at his or her job (and a large proportion did), a reflection of Harris's own values, and fair notice that the titles were not honorific. And third, that the individuals chosen reflect Harris's own intention of seeing party reforms become a reality. The later anguish of many party regulars indicates that they chose to ignore the warnings of the oncoming storm.[13]

Senator George McGovern was chosen to head the more critical of the two groups, the Commission on Party Structure and Delegate Selection. McGovern, considered a representative of the left, had briefly contested for the presidential nomination in 1968. He had immediately and publicly endorsed Humphrey as soon as the latter won the convention's nod, and he was a personal friend and former neighbor of the Minnesotan. McGovern appeared to be a happy choice.[14] The vice chairmanship of the same commission went to Senator Harold Hughes, a man identified with reform since its inception; Hughes's candidacy for the top position had been sabotaged by Humphrey, who had resented Hughes's begrudging endorsement of his presidential race. Party regulars feared the purity of his commitment to reform. Hughes labored under a double curse.

The twenty-eight-member group consisted of party notables, party office-holders, elected officials, labor representatives, and two academicians. Among the best known were Indiana Senator Birch Bayh and Illinois Senator-to-be Adlai Stevenson III, I. W. Abel, President of the AFL-CIO United Steelworkers (who chose not to participate in the commission deliberations), Aaron Henry, black civil-rights leader from Mississippi, and former Florida Governor LeRoy Collins (who contributed less as the years went on). Fred Dutton and Donald Fraser (as well as Harold Hughes, of course) were members of the original Ad Hoc Commission.[15] David Mixner, a young antiwar activist, was included as a representative of youth. Three of the commission representatives were women, three were black, and three (among the least active) were Latin American. On the whole, the membership, while skewed heavily toward party professionals, had an intrinsic balance and constituted a fair-minded and generally progressive group.

Congressman James O'Hara of Michigan, an expert parliamentarian and a leader in the House of Representatives who was sympathetic to organized labor (an ironic twist, as matters turned out), was chosen to head the second of the major reform groups mandated by the national convention, the Commission on Rules. O'Hara clearly met the convention resolution's proviso of being "knowledgeable in matters of parliamentary procedure and familiar with Convention procedure." The qualifications of the other commission members were less clear in this regard. Joseph Crangle (New York), James Hunt, (North Carolina), Irving Kaler (Georgia), and Stephen Mitchell (New Mexico), all prominent in promoting the reform alternatives at the convention, were represented among this group's membership, as was former (having lost the intervening election) Illinois Governor Sam Shapiro, the chairman of the convention's Rules Committee. Donald Peterson, who gained attention as a leader of the Wisconsin delegation and who had been one of the most articulate in expressing the rage of many at the convention, won a place on the committee, as did Clarence Mitchell III, the NAACP lobbyist in Congress, John Powers, a venerable pro from Boston, and Hodding Carter III, young scion of a Mississippi publishing dynasty. Among the most easily recognized of the appointees were Herman Badillo, congressman and mayoral candidate from New York City, former Kentucky Governor Edward T. Breathitt, Senator Thomas Eagleton (McGovern's aborted running mate in 1972), United States Representatives Patsy Mink of Hawaii and Charles Vanik of Ohio, and the Reverend Channing Phillips, black leader from the District of Columbia. As in the McGovern-Fraser Commission, many of the better-known names (Mitchell, Badillo, Eagleton, Mink, Vanik, Phillips) participated only occasionally in the deliberations, the burden being carried disproportionately by nationally unknown individuals (Bjorlie, Crangle, Hunt, Kaler, Auerbach, Peterson, McDiarmid, Sylvester, etc.) and the chairman. On the face of it, the new Commission on Rules appeared more liberal than its sister creation, the McGovern-Fraser Commission. Among the twenty-four members[16] were five women, three blacks, two Spanish-speaking representatives, one spokesman for youth (Dennis O'Toole), one representative of organized labor (Joseph Keenan), four members of Congress, and four state legislative officeholders. Paul T. David of the University of Virginia, the most learned academician specializing in convention proceedings, was designated the permanent consultant to the commission.

O'Hara and his committee received little attention from the media in the early stages of the reform drive. The focus was on the McGovern-Fraser Commission, rightly considered to have the broadest mandate and the greatest potential for explosive change.[17] The commission's rapid start on party structure and delegate selection did nothing to disappoint observers. Within two weeks of its creation on 8 February it had hired an intelligent practitioner of the art of politics, Robert W. Nelson, as staff director. Nelson, an official in the Interior Department and a former McGovern campaign manager in South Dakota, was followed in short order by legal counsel in the form of Eli Segal, and then, in June, with an aggressive research director, Ken Bode; these three formed the nucleus of a permanent staff that was supplemented by hordes of volunteers, who came to characterize the commission's feverish activity.[18] By the end of March the commission had held its first full meeting and was threatening to crisscross the nation to tap grass-roots sentiments as to what needed change. The leisurely O'Hara Commission, faced with different problems and a more relaxed time schedule, did not meet until May and did not begin its real work for another year.

The McGovern-Fraser Commission's Work Begins: Defining the Target

The national chairman called on the new group to "begin promptly to carry out their work."[19] They needed no such prodding. Within three weeks they held their first meeting, a gathering that set the tone and broadly defined the ambitions that guided the commission over the next four years. In many respects the meeting on 1 March was historic: it was at this point that the convention's mandate was provisionally interpreted; the ground rules for deliberations and decision-making were set; the structure of committee activities was authorized; and an ambitious timetable for the completion of the various phases of the work was adopted (see table 2.1). And the divisions within the group became apparent.

The beginning of the meeting was pure McGovern. First, he called on Anne Wexler, who had coauthored the "Minority Report of the 1968 Rules Committee," to review the history of the group's formation and to interpret the critical wording of the convention resolution establishing it.[20] This stratagem assured an early and sympathetic hearing of record for the reformist point of view. Predictably, Wexler took a hard line. McGovern then moved that her version be adopted as the commission's official guidelines. Objections followed. Particularly at issue was the meaning of the phrase "all feasible effort" in the mandate. The Wexler view was that a state party that failed to achieve all the specified changes could satisfy this criteria *only* in situations where state laws had to be modified and the legislature was Republican controlled. After debate, a majority of the commission supported this interpretation. The escape clause was thus narrowly defined, although the issue was far from settled. More significant, and less noticed in the debate, was the assumption that the commission

Table 2.1
Chronology of the McGovern-Fraser Commission
Adopting the Guidelines

Date	Event
1968	
4 August	Creation of Ad Hoc Commission on the democratic selection of presidential nominees; Harold Hughes named chairman.
26, 27 August	Democratic National Convention adopts resolutions establishing reform commissions.
1969	
14 January	Democratic National Committee passes resolution numbers 11 and 12, authorizing McGovern-Fraser and O'Hara commissions; Senator Fred R. Harris named national chairman.
8 February	Harris appoints two commissions and their chairmen.
24 February	First staff member hired.
1 March	First meeting of full commission.
25 April	First of seventeen field hearings.
11 August	Field hearings end.
23, 24 September	Full commission initially reviews guidelines and tentatively adopts some; final action postponed to November.
October	Proposed guidelines and consultants' report on two, B-6 and B-7, widely circulated for appraisal.
18, 19 November	Full commission adopts final eighteen guidelines.
December	Guidelines distributed to state parties.

had the authority to both set standards and work toward their implementation. The final arbiter, of course, would be the Credentials Committee of the next convention, but the burden was being placed on the state parties early to change their practices to fit a yet-to-be determined model.[21] Remember that this took place at the opening of the very first meeting! The commission made some broad organizational decisions, touched on some potential substantive issues, and adjourned, all in less than three hours.

Two themes predominated, one of moderation of application, and the other of seriousness of intent. The tone of the proceedings is best captured in the chairman's remarks. For example, McGovern, while stressing "openness" of party procedures (suspiciously close to the participatory theme of the McCarthyites that had so irked the party regulars the year before), promised that no one group, section, or individual would be singled out as a scapegoat. It was a pledge on which he, the other commissioners, and Nelson would consistently attempt to deliver, despite consistent provocations. McGovern's ministerial background could find solace in his statement that the body's mandate would be fulfilled "by appealing to reason and our sense of justice"—although McGovern the practical politician asserted himself to caution that he believed such a course to be dictated also by "political necessity." Whatever the obstacles, the principal emphasis was clearly on achieving substantial changes in delegation selection methods.

McGovern struggled to outline the antecedents that contributed to his group's authority (something he never really mastered), including the auspicious role of Richard Hughes's Special Equal Rights Committee. While his presentation was murky, McGovern at least satisfied himself that his unit had "a clear mandate to fulfill" that was of a magnitude such as had never before been entrusted to any party commission. The chairman vowed that his group would meet the letter and spirit of their authorization, both of which that particular meeting was in the process of clarifying.

The chairman's remarks are noteworthy for setting the tone of the inquiry as well as for dedicating the group to producing something more than symbolic recommendations, the normal output of a party committee. The broad interpretation of the committee's role, as reinforced by the Wexler report, explains much of the body's later assertiveness. The remark to the effect that the commission's authorizations were broader than any previously assigned to a party agency were true enough; the group's powers had few—if any—parallels in the long history of the major parties in this nation.[22]

The commission had obviously chosen to take a strong position. Such an approach was extraordinary in a national party system renown for its chaotic decentralization and its complete disregard for any common standards of performance. The group's position could not be expected to go unchallenged, and opposition did in fact arise—at the meeting itself. Led by the persuasive Will Davis of Texas, opponents argued that such a forceful line was unrealistic or worse, and that it would not be tolerated by the states. The majority was in no mood to be influenced by the dissidents, but the issue would be raised again.[23]

The state parties would not surrender as easily as the commission's outmaneuvered minority. The local parties would resist; some could be counted on to employ any manner of stratagem to avoid what the commission came to believe was their responsibility. Their hope, of course, was to negate any real reform. Before the battle of wills could be resolved, every party agency as well as the three major branches of government would in some way be involved. In dealing with the problems it found within candidate selection procedures, the commission in effect reordered the priority of relationships among party levels. Normally power is centered in the unit closest to the voter, the locality, or, on rare occasions, the state, depending on the strength of traditions and the unprogrammed growth of organizational forms. Never in any meaningful way, however, has power—the ability to command acts of allegiance or to employ standards of party conduct—centered in a national party organ.[24] In effect, a delegated agent of the national convention with a dubious (or at best unclear) specification of powers was taking it upon itself to set rules to which the plethora of local duchies and minor political lords would have to comply in order to have any say in the nomination of presidential candidates. The audacity of the move is striking. Less clear at this point was the effect it would have upon the vitality of party operations. The commission's efforts could seriously affect the election of party nominees (the regulars' raison d'être for a party's existence), should basic differences arise as to the interpretation or application of the new rules. At this early stage, even the cooperation of the Rules Committee for the upcoming convention (the agency that would ultimately be entrusted with enforcing the commission's judgments) was in doubt. The road was to be long and uncertain, but in its own way, a quiet revolution had begun.

Such, then, were the stirrings of the McGovern-Fraser Commission. The commission was not destined to meet again until September and, as fate would have it, actually met relatively few times over the next four years. Spurred by this initial gathering, things happened quickly. Seventeen public hearings were held throughout the country between 1 April and 10 July. By September the commission felt prepared to adopt tentative guidelines. By November it had completed the consultation and decisional process and formally ratified the eighteen guidelines that were to serve as national party law. Within a year of its founding, the commission was hard at work enforcing its own handiwork, a set of proposals that, when applied within the states, would permanently alter the nature of presidential nominating politics.

The Executive Committee and the Staff

A number of organizational decisions flowed from the commission's first meeting. An executive committee was established.[25] This group of ten met in March and three more times before the fall gatherings of the entire commission. It assembled periodically thereafter, giving loose supervision to the reform agency's affairs. It provided a vehicle for continuity between the infrequent full meetings of the entire membership, and it served as a means of communication between commission leaders, staff, and members. Its greatest single contribution was in choosing a successor to McGovern when the senator departed to pursue his presidential ambitions. On 7 January 1971 the executive committee selected one of its own, Donald Fraser, one of the earliest reform advocates, to lead the group during the sensitive implementation phase. Beyond this, the executive committee fulfilled primarily a symbolic function. It provided a consultative process broadly representative of the membership, one that could be brought together on short notice and at limited expense. It could serve as a sounding board for proposals and it had the authority to make decisions in the lengthy interim between commission meetings. The chairman and the staff had de facto the same power, and their operation was considerably less cumbersome. The executive committee also initiated a way of overcoming the geographical diversity of a membership with a limited common focus.

Five of the ten members lived in the Washington, D.C., area and, given the fact that three others seldom attended, the balance of power in decision-making was centered there. Perhaps most important of all, the executive committee helped to protect the chairman (and, through him, the staff) from unnecessary abuse by bestowing a sense of legitimacy on decisions he and it initiated. The executive committee, while a useful organizational tool in broad terms, was not a key factor in explaining either the group's success or its operations.

The March meeting provided (basically through passive consent) authorization for an expanded staff to meet the ambitious schedule. The enlarged staff proved to be the driving force behind much of what the group accomplished. Augmented by an enormous influx of summer workers, it coordinated the complicated array of field hearings and supplied the research necessary to justify the proposals given to the September commission meetings. The principal staff and commission members determined the thrust and wording of the original nineteen guidelines (one was eventually dropped), a responsibility that set the limits of the debate as well as its substance.[26] This initiative proved a major influence in setting the final recommendations.

In the second phase of the reform operations, a severely curtailed staff[27] (in concert with first McGovern and then Fraser, and, to a lesser extent, the executive committee) handled the enormous responsibility of implementing the fundamental changes demanded of the state parties. This aspect of its work, unlike the dramatizing of the party's difficulties in the publicity-oriented first stage, required a professional skill, a sense of timing, and a prolonged self-discipline seldom found in public advocacy groups seeking to transform a political order. The effort had to be made while insuring that national and state party leaders were not unduly agitated; that the press was kept abreast of affairs (if not enthusiastic, its criticisms at best would be reasonable and accurate); and that the vast number of people who held a stake in the outcome were not overlooked. It was a sensitive job.

The work of the staff and the committee officers was overseen in a desultory manner by the full commission membership. Meetings of the entire group, in fact, were later needed to clarify the intent of its directives and to provide a vote of confidence in staff operations. In truth, however, the commission itself played a minor role during the enforcement period. The determination of the staff, combined with a political resourcefulness and sense of restraint, contributed directly to an environment conducive to enactment of the guidelines. This professionalism, and the backing of a majority of the commission plus the national chairman (on the occasions he was called on to declare himself—especially significant in the early phases of implementation), accounts for the almost total adoption of the national rules.

The Subcommittees: Road to Nowhere

A third area of organizational decisions proved less effective. The commission, in its meeting on 1 March, divided its membership among three subcommittees—delegate selection, grass-roots participation, and party structure—intended to do the real work of the full body.[28] This was not to be the case.

The subcommittee on delegate selection was particularly short-lived. This subcommittee was the first casualty because its work became the major concern of the entire membership. As the commission's focus clarified over the next several months, the commission coopted the area originally designated for the subcommittee on delegate selection. The public hearings began to cue the members to the most persistently sensitive of the issues of concern to party members and the one (unlike campaign financing or eased registration practices) that was amenable to *party* change. As the commission's resolve in regard to initiating concrete proposals on delegate procedures hardened, the subcommittee became superfluous.

GRASS-ROOTS PARTICIPATION

The story of Adlai Stevenson's subcommittee stands in sharp contrast to that of delegate selection. The group and its small staff worked hard, yet the more hours they put in, the clearer it became that the problems given them for exploration necessitated major inquiries well beyond their resources or even those at the disposal of the full body. The more intensive their investigations, the farther they diverged from what was emerging as the mainstream of the commission's deliberations.

Perhaps the enormity of the undertaking as well as the hopelessness of accomplishing significant change within the structure in which they operated should have been apparent from the beginning. The broadness of the mission charged to their small group does provide an indication of how unstructured the parent body's goals were at the time. Stevenson's group investigated and recommended improvements in such areas as registration laws, campaign financing, and the involvement of youth, blacks, and women in party processes. If this charge was not enough, the subcommittee (as do most political groups) cast itself in an action mold. That is, not being content to develop a case in favor of specific resolutions, the Stevenson subcommittee saw itself as a prime mover in encouraging community-level political involvement.[29]

The Stevenson subcommittee fell victim to the rush of events, as did the others. In addition to the press of time, however, it had to grapple with a broad set of problem areas, including registration procedures, a topic on which it produced a creditable report. Yet the overall impact of the group was limited. Registration, an important adjunct of delegate selection, did not receive—and, given the operating conditions, probably could not have received—the full attention it deserved. The subcommittee's intention to reach out through party structures and the media to welfare groups, youth, and minorities to motivate people to involve themselves in politics was more ambitious than practical, and far more than the beleaguered reformers could hope to achieve.

The McGovern-Fraser Commission did eventually adopt a policy position on each of the charges put to the subcommittee. Guidelines A-1 and A-2, the "quota" proposals on women, blacks, and youth, were taken from the more forceful promulgations of the Special Equal Rights Committee. The parent body, adding insult where it was not needed, created another "Youth Task Force" under McGovern's leadership. The new group's one contribution can be found in a well-attended, extensively publicized hearing on the difficulties inherent in young people entering the electorate (held immediately after the eighteen-year-old vote had been legalized).[30] The commission "urged" (not "required," thus depriving the proposal of the force of party law) that registration burdens be alleviated, and it called attention to the able report of its subcommittee. The full body did "require" the removal of all excessive fees in delegate selection, and it "urged" that ways be found to ease the overall financial burden on delegates. The proposals on financing were harmless enough and fell within the commission's limited mandate on the question. In the post-Watergate period they border on the naive—although they proved to be more ambitious than the Democratic party could handle during the election year.

PARTY STRUCTURE

The most consistently interesting of the subcommittees was created to explore the party's organization and to recommend means of making it more accessible and responsive to its constituents. Similar to that of the delegate selection subcommittee, its area of expertise traced back to the convention's mandate and constituted one-half of the McGovern-Fraser body's presumed jurisdiction (and one of the two main emphases in its title). Its responsibilities were narrower than the Stevenson subcommittee's, and change could be achieved through internal party corrections. The task force found an aggressive leader in Donald Fraser, who believed it imperative that party structures be revitalized and made more responsive to the demands of an increasingly policy-conscious electorate.[31] The new chairman, like Stevenson, worked hard at his job, and the limited subcommittee staff initiated investigations into areas of party operations seldom clear even to professionals.

Despite all it had in its favor, it failed. The reasons, in part, were similar to those underlying the futility of the Stevenson task force's limited yield. Events moved too quickly for the subcommittee structure to perform effectively. The principal focus remained on the full commission, and the demands of its work left little time, staff resources, or funding for complimentary efforts. The main commission focus presented opportunities ambitious enough to fully occupy all of its members.

All of these reasons apply, but there is more to the story. The entire question of restructuring the party organization (in contrast to determining practices for choosing presidential candidates or for modernizing the convention) came to occupy a no man's land between the two appointed reform groups. The Fraser task force recognized the difficulty.[32] Both commissions had legitimate aspirations in the area and, worse, both could claim convention authorization for their involvement. A self-conscious indifference resulted. The McGovern-Fraser and O'Hara commissions independently pursued their chief objectives with the intention of turning to questions of party organization at a later date. The two commissions belatedly joined forces in a last-minute effort to accomplish something. With Fraser taking the lead and the McGovern-Fraser staff under Nelson's direction providing the key background work, the combined groups announced in late spring of the 1972 convention year a laudable but highly ambitious "charter" intended to transform the Democratic party into an instrument through which the people could exercise an effective control over their leaders.[33]

Time was indeed short. The charter received scant attention from the press, citizens, or party members, overshadowed as it was in the furious climax to what had become a nasty contest for the presidential nomination.

The charter surfaced at the convention, where a nervous McGovern command agreed to postpone a decision on it until the last session. Working frantically up to that point, Fraser, O'Hara, and Nelson, in consultation with major party leaders, attempted to reach an acceptable compromise. The results were not satisfying. A fight of sorts—akin to a filibuster—occurred when the package came to the floor. A bored media ineptly covered the give-and-take that followed as more of the "party business" the networks appeared to detest. The fracas did contribute to the delay of McGovern's acceptance speech to the midmorning hours.[34] The compromise, as agreed to by the convention, realigned and enlarged the National Committee; it provided for a national conference (akin to a convention, though without its nominating functions) to meet in the off-year between presidential elections. And it created a new reform commission, the Charter Commission (eventually to be chaired by former North Carolina Governor Terry Sanford), to complete the work begun by Fraser's subcommittee several years before.[35]

All of this, of course, would occur well in the future. The subject matter held importance, but it fell beyond the resources of the subcommittee whose performance (due to factors it could not control) ranked somewhere between the extinct delegate selection and the too-broadly oriented but somewhat productive Stevenson task forces. It is hard to give this small group credit for any of the later developments. Its principal contributions were to emphasize Fraser's concern with the problems raised and to move him to think in earnest about possible remedies. Beyond this point, it served only to highlight the difficulties that would be encountered in a future area of contention between the two party commissions.

The subcommittees never functioned as they were intended to. They were submerged by the rush of attention given, in particular, to the enormously successful public hearings, and by the pressure to reach agreement on the proposed national standards before the end of the first year of the commission's existence.

The Public Hearings: An Effort to Be Responsive

Bitterness and distrust shrouded the birth of the reform movement. The anger of Chicago carried over into a sullenness of mood and a depression of spirit that the creation of the commissions did little to alleviate. The public hearings, which were to be held throughout the nation, were conceived as a means of penetrating this residue of ill will and providing a healthy outlet for the emotions that weighed down party spirits. The commission would go to the people—a novel approach for any quasi-governmental body. Further, unlike the perfunctory staging of many such efforts, the meetings would truly be open and well publicized, and would afford an opportunity for everyone to present grievances. The commissioners might receive an education. Everyone, even those ". . . not necessarily sympathetic to its [the party's] goals," would be welcome.[36] The linen would be cleansed publicly. In the process some of the disillusionment fostered by the previous year's presidential race might be moderated. In turn, the commissioners would discover the exact dimensions of the problems most affecting party members, and they might also stumble upon some recommended changes of merit. The long restorative process needed to recharge party spirits (and, eventually, its fortunes) could begin in no more appropriate a setting. These were the hopes.

Enormous success crowned these efforts. People came, more than four hundred fifty witnesses in all and, for one hearing (in Chicago), one hundred fifty spectators (unimpressive compared with other types of events, but highly gratifying for a party hearing). The meetings were carried off expeditiously, seventeen being held in less than four months (see table 2.2). And the media paid attention. The view of party operations depicted for the members was not pleasant, though admittedly the nature of the hearings was designed to tap discontent rather than laud party performances (the state and national conventions, state and national committee meetings, and virtually every other party-sponsored meeting or publication dunned the public on this score). Still, accepting the bias, party misconduct, the laxness and irrelevance of party proceedings, and the arrogance and indifference of party leaders (as the following excerpts make clear) were far more widespread, penetrating every level of party management, than anyone dared imagine. It may well be that the public hearings proved the catalytic ingredient that moved the commission inexorably from a well-intentioned assemblage of reasonable people to a group truly determined to produce needed changes. Similarly, the range of problems and the intensity of the discontent brought vividly to the agency's attention considerably weakened the nature of the opposition that less-enthused members could raise within the group itself. In fact, judged by the severity and range of the difficulties encountered, the committee's actions could be considered moderate.

Table 2.2
Public Hearings of the McGovern-Fraser Commission

Date (1969)	Place	Date (1969)	Place
April		June	
25	Washington, D.C.	7	Chicago
26	Detroit	11	Portland
May		14	Houston
3	New York City	16	Atlanta
3	St. Louis	21	Los Angeles
5	Minneapolis	July	
16	Phoenix	10	Boston
22	Jackson	19	New Orleans
24	Philadelphia	August	
28	Denver	11	Nashville

The hearings performed one other service that pushed the reformers toward change: the press and the rank and file had been alerted to the need for and significance of reform in the most explicit terms. Any failure of will before meaningful structural modifications had been attained would be met with hostility from the very audiences the national party, through its reform mandates, were attempting to conciliate. The general outcome (although not, of course, the specific recommendations) had become inevitable.

The hearings dealt with real people reciting specific grievances. Although obvious, this point is important. Everyone who had lived through the Chicago convention preferred to suppress the memory of it. The need was to establish, to the satisfaction of the party professionals, that the problems encountered in Mayor Daley's city were indicative of a sickness within the national party. They were not aberrations solely explainable by the peculiar nature of Chicago politics or the make-up of the insurgent coalitions. Remedies could not be simply effected by a change in or avoidance of a locality; national action of relevance to all party members was required. The hearings accomplished this goal many times over by bringing to light local travesties of responsible party action in every state examined. What was heard went well beyond the body's mandate. Yet the concrete nature of the episodes revealed grievances party regulars could easily comprehend, of a significance they could readily appreciate. They could relate to and they knew how to rectify problems such as these.

A voluminous record of each of the hearings exists. Between the transcripts and the generally extensive press treatments, any interested person can catch the flavor of what transpired. Nonetheless, the one element ignored in most controversies over the value of party reform is the specific nature of the outrages encountered. The following gives some example of these, in the spokesman's own words where possible.

Covering the State Parties

The seventeen hearings began in the nation's capital in late April with the familiar (at least to that city's politics-watchers) parade of notables—presidential contenders, United States senators, spokesmen for citizens' groups, national party officials—offering their views as to what ailed the party. The meetings then hopscotched across the country, touching down in such places as Nashville, Denver, Portland, Oregon, and Austin, Texas. Most participants recited irregularities from the previous year's presidential nominating battle that still rankled; others lectured the subgroup of five or so representing the full commission as to what reform should or should not do; a few officials gave bland presentations, attracting some media exposure while not unduly alarming anyone, and fewer defended party operations. One man went so far as to leap from a seat in the audience and leave the meeting, shouting he could stand no more such heretical one-sidedness. An excellent feeling of the hearings—and the most compelling glimpse of party operations—can be drawn from a sampling of the descriptions offered by witnesses.[37]

A Presbyterian minister who headed an antiwar group determined to work within the state party commenting on nominating politics in Tennessee:

We were refused the floor in county conventions. In some, our delegates could not nominate state delegates. At district caucuses the morning of the state convention, each district chairman "naively" presented his caucus with national delegate nominations; these supposedly had been worked out in district nominating committee meetings that morning. Actually, we . . . had the list days in advance—from someone in the Governor's office!

The state convention's Permanent Chairman had promised me the floor—I was an official delegate from Greene County—to speak against the unit rule and appeal for representative support for Senator McCarthy and/or an open delegation. When the convention was under way, I tried at the appropriate time to get the floor. I was literally ignored by the Permanent Chairman, who amid a chorus of resounding boos and shouts of "no," declared the Governor a favorite son and adjourned the Convention. We walked out, while TV cameras showed the state what had happened.

Also in Tennessee, an investigation into voting in a state primary in Davidson County uncovered a most involved electorate: in eight precincts where the records were retrievable, 120 percent of those legally enrolled voted. A sampling of just under half of the precincts in the district found that only one-quarter had adequate voting records, and in another quarter of the precincts, records were either missing or left blank. Apparently party elections within the county experienced such lapses regularly.

Two Florida Democrats drew attention to the unresponsiveness of their state party. They illustrated the situation by describing the structure of their state central committee and its depressing effect on representation:

The State Executive Committee is elected without any relationship to population; this lack of representation becomes more disproportionate as the state grows increasingly urban. Our counties range in population from 2,900 to 1,200,000; yet, each county elects two representatives to the Executive Committee. This rurally dominated committee[38] then elects the party leadership, which accounts for its neanderthalistic character. The National Democratic Committeeman and Committeewoman are also selected by the Committee, further removing this choice from the people.

Unfortunately, Florida's Democratic Party does not have the benefit of any semblance of minority representation. Minority groups and opinions are essentially ignored by the controlling leadership of the party.

Of Florida's 880,000 Negro citizens, not one has been selected to the Democratic Executive Committee since Reconstruction. For the sake of form, a few blacks are usually hand-picked to be included in the convention delegation. However, it should be clearly understood that these Negro delegates in no way can be said to represent the eighteen percent of Florida's population which is black. *During the 1968 Convention, the four Negro delegates joined their white compatriots in supporting the Maddox delegation;* [39] *and, indeed, voted against the seating of all disputed minority delegations.* (Italics added.)

Malapportionment of state party bodies was not confined to the South. The national committeeman from Oregon (which was, paradoxically, widely considered to be one of the most inclusive and commendable of state parties) reviewed one of the less desirable aspects of his state party, the incredibly uneven representation given party supporters: "The 'one-man, one-vote' concept is badly abused in both county and state central committees. . . . in Benton County, a precinct committeeman in Lobster Valley represents eight registered Democrats while a precinct committeeman in Mountain View, having an equal vote in the central committee, represents 230 registered Democrats, a 27 to 1 discrepancy. In the State

Central Committee, the Chairman of Wheeler County represents 248 registered Democrats while the Chairman of Multnomah [Portland] County represents 88,145 registered Democrats, a 355 to 1 discrepancy."

Also at the Portland hearing, an affluent suburban housewife reported on the "stranglehold" party leaders have on organizational positions and the threat newcomers pose to them:

> In our county active McCarthy workers were overwhelmingly rejected by the Democratic Central Committee when they sought appointment for unfilled precinct committee positions last Spring. The politicians controlling the county party structure were more interested in maintaining their positions than in adding new strength to the party. In many instances they sought out alternate committeemen for the same precincts to shut out the activists who were seeking appointment, while leaving unfilled many other precinct posts. *Ironically, the replacements they appointed were in the main not active during the election nor have they been seen since.* (Italics added.)

As to the paranoia and excessive secrecy that mock democratic procedures, here is testimony from an Arizona precinct committeewoman: "The Maricopa County [Phoenix] Chairman and his advisers cared so little for anyone's opinion that they simply refused to submit their secret slate of national delegates to the elected state committeemen, *even though the leadership had enough votes to have their list approved.*" (Italics added.)

The discrepancy between form and reality (appearing democratic while in practice being autocratic) was (unintentionally) underscored in the presentation of a party official from Wyoming. A quarter of the delegates to the national convention are elected by the state convention. The other 75 percent of the positions are filled by candidates who had to apply to a nominating committee chosen by the state chairman with the approval of the state central committee. Each potential nominee must be endorsed by his county committee or county convention. Under party rules, the nominating committee "shall give consideration to the length of party service, geographical distribution, occupation and other factors so that labor, industry, agriculture, business, the professions and Young Democrats shall be represented": everyone, it would appear, except newcomers, party dissidents, or those supporting a candidate or policy view to which the party functionaries took exception. The final slate required state convention approval. The state chairman assured his listeners that the process achieved a "reflection of the majority decision behind which all groups can, and must, unite."

On the organizational control of representation, testimony came from a number of states. In Iowa, for example, an estimated 40 percent McCarthy showing in the local caucuses was reduced to 8 percent of the national convention delegation strength in the state convention. In another state, a caucus chairman pulled 400 proxies from his pocket to counter an adverse vote from the floor. In Kansas, a witness complained of the tenure of the precinct leader (forty-four years) and her failure to call any precinct meetings. County meetings were initiated at the pleasure of the chairman and were limited to the party regulars. When the same incumbent later volunteered to work for the national ticket, he was told only paid workers were used in the county and his one and only contribution would be his vote on election day (needed to keep the same officials in power). Such stories were commonplace. Yet even with such competition, some states or localities excelled in horror stories. A close look at these offers some insight. A few of them are explored here.

Missouri, a border state containing a mixture of the southern penchant for a formlessness of party structure and a northern bossism, provided examples of a variety of problems, many common to other states, others bearing the distinctive imprimatur of the state's politics. Known for its backroom politics, Missouri did not disappoint when it came to presidential delegate selection. Among the abuses reported were: party bodies and electoral districts drawn in no relation to population;[40] multitiered selection methods for state committeemen and state chairmen that effectively freed these individuals of any control from the grass roots; party laws fixed by legislative statutes and therefore exceedingly difficult to change;[41] no voter registration by party; no rules as to eligibility to attend party meetings or national conventions; inadequate notice of relevant meetings for delegate selection; absence of clear procedural rules for the conduct of party meetings; unlimited proxy voting in party meetings; no provisions for minority representation; party leaders, elected for four-year terms and out-of-touch with the presidential candidate sentiments of voters, automatically attending national conventions; no rules or constitution governing state party actions; precinct caucuses held in rooms too small to accommodate all of the participants, with the moderator deciding arbitrarily who could or could not participate; precinct leaders appointing disinterested friends to delegations to state and county conventions rather than opening them to others; and some extraordinary procedures once the delegates reached the national convention.

In the last regard, Missouri Governor Hearnes cast his delegation's national convention votes without bothering to poll the delegates or ascertain their sympathies. When a delegate challenged this and asked the chair for a roll call—a right he had under the convention rules—he was ignored. When a McCarthy delegate challenged the governor on one vote tally, Hearnes admitted he made up the vote and in the process ". . . threw in some extras [McCarthy votes] to show how fair he was." Having fought hard to get to the convention, the delegate was shocked.

The Missouri State Democratic Chairman estimated that past members attending precinct, county, and district caucuses made up 5 percent of the total. Others believed this figure "generous." Perhaps the low turnout can be explained. One witness related that "it is not at all uncommon to announce the meeting for seven-thirty and have the presiding officer get there at seven and the meeting is over at seven-thirty when the mass of people come . . . this is fairly common procedure." One woman, unable to acquire information from any other source on delegate processes, researched law books obtained from the local library to find the relevant statutory provisions. She discovered that ward conventions were required, but when she called her local party officer she was told that "we haven't had them in several years . . . we usually just get together before we go into the county convention."

The experience of another prospective delegate in Jackson County, Missouri, adds a little drama to the normal account:

> I received notice of the meeting the day before it was to occur. . . .
>
> I arrived at the meeting over a quarter of an hour early. Since the entrance to the meeting (which was held in a private home) was through a garage and a back door, I stationed myself in front to direct those of my associates I knew would be coming later. When I came to the door to gain admittance at five minutes before the appointed hour, I found the door to be locked and several others of my associates unable to gain admittance. Upon gaining admittance by one of my associates opening the door from the inside, I found that a temporary chairman, Mr. ——, had begun the meeting early. He had proclaimed himself permanent chairman without taking a vote or allowing other nominations for the position. He had appointed a nominating committee without asking for any further nominations to that committee, or for calling a vote. He then asked for a vote on the report from the nominating committee on the subject of delegates to the county convention, without reading the names on the list. A vote was taken without asking for the "no" votes, without asking for further nominations, and without any semblance of order on the floor at the time. Having obtained a less than majority response of "yes's" Mr. —— then struck me in the jaw and knocked me down escaping with the list and, I presume, having ended the meeting.

That unrepresentative delegations should emerge from such practices is not surprising. As one observer noted: "One family in the city of St. Louis had as many . . . national convention votes as the entire black population of Missouri."[42]

Most of the hearings dealt with themes such as these, which were endemic to the state parties. Some state parties proved more troublesome than others, either in the intensity with which a given practice was adhered to or in the pervasiveness of the problems throughout the party system (as examples, the unit rule in Texas or the delegate apportionment process in Georgia, which in contrast made Wyoming's or Missouri's appear progressive). Amid the recital of the barriers experienced, the problems in two areas stood out. Chicago with its politics proved to be a glimpse of the worst the North had to offer. Parties in Connecticut, Indiana, Oklahoma,

Pennsylvania, and elsewhere could see their mirror image in some of the practices found in Chicago, and in this regard Cook County's paternalistic organization is instructive. But in the range of abuses uncovered, it remains unique, a warning of what a truly closed system can become.

The other area is the South. The injustices in a Chicago-type approach depend on extensive organization and a powerful leadership that is unresponsive to disorganized public sentiment and that, in fact, is capable of bending grass-roots support to its own ends. Neither condition necessarily prevailed in the South. The problem in these areas remained the crudity of democratic forms of expression. Rather than precisely articulated party forms, investigations in the South found either the total absence of any real party structures or the nascent, primitive state of their evolution. In the process of illustrating these patterns the cumulative impact of the seemingly unrelated abuses publicized by the hearings becomes clearer. First, Chicago.

Chicago: The Worst Writ Large

Little factual discrepancy exists in the Chicago testimony. The points in controversy settled on interpretation; that is, a judgment had to be made concerning whether the practices unveiled were intrinsically "good," or whether they were grossly unfair to the degree of being antidemocratic. For sheer excitement and publicity value, the Chicago hearing provided the highpoint of the seventeen public airings. To some, Mayor Richard J. Daley personified the apogee of American politics. To many, he had emerged as the culprit responsible for the disastrous national convention. For still others, Daley assumed the proportions of a folk hero—the professional politician inviolate, the voice of realism and the symbol of unwavering authority in a time of anarchy. Each of these perspectives overrated the portly mayor. One thing did appear certain. A confrontation loomed. The press was titillated. Holding a hearing of the McGovern-Fraser Commission in Daley's backyard presumably constituted a direct challenge to the most inflammatory figure to emerge from the convention. The Mayor's prepared response unnerved a lot of people, but the spectacle the media anticipated had simply been delayed.

Appearing before a tense group of commission representatives, Daley took the initiative. He went farther than the reformers ever intended to go, proposing that everything in sight be changed: more citizen participation, direct election for as many party offices as possible, reform of the National Committee, regularization of convention procedures, a reexamination of the electoral college, open party deliberations, the "one man, one vote" principle applied to all party agencies, and so on. As the mayor talked on, it became clear that these proposals were directed to other states, since Illinois fell heir to none of the abuses outlined. Daley ended on a distinctly accommodating note, asserting that the purpose of the convention (and, implicitly, other party forums) was not only to field a winning candidate but also to "help provide understanding between opposite viewpoints; to resolve differences; and to achieve unity."

Daley then entertained questions, in itself a novelty.[43] The inquisitors were circumspect and permitted the Cook County party leader to engage in a long and rambling defense of Illinois election procedures. The explosive moment had seemingly passed without the expected fireworks. Not so. McGovern, chairing the session, took the opportunity to advance gingerly "an expression of sincere concern" to the effect that it would be nice if the Mayor would use his influence to terminate the city's pursuit of "continuing indictments and harsh legal actions" against "people who were caught up in the chaos of last summer." Daley exploded: "I make no apology to you or anyone else." In Daley's view, outsiders came intending to cause trouble. They succeeded. They violated the law in the process and they would be prosecuted. The acrimony started long before the convention and "it was built up intentionally by [the] leaders of our party [McGovern?]." The infuriated mayor tore into the dissenters, defended the police, relived his upbringing near the famed stockyards and, to the expressed delight of onlookers, inadvertently coined another Daleyism: "I am not for oppressiveness, just for oppressive purposes." The media reporters were happy. The story went out. The mayor, McGovern, and the Democrats had performed as expected.

The real story of the Chicago hearings gained little public notice. The picture of political operations that emerged from the testimony did little credit to anyone, and certainly not to America's most honored mayor, the most powerful man within the Democratic party. Anyone who believes that politics involves more than the advancement of naked self-interest and that democratic assumptions have some relationship to the execution of the public's business had to be disheartened by the recitation of abuses inherent in the everyday operating procedures of the Chicago party. The hearing was thorough in this regard. Many people, a number practicing politicians, welcomed the opportunity to be heard. What they had to say was not comforting.

Two witnesses, one a United Auto Workers' organizer and the second a renegade suburban committeeman, gave particularly precise and knowledgeable accounts of the operations of the Cook County machine. These reports are worth drawing on.

The UAW representative began by explaining to the commission members why other labor officials were absent: "I am here on my own initiative. Mayor Daley didn't tell the other labor leaders to appear, so they are absent."

He then went on to describe the role of the machine in several areas of concern.

(On nominating candidates for public and party office)

There has not been a significant statewide primary contest since 1960 [as of 1969]. Candidates are slated for office in meetings closed to [the] press and public, the power and resources of the Party are placed at the disposal of slated candidates and the primary election becomes a statutorily required formality. . . . the primary turnout [is] principally a test of party discipline. Petition requirements for some party offices are far higher than for general elective office. Indeed, *in one recent contest for township committeemen, there were not enough qualified voters in the township legally to put both candidates on the ballot.*[44] (Italics added.)

(On patronage resources)

A significant proportion of public employment is controlled by the political parties. A party officer will participate in deciding whether a man is hired, disciplined or advanced, he can have the employee fired or "viced," and if the job becomes vacant that party officer will select another, because the job is his. . . . Nor are jobs the only reward. There exists a structure of homage and fealty in exchange for the dispensation of judgeships, appointments as special receivers, insurance business and the like.

(On financing party activity)

A Democratic Cook County Central Committee dinner will have 6,000 people in attendance at $100 a plate, although neither those who attend nor, indeed, most of the members of the Cook County Central Committee will ever be advised as to how much was raised or, more importantly, how this half a million dollars or so will be spent. . . . one who seeks, in a primary contest, to oppose a slated candidate must fight not just a candidate but an entrenched and well endowed political apparatus.

(On selecting delegates to the national convention)

Two delegates to the national convention are elected from each congressional district during the primary election. The ballot does not indicate the delegate candidate's preference for a presidential candidate. In any district . . . the township committeemen traditionally take turns being elected. The majority of the delegates are selected by the state convention. The slate is prepared in advance and many delegates learn of their selection, which they did not seek, by reading of it in the newspapers.[45]

(On the relationship between policy, issue-oriented groups, blacks and non-Chicago Democrats to the organization)

With Democratic voting power concentrated in Cook County [Chicago and suburbs], party policy too often becomes an adjunct of metropolitan politics and municipal administration . . . [and] an increase in the city sales tax becomes more important than an equitable tax structure. Black legislators are successfully pressured into voting for measures, such as stop and frisk legislation, which they believe will be disruptive to their communities. . . . Downstate legislators vote for election bills which will leave downstate Democrats weak and prostrate . . . because the measures will benefit Democrats in Cook County. . . . the system has fostered the political colonialism of black neighborhoods through welfare and patronage politics. Lacking ideology, it has excluded the suburban

Democrat. It has made downstate political efforts exceedingly difficult. By its emphasis on regularity and loyalty, it has created a profound distrust of those who question, [those] who will support one candidate but not another and who express dissatisfaction with the Democratic Party as it is now constituted in Illinois. There is a basic premise, often expressed and often acted upon, that Democrats and Democratic groups who are not part of the precinct organization regardless of their credentials, really are not part of the Democratic Party, that there is a "we," the organization, and a "they," those other people who call themselves Democrats. . . .

Many who consider themselves Democrats in national campaigns and on national issues, particularly younger voters, believe there is not a way for them effectively to participate in state elective politics.

(On the reactions of the party and its leaders to reform legislation)

Democratic legislators did not want slating meetings open to the public. They did not want changes in petition requirements for party offices. They did not want provisions to make registration easier. They did not want election of county chairmen. They did not want election of delegates to state conventions. . . . They did not want authorization for national delegate candidates to express preferences on the ballot. They did not want restrictions on party officers dictating the hiring, [disciplining] and firing of public employees or restrictions on public employees engaging in political activities during working hours.[46]

(On the differences in thinking between independent and organization Democrats)

The suppression of diversity within the delegation to the [Democratic] National Convention is only one aspect of the monolithic structure of the Democratic Party in Illinois which has resulted in its becoming the minority party in the state. The party structure and leadership have discouraged the entry into politics and public life of many independent and progressive individuals, and have impeded the rise to positions of influence of those who have entered. . . .

Many of the party leaders at all levels seem to think that a tight party organization is a strong one. But, in fact, a strong political organization is an open one. How can a political organization expect to grow and change with the changing needs of society and with the changing views of the electorate unless it is open to the participation of the electorate? (Italics added.)

(On the representation of blacks within the local party)

[While] 37.5 per cent of the city's [Chicago's] Democratic vote is provided by Blacks, only 18 per cent (9) of its (50) Democratic Committeemen are Black, and 19 per cent (7) of its (36) elected delegates and alternates to the last Democratic National Convention [and] an even smaller percentage of those appointed were Black. [While the Democratic presidential nominee Humphrey won 86.7 percent of the vote in the black wards against only 51.5 percent in the other wards of the city, both the black vote and black registration were down (22.5 percent and 14 percent respectively) from four years earlier due to] the deliberate discouragement of the Black constituency by the power structure of the Cook County Democratic Party.

(A Cook County Democratic Committeeman on the duties and emoluments of his office)[47]

The committeemen are nominally elected in primary election by their constituents and while they are formally charged with the selection of county candidates and the determination of party policy, in fact *during my three years of tenure, no issue has ever been discussed, no challenge ever raised to the nomination of any candidates.* The Central Committee is, in fact, a rubber stamp. The committeemen of the various congressional districts select the congressional candidates and they select the minority number of delegates to the national convention, those 48 who are elected out of the total of 118. While formally it is possible for others to run against the nominees of the committeemen, any such candidate has to reckon with the committeemen's control of the patronage workers and of the funds which flow from them. In consequence, a primary contest is a rare thing and an almost impossible obstacle to any Democratic candidate who is not selected by the committeemen. (Italics added.)

(The same speaker on the relevance of patronage to party operations)

The committeemen control the hiring, promotion, demotion and firing of thousands of government employees. Before I made it clear that I was personally opposed to the system, I received telephone calls from time to time from the Democratic headquarters saying, for example, "There are two forest ranger jobs in the forest preserve which are yours. They pay $375 a month. Do you want them?"

During the summer months I receive telephone calls from students who tell me that they have been offered jobs by road contractors subject, however, to my political endorsement.

It is not the public officials who are in a position to know whether an employee does good work in his job who determine who is to be hired and who is to be fired, but rather the committeemen.

The government workers selected by committeemen are expected to contribute some portion of their government salary each pay day. Typically, the amount is two per cent. . . . in the black wards in Chicago where jobs are scarce, the rate is higher. . . .

The patronage workers are the precinct captains. They are expected to do precinct work so that they provide both regular work in the precincts and political funds.

Many of the committeemen are, themselves, job holders, but even if they were not, they acquire an obligation to go along at the risk that if they don't, many of the people whom they have sponsored for jobs might be fired.

The total result of this system is the control of the party apparatus by a handful of people who are able to exclude, and in fact, do exclude from party decisions and the selection of candidates everyone who is not part of the political patronage system.

Little more need be said. These tales of greed, abuse of party office, meaningless elections, closed party forums, and servile decision-makers suggest something close to a disembodied whole with a maintaining and regenerating system peculiarly its own. Its lifeblood is patronage workers.

Its objective is winning elections. Its rationale is: electoral victory means public office means money. The redeeming quality of the Chicago operation, if there is one, is the clarity, totality, and precision of its workings. The Cook County party has an advantage over its rivals in that it has "pulled it all together." The techniques employed (with some variations, of course) and their consequences (allowing for less precision and other motivations—power, the advancement of a presidential candidate's fortune) are familiar, in part, to other state parties. This the hearings made unmistakably clear.

The South and the Beginnings of Representation through Parties

One-party areas present problems in direct opposition to those encountered in the discipline of a Chicago-styled organization. In states where the party has been dominant (Mississippi, Alabama, and Georgia, for example), the generations of being without viable choices in general elections have contributed to a total corruption of the political fiber. Public officeholders maintain themselves in position through a corps of private followers and client groups who directly benefit from their tenure. Even the loose discipline of a party with a common stake in the actions of its elected officials is absent. If they exist at all, party structures are loose groupings of old-line regulars with few responsibilities and no accountability. The anarchic parties remain irrelevant to most of the major decisions and policy choices made by an electorate. The real battles are waged over primitive but essential democratic rights (such as the opportunity to vote). Anything beyond this first stage represents something of a luxury. That every conceivable abuse could fester within such political systems is not surprising.

The field hearings tapped these strains. The problems are clear enough. The solutions proposed by the witnesses were all-inclusive, ranging from means for protecting individual voting rights to proposals for items to be included in auxiliary group charters. A few examples convey the totality of the confusion.

Alabama serves as representative of one type of difficulty. One E. D. Nixon struck at the core of many southern problems. Nixon, a former sleeping-car porter active in registration work, related the barriers to simply getting people qualified in some parts of Alabama to participate in party or general elections. As to the problem of registration, he said, "The difference between the white ones that was [sic] dead or left town, [is that they] were still able to be voted [sic], when the live negroes who were there were not able to vote." The registration books in Montgomery open after blacks go to work and close before they return home. Registrars required blacks to fill out applications with twenty-one questions. Should the individual overcome this hurdle, he could still be refused enrollment.

Once registered, there remained the possibility that the "keeper" of the local polls would put his hand across the door and say, "This is a white primary and no Negroes are allowed to vote here today," an experience Nixon said he had. This type of problem, of course, constituted a first step in self-governing, and was beyond party jurisdiction.

As to party operations, the Alabama state chairman of the faction closest to the national Democratic party, in his fashion a supporter of the reform attempts, told the commissioners that even the much-maligned unit rule would represent a sign of progress for his chaotic state party. The chairman, Robert Vance, contended that, in Alabama, "every candidate, every voter, every political leader and ultimately every delegate can (and often does) 'do his own thing.'" Doing his own thing included running two slates of electors in the just-past presidential election, each claiming to be the "true" Democrats. Each slate even had its own party symbol: the donkey for the nationally oriented Democrats, and the traditional Alabama emblem, the rooster (which accompanies the motto "White Supremacy—for the Right"), for the Wallace Democrats. Perhaps the state's Democrats were attempting to make amends for several previous elections (most notably those of 1960 and 1948) in which the state's citizens were denied the opportunity to vote for electors pledged to the national party's presidential nominee.

A black activist and leader of his own splinter Democratic faction, Dr. John Cashin, charged that the person sympathetic to the national party confronted in Alabama "the most confused and complex situation imaginable." He contended that the problems went well beyond what one panel could absorb in one day of public hearings, which was probably a fair assertion. Some of the problems as Cashin saw them included: a convention delegation, pampered by the national party, that came out and campaigned for the Wallace ticket; a seventy-two-man, lily-white state Democratic executive committee that was selected from congressional districts gerrymandered to dilute the black presence; a completely open (there is no party registration) Democratic primary that allowed "a Republican racist white block vote" to select party nominees; counties with over 100 percent white registration; and party candidacy that, for obvious reasons, offered no incentives for blacks to register and organize politically. Such disorderly politics are imposed on an electorate least able to handle them, an electorate characterized by little formal schooling (a mean of eight years for whites and less than five for blacks) and low per capita income. It is Cashin's contention that "it is in their [the state's party leaders] best interests to keep the situation as confusing as possible . . . so that ignorant people will not be able to wander through the maze."[48]

There are two sides (and, in Alabama, at least this many) to every story. Angered by the implicit accusations, the loyalist state chairman (Vance) recounted his problems in simply trying to have a "donkey label" placed on the ballot to help guide illiterates as well as the formidable resistance he encountered in attempting to pursue a campaign on behalf of the national party's nominees.[49] Whatever the truth of the allegations, the dimensions of the problems themselves become clearer. The challenge in Alabama and related states poses a more fundamental question than those found in Illinois or other states with similar practices: How can one insure that people will have the freedom to cast an unfettered ballot for candidates that offer representative choices? The difficulties, in short, far exceed the ability of one party or party agent to institute significant change.

The tales of abuse uncovered in delegation selection in Mississippi speak to the worst to be found in the states, southern or otherwise. As enumerated by the young delta newspaper publisher Hodding Carter III (a member of the Commission on Rules), among others, these read like a primer on corrupting the process: official attempts to maintain a white-based system; malapportioned party structures from the precinct to the state level, designed to represent areal units rather than population; party meetings held on workdays, during business hours, to maximize the inconvenience of attending; an arbitrary role by the governor in delegate selection; use of the unit rule at various levels of party decision-making to bind convention delegates; lack of representation for minority candidates or issue positions; acceptance of delegates without clear indications of their presidential candidate; keeping secret the times and places of meetings concerned with delegate choice; reluctance to register new voters or include them in party business; failure to educate prospective voters as to their role in delegate selection or the options open to them; the same people ("the courthouse crowd," as one speaker put it) year in and year out making the significant decisions; polls closing while lines of people still waited to vote; prohibiting illiterates from participating in elections; exclusion of blacks from political processes "by intimidation, trickery, and blatant disregard for the established procedures"; candidate support dictated by plantation owners; excessive filing fees (of, for example, $100 to $500) to ban the poor from seeking public office, especially at the local level (contests for positions on the school board, justice of the peace, etc.); intimidation of voters at the polls; threats to teachers (especially black teachers) of loss of jobs for engaging in minimum political actions (registering and voting); replacement of state executive committee members who die or resign by the remaining committeemen; and absence of any enforceable guarantees as to participation or representation at any level of the political system.

A sorry picture of party performance emanated from these hearings. The parties and their leaders seemed more concerned with thwarting the democratic will than with acting as an agent to expedite the people's control of their government. The point, as one speaker at the St. Louis hearing put it, is that "the more dramatic abuses, the ones that hit the front page of newspapers, really were made possible by abuses of democratic procedures that weren't very dramatic." The most visible outrages were built on an accumulation of acts of misrepresentation.

The unique set of hearings provided massive information on the functioning of local parties. Although uneven, they still could lay claim to being the most extensive ever held. The view of party operations offered few encouragements—except the willingness of people to tell what they had encountered and the implicit assumption that a constituency awaited a drive for meaningful improvements to begin.

The McGovern-Fraser Commission had set out to tap "grass roots sentiments on what the Democratic party does and what it should do."[50] The first part of what the party undertook (at least what it did that caused the greatest reaction) was consummated successfully. The second half of the committee's intentions was not so happily concluded. Before starting the reformers had promised that "the testimony taken at the hearings will be the Commission's fundamental ingredient in fashioning its recommendations."[51] In a sense, this was true. The problems brought to their attention would constitute the agenda for reform. But if the committee entertained a literal belief that the proposals advanced in these public meetings would emerge as the basis of their guidelines, they had to be disappointed. Those who appeared before the regional panels impressively articulated their grievances and personalized for those present the types of barriers they found in attempting to achieve representation within the party. This dimension of the hearings was moving. When the same witnesses turned to suggesting what should be done, they were less convincing. A number avoided the subject. Others endorsed general principles of fair play or simply called for something (left unspecified) to be done. Still others advanced vague plans of the type that serve as currency in political rhetoric (a national presidential primary, the governmental funding of elections, biennial conventions, uniform registration qualifications, fair representation for blacks). And others argued with equal fervor for specific points they felt to be important (a population base for the apportionment of party agencies and conventions, prohibiting media access to the convention floor, a ban on proxy voting, an end to open primaries). Few novel or well-documented reform alternatives were forthcoming.

Witnesses did pinpoint difficulties that fell within their mandate on which the commissioners were receptive to advice. The testimony given in the public hearings also covered every aspect of political reform in any way related to the party system. And while the commission staff assiduously mined the testimony for any and all materials that might assist them in the deliberations to come (thus fulfilling the early pledge), the quality of the testimony—as could be expected from open hearings involving all strata of the party and the public—varied greatly; little that was presented met the specific yet comprehensive review of a problem area with a reasoned advocacy of a given position or alternative. For most, advancing reform proposals was a minor stimulus underlying their appearance. A great deal of staff energy was devoted to organizing and interpreting the results of the hearings. Their impact on the commission, however, was more in the intensity of feelings conveyed during the meetings and the unique, and more often than not disturbing, glimpses into party operations that the hearings afforded. The distaste for party operations that were deployed to limit participation was vividly and repeatedly articulated. The remoteness of party officials and the antiquarian nature of party institutions was consistently underscored. If any commissioner had felt, prior to the hearings, that the discontent of the previous year was a passing fad, or that no fundamental reform of operating procedures was necessary, the field hearings disabused him of any such notions.

Beyond recommitting the group to their task and emphasizing the urgency of the changes needed, the regional meetings made several other contributions. Each of the hearings was well publicized locally and nationally. After forcefully drawing public attention to some of the most unsavory of party practices (thus reinforcing much of the dissatisfaction expressed during the earlier presidential election year), it was unthinkable for the party to permit affairs to remain unchanged. The monitoring of a suspicious press alone would make such a course of action unlikely. For much of the press, as for the attentive public, the question more than ever became, not what problems existed, but what the party intended to do about them. Pressure on the national party increased, giving added significance to the fall sessions of the McGovern-Fraser Commission, called with the intention of framing recommendations. If there ever had been a road back from significant change, the regional hearings virtually assured that the party could not take it.

The public meetings represented an act of faith, a symbolic gesture of inclusion. Views and opinions on decisions yet to be made were sought from anyone who cared to offer them. The patronizing aspects that engulfed much of political decision-making and that are common to most party deliberations, the belief that "we" know what is best for "you" and therefore as reasonable people have acted (or will act) in your best interests, was effectively removed from the McGovern-Fraser Commission deliberations. Overconfidence, a sense of arrogance, or a feeling of being divorced from or out of touch with the constituencies they sought to represent were not charges that could appropriately be directed against the committee's operations. If anything, the reformers could be faulted for expecting too much specific guidance from their clients. The public hearings added a legitimacy and credibility to their operations. While the final outcome of their work remained uncertain, the first of many bridges had been crossed, and steps had been taken toward establishing a climate receptive to their work.

The regional meetings also had a cathartic effect. There is an independent value in being able to say publicly what you want, to accuse or defend, and to feel that someone is listening. And while a reservoir of new ideas was not tapped, emotions certainly were. The hearings provided a gauge to the mood of those most concerned with party affairs.[52] For those who still failed to get the message, the following aptly summarized the feelings uncovered:

I come here with a very simple message. There are two Democratic parties in this country. One is the Democratic Party of the people: the people who work and vote and sacrifice for it, the people who look to it for leadership and assistance, the people who decide whether it will sit in the seats of power. The other Democratic Party is a collection of offices and machinery, with fancy titles. It issues press releases. It was, in 1968, completely and thoroughly separated from the people of the real Democratic Party. It is still separate today. It is your job to return the machinery to the control of those who are its rightful owners.

The words of a disgruntled suburbanite in Philadelphia? A housewife in California? An angry civil-rights worker in the South? Hubert Humphrey, the candidate of the party regulars and a victim, perhaps more of a victim than any other, of the ferocious party infighting of the previous year, issued the challenge to the group he helped create at its first open hearing. Later testimony reiterated in detail the problems Humphrey had so aptly described.

THREE

Adopting
the Guidelines

WITHIN SIX WEEKS of the last public hearing the commission was prepared to act. The staff had been busy. The voluminous records of the hearings were thoroughly indexed to reveal the most common violations raised and the solutions that had been generally favored. The nineteen recommendations that the staff initially formulated were based on the successfully concluded hearings, a nationwide system of correspondence with politicians, academicians, and other interested citizens (used at critical points by both commissions to broaden the consultative process), and a surprisingly adept review of the morass of state laws and party regulations that existed concerning delegate selection. The staff had indeed been busy.

Pulling Together Loose Ends: A Set of Recommendations

The preliminary rules thus drafted were presented to the executive committee on 28 August and again on 11 September. These were adopted with some modifications, and a copy of them was mailed to all commission members in anticipation of the climactic meeting of 23 and 24 September.

The late September gathering proved as significant as expected, though the group did not complete its work. The intricate and controversial ramifications of the proposals it was dealing with precluded any final judgments on any of the matters on the agenda at this first session. It did manage to adopt over half—ten—of the requirements in relatively definitive form, and it made provisions for a ratification and influence process that would carry over into late November. It also locked horns on two vital questions that in one form or another arose at every one of its caucuses: its conception of the powers entrusted to it (or what did the convention mandate really mean); and its expectations in promulgating delegate selection rules and what burden could reasonably be placed upon the state parties. Those controversial points constituted a continuing dialogue for the commissions and their opponents and supporters. They never were resolved (and, given the nature of American politics, never could be) to the satisfaction of all the participants. The September meeting took significant steps toward achieving conscionable standards meant to insure the panel's objective, "a process through which all Democratic voters had full, meaningful and timely opportunity to participate."[1]

Strains did exist, of course. Because their long-term objectives were continually in question and because of the significance of the process being examined, controversy was bound to occur. Matters were not helped by the awkward phrasing of the proposed standards, a difficulty the originators never overcame in the four reform years. The vagueness and mystery that surrounded party processes continued despite the hearings (which constituted an unsystematic tapping of the problems bothering participants) and the hurried work of the staff (which necessarily concentrated on the formal rules and written publications of the states). These publications did not constitute an accurate guide to the actual operations of the system—this much the public meetings clearly established. And there was the problem of having a large body of people on varying backgrounds, interests, and commitments attempt, under pressure, in full public view, and within a restricted time frame, to make decisions on items that would affect party capabilities for years to come. There was little to guide the panel, yet much was at stake. This last point was not lost on the participants.

THE SEPTEMBER MEETING

The healthy combativeness of the group at this juncture was evidenced in the proposals put forward, but it was even more evident in the interpretation placed on their "mandate" by the members. The commission followed the "operating definition" of the convention's grant of authority to the panel first put forth in the executive committee in August and reiterated in the same group's meeting on 11 September. The commissioners argued that any narrow reading of the phrase "full and timely opportunity to participate" would be inconsistent with the parent body's intent, a violation of the spirit of the minority report as adopted by the full convention. In effect, the early work of the March gathering had paid enormous dividends. The commission was now prepared to claim that in reality this wording of the mandate was intended to be interpreted like the clauses guaranteeing "equal protection" and "due process" in the Fourteenth Amendment to the United States Constitution.[2] Of all the words in the loosely construed Constitution, these are among the broadest of the broad. They have been employed to apply the Bill of Rights to the states on a discriminate basis. The commission's interpretation of the phraseology in its mandate could not have been more encompassing. This was a heady contention for a bullish group.

No one takes party committees seriously, at least to the extent that they content themselves with holding meetings, issuing reports, and generally doing the timeworn things party politicians have come to expect them to do. Consequently, no one chose to challenge such a sweeping declaration of authority. It was on the record for all to see, and, during the implementation phase of the commission's work, many would come to wish that they had raised objections at this more vulnerable juncture of the reform process.

The proposed standards were awkwardly classified in three divisions: abolishing rules or practices that inhibited access to the delegate selection process; diluted the influence of the Democrat in the delegate selection process; or did both. This arbitrarily confusing classification was retained throughout the period of adoption and implementation. Unfortunately, it did little to further understanding. The proposals themselves were extremely broad, just as the nature of the inquiry had been to this point.

During its two-day session the commission adopted in September all the proposals in the first two categories except those relating to the intrastate apportionment of delegates and the representation of all significant political positions within selection processes, two touchy issues of obvious political consequence. On these items, debate was unusually spirited and inconclusive.[3] The seven combined standards could not be reviewed in depth because of time limitations. The staff circulated to its national panel of friends explanations of the ten standards agreed upon, working papers on the two in question, and a summary of the seven yet to be debated. Those materials, in line with McGovern's dictum to secure "thoughtful, orderly changes,"[4] were mailed in early October to over three thousand party leaders, public officeholders, academicians, and party members in anticipation that some useful feedback could be obtained before the full commission convened for another session in late November.[5]

The presidential nominating process is complex. Attempting to superimpose some rationality on the system while being fair to all party factions as well as party members and prospective candidates can be a trying job. Practical objections were raised to a number of proposals. Others were questioned on theoretical grounds—the inherent rights of the state parties, past traditions, the real meaning of equitable democratic processes, and so on. Disputed political advantages were raised in objection to still others. Virtually every one of the proposed standards stimulated debate.

The "winner-take-all" primary, which would cause deep wounds in the next presidential nomination fight, stirred one debate. California was the testing grounds. Many objected to Robert Kennedy's capture of the full delegation (174 convention votes) with only 46 percent (to McCarthy's 24 percent) of the primary vote. Several members pointed out that forcing a change would bring the commission into conflict with the laws in South Dakota, Oregon, Massachusetts, Maryland, and Indiana. A handful, led by

California's Fred Dutton ("I am shocked at this idea that the Democratic party wouldn't be for 'winner-take-all' primaries in all fifty states"; "I believe we're only building in factionalism, . . . divisiveness [in outlawing such primaries]"), argued that these contests programmed a decisiveness and drama into prenomination campaigns that stimulated higher turn-outs.[6]

The hassle over the quota concept (future guidelines A-1 and A-2) is instructive. One of the Texas representatives, Albert Pena, castigated the provisions for omitting Mexican-Americans, an issue he raised in a challenge to his home state's delegation to the previous year's convention. Others tried to distinguish between the need to include blacks and youth, possibly, and the need to push hard for women's participation, a stand that "appalled" California's Carmen Warschaw. Some members talked about expediency, others, morality, and some even spoke of politics. Some discussed representation in terms of percentages (the quotas); others questioned the validity of such formulas. Some spoke to future potential, others spoke of past obligations or neglect. Many ruminated about enforcement: Could the body really require such actions? One member argued that reason had been left behind in assigning mandatory proportions of delegations to vaguely described groups. Could or should demographic groups and minority political views be equated? Would and legally or morally could the public's right to choose its representatives be abridged by such a policy request? Others rebutted that the proportions were not really mandatory (a point the commission footnoted when it promulgated these provisos), but that they of course would be interpreted and acted upon in that manner. Who would enforce what type of penalty? Who would oversee the process? Confusion and a good deal of irritation marked the lengthy debate. The issues, of course, were never resolved satisfactorily. The rules on nonmandatory mandatory quotas became the most controversial among the standards adopted. In the years ahead the staff would require a careful reckoning of the intent of the commission, and the upcoming convention and its committees would be left to deal with the matter as best they could (and, as it turned out, in a manner mostly— although not totally in every state delegation—supportive of a hard-liner stance).[7]

Intricate points of law, procedures or wording and its intent, repeatedly surfaced and were debated with full vigor. The results did not always lend themselves to clarity or alertness. For example, a turgid but important discussion of exactly what the group was asking the states to do at one point led to both the now familiar cursory examination of the mandates and a serious attempt to assign precise meaning to the awkwardly phrased statements in the staff's requirements. The debate over the interpretation of "called upon," "recommends," "require," and "all feasible efforts" was resolved through a motion put forth by former Florida Governor LeRoy

Collins. To clarify its purposes Collins fashioned, and the commission adopted, the following: "When the term 'called upon' is used herein, it is meant to carry the full authority of the Commission to obtain the accomplishment of the stated purpose. Where the Commission does not have authority to mandate the deserved [or] the desired changes, the term will be construed to call upon all those having such authority to use all feasible efforts to accomplish the change." To further understanding, the governor added: "And I suggest that we adopt this as the definition and then that we not use that language about 'all feasible effort' from time to time as we agreed heretofore that we would."[8]

A lawyer's delight! Imagine attempting to follow all of this orally and in different forms in each of the standards being weighed. The members did survive.

The press, a group Vice-Chairman Harold Hughes described as generally supportive but cynical that anything of consequence could be accomplished,[9] were fascinated (if that word can be applied to reporters) by the proceedings. The assessments were guarded, evidencing that combination of practicality and suspension of belief that Hughes had touched on. One observer in the press cautioned that the commission's actions remained only the "first step in . . . [a] complex process" by a group still unsure of its own powers. Other reporters drew attention to what they believed were the schisms in the body, a revival, as one put it, of "the controversies and rivalries which embittered the 1968 nomination and contributed to the party's defeat." In one dispatch the representative of the *New York Times* raised the specter of a McCarthy-like takeover of some party organizations by the young, and in another warned that the agency's job "is [so] complex, contradictory and controversial it may never get done."[10] To balance the assessments, reporters did find that the proposed changes amounted to "the most comprehensive and far-reaching blueprint for party reform proposed in this century." They made note of the fact that even the less controversial (as judged by intracommission divisions) proposals would eliminate many of the "dirty tricks" that had led dissidents and minorities to charge party regulars with unfair and exclusionary practices a year earlier. In sum, the consensual recommendations, if enacted, would alone accomplish many of the goals envisioned in the initiation of reform. Overall, there was agreement that the proposed actions did indicate "that the commission's leadership . . . [was] determined to press for sweeping party organization," an assessment with which it is difficult to quarrel.[11] Although the outcome of the effort remained in question, the scope of the movement and the reformer's objectives were correctly perceived.

THE NOVEMBER MEETING

The commission reconvened on 19 November, and the two-day session reopened the business left pending with "long-winded earnestness."[12] A

summation of the commentaries received from the circulation of the preliminary report had been reviewed. These reactions varied widely, agreeing
only that the proposals as written were unnecessarily ambiguous. Some
clarity needed to be introduced. The standards left undecided had to be
resolved, and the final seven recommendations had to be disposed of. The
members had been reflecting for two months—they came back ready for a
fight on the most significant of the issues before them.

First, the quota, a question needing further review because of the intense interest and confusion that surrounded it. Fred Dutton, backed by
McGovern and Carmen Warschaw, took the affirmative. The quota idea
was an effort to encourage (rather than command) the presence of youths,
women, and blacks on state delegations. Its intent was to smash the
tyranny of white middle-aged males.

The forceful Will Davis of Texas, supported by Professors Austin
Ranney (University of Wisconsin) and Samuel Beer (Harvard), among
others, led the attack. Political views, rather than age, sex, or race, should
constitute the basis for proportional representation, they argued. The provisions were in truth mandatory quotas. Adequate representation could be
provided through other means—a contention that the youngest member of
the decision-making body, David Mixner ("I've worked for ten damned
years in the Democratic party, and still the institutions don't respond"),[13]
found particularly galling. What relevance did group characteristics have
for processes intended to provide parity for all significant shades of political views? How could requirements for electing delegates be reconciled
with filling arbitrarily designated quotas assigned to specific groups?

The exchange was heated. A proposal to strengthen the proviso, *requiring* states to represent the various groups, was voted down with only
Mixner, Hughes, and Patti Knox, the vice-chairman of the Michigan party,
in favor. With the air thus cleared, the commission voted thirteen to seven
in accepting Dutton's motion to give women and youth, along with blacks,
a proportionate share of states' convention delegate votes, and ten to nine
in supporting Senator Birch Bayh's compromise that they must bear "a
reasonable relationship to the group's presence in the population of the
state." No percentage requirements were instituted, and the commission
later voted sixteen to zero to clarify that its action did "not envision the
imposition of a quota system." The divisions within the body on the issue
were deep and readily apparent. The compromise offered no indication of
how it was to be implemented or what could reasonably be expected from
the state parties.[14]

Another point of controversy, held over from the September meeting,
was the "winner-take-all" primary. The real focus remained on the primary as practiced in California, the state with the largest delegation and
the last major prize that could be won in open combat prior to the national
nominating convention. The political significance of the state, great by any

calculation, was magnified by these factors. Californians loved the "winner-take-all" primary for this reason. Others resented the principle (which they saw as a form of unit rule), the advantage lost (one-third to one-half of the delegation, or up to 135 convention votes, for a losing candidate who ran strong), the high cost of California campaigning (again, on the presumption they might end up with nothing), or simply past performance (the McCarthy people were sensitive about the loss to Kennedy that effectively ended the Minnesotan's candidacy).

Dutton paraded the familiar arguments—with the symbolic decisiveness, excitement, and competitiveness that marked the campaign—first made before the Ad Hoc Commission and repeated since as warranted. Mixner called on his experience to buttress his case, and others joined in on both sides. The sentiment of the commission seemed weighted against the practice when, in what may have been the pivotal argument, George Mitchell, national committeeman from Maine and later a leading supporter of Edmund Muskie's presidential bid, raised a novel point. Endorsing the proposed ban against such primaries constituted a radical innovation in party thinking, a revolution in nominating practices that was well beyond the commission's powers (a contention made by anyone opposing anything the commission supported). Mitchell's argument was that anything so drastic should be thoroughly debated by all segments of the party. This latter strategy carried weight, although in reality the nomination procedures of one state represented the target of the amendment. It is likely that the commission was not prepared for the outburst it encountered on the point, and that the technical and theoretical points raised (as with so many other issues) were difficult to assimilate and pass on in such a short period. In the end, a motion calling for proportional representation in such cases gained the support of only Mixner, Hughes, and Knox. A compromise proposal drawn out of a welter of conflicting provisions was finally accepted by a twelve to five division. This version "urged" state parties to "encourage as full a representation of minority views" on presidential candidates (the rubric under which the debate took place) as possible, and "urged" the next national convention to ban the practice. California's Democratic politicians, of course, were not listening. They had won their battle. The failure of the party, through its agent, to come to grips with the problem effectively, decisively positioning itself on one side or the other, was to cost the party dearly in the next election.[15]

The third major controversy that faced the embattled commissioners involved the intrastate apportionment of convention delegates. The issue was a delicate one. Prior to this point, such a distribution of votes had been totally within the preserve of the state parties. No one was quite sure how it was done in all of the states (this was one of the continuing mysteries of the nomination process), but they were confident that any promulgation on the subject would be resented by state and local party leaders. They also knew from their field hearings and their limited investigations that the practices in some states went back generations and were based on grants of votes to local entities (townships or counties) with no regard for population or Democratic strength. It would appear that a decision on this matter fell into the range of marginal issues that came under the commission's jurisdiction and could, in fact, overlap the concerns of its sister reform agency, the O'Hara Commission, which had clear responsibility for interstate delegate allotments. Nonetheless, the members persisted. In part they were beating the O'Hara Commission to the gun, and they hoped they were even influencing its yet-to-be-made decisions on interstate formulas for distributing delegate votes.[16] The O'Hara Commission would encounter a *fait accompli.*

The two formulas for the computation upon which to base apportionment of votes that attracted the committee members were Democratic strength and population. Allotments based solely on areal subdivisions invited little backing. Major considerations had to be resolved before either formula could be made workable. How do you measure "Democratic strength"? How do you determine what a "Democrat" is if your calculation is to be based on party membership? Does one measure or another of party success unduly benefit given groups within the party or bias representation? Concerning population criteria, why should Republicans and Independents help choose Democratic presidential nominees? Answering such questions requires much thought and a solid background investigation, more than a badly pressed panel could afford to do. Confusion is bound to result, and the most likely outcome is compromise.

At one point the group adopted, on an eight to six vote, a division of convention seats tied to "Democratic-ness" (party strength in national, or, less desirably, state, elections). Having done this, the commission immediately voted, by a ten to five margin, to reconsider the proposal. The members then ratified a complex formula that provided for an intrastate distribution of national convention votes based on both population and "Democratic-ness" (as measured by the party vote in the previous presidential election).[17] Having arrived at a working formula, they exempted, by a nine to five vote, all but statewide conventions from the provision. In a state convention or committee appointment system (the latter was frowned on but not banned), the state parties were required to adopt some scheme based on population *or* the Democratic vote (measured, at the state's discretion, by the presidential, senatorial, congressional, or gubernatorial election returns) *or* party enrollment figures. Additionally, in states with convention systems, 75 percent of the delegates chosen had to be selected at the congressional district level or below, a confusing solution to a demanding problem.

These debates consumed the major share of the two-day meeting. A number of other changes of consequence were adopted in what came to be the commission's final session on molding their recommendations. The committee voted to exclude all ex-officio delegates (those awarded their places based on their public or party office—senators, governors, congressmen, state chairmen—rather than on some form of open selection) from future conventions, only to find out that the largest number of such votes resided in 110 members of the Democratic National Committee. Predictably, the National Committee representatives, the bulk of whom were elected four years prior to any convention, proved exceedingly reluctant to surrender one of the few prerogatives of their inconspicuous office.[18]

The group's work had other objectives that were less visible. For example, the members believed they had undercut, through a variety of provisions (and especially the outlawing of the unit rule and the banning of instructing delegates to vote against their own preference), what are euphemistically called "favorite son" candidates for the presidency. Such candidacies can consume much of the national convention's time. More significantly, the commission believed they did not permit a state's party membership to vote a meaningful and direct choice among the principal contenders for the party's nomination. The designs of such candidacies were considered self-serving. They allowed states' delegation leaders to barter "their" bloc of convention votes for favorable treatment or policy commitments from a prospective president or for the promise of an appointive office (the vice-presidential nomination when the votes are critical to the presidential contender's success, a cabinet or other power-level position otherwise). The delegates from such a state were instructed to vote for the "favorite son," and most could be counted on to follow the delegation leadership in supporting another contender once a bargain had been struck.[19]

Finally, the panel attempted to tighten and simplify the message it sent the states. The torturous use of "call upon" was dropped. In its place, the word "requires" was employed when the commission demanded action. In states in which statutes impeded change, "requires" was linked to "all feasible effort," providing a gauge with which to measure the final outcome. Beyond this, the group chose the verb "urge" to indicate an end that was desirable but, because of time limitations, the magnitude of the problem, an unclear grasp of the issues involved, or the belief that the matter fell into a marginal area of the body's concern, unattainable. An occasional "recommend" was thrown in for diversity.

It was believed at the time that a full headquarters staff would be needed in Washington to give these words reality. Field task forces, in addition, would be formed to work with the state parties in clarifying and applying the rules as adopted. These, then, were the objectives. The committee's visions badly outstripped its financing. The status of the commission's funding as revealed by McGovern—$900 in the bank, $35,000 in debts outstanding—spoke more convincingly to its future. A shoestring operation would assume the major responsibility for directing the implementation of the reform proposals.

The November meeting had accomplished much. It had adopted, in final form, the commission's eighteen recommendations, clarified the onus to be placed on the state parties, and tentatively projected the group's operations into an uncertain future. Battle-wearied, its members could return home, taking some pride in the group's accomplishments. The immediate reactions of participants, press, and onlookers quite predictably covered every shade of opinion. One disheartened young reformer concluded that the results were "at best, a compromise with the 'old politics'—at worst, a failure."[20] "We simply underestimated the difficulties of achieving broad scale reform. . . . We tried to launch a teapot in a tempest."[21] His disillusionment was shared by others. Aaron Henry, the black activist chairman of the Mississippi Freedom Democratic party, lashed out at his colleagues: "We don't look very reform-minded. We have continually eroded to the most conservative position on every major issue. . . . The guidelines do not at all reflect the positions that all of us agreed on in private."[22] To add ideological balance, Will Davis also castigated his confreres. The reforms, the Texan contended, "[may be] so radical and extreme that they will never be adopted—you've [the other commissioners] gone too far."[23]

McGovern and Hughes both placed the commission's work in a more positive light. Both saw the outcome of the meeting as a series of "historic steps" toward a more open party system, although both appreciated the dangers inherent in the process of implementation and the probable need to institute challenges to some states before the next national convention.[24] McGovern concluded that "what we have done—that is, to look very critically at our procedures and to make substantial recommendations for reform . . . —I am convinced . . . will open up the national convention for many people who would not participate in the past."[25] True enough. But before this point could be reached, many problems needed resolution. The next step is to examine precisely what the guidelines the commission enacted were asking the states to do, and what evils they were designed to correct.

The Guidelines

As accurate an assessment as any of the fruits of the committee's work was that its "guidelines" represented "painfully wrought compromises,"[26] recognizing all that such an observation involving political compromise implies. Just as anything that is ever accomplished in politics, the guidelines satisfied few. The standards proclaimed were, nonetheless, "historic" (as claimed by McGovern, Hughes, and others) and, possibly more significantly, practicable. They struck an admittedly awkward balance between the aspirations of many people; they provided a serviceable format for the state parties to follow in amending their procedures (although not one clear of ambiguities); and they recognized and responded to a need for meaningful change. They also embodied far more innovative attacks on traditional problems of representation within a political party than anyone could have prophesized amid the recriminations and outcome of an embittered nomination fight little more than a year earlier.

The process of adoption was specific to the point of distraction, including constant haggling (most familiar to lawyers) over the connotations of words and repetitive attempts to protect the interests of real (or imagined) groups. Still, a reading of the guidelines finally decided upon begins to build an appreciation of the subtlety of the proceedings involved. Prior to the work of the reformers no one had commanded a knowledge of how the election procedures operated. They remained primarily obscure practices, relying on unfamiliar state laws or customs for sanction and local party operations for execution. They were called into play once every four years, and their complexity as well as the infinite variety of conditions in which they were used defied comprehensive evaluation. The guidelines did *not* establish a system for selecting delegates to the national convention; this would have introduced an order, a logic and sameness, foreign to an American experience that relied on highly individualized, often eccentric, party practices to function. Such a reformation was not the intent. Rather, the reformers hoped to establish criteria of fairness, both in relation to the procedural aspects of the practices employed in choosing delegates and in relation to passing judgment on the final outcome. The objective was to give every party member, not just officials, the opportunity to exercise direct influence on deciding who would represent the party as its presidential nominee. This participation was to occur during a period in which the candidate and issues were known, thus insuring a timely and meaningful choice.

The results of these actions were expected to be representative. They were to reflect the will of the party's majority. There was to be visible evidence that the outcome represented in some manner the wishes of known groups of political consequence in the electorate, including those believed to have been previously underrepresented in the selection process (blacks, ethnic minorities, women, and youth).

These are difficult-to-realize objectives, and it is an open question as to whether (and to what extent) the commission succeeded in its quest. Some goals are quite possibly contradictory (assured voices for specified groups versus the prevalence of the popular will, to cite one of the most troublesome examples), a point that caused endless problems for those most concerned with maintaining equitable standards. If an elected slate blatantly distorts the characteristics of the voting population, does it constitute the free choice of party supporters or an unrepresentative selection of delegates? Obviously there are different conceptions of democratic appropriateness mixed in unequal parts among the standards. Such confusion does not encourage an economy of application or a clarity of judgment as to right or wrong—the confusion that accompanied the choice of delegates and the unusual number of challenges in 1972 vividly dramatizes this point.[27] The inherent conflicts in assumption and political advantage that lay behind some of the guidelines encouraged attack. Those who wished to confuse or subvert the issues raised were given ample grounds on which to question the logic of the standards and ample ammunition to accompany these questions with implicit or quite pointed attacks designed to nullify the entire package.

One problem in assessing the guidelines is that their authors were attempting to mold them to meet the difficulties they knew would result. The rules are not, for the most part, dogmatic. The effort was to create reasonable criteria that well-meaning individuals could apply within their own situations. The commissioners were cognizant of the limits of political reality; most were practitioners of the art of politics. They could only go so far without jeopardizing any real hope of affecting change. If the demands were unreasonable, they would undoubtedly be ignored.

Consequently most of the provisions are not overly precise, but the reformers attempted to impart the spirit and intent of the criteria. The individual guidelines, then, are necessarily flexible. Less promising aspects are that they are repetitive, they overlap in many respects, and, as noted, they provide grounds for contradictory interpretations. If the outcome of the commission's work is perceived, as it should be, as the culmination of a series of different stages of political compromise intended to accommodate a multitude of known (as well as not so familiar) practices and as an effort to modify an ongoing series of politically interdependent mechanisms, then the nature and wording of the final recommendations are both clear enough and broadly impressive. If the balance of the guidelines are taken, as many party regulars and challengers chose to take them, as literal statements of what would be accepted (something akin to law), then an endless series of difficulties was possible. The key to application was that the changes, where needed, would be instituted by well-intentioned men who placed party harmony and (presumably) future party success above short-term commitments. Where such a condition was not met, where indifference or a desire to perpetuate actions that favored one group or another drew paramount attention, serious problems arose.

A number of things should be kept in mind when approaching the McGovern-Fraser guidelines. Considerable variety exists among the guidelines as to intent and specificity. Some of the proposals are weak and vague, while others are clear to the point of being rigid (for example 10 percent committee selection, 40 percent quorum); some verge on being meaningless ("urge"), while others have a quite apparent, immediate, and significant impact (A-1 and A-2 on "quotas"); some require state parties to change state statutes (a major undertaking), while others only affect the more amenable party regulations; and some constitute direct affronts to privileged sanctuaries (the ban on ex-officio participants and the requests for written notices and even published organizational rules), while others treat all with a Lombardi-like even-handed severity. And not all the rules demand action by each of the state parties.

In establishing the changes they wanted enacted immediately, the committee weighted the proposals in specifying the kinds of action they hoped would result. All or parts of five regulations were "urged" or "recommended." The difficulties posed by these proposals remain consequential: an inclusive system of voter registration; an alleviation of the financial burdens imposed by political involvement; a proportionate representation at all stages of delegate selection for candidate or political views not held by a majority of the participants; a confinement of selection procedures to party members, while leaving them accessible to those of good faith who wish to enter the party; and a prohibition of party committees from directly choosing national convention delegates.

The difficulty as seen by the party representatives was the severe psychological or legal readjustment demanded within a limited period of time (e.g., quasi-open selection instruments, the influence of party committees in the process); the group could not divine adequate solutions in the brief period they grappled with the problems (e.g., a faithful rendering of less than majority political views, and also the open-closed party mechanism issue which the commission firmly straddled); or the scope of the undertaking, as the committee's limited investigations alone should have demonstrated, went far beyond the commission's ability to affect answers within a restricted time reference. These fervent "urgings," then, amount to little more than expressions of sentiments and indications of future trouble spots.

Another factor implicit in the commission's deliberations surfaces. The balance of individuals most involved with the work of the reform were men of action—elective politicians, party officers, lawyers, businessmen, labor organizers, and minority spokesmen—intent on changing a system they found wanting. The emphasis was on doing. Once committed to the task, they sought immediate results. Vague hopes projected to some distant future had little place in their thinking. Politicians in particular personify this quality. Politics has a notoriously short time perspective. The "now" is of immediate consequence, and it receives priority. In an overly volatile and virtually unpredictable profession, the political realities of the present demand first and total recognition. Many find it difficult, for example, to project as far as from one national convention or election year to the next. This mood, with its accompanying need for quick action and the desire to see tangible results, fed a perspective limited to what could be reasonably achieved. This ambiance led the commission to emphasize thirteen full and two partial recommendations from the original eighteen. The "urgings" never came to more than that.

The set of proposals was divided into the same three rather curious groupings that were derived from the first listing—those inhibiting access (A), those diluting influence (B), and those combining parts of both of the first two sections (C)—significant only in that each rule came to be referred to in shorthand by its standing (A-1, B-1, C-1, etc.). In introducing the individual regulations and the problems they were meant to alleviate, I have retained the original listing.[28]

GUIDELINE A-1: RACIAL DISCRIMINATION

Discrimination intended to keep blacks and other minorities from participating in elections is an old problem in American politics. The battle against discrimination has been fought for a long time, and in recent years victories have been "won" repeatedly, but the issue, although more latent now, remains a sensitive one. Many believe the struggle for equal representation is over. For that reason, the story has to be continually updated. The grossness of the misrepresentation is appalling.

The 1890s, the years of the legal acceptance of the first statutes designed to prohibit blacks from voting and taking part in party affairs, were also the years that saw the beginning of a long and tangled series of encounters in the courts over attempts to open politics to blacks. The objective was legally achieved in the 1944 Supreme Court decision of *Smith* v. *Allright*. In 1948 the Democrats figuratively offered platform concession to blacks, leading to the Dixiecrat walkout from the national convention. The Mississippi Freedom Democratic party's 1964 credential challenge to the old-line party regulars from that state provided that convention's only minicrisis, leading, eventually, to equal access to convention delegations. This year effectively marked the end of the Democrat's tolerance for a racially prejudiced selection process. The convention established the Special Equal Rights Committee, first led by powerful Pennsylvania Governor David Lawrence and then by New Jersey Governor Richard Hughes. The special committee adopted the "six basic elements" intended to end party discrimination based on race. These "elements"[29] are broadly suggestive of the more elaborate requirements evolved by the McGovern-Fraser Commission (and, as a matter of record, are specifically incorporated in A-1). The special committee's boldness in meeting its problem and its maneuvering in implementing its recommendations served as a model for the later reformers. The "elements" were distributed to the state parties, and with their adoption by the National Committee and their incorporation in the call to the 1968 convention (as well as the selection of Richard Hughes as credentials committee chairman), the party served irrevocable notice that black party supporters would have full opportunity to influence party actions.

To some the action may appear to have been taken extraordinarily late. Political parties are agencies that strive for consensus; however, they are most reluctant to institute change. The second of the major parties saw its own, more limited, reform emphasis, intended to parallel the McGovern-Fraser thrust, come to grief over the same issue. The lesson appears to be this: if a party is willing to make a serious and binding commitment, regardless of timing, it should be welcomed and applauded.

The Democratic record up to this point was unimpressive. Black participation in prior national conventions had been minimal. The first black (a Reconstruction United States Senator from Mississippi) did not appear at a Republican convention until 1880, and no blacks participated in a Democratic convention until 1936! The proportion of black delegates in Democratic national conventions in 1952 and 1964 was 1.5 and 2.2 percent respectively, rising to 5.7 percent in 1968 and to 15.5 percent in the reform convention of 1972. Before 1972 no black had ever served as chairman of a major convention committee or sat as the convention's presiding officer.[30]

The 1960s, as a direct consequence of the congressional civil-rights legislation (most conspicuously, the 1965 Voting Rights Act), witnessed a resurgence of black registration and voting, especially in the South. In turn, the black vote, important to the Democrats since the New Deal, became even more party oriented.[31] The pressure on the party increased.

As the acting director of the United States Commission on Civil Rights told Congress, "The history of white domination in the South has been one of adaptiveness."[32] The record bears him out. The old order hung in as best it could. A report of the Civil Rights Commission tells the story.

Officials charged with managing elections in some areas of the South have withheld information from black party members about party precinct meetings and conventions or have prevented them from participating fully; omitted the names of registered Negroes from official voter lists; failed to provide adequate voting facilities in areas with greatly increased Negro voter registration; refused to provide or permit adequate assistance to illiterate Negro voters; given inadequate or erroneous instructions to black voters; disqualified ballots cast by Negroes on technical grounds; failed to afford black voters the same opportunity as white voters to cast absentee ballots; established polling places in locations, such as plantation stores, likely to discourage voting by Negroes; and maintained racially segregated voting facilities and voter lists.[33]

The events surrounding the election that led to the formation of the McGovern-Fraser Commission were not calculated to enhance trust. The incidents are specific to one county or state, but the pattern is familiar. Incumbents of party offices in Alabama extended their own tenure by fiat simply to avoid giving blacks the opportunity for election to these positions. One Alabama county party switched from district to at-large elections in order to deny the black voters the opportunity of electing their own party representative.[34] The state legislatures of Alabama, Mississippi, Georgia, and Arkansas extended the terms of some state and local offices under their jurisdiction and made others appointive rather than elective to prohibit black access to them. Filing fees for some positions were increased, and others in danger of being captured by blacks were abolished. The Alabama Democratic State Central Committee continued to employ districts grotesquely malapportioned (although they had been voided by the courts years before for use in elective races) to maximize the white vote and elect its committeemen. The districts had not been reapportioned in thirty-seven years. Predictably, the state central committee remained "lily-white." Louisiana elected its Democratic state committeemen from parishes (counties) gerrymandered to deny blacks representation. The Louisiana legislature, in addition, under the prodding of the legendary racist from Plaguemins County, Leander Perez, required by law that each parish have at least one committeeman, effectively minimizing both the black and the urban share of seats in the state party organization. The United States Commission on Civil Rights reported that in the 1968 presidential election year, less than six-tenths of one percent of 1,700 state committee positions in ten southern states were held by blacks.[35]

If a black candidate overcame such obstacles, more could lie ahead. A Greene County, Alabama, judge refused to print the names of several black candidates on the official ballot. Physical and economic intimidation took place in some quarters. Black registrars in Alabama were threatened with physical harm, and in some cases, run out of the county. Shots were fired into one black registrar's house in Mississippi, and another's was bombed.

Predictably, discrimination was not confined to the South. Participants in the New York hearing charged that state with employing literacy requirements, which, in substance and through the manner in which they were applied, effectively intimidated blacks, Puerto Ricans, and anyone else to whom they were applied. The McGovern-Fraser Commission heard testimony in Los Angeles that no black there had ever served as county chairman, and in Philadelphia it was told that congressional districts had been gerrymandered to deny blacks a proportionately equal share of representation.[36]

RESOLUTION. The problem was stickier than it appeared (given previous national convention actions), and the manner in which the McGovern-Fraser group resolved it (and the question of the representation of women and youth) stimulated the deepest divisions within the commission; this resolution was also more difficult to enforce than any other. First the group reaffirmed and again "required" the "six basic elements" of the Richard Hughes Special Equal Rights Committee. They had little choice in this regard. Next, after intensive debate on several occasions, it required the state parties to employ "affirmative steps" to increase minority representation within the party and on the national convention delegation "in reasonable relationship to the group's presence in the population of the state." It appended the notation that this wording did not signify a "mandatory imposition of quotas," although the state parties interpreted it as such and, although no action was taken, later commission debates over what percentage deviation from full compliance the commission would allow a state party did little to relieve their anxiety.

AFTERWORD. Despite the intense controversy surrounding it, the provision did have a substantial impact on the convention. Guideline A-1 complimented and reinforced the changing mood of the party. There were three times as many black delegates at the 1972 national convention as there had been at the convention of 1968 (15.5 percent and 5.7 percent). The Ad Hoc Commission had found that Mexican-Americans, Indians, and other racial minorities remained "all but unrepresented" in the 1968 national convention. The 1972 convention produced traces of representation for some and considerably more for others: Latinos or Chicanos held 5 percent of the delegate seats, American Indians one percent, Asian-Americans less than one percent (seventeen representatives), and Eskimos had two kinsmen to speak on their behalf. Twenty-two percent of the delegates were nonwhite, a considerable improvement in a four-year period.

Minorities had become too great a force and too diversified in their views to be satisfied with a few token convention appointments at the 1972 meeting. Blacks did, in fact, manage to gain a number of positions of real influence and high visibility in the proceedings. California legislator Yvonne Braithwaite Burke shared the convention's presiding officer duties with National Chairman Lawrence O'Brien; Mrs. Patricia Roberts Harris, former ambassador, member of the Eisenhower Commission, and law school dean, authoritatively presided over the troubled sessions of the Credentials Committee; Kenneth Gibson, the mayor of Newark, effectively chaired the final (crucial) sessions of the Platform Committee, receiving for his efforts a spontaneous demonstration of support led by no less than the George Wallace delegates from Florida; and Basil Patterson, a former state legislator and candidate for lieutenant governor in New York, was elected vice-chairman of the National Committee at its meeting the day after the convention ended, the first black in either party to hold one of the two top elective positions.

The most pronounced changes were felt in states with the greatest percentage of black residents and, not accidentally, the fewest (proportionately) black delegates (table 3.1). The average increase in black

Table 3.1
Black Representation in Delegations from the Eleven States
of the "Old Confederacy"
1968 and 1972 Democratic National Conventions

State	Percentage of Black Delegates		Percentage of Increase, 1968–1972	Percentage of State Population Black
	1968	*1972*		
Alabama	4	19	15	30.0
Arkansas	2	44	42	21.8
Florida	7	42	35	17.8
Georgia	5	32	27	28.5
Louisiana	18	34	16	31.9
Mississippi	2	44	42	42.0
North Carolina	6	47	41	24.5
South Carolina	13	25	12	34.8
Tennessee	11	49	38	16.5
Texas	4	30	36	12.4
Virginia	6	38	32	20.6
Mean Percentage	6.9	36.7	29.6	25.5

representation in these eleven southern states was 30 percent, while the mean gain for all the 1972 state delegations was 10 percent.

The figures are impressive.[37] Nonetheless, it is well to remember that the debate within the commission did not center on the desirability of increased minority influence within the convention but over the formula to be enacted and whether an arithmetic standard (i.e., mandatory quotas) was consistent with conceptions of just democratic representation.

GUIDELINES A-2 AND A-3: FEMALE AND YOUTH REPRESENTATION

The tensions that plagued the commission in resolving A-1 arose again in relation to the participation of youth and women. The problem, the underrepresentation of both groups due to the arbitrariness or indifference of those with power, was also similar. The process was more subtle, however, since it depended upon latent attitudes and ingrained social prejudices rather than on overt exclusion through discriminatory rules or laws. Once the initial barrier of gaining commission attention for the difficulties youth and women encountered was broken, the debate over resolving the issue became joined with that on black discriminatory practices. The resolution was also identical, although the absence of a precedent of "six basic elements" makes the reformers' decision in these cases more venturesome (and, if anything, less well received) than their judgment on race.

It may well be that the party's trustees blundered—or, to be more discrete, backed—into a stand on the problems raised. Both political parties believed they already adequately represented women. Women have traditionally filled a well-defined role within both parties, and they do have available the fruits of what could be referred to as a "mirror-image"[38] party organization at all levels, although they of course occupy the less powerful, basically honorific posts, such as vice-chairman or assistant or deputy chairman of the county or state party. Both parties have had (and continue to have) women's auxiliaries (the National Democratic Woman's Club, the Democratic Woman's Club of Cook County, etc.), although their function remains primarily social. The national committees have had women's divisions that can be helpful in meeting traditional political problems, but they are seldom vigorous advocates on behalf of reform of social problems of dominant concern to their sex. Given the party's obvious provision for their needs, what else could women possibly want? Both parties were soon to find out.

Women constituted about 53 percent of the adult population in 1968. However, they accounted for only 13 percent of the 1968 Democratic delegates and 17 percent of the Republican. Led by Ohio's, South Carolina's, and West Virginia's 5 percent, the Democratic convention contained twelve state delegations in which less than 10 percent of the members were women. Only one state delegation, Florida's (in which 56 percent of the members were male), approached equity. A woman headed one of the four convention committees, the innocuous permanent organization (which the O'Hara Commission could find no good reason for maintaining), and one of the fifty-five convention delegations (Oregon, one of the states historically more sympathetic to female equity)did have a female chairperson.

The Republican convention did no better. Three delegations (New Hampshire, West Virginia, and the Virgin Islands) had no female delegates at all, and eleven did not have a sufficient number to fill the seats on the four convention committees assigned them. Women were ornamentation. The males patronized them and subtly denied them opportunities for effective power.

The representation of youth had not been a subject of controversy within either party, despite the persistent youth-oriented crises of the previous national election year. The youthful volunteers (McCarthy's "kiddie korp" or "children's army," as some referred to them) had captured the begrudging respect of the professionals for their efforts on behalf of their candidates, but they had also won their enmity for supporting so vehemently the candidacies of the insurgents (Eugene McCarthy and Robert Kennedy). For many regulars the youth issue translated itself, unfortunately, into "those on the inside versus those on the outside wanting to get in." Besides, both parties had again made allowances for the youth vote, maintaining special divisions and such agencies as the Young Democrats or Teen or College Democrats (or Republicans), even though such organizations were normally politically impotent groups whose original goals had been prostituted in the political wars over the decades. Be that as it may, the party regulars were content—and basically unprepared for the intensity and comprehensiveness of the assault that followed.

The debate took place during a national mood of puzzlement. As with the question of representation of women, it represented one aspect of a movement of far larger social concern. Student rebellions on the nation's campuses were peaking; the youthful demonstrations against the Viet Nam War and the repetitive mass marches in Washington had seemingly accomplished little beyond getting Richard Nixon elected; the Chicago convention had been as bitter an experience for newcomers as for regulars; and the independent movement for an eighteen-year-old vote faltered, collecting more than its share of clay-footed advocates in Congress and persistent rejections at the hands of voters in state referenda. Among these activities, the actions of the reformers were of a lower order of significance, although still of symbolic importance.

Those campaigners for representation of youth (defined as eighteen to thirty year olds) could argue convincingly that the present system prejudiced their case. Less than 4 percent of the better than twenty-five hundred delegates to the 1968 Democratic National Convention had been under the age of thirty; eight states had an average age for delegates of more than fifty; only three states selected any delegates under the age of twenty-one; nineteen of fifty-five delegations had no member under thirty, and a solid majority had no more than one member under thirty. Only Nebraska, Nevada, and West Virginia had 10 percent or more in the younger age range. The Republican National Convention skewed even more noticeably to those who were middle-aged or older. A whopping forty-two state delegations had no representative under thirty, and one, Connecticut, had none under forty. Eight other delegations had only one member under thirty, and the average age for twenty-two of the delegations was over fifty. Not surprisingly, a meager one percent of the Republican delegates were thirty or younger. Eighty-three percent were forty or older. Bad as things were for women, they did outdistance youth. At least females were visible at both conventions. Youth played no significant role in either convention, although they clogged the streets outside at Chicago. In short, their grievance appeared legitimate.

RESOLUTION. The McGovern-Fraser Commission's remedy paralleled its remedy for blacks. State parties were required to eliminate discrimination and to take "affirmative steps" to encourage representation for these demographic groups in (again) "reasonable relationship" to their proportion of the state's population. Eighteen year olds were given full access to all party affairs, and the state parties were required to make "all feasible efforts" to overcome barriers imposed by state laws. The disclaimer of this being a quota was not noted as with race, possibly through oversight and possibly in the implicit understanding that the assertion applied to both A-1 and A-2.

AFTERWORD. Judged by previous showings, the non-quota quotas on youth and women were distinctly successful (see table 4.4). They forced the Democratic party (and coincidentally the Republicans also) to seek out females and young people (as one wag put it, "young, black females would be in great demand") to serve on the delegations, theoretically making them more representative of the electorate. The results are striking. Forty percent of the Democratic delegates were women, well short of an even split but tenfold greater than four years earlier. A woman came close to unseating the national chairman as the convention's presiding officer in a minirevolt on the Rules Committee, a woman chaired a convention Credentials Committee hearing, a woman finished second to the eventual nominee in the race for the vice-presidential position, and Shirley Chisolm ran as a minor candidate for the presidential endorsement. The vocal Women's Caucus made itself heard throughout the convention, most significantly in the forming of the party's platform.

Youth fared better also, but more along the lines of the role played earlier by women—they were visible in the proceedings but not significantly influential. The representation of those thirty or under increased over fivefold (to 21 percent). Only seven states had 10 percent or less of their delegations composed of "youth" delegates, and a surprising thirteen states had 30 percent or better made up of people up to thirty years old. The bonds holding youth together as a distinctive group within the political arena seem considerably weaker than those tying women together in a community of interests. Once the eighteen-year-old vote had been achieved and the Viet Nam War had faded as an issue, the raison d'être for a "youth group" paled.[39] In terms of representation, however, major attrition is not likely to set in for either group. Once the barriers have been lowered, the gains are usually permanent.

GUIDELINE A-4: THE FINANCIAL COSTS OF BEING A DELEGATE

Political activity is expensive. The election year of 1972 "cost" over $425 million. President Richard Nixon expended more than $60 million as an incumbent seeking reelection. People are duly impressed by sums of this magnitude. What they fail to appreciate is the financial expenditures required of the "little man" who dares to venture into political combat. This less-recognized problem was what the reformers attempted to alleviate.

There are many dimensions to the problem. Some of the minor infringements the commission could and did void. As to the fundamental difficulty, the group could only once again draw attention to the varied inequities. For example, professionals realize the significance of "starting costs" in seeking any political office. Consequently, in many jurisdictions petition requirements are unusually high (especially for people not supported by the major parties), and excessive fees (some, such as "customary" or "obligatory" "donations" to a state party's treasury, are hidden; others are tacked onto the state's requirements for filing nomination papers) are not unknown. Most are not part of general public knowledge, but constitute little surprises for those seeking delegate status. There are numerous illustrations, ranging from onerosity to nuisance.

Concerning petition requirements, there are the following: Pennsylvania, New Hampshire, Nebraska, and the District of Columbia demanded only between 25 and 200 petition signatures; Connecticut and Massachusetts refined the art, the former demanding the pledged support of 5 percent of the registered Democrats in a township and the latter, either the endorsement of the party's state central committee or 2,500 petitioners, with no more than 500 from any one of twelve counties to enter a slate; New York specified 500 (except for New York City, where the total was 750) names per congressional district; New Jersey called for a modest 100; Ohio law stipulated 1,000 signatures to run statewide and 100 to seek delegate office within a congressional district; Rhode Island required 500 statewide, with at least 25 from each county; and Oregon, with a further variation to a confused theme, accepted 1,000 petition names or 2 percent of the last Democratic vote, whichever was less, in lieu of a $15 fee. The time for collecting such signatures also varied dramatically by state whim, from a low of ten and sixteen days (Rhode Island, Connecticut) up to two and three months (California, New York).

The same capriciousness faced a presidential contender seeking to qualify as a candidate in a primary. Four states (Oregon, Nebraska, Rhode Island, and Wisconsin) relieved the candidate of the decision, lodging the power to place a contender's name on the ballot in the secretary of state or in a specially designated, nonpartisan committee. Presidential aspirants do not always appreciate having state agencies determine their individual state strategy for them, although their options in such cases are limited.[40] Massachusetts welcomed any names submitted by the state chairman, but required 2,500 petition signatures, divided by county, for others; Indiana followed the same course of action, only stipulating a larger total, 5,500, with at least 500 from each of eleven congressional districts; New Jersey accepted 1,000 designated supporters, and New Hampshire, only 50 from each of two congressional districts, *if* they were individually notarized.

The range and severity of the free provisions also varied: Connecticut allowed the official slate of the state party free access to the ballot, while imposing filing fees totaling $14,000 on any statewide challenging slate; Florida collected $50 from all at-large delegate candiates and $25 from those at the congressional district level; Nebraska levied $25 and $15 fees on prospective delegates and alternates respectively; Hawaii required $25 and Connecticut $15 from those seeking to be delegates to the state party convention, a step in the delegate selection process; West Virginia demanded an amount calculated at equivalent to one-tenth of the president's salary for a contender for that office to appear on its primary ballot; West Virginia also charged at-large delegates $20 and district-level delegates $10 for filing; the South Carolina Democratic party assessed its delegates $15 to help defray the party's expenses, which was arbitrary when compared with requirements of states without such a tradition, but cheap when contrasted with similar state party requirements of $250 (instituted by the Indiana and Iowa Democrats); Indiana's, a state party that has forged a reputation in this area,[41] pushed a good thing a little farther, demanding another $250 from its Democratic delegates to maintain a hospitality suite and delegation headquarters in the convention city; Pennsylvania, Maryland, Oregon, New Hampshire, Alabama, Nebraska, and Oregon made fees of $10 to $25 a condition of seeking delegate status, although New Hampshire and Oregon would specify a certain number of signatures in place of the fee; and Wisconsin and Iowa required a $4 dues and a $5 registration levy to participate in caucuses or conventions relating to delegate selection. In a welcome contrast to the country's norm, in North Dakota, a state with a number of other forward-looking political traditions, a delegate was provided with up to $200 by state law to meet his travel and personal expenses in attending the convention.

Another aspect of the cost problem—one that infinitely muddied it—centered on the economic class structure of conventions. Economic considerations (among other factors) unquestionably hindered less affluent people in attending conventions. These gatherings were significantly more representative of the economically comfortable middle classes, a point that can be easily illustrated. The parties do not keep information of this nature, but one can review the rosters of the conventions of both parties and make judgments as to the economic and social status of delegates from their occupations or residences. The most specific data available are for the conventions of 1948 and 1964 and the reform gathering of 1972.[42]

Only 21 percent of the Democratic delegates and 16 percent of the Republicans attending the 1948 conventions earned less than $5,000 annually. Fifty percent of both conventions made $10,000 or more. By 1964 the figures pointed to even more discriminatory representation. With a national median income of under $6,000, 85 percent of the delegates of both parties made $10,000 or more. Less than 3 percent in either convention made below $5,000. The median income for Democratic delegates was a high $18,000, and for Republicans, $20,000. For the Democrats, in 1968, 40 percent of the delegates made over $20,000 (compared to 12 percent nationally) and a low 13 percent had incomes below $10,000 (as against 70 percent nationally).

Finally, there were the costs involved in campaigning for the office and in traveling to the convention city and meeting one's living expenses once there. The range of campaign costs personally borne by the delegate in 1964 was modest (ranging from $50 to a little over $150). Delegate living expenses for the same year came to a more substantial amount, between almost $350 to over $700 (depending on region of the country), and averaging $455 for Democrats and $647 for Republicans.

RESOLUTION. The commission was perhaps at its most ineffectual in finding solutions to the economic difficulties faced by prospective delegates. It did what it could, but it dealt with only the fringes of the problem, and even then its remedies lacked authority.[43] The commission required state parties to remove all "excessive" costs and fees (over $10) and to waive any others that might constitute a financial burden. Mandatory party assessments were voided. State parties were also required to eliminate "excessive" (over one percent of the registered or voting Democrats)[44] petition requirements, and were "urged" (and therefore not bound) to seek ways of better handling the financial strains placed on delegates.

AFTERWORD. The problems of economic class representation and personal traveling, living, and campaigning costs are not dealt with in these recommendations, although they influenced the reformers. Some of the harshest criticism levied against the guidelines resulted from the economic imbalance that supposedly resulted from their application. The 1972 convention was unquestionably skewed toward economically better-off persons.

The only effective way of dealing with the problem would be to employ the "reasonable representation" formula that caused so much turmoil when applied to other demographic groups. As to individual costs, a good deal of elaborate planning (national party-initiated state quotas to help

Table 3.2

Family Income and Campaign Costs of 1972 Convention Delegates

Family Income of Delegates

Income ($)	Percentage of Democratic Delegates (N = 1,550)	Percentage of Republican Delegates (N = 807)
Under 4,999	4.4	0.9
5,000–9,999	10.7	4.5
10,000–14,999	20.3	11.6
15,000–19,999	18.6	11.6
20,000–24,999	13.6	15.0
25,000–29,999	8.8	10.5
30,000–49,999	13.4	21.8
50,000 or more	10.2	23.2
	100.0	100.0

Costs Incurred in Running for Delegate Position

Costs ($)	Percentage of Democratic Delegates (N = 1,505)	Percentage of Republican Delegates (N = 749)
0–49	66.7	79.6
50–199	20.5	13.6
200 or more	12.8	6.8
	100.0	100.0

SOURCE: Based on a sample of 1972 convention delegates.

needy delegates, low-cost dormitory and inexpensive hotel arrangements, busing, provisions for cafeteria meals, day-care centers) by the Democrats (and, to an extent, the Republicans) failed to deal adequately with what remains a serious problem.

The economic composition of the 1972 convention, shown in table 3.2, appears to be little changed from its predecessors. As in 1964, 85 percent of the delegates made more than $10,000. The modal category of income was $10,000 to $15,000, and the majority of Democratic delegates made between $10,000 and $25,000. The distribution looks fair only in comparison to Republican delegates. Only 5 percent of them made below $10,000, and a majority earned more than $25,000.

The costs of campaigning for delegate positions in 1972 seems to be in line with those of earlier conventions. Two-thirds of the Democrats (and three-fourths of the Republicans) spent a modest amount (less than $50) on their campaigns, and only one in eight Democrats was required to invest $200 or more in the effort.

GUIDELINE A-5: PARTY RULES

The content and availability of formal party rules within a state fall into the sphere of arcane knowledge known only to the political cognoscenti. The substance of such rules, whether they are found in state statutes or party by-laws, may control every element of participation within a state party explicitly or by indirection (leaving local officials to implement the regulations and fill the void). Political professionals appreciate this fact of life, and so did the commission. This particular guideline, rather omnibus in its inclusiveness and significant in its ability to predict later recommendations, represented one of the most significant (although least commented on) in the range of those presented.

The group's position, as put forward in a staff memo, was quite clear: "A Democrat can enjoy full and meaningful participation only in a system that has been comprehensively defined by party rules and/or state laws, which have been adopted well before the process is scheduled to begin. These party rules and state laws must define every aspect of the delegate selection process down to the time and place of every precinct caucus. Furthermore, there must be no provision in the rules which permit party authorities to alter or amend the delegate selection process before or during the procedure."[45] The process should be stable (last-minute changes at the whim of party officials had to be avoided), open (assured through specific by-laws), well publicized (full public notice of date, time, and place of meetings), and not subject to modification or discretionary abuse by party officials (for example, the realignment of delegate apportionment formulas or the choosing of alternates or filling of vacancies in a delegation by unaccountable party officers). Furthermore, the wording and tenor of most party constitutions should not (though they did) go beyond the ready comprehension of most laymen.

The commission judgments on this matter were unusually clear and inclusive and provoked little internal disagreement. The effort was aimed at avoiding instances similar to that reported by a Louisville party member whose "precinct meeting is always held out-of-doors in December in what appears [to be] an effort to discourage participation."[46] As far as could be determined, eight states had no party rules (Ohio, Louisiana, Illinois—which fought this provision until after the delegate selection for the next convention—South Dakota, Missouri, Kansas, Utah, and Washington—which did have state committee by-laws). Massachusetts and Wyoming appeared to have difficulty in finding their party regulations, and one state made theirs available only on payment of a modest fee. This review says nothing concerning the substance and provisions of the rules. Most states allowed party leaders at various levels a substantial amount of discretion in these activities. At least three states (Louisiana, Missouri, and Alabama) had no standing regulations applicable to delegate selection. These were issued by call or resolution immediately prior to the commencement of the processes. The trust invested in the judgment and loyalty of party officials can be enormous in such cases. In Alabama, as an example, the state committee had the option of choosing even the method of selection (primary, convention, committee, or some combination). Four states (Alabama, Connecticut, Delaware, and Tennessee) permitted local party functionaries total discretion in the delegate selection procedures they chose to employ. The party's town committee in Missouri or Connecticut or its county officials in Tennessee determined the place and time of delegate selection meetings.

The jockeying of the specific rules covering local meetings (usually within a broader set of state regulations that applies some limits to the total process) was a more familiar stratagem, common to state parties. New Hampshire permitted all towns to determine their own polling hours in primaries, and, although it undoubtedly increased confusion, New York had different hours for rural and urban counties and Rhode Island legislated varying times for each of its towns. New York and Connecticut required different times for poll openings and closings in primary and general elections, and in Utah and North Carolina the time and place of local caucuses were established by the county committee. Texas allowed a modified local option, placing time limits on the meetings (no early morning or midnight gatherings). As to place of caucuses, Alabama, a state notoriously lax in such requirements, demanded only that they be held in the vicinity of a polling place. The information gathered on Missouri practices in the field hearings—the accusations of caucuses being held in secret places, behind doors closed to all but the faithful, at hours earlier or in locations other than what was publicized—revealed one of the most systematic statewide perversions of these practices, and gives some inkling of the problems encountered on a more limited scale in the other states. RESOLUTION. The commission's skepticism of current practices led to an unusually explicit and forceful set of proposals; most of the following guidelines are simply efforts to codify and specify provisions outlined in this section. State parties were required to adopt precise written rules on delegate selection and to make these readily available. These were to provide for the apportionment of delegates and distribution of votes within the state; the means for choosing delegates and alternates; the manner through which alternates succeeded delegates and vacancies were filled; the dates, times, and places of all meetings, which (with the exception of rural areas) had to be uniform within a state in a given year and over a period of years; the procedures for selecting convention committees and their responsibilities; the methods for instituting and handling credentials challenges; and the provisions for minority reports. Furthermore, the state party was told to "facilitate maximum participation among interested Democrats" in the nominating system and to gear all of their actions and regulations toward this end.

GUIDELINE B-1: THE USE OF PROXY VOTING

The proxy arrangement ideally allows someone not present at a proceeding to have some influence on the outcome. While useful and sometimes even necessary (many meetings in rural areas would be hard to conduct without it), proxy voting can be subject to gross abuse. A Honolulu newspaper reported that proxy votes from unorganized precincts were being cast—including a precinct consisting of vacant lots razed in an urban renewal project! At a county convention in Cleveland County, Oklahoma, one member held 123 proxies, enough to outvote everyone present. In one state where proxy votes had been employed to control a local meeting, a later examination showed that many of the proxies had not been notarized, and that many represented unregistered party members, thus invalidating them. But the damage had been done. In one case in Missouri, a state subject to an inordinate amount of party abuse, a test vote in a Clayton Township (St. Louis County) meeting showed the insurgents in control, 140 to 111. A party regular then voted a comfortable 492 proxies (which his opponents were not permitted to examine) to elect his candidate as chairman.[47]

RESOLUTION. The commission outlawed proxy votes.

GUIDELINE B-2: OVERLAPPING SELECTION PROCEDURES AND CLARITY OF PURPOSE

Party meetings or primaries that select national convention delegates also conduct other party business in at least thirty-two states. Party members in some areas are forced to influence the choice among presidential contenders most indirectly, selecting among party officials for positions in which one of their many functions will involve a role in selecting national convention delegates. Such practices dilute and obscure the impact of the individual party member. Illustrations of the widespread practice are numerous. Indiana, Utah, and Kentucky had state conventions that both selected national convention delegates and determined party nominees for state officers (the latter a far more critical set of decisions). Precinct committeemen elected in the off year in Idaho were responsible, along with their own local party duties, for a great part of the presidential delegate selection process. A combination of party agencies in Arizona, Louisiana, New York, Oklahoma, and Pennsylvania had a direct hand in choosing national delegates. Party primaries are vehicles for resolving many party issues, a fact that muddies the process of delegation selection. Some primary states do not permit a potential delegate to list his presidential preference, thus adding another layer of ignorance to the entire process.[48]

RESOLUTION. The commission promulgated a general standard and left it to the goodwill of the states and the skill of the staff to enforce it. A state party was required to make "clear to voters to vote how they are participating in a process that will nominate the Party's candidate for President." Presumably this meant, in part, that candidates for delegate would designate whom they favored. The state parties that employed convention or committee systems were required to clearly designate national convention delegate selection as such.

GUIDELINE B-3: THE MATTER OF A QUORUM

State party rules varied (or were nonexistent) concerning the minimum number of people necessary at a meeting before business could be transacted. In effect, this permitted unrepresentative, small gatherings of "cronies" to act in the name of the party. Arizona party by-laws allowed as little as 25 percent of the membership of the state committee, and New York, 33 percent, to be present to appoint convention delegates. North Carolina was satisfied that representativeness had been accomplished if as few as ten registered Democrats attended a party caucus. The state party in Maine authorized 2,223 to attend its state convention. Many smaller towns did not send representatives, and only 846 voted in the convention's only roll call. Only 23 percent of the seventy-two-member Alabama State Central Committee attended the meeting destined to choose its national convention delegates.

RESOLUTION. The commission debated setting as a quorum 50 percent of the party base (however determined), but settled for requiring 40 percent.[49]

GUIDELINE B-4: SELECTING ALTERNATES AND FILLING DELEGATION VACANCIES

This provision, like many others, is an elaboration of guideline A-5. State chairmen or state central committees, a presidential candidate's nominating committee, delegation chairmen, the delegation, or even the delegate himself are permitted by some states to select alternates or to fill vacancies that might occur in a convention delegation. Knowledge of these practices employed in this backwoods of politics was limited, and any sense of regularization of methods was entirely absent. Rhode Island law permitted the state committee to fill vacancies in the delegation and to select delegates if insufficient numbers filed in the primary. Wisconsin, Arkansas, and Maine followed related practices. The state chairmen in Connecticut and Massachusetts were empowered to complete delegations. Under this rule the Connecticut Democrats (by leaving their delegation choices incomplete) gave their state chairman authority to appoint directly four delegates and up to eight alternates. North Dakota, Maryland, Michigan, West Virginia, Florida, and Oregon allowed the national convention delegation to choose its own alternates and to fill vacancies as they occurred. Nevada gave the county central committee power over decisions on alternates and filling vacancies, a grant they exploited fully, right down to the precinct level.

Any sense of representativeness is lost in such juggling. The entire concept of "alternates" is questionable. Legislators do not have shadow substitutes, for example.[50] If the parties did not feel they needed to work so hard in attempting to reward as many members as possible by including them in conventions, and in particular, if they did not allocate such posts to the party's "fat cats," the heavy financiers of campaigns, there would be little argument for keeping these honorific positions in an already bloated convention body.

RESOLUTION. The commission's solution rested in restricting the methods of choosing alternates to one of three specified in the convention call (primary, convention, or committee), and specifying that vacancies be filled by a "timely and representative committee," the original body that chose the delegation or the delegation itself acting as a committee (an individual member could not choose his successor).

AFTERWORD. The rulings are general and have had no significant impact. They present no particular constraint on state parties, although they do void several of the most arbitrary practices concerning replacement (the uncontested role of the individual delegate or the state chairman, for example, although the latter's power is de facto left intact by the implicit approval given to state central committees).

GUIDELINE B-5: THE IGNOBLE "UNIT RULE" REAPPEARS

Again, a seeming redundancy. The unit rule was outlawed by the 1968 convention, and by action of that body the prohibition was extended to any stage of the deliberative process leading up to the 1972 convention. Enough had been said on the matter. The commission concurred in negating the unit rule—"the practice of instructing delegates to vote against their stated preferences," a far broader interpretation, but one consistent with the convention's action—at any point in the delegate selection process.[51] The latter phraseology (like the 1968 convention's) places only a moral sanction on a bound delegate. It was left to the individual to decide how he would fulfill his "instructions" from a primary electorate, a state convention, or any other body.[52] The commission did stretch the prohibition, choosing to apply it in a questionable manner to "favorite-son" candidates, a problem that fell more comfortably within the jurisdiction of the O'Hara Commission.[53] It simply noted in an addendum that the ban included delegates "instructed" to vote for a favorite son. If extended to its logical extreme, as these departures threatened to do, no candidate, major or minor, could count on any delegate's support, regardless of how binding his selection procedure had been.

As with many practices in politics, once examined closely, the seemingly familiar turns out to be far more complicated than originally expected. The delegates who prohibited the unit rule knew exactly what they had in mind: outlawing the arbitrary use of power to distort representative institutions (nicely personified by Texas in the convention that voted the ban). The presumption was that the edict applied to the approximately fifteen non-primary states who employed it (usually in a limited fashion). However, if the extension to primary states is undertaken, then the whole problem of "bound" delegates is opened to question. Of greater practical significance, the "winner-take-all" primary (most notable in California) is then illegal.[54] Admittedly, the concept is being stretched. The commission in its policy-making sessions had deliberately avoided taking a direct stand on the California-type primary, much to the party's later chagrin. The commission waffled on the issues involved and on the wording of the proposal as to its application, an indecisiveness or a lack of political courage that would prove costly.

RESOLUTION. The commission ratified the ban on the unit rule and, through a notation, applied it also to favorite-son candidates.

GUIDELINE B-7: THE DIVISION OF NATIONAL CONVENTION
DELEGATES WITHIN A STATE[55]

Employing the arguments that the reformers had been mandated to recommend changes that would "assure even broader participation in the nominating process" (which was true enough) and that quality of such participation is directly affected by the intrastate apportionment of national convention votes (a tenuous link), the commission prepared to endorse specific allocation formulas as being more representative. The systems devised by the state parties for apportionment ranged from something approaching whim or temporary political advantage to reliance on traditional distributions, emphasizing geographic units (e.g., the township in Connecticut, counties in Pennsylvania, Maine, Louisiana, Idaho, and

Hawaii, or congressional or other districts in other states), the number of people voting for Democratic candidates in specified elections (not always presidential),[56] or rewards for evidence of party success (extra bonus votes is one illustration). The impetus supplied by the series of court decisions on reapportionment gave these hitherto-unexplored problems a greater sense of urgency.

Two basic areas of decisions emerged from the morass of questions vying for commission attention: the desire to specify a formula for national convention delegate apportionment within a state, and the effort to prescribe a balance between local (normally defined as the congressional district, although county, city, town, etc. could be used) and statewide (at-large delegates) interests. By mutual (and basically silent) consent, an allocation formula resting on geographic subdivisions regardless of population was not given serious attention. The bulk of attention was devoted to schemes emphasizing population or some calculus of Democratic strength (for example, party registration or the Democratic turnout in a presidential or some other race) as a base.

Each alternative had its strengths and its weaknesses. A population criteria includes Republicans and Independents as well as Democrats in devising a process of selection that is exlusively party oriented. Not all states have party registration, and even for those that do the practice is not necessarily statewide, requirements varying in severity and in the fidelity of their application from one community to the next (thus including voters in one locality that could not vote in another), and figures are not necessarily reliable or current. A party's manifestation of strength in a state or congressional race can have little relationship to its presidential vote (the difference between the congressional and presidential returns by district in Florida, for example, approached an average of twenty thousand votes; the 1968 Democratic gubernatorial and United States Senate nominees in Louisiana captured an incredible 100 percent of the vote, and the Democratic United States House contenders, on the average, 81 percent, while in the same year the presidential candidate of their party could claim only 28 percent,[57] and the variations in patterns of support within a state from one Democratic presidential nominee to the next can be extreme indeed (in Burt County, Nebraska's Democratic presidential vote fell off by 50 percent between 1964 and 1968, and those of Independence County, Arkansas, and Knox County, Tennessee, by approximately 40 percent). What was to be done, then?

Consultant Richard Wade put the issue of the principal choices hanging in the balance well in a report prepared for the commission: "The problem of apportionment is clearly very complex. In the broadest sense, finding a solution requires an adjustment between past performance and future expectations. A rigid apportionment system based on previous results would, of course, maintain party integrity and reward those who have a sustained commitment to the party. But a reliance on old statistics may also inhibit future growth. . . . In this inevitable tension, perhaps prudence dictates a tilt toward the future."[58]

The presumption exists that the smaller the geographic unit of representation, the more reflective the elected officeholder is of the wishes of the constituency. By such a standard, an at-large delegation employing the state as the electoral unit in caucus or convention states or that old bugaboo the "winner-take-all" primary, with delegates elected statewide, symbolizes the ultimate divorce of the delegate from his electors.[59] A delegate chosen under these conditions is hypothetically the most unresponsive to individual and community pressures for which he should act as a trustee.

These thoughts blended with the differing conceptions of representation that the commission constantly flirted with but never openly addressed. The mixture of assumptions (never articulated) as to what constituted the ideal representative contributed to the complexity of the choices placed before the reformers. With only vague standards to guide judgment, confusions persist and overlappings and even contradictions in intent occur. Perhaps attempting to shape reality to criteria (however imprecise) within the time limits allowed proved enough of a challenge.

The situation in New York State demonstrates the nature of the problems being addressed by a group that had no clear idea of the type of representation it wanted to promote. The state received 190 votes in the call to the 1968 convention. State party rules reserved 5 full votes for party functionaries. These rules also assigned 3 to each congressional district (41 districts accounting for 123 votes). The remainder of the delegates were selected at-large by the state committee, which also had the option of assigning, at its discretion, each member thus chosen a full or fractional vote. As a consequence, 62 national convention votes were stretched to include 105 people.

Party professionals in New York appreciated the discretion they could exercise in awarding national convention seats. The commission was set on limiting it. The state party representatives especially appreciated the five full votes awarded automatically to officeholders.[60] The commission frowned on the practice. The congressional district provisions in the New York plan accurately represented population differences (due to the reapportionment decisions), and thus were acceptable in this sense. These same districts, however, badly distorted party strength (the Democratic vote of one constituency was 280 percent that of another), giving ardently Republican areas an equivalent voice in party affairs to those with strong Democratic sympathies. This inequity the reformers hoped to alleviate. The commission intended to severely restrict the major role of the state central committee (believed to be considerably less reflective of grassroots sentiments than either conventions or primaries) in choosing delegates and supervising the distribution of convention votes. The commission also came to find the selection of 35 percent of the delegation from a constituency larger than the congressional district excessive.

RESOLUTION. After considerable soul-searching during the fall of 1969 (comparable only to the nondecision on adequately protecting the concerns of all presidential contenders with a significant following and the "quotas" that bedeviled the commission to its liquidation) the group endorsed an apportionment formula divided fifty-fifty between population and Democratic strength within a state. Initially the calculation of party "strength" was left open to state option (limited only to the presidential, senatorial, congressional, or gubernatorial vote in the preceding election or to party registration). Such leeway delayed a choice among the alternatives involved and built considerable slippage into what should have been standards of comparative equivalency among the states. The situation was intolerable, and no one was pleased with it. A move began almost immediately after the November meeting to tighten the requirement, restricting it at first to presidential returns from the prior election. Then, in an ingenious attempt to provide a fair and reasonably stable criteria of national significance, the mean Democratic vote for president in the past *three* elections was substituted for the earlier formulations.

GUIDELINE C-1: PUBLIC NOTICE OF MEETINGS
CONCERNED WITH DELEGATE SELECTION

This provision is an extension of three (of the total six) rules adopted and circulated to the state parties by the Special Equal Rights Committee in July 1967 and by the national committee in January 1968 and made binding on delegations through its call to the convention. The regulations demanded a number of useful innovations: the "timely" publicizing of the location and hours for all party meetings in places accessible to all and the full public disclosure of all legal and traditional procedures for selecting national delegates at all stages and of the qualifications for contesting each office in the process. While well intentioned, quite obviously the new rules had been ignored. Furthermore, no penalties had accrued to the violaters of these edicts. The Credentials Committee under Richard Hughes (also chairman of the Special Equal Rights Committee) found these party bylaws impossible to apply in decisions not involving gross misrepresentations of blacks. If nothing else, a reemphasis of the provisions was needed.

The commission was further concerned with the failure of prospective delegates to indicate the candidate they would support (thus giving party voters a reasonable choice) and the lack of standardization within the states of methods of educating voters to the choices they faced. Ten of the sixteen primary states failed to permit candidates for delegate positions to indicate on the ballot the presidential aspirant they supported. In twelve states party voters elected state committeemen with no formal advance notice that one of their duties consisted of partially or completely selecting the state's national convention delegates. In some states the process began so early and was so indirect that it deprived party supporters of any say in the outcome. Idaho Democrats voted for precinct committeemen two years before a national convention without realizing this constituted the first step in the unwieldy delegate selection process. Oklahoma likewise allowed their congressional district committees to choose half of the national delegation. The county chairmen (and co-chairmen) who sat on the district committees were selected by precinct committeemen who were in turn elected by party voters a year and a half before the presidential convention. What voice did an Oklahoma Democrat have in deciding the membership of the delegation thus chosen or in influencing their commitments?

A minimum of six states did have provisions that met the "public notice" guarantee, although a number would have to be considered pioneers in rendering these impotent. California required a list of candidates and a notice of elections to be published, but in no more than two newspapers per county. Pennsylvania, Missouri, and Connecticut favored notices in small print tucked in inconspicuous corners of newspapers. Connecticut (and many others, as the regional hearings made clear) went on to hold what were, effectively, closed sessions.

RESOLUTION. The commission restated the "public notice" requirement and required that a clarification be made available to party rank-and-file in advance, detailing the relationship between delegate selection and whatever party business was to be considered. It also required every delegate hopeful in a primary election or those running for offices with a hand in the process to list their presidential preference on the ballot (including a statement of "uncommitted," if this described their position at the time). This last twist particularly irked party regulars determined to withhold any endorsements (and thus maximize their bargaining positions) until well into the convention.

GUIDELINE C-2: THE EXCLUSION OF EX-OFFICIO DELEGATES FROM THE CONVENTION

Every state delegation to the national convention contained ex-officio delegates. The practice is an old one, much treasured by party officials who regard it as one of the prerogatives of their office. Its advantage can be subtle. For example, in a primary election, the slate committed to an incumbent president, a front-runner, or a favorite son, or which is designated "uncommitted" but receives all the attention, is stacked with the senior politicians of the state party. It is elected and so are they. A state convention selects a delegation. The party faithfuls obviously desire to reward their leadership with convention seats, and do so. Neither the primary nor the convention practice is unacceptable. Although some may have wished for a more open competition for the national posts, the party leaders were nonetheless elected in a perfectly legitimate manner.

Less subtle is the practice whereby a state party would include, with full voting privileges, on its national delegation a party or political officer by virtue of the position he held. These were the ex-officio delegates the commission attempted to ban. The arguments against their inclusion were many: the automatic selection of such members excluded "meaningful" participation by party members in filling the seats; the awards were not subject to any challenge; the call to the convention specified only primary, convention, or committee appointment of delegates (an unconvincing legalistic argument used frequently in support of the commission's position and meant to imply that because automatic delegates had not been explicitly authorized they were prohibited);[61] ex-officio delegates were normally selected prior to the convention year and thus were "untimely" (a violation of C-4); ex-officio party and public officials were chosen for their duties with no thought given to their role in a national convention; and, for election officials, all voters (not just Democrats) helped chose them, thus complicating procedures intended only for party members. Such positions were effectively removed from the control of the party membership, and members were unquestionably awarded national delegation posts on the basis of considerations other than their support for a given presidential contender or their views on issues facing the national convention. Further, and less explicitly stated, once at a convention, their power, seniority, and expertise virtually guaranteed that they would control the delegation, effectively dominating its actions and neutralizing the influence of the bulk of the delegation's membership.

The issue continued to be a sensitive one throughout the debate over reform. Several themes were repeated in the arguments of supporters. Most significantly, party leaders believed such positions were rightfully theirs, and they had no intention of relinquishing them. As one advocate noted, it is unfair to penalize people who have devoted themselves to party affairs, often continuing the less glamorous but necessary work of the party between elections, when others are too preoccupied or disinterested to lend a hand. Such hard work and unquestioned loyalty should be rewarded, and a pass to the national convention was the normal means of accomplishing this.[62] Others argued that elected officials and older party leaders insured a continuity important to the party. Congressman Jim Wright of Texas, in a communication to the group, expressed the feelings of many officeholders when he wrote that elected officeholders more than likely represented "a majority of the Democrats in an area," and that excluding them was deliberately "borrowing trouble" (a charge that turned out to be true enough for both reform commissions), "meddling," and unnecessarily "placing an onus upon the fact of being an elected official."[63] The questions to be answered revolved around the true nature and intent of delegation selection for a national convention and the priorities to be emphasized. Experience and professionalism (as well as incentive to continue in the mundane workaday world of local politics) were significant factors to be considered in a national convention. But so also was a truly representative body, one that reflected opinions of a grass-root electorate in an election year.

Unquestionably, the state parties had grossly exploited their advantage. Since party leaders exercised the chief influence in framing party by-laws or in choosing a delegation, it could be expected that they would make adequate provision for themselves. In some states they accomplished their goals with a vengeance. The Missouri State Central Committee offered automatic positions to former President Truman (declined), the two United States senators (one declined), the governor, and the state chairman. New York party rules awarded the state chairman, vice-chairman, party secretary, party treasurer, and the head of one of its committees with ex-officio positions. Georgia's Rule 55 allowed the governor and state chairman to appoint themselves delegates, which they did without fail. The state committee of Washington allocated 25 percent of its convention vote to ex-officio delegates. Maryland reserved 27 percent of its total (adding such officials as the attorney general and state comptroller to the positions more commonly associated with the practice) and Colorado, 14 percent for ex-officio designations.

The custom had a greater hold on the delegate nominating system than first realized. One step further removed, ex-officio delegates were often included in state bodies instrumental in choosing the final national delegation. Minnesota and Wyoming gave several party leaders an uncontested voice in the state convention. In Kansas the county conventions were limited only to precinct chairmen, and Montana restricted the entire nominating process to party officials. Michigan awarded all incumbent Democratic state legislators seats in its state convention, and the state committee in Washington specified twenty-one names in its call to the state convention to be given ex-officio status and placed the authority to choose ten more in the state chairman.

Idaho provides another example of the practice as it affected the nomination of national delegates. In this state and by state law, all legislative district chairmen, county chairmen, state committee members, and incumbent state legislators are ex-officio delegates to the state assembly, which in turn chooses the national convention delegates. And of course every state had its national committee representatives sitting as ex-officio delegates with a full convention vote, which was bestowed on them by their own action and certified in the convention's call.

RESOLUTION. The commission prohibited ex-officio delegates, requiring that all delegates be chosen by a process that allows every Democrat a full and meaningful opportunity to participate. The process was to take place within the calendar year of the national convention and was to be limited to primary, convention, or committee nomination.

GUIDELINE C-4: THE QUESTION OF "TIMELINESS," OR PREMATURE DELEGATE SELECTION[64]

One of the most striking findings of the McGovern-Fraser Commission and its spiritual ancestor, the (Harold) Hughes Ad Hoc Commission, focused on the discovery that the delegate selection process began too far in advance of the convention for people to know the issues or probable candidates, for widespread interest in the procedures and their outcomes to be stimulated, and for the rank and file to exercise any direct influence on events. *Mandate for Reform* made the point starkly: "The day Eugene McCarthy announced his candidacy, nearly one-third of the delegates had in effect already been selected. And, by the time Lyndon Johnson announced his intention not to seek another term, the formal delegate selection process had begun in all but twelve of the states. By the time the issues and candidates that characterized the politics of 1968 had clearly emerged, therefore, it was impossible for rank-and-file Democrats to influence the selection of these delegates."[65]

The process of delegate selection is extraordinarily intricate and subtle. In its general estimates the commission was referring to all aspects of the system: the twelve states in which a state central committee and the one state in which a nominating committee (composed of county party officials) apportioned intrastate delegate seats; the three states in which a state chairman or state committee participated in slatemaking or endorsed nominees for delegate positions; the ten states that set in motion at the local level the labyrinthine methods that eventually wound up through the party bureaucracy and culminated in delegate selection for the national convention; the four states in which an elected official who last faced the voter years before the convention played a predominant role in choosing national delegates; and of course the numerous states that permitted a state committee or state chairman to select alternates or fill vacancies (B-4), or that chose to permit, through party action or by-laws, ex-officio delegates to attend the national convention (C-2).[66] The "first event," as some call it, in delegate selection can occur one to four years prior to the convention, yet it has a potentially significant impact on the membership of the delegation and, hence, on the presidential nomination. This "first event" varies by state, consisting in some primary states of the filing dates for potential nominees or presidential contenders to appear on the ballot; in others it is the election of a committee within the party to appoint, elect, or endorse the names of prospective nominees to place on the ballot; it can also be the beginning of slatemaking by the supporters of a presidential aspirant. In non-primary states this "first event" can be the process of selecting precinct and ward committeemen who in turn appear as (or appoint) representatives to the county, district, state, and even the national convention itself.[67] In all, the commission estimated that all of the accredited delegates in eleven states, and on the average, over 50 percent of the national delegations in thirteen other states, were selected in an "untimely" manner. Additionally, the 110 national committeemen selected four years prior to the convention were given a free pass, thus swelling the number of delegate posts the views and commitments of whose incumbents party members had little or no opportunity to influence directly. Universally, and despite the unusual problems implicit in sorting these processes out (one-fourth of the states affected would require a change in state laws), the practice was deplored.[68]

RESOLUTION. The earlier national convention had in fact recognized the difficulty and acted upon it, directing that delegates be "selected through party primary, convention, or committee procedures open to public participation *within the calendar year of the National Convention.*"[69] (Emphasis added.) What was left to the McGovern-Fraser Commission was to go a half step farther, clarifying and extending the prohibition, and, in the process of adopting it, reemphasizing its significance and giving the staff jurisdiction to supervise its enforcement. This it did by banning officials chosen before the calendar year from participating even indirectly in the process.[70]

GUIDELINE C-5: THE USE OF PARTY COMMITTEES IN THE SELECTION PROCESS

The commission obviously disapproved of the role of committees in delegate selection, believing they offered the party supporter little opportunity to influence the outcome of the election. But the 1968 convention had specified that conventions, primaries, *and committees* were the proper vehicles for national delegate selection (see above) thus tying the group's hands and seemingly limiting the reformers to simply expressing their displeasure.[71]

Six states and the Commonwealth of Puerto Rico employed committees that were predominant in choosing the final national delegation (table 3.3).[72] At least two states (Arizona and Louisiana) were authorized to select the entire delegation, and at least three more (Arkansas, Georgia, and Rhode Island) had practices that were potentially even more restrictive, centering power in the hands of one or two key officials (the governor and state chairman) with, in some cases, the power to review the results lodged in a compliant state central committee. Seven states granted the state committee (or, in one case, a congressional district committee) authority to fill part of the delegation, to provide replacements if necessary, or, in the case of Wisconsin, to salvage what it could (with the approval of the actual winner) if none of the candidates listed on the

Table 3.3
State Selection Processes, 1968

Convention Systems		*Committee Systems*	*Primary Systems*
Alaska	Missouri	Arizona	Alabama
Canal Zone	Montana	Arkansas	California
Colorado	Nevada	Georgia[a]	District of Columbia
Connecticut	New Mexico	Louisiana	Florida
Delaware	North Carolina	Maryland	Massachusetts
Guam	North Dakota	Puerto Rico	Nebraska
Hawaii	South Carolina	Rhode Island	New Hampshire
Idaho	Tennessee		New Jersey
Iowa	Texas		Ohio
Kansas	Utah		Oregon
Kentucky	Vermont		South Dakota
Maine	Virginia		West Virginia
Michigan	Virgin Islands		
Minnesota	Wyoming		
Mississippi			

Mixed Systems

Illinois: Two-thirds of the delegation was selected by convention and one-third by primary.
Indiana: The delegation was selected at a state convention, but was bound by the results of the presidential preference poll.
New York: One-third of the delegation was selected by committee and two-thirds by primary.
Oklahoma: Half of the delegation was selected by convention and half by committee.
Pennsylvania: One-fourth of the delegation was selected by committee and three-fourths by primary.
Washington: Two-thirds of the delegation was selected by convention and one-third by committee.
Wisconsin: Most of the delegation was selected by either the State Administrative Committee or Senator Eugene McCarthy, the winner of the presidential preference primary in eight of ten congressional districts and at-large.

NOTE: In some states, statutes and party rules allow considerable discretion to the state committee to choose which selection system will be used in each presidential election year. This table reflects the system the state parties used in 1968. In several states, new statutes and party rules that date this chart considerably have already been adopted.
[a] The chairman of the state Democratic Executive Committee chose the entire delegation, with the advice and consent of the governor.

primary ballot won—an extremely unlikely situation.[73] Another six states at least permitted town, county, and district committees to exercise a potentially dominant hand in appointing delegates to a state convention that in turn chose the national representatives.[74] The commission would have liked all state parties to move toward a convention or primary system at all levels, but seemingly had little authority in the matter.[75]

RESOLUTION. Inventive as the commission was, it found a way out. The national convention had said nothing about the proportionate distribution of choices by each of the three party vehicles they had named. The McGovern-Fraser Commission seized upon this omission to require that no more than 10 percent of the convention delegation be picked by committee procedures. The guideline also agreed to reemphasize the clarity principle (B-2) as it applied to the process through which the committee itself was selected.

GUIDELINE C-6: EXTENDING PROTECTIONS TO THE PROCESS OF NOMINATING PROSPECTIVE DELEGATES (SLATE-MAKING)

"Let me do the nominating," one old-time party boss reportedly declared, "and I don't care who does the electing." On this point, the commissioners were believers. As they noted, in many states a slate of prospective delegates was presented to the agency—usually a convention or the party membership through a primary election—officially designated with the power to make the final choice. This body could adopt the slate presented or choose among competing slates formed by others. Once decided upon, the composition of these slates was extraordinarily difficult to change, effectively removing this level of choice from broader party consultative processes.

Party rules in the various states protected in one manner or another the power of the regulars to choose a slate, remove it from effective challenge, or give it preferential treatment over competing slates. The principle and its significance should be kept in mind in evaluating the usual diversity of state practices. Massachusetts regulations permitted the state committee to form district and at-large slates. If the at-large candidates remained unopposed (as often happened) they became delegates (nomination explicitly became election in this case). The New York and Pennsylvania state chairmen submitted a slate of names to the state committee, although in the latter case each individual nominee must have been approved by a majority vote of the assemblage.[76] California allowed any committee of three or more party members to organize a slate and seek a presidential candidate's endorsement of it.[77] Believing geographical dispersion important, the state statutes provided for a rigorous apportionment of prospective delegates by locality. Town committees or town caucuses in Connecticut had the authority to choose and endorse slates when local challenge primaries were held. This "official" slate would be opposed by an insurgent slate (the reason for the primary). At the state level, the slate was chosen by the state chairman and presented to the state convention with no opportunity given to individual delegates to make nominations from the floor. A similar process was employed in Indiana, although the role of the state chairman and the central committee in initially establishing the slate was more subtle. Missouri's at-large delegation was decided by a nominating committee of the state convention. Maine provided a variation on the same procedure, permitting a nominating committee composed of two delegates elected from each of the counties to make a slate for the state. Again, nominations were not permitted from the floor. The convention could reject the entire panel, though, and then the nominating committee reconvened and proposed another. The process was repeated until a satisfactory compromise group could be selected. Minnesota provided for a nominating committee of two representatives from each congressional district to choose an at-large delegate slate, and allowed the candidates to fashion their own slates for the county convention. Michigan ensured some harmony among factions by holding an unauthorized "midnight" caucus among state officials, representatives from each congressional district, and black and labor spokesmen to arrive at a compromise slate satisfactory to the party's major constituent groups. Kentucky, North Carolina, Virginia, and Indiana state convention delegates caucused by congressional district, and the slates they appointed were automatically endorsed by the full body. Iowa had a similar system, but allowed nominations from the floor of the convention. In North Carolina incumbent Democratic governors reportedly exercised considerable influence and had the power to select the at-large slate themselves. In Georgia the governor's role was not even subtle. The incumbent chief executive eliminated from the delegation proposed by the state chairmen the names of an ex-governor and the mayor of Atlanta, both of whom he disapproved of, and then personally announced the results to the press and public.

In a number of other states, although the variety that characterized this nation's party procedures was present, the emphasis was quite different. Wisconsin preferred that a presidential candidate select his own slate of delegates. If for some reason he failed to do this, the state or congressional district committees could name the slate, subject to veto and replacement by the presidential contender. New Hampshire and Oregon opted for a highly democratic system, but its pitfall lay in its emphasis on the value of some type of slatemaking provision. Both states allowed candidates for delegate to file on their own for ballot spots. In Oregon, although they were pledged to presidential contender X, delegates had to vote in the national convention and support candidate Y if the latter won the state primary, a most unhealthy situation. Lyndon Johnson found that there was no effective way to limit the number of prospective delegates who filed on a candidate's behalf in New Hampshire. Thus, in the primary contest with Eugene McCarthy, almost twice the number of delegates who could be elected filed committed to the president, diluting his support by spreading his votes among over forty candidates contesting for twenty-four positions. The McCarthy people closely supervised their filings, limiting their candidates to the precise number of seats at stake, and won over 80 percent of the representation on the national convention delegation—although they captured only slightly under half of the vote in the advisory presidential primary. In other states with similarly permissive requirements, it had been rumored that supporters of one candidate with little public support or public officials who were not enthusiastic about any contender in particular would file on behalf of the prospective nominee most likely to win in their locality, thus giving them the opportunity to attend the national convention and do what they could when there. Delegates at the state conventions in Vermont and North Dakota, attempting to be as scrupulously fair as possible, sponsored straw polls to test the presidential candidates' strength, and then divided their national convention delegations proportionately. The secrecy surrounding unpublicized nominating committee meetings, the lack of public recognition of their function or its significance, and the difficulty of effectively challenging nominees entered on a slate (or the entire slate if necessary) made this one of the least representative aspects of the entire delegate selection process.

RESOLUTION. The commission's requirements in this regard were widely misinterpreted. Basically, the reformers attempted to point out the key significance of the practice of slatemaking and then to enforce minimum safeguards that would open the process, making it representative of and responsive to election-year sentiments. The commission's provisions are both modest in tone and unspecific, although if they had been conscientiously applied, they should have laid the basis for inclusive and reasonably fair slatemaking procedures. Given the manner in which these proceedings were usually held, the realization of this objective might in itself have been enough to constitute something of a revolution. A later failure (or unwillingness) to appreciate exactly what the commission had said and, more significantly, a desire of party professionals to control so vital an action resulted in a decided reluctance to comply with this ruling, ranking it among those most consistently (although least publicly) attacked parts of the total report.

Specifically, the commission required "State Parties to extend to the nominating process all guarantees of full and meaningful opportunity to participate in the delegate selection process." The committee took this to include, among other things, dictums that groups performing a slatemaking function should do so with adequate public notice of their intent, that there should be popular involvement in the process, that provision should be made for the right to challenge the final recommendations, and that a slate on behalf of a presidential contender should be chosen in consultation with the candidate.

Overview

At the end of 1969 the commission had completed its work on the substance of the reform proposals—no mean achievement, given the pessimism that opened the year and the magnitude of the effort that had been initiated. A number of difficulties had beset its operations. One was simply gathering a professional staff with the acumen and drive to accomplish what needed to be done. Others were convincing both the party regulars and the disenchanted novice that the commission was serious about its mandate, that some of the grievances put forth should offend anyone's sense of fair play, and that "reform" (within the limits that the commission would propose) could be accomplished and, more significantly, was in the best interests of all concerned. Time demands added a further complication. The groundwork for organization decisions had been laid in March and April. Information-gathering, the cathartic public hearings, the education of the party's constituencies to the desirability of change, and the fundamental research required to penetrate the ignorance surrounding state procedures on delegate selection had been accomplished between April and August. Between September and December the emphasis was on reviewing and clarifying the proposals and deciding exactly what could reasonably be required of the state parties. All this was accomplished by a group that was unsure of its exact powers and the specific objectives it should hold before it; a large group composed of varying backgrounds and interests attempting in full public view to make decisions on items for which there were no precedents; a group seeking to keep itself solvent and attempting to establish reasonably harmonious working relationships among a membership adroitly pulled from major segments of the party. Although the group was composed of strangers hoping to accommodate others, each group member also served in some form as a spokesman for his or her loosely designated constituency. While a party agent acting, presumably, in the name of all Democrats, the body experienced an awkward relationship with the National Committee and held no formal authority over the state parties it was attempting to lead. Even though it was subject to these strains, the committee managed to perform in the public eye, holding all meetings in the open, encouraging an ambitious schedule of field hearings throughout the country, and fulfilling its obligations while necessarily experimenting with structural innovations (such as the aborted subcommittee structure). It was a virtuoso performance that within ten months resulted in framing a package of resolutions that, if accepted by the states, would revolutionize (in a quiet and professional manner) the practice of politics in the United States. In particular, an enactment of the committee's proposals would push forward the bounds of participation, providing for an inclusiveness foreign to an area that had been, for all intents and purposes, a closed party preserve. The precedents established by the group and the impact of the reforms, once they were administered, would insure that the American party system would never be quite the same.

Yet a review of the proposals themselves is something of a letdown. Read in order, they appear to be what they are—a practical set of ground rules, quite obviously the product of extensive compromise, meant to deal with mechanical difficulties within a broadly-based system. Working under the pressures it did, it is not surprising that the commission blundered into difficulties that, with more forethought, could possibly have been avoided, and that it failed to resolve satisfactorily key issues bound to arise in a project of that scope. In truth, the guidelines represented a mixed bag. They ranged from proposed major changes to minor tinkerings, from the precise to the hopelessly vague (a difficulty compounded by the needlessly prolix language in which they were couched), from pious statements of commitments to blueprints for the significant alteration of existing institutions, and from unquestionably new petitions to overlapping (and, at several points, virtually interchangeable) standards. The final regulations were not a model of coolly logical deductions derived from basic democratic norms. Yet, once having decided on its objectives, the commission appeared remarkably pleased with its grand design: it was to meet in full numbers only twice more, to clarify points of interpretation (basically to peruse questions relating to its implementation power and the actions required of the state parties concerning the "quotas"), in the three ensuing years. Satisfied with its endeavors, it left the job of enforcing its provisions to the staff, a group that, in the months ending the first year of reform and beginning the second, underwent the same decompression process that affected everyone else.

The frantic initial year over, the commission and regional hearings completed, the decisions made as to the rules to be fought for, the touchy process of providing an emotional outlet for the frustrations of the earlier presidential year brought off reasonably well, the staff itself underwent a metamorphosis. All but a few of the volunteers melted away. The National Committee, feeling the pinch of its $9 million plus debt and regarding the final phase of the commission's work as a fairly passive monitoring of state actions, severely reduced the always uncertain payroll. And the media, with its notoriously short attention span, turned to more pressing matters. The next three years witnessed the endlessly trying job of pressing the state parties to conform in some manner to the regulations promulgated, which devolved on the staff director, Robert W. Nelson, and his chief lieutenant (and new research director), Carol Casey. A year later a new ally was added. Congressman Donald Fraser of Minnesota, an original member of the Hughes Ad Hoc Commission, was named to replace the retiring McGovern as chairman. Fraser proved to be a quiet, intensely concerned leader who gave his time to a matter he believed to be critically important.

The operation was surprisingly small, but it was sophisticated, and it proved to have unparalleled success. It involved, among other things, constantly prodding the lagging party chieftains throughout the country; attempting to safeguard the integrity of the reform spirit from the endlessly clever deviations put forth by one state party after another; cultivating a fickle press interest while trying to nurture some sustained reporting of what the reformers were doing; guiding the states through the maze of difficulties to the goal of enacting an acceptable core of changes; insuring to the extent it could that no one connected with the reform movement did or said anything foolish enough to provoke an attack from those all too willing to engage in such diversions; and warding off the guerilla attacks of the left and right (a constant battle) while holding the center of the party fully in line (with the help of a national chairman unwilling to see his party polarized anew). Change is difficult to enforce. When the vehicles of that change are stubbornly independent political spirits who are at best begrudgingly convinced of its propriety, the effort is particularly trying. Yet a skeletal staff operation, in concert with a seriously committed and persuasive commission chairman and hundreds of concerned individuals of every political viewpoint scattered throughout the states, was destined to accomplish some remarkable feats.

All of this lay in the future, which was highly uncertain at the time. The immediate reaction, after the guidelines had been adopted, was to lay back and assess their significance as the results of the first whirlwind year. It would be difficult to disagree with the comments of one observer of the proceedings, who said that "the McGovern Commission guidelines are modest thrusts at change, not nearly so radical as some of its members had envisioned or as some state chairmen have feared. *The basic element is a call for fairness.* . . . If the party's leaders cannot swallow most of this without indigestion, then they are as corrupt as their severest critics have claimed."[78]

It is one thing to legislate, another to enforce. Next lay the second phase of the commission's activity, implementation.

FOUR

Enforcing
the Guidelines

"I CAN'T TAKE this stuff back to Texas and sell it," Will Davis admonished his fellow commissioners. "It's totally unrealistic!" Many agreed.

A few years later Davis, a former state chairman, a Connally supporter, and perhaps the most articulate or persistent (or both) of the conservative critics on the McGovern-Fraser Commission, was leaning over from the stage of his party's San Antonio convention (a mammoth 7,782-member, seventeen-hour affair) in the wee hours of the morning to prod a national reporter to "tell George it works pretty well after all," adding, "And tell him I was the one who fought it out."[1]

The time from the commission hearings in the fall of 1969 to the preconvention maneuvering in the early summer of 1972 represents a relatively short period in the life of a major party. Yet dramatic changes occurred during these years; the ever-flamboyant Texan makes up but one of fifty examples. The purpose of this chapter is to trace the evolution of these changes.

The Implementation Period

The recommendations framed by the commission remained somewhat fuzzy as 1970 began. It would be up to the committee's chairman and its staff, with the implicit backing of the full membership, to tighten these requirements as the months progressed. Their authority to implement (a mild-sounding word favored by the commission) the guidelines was equally vague, despite the loud reassurances of the reformers to the contrary. However, two things were clear. The commission was deadly serious in its enforcement attempts, and the "implementation" or lack of it of the new rules would provide the true test of the success of the reform effort.

The real story of reform, then, lay in the enforcement; in the movement to force fifty state parties and the District of Columbia's party to accept rules promulgated by a national party body. The McGovern-Fraser Commission would push, cajole, threaten—in short, do whatever was necessary, to compel the full range of local parties, from political baronies in the Northeast and Midwest to the leaderless aggregations of voters in the South and Far West that shared little beyond a party label, to adopt and then live by rules the commission felt to be just. Such an undertaking was unparalleled in the history of American party politics. It was bound to be difficult. Yet, in less than three years, the McGovern-Fraser Commission wrought a political miracle.

Until early 1970 the work of the group could be dismissed as a publicity-oriented campaign intended, through skillful development by the media, to soothe the angry while avoiding any infringement of the prerogatives of the traditional centers of power within the party. Countless other ineffectual party committees at the national level over the years had employed the same tactic: ameliorate short-term difficulties as far as possible, and work to restore party spirit. Such committees gave the people at the national level—divorced as they were from "real politics," the electoral needs of the grass roots—a semblance of meaningful activity with which to occupy their time in the dull months between conventions. Or so many would assume. Even if McGovern, Hughes, Harris, and some of their allies chose not to be dismissed so lightly, the fruits of their labor could amount to little more than pious generalizations. Party regulars—the Daleys of Chicago, the Lawrences of Pennsylvania, the De Sapios of New York, and their successors and equivalents—would publicly embrace and loudly acclaim the proposed changes, and there the matter would end. The party would go on record in favor of "fairness," "openness," and "democratic representation"; nothing would change; and the politics-as-usual would be the order of the day. This line of reasoning came to even less than wishful thinking. The commission and the national party were both presumed to be impotent. They had done their best over the years to avoid controversies with their state units. They had no real power over any state entity; an enforcement process without sanctions could be ignored as meaningless.

One could find little solace among knowledgeable observers. It was possible to choose any of several probable outcomes of the reform movement, depending on the source of information and his pessimism ("realism")/optimism at the time, whom he had happened to speak to last, or, in the case of a national columnist, his ideological commitments.[2] At the first meeting of the commission McGovern had vowed, "We will not be weak-kneed on the hard questions of political reform."[3] Although many would have preferred a weaker commission (in fact, the reformers had proved unwilling to face several issues), the reformers were determined to see the state parties enact what they had managed to agree on.

Sniping at the Reforms: The State Parties

The recognition that changes would be required of all state parties came painfully slowly.[4] Those who did not favor the changes, or who looked

with scorn on a national commission attempting to force them to do anything, subtly but effectively resisted by doing substantially little. No matter
what they had agreed to verbally or under pressure, if they chose not to act
there was no way the national party could step in and execute the needed
modifications of party rules or state laws.

Not many states fully comprehended what was under way, and few
totally resisted the advances of the national party until the comprehensiveness of the regulations and the seriousness of the movement became un-
mistakable. Surprisingly, the full meaning of what was occurring did not
strike the state party leaders until six months before the national convention. At this point, and belatedly, it appeared that everyone objected—
several state party leaders attempted to take their opposition to the
extremes of federal and state adjudication (a curious posture for regulars
who stressed loyalty to party, unity, and cohesion above all other virtues).
A small number of state parties had fought the entire concept of "reform"
from the beginning, and had done everything in their power to assure that
it accomplished little. Fortunately for the reformers, the state efforts opposing the work of the commission were disorganized. They received little
support from the other state parties, which were absorbed with the day-to-
day business of politics and were waiting to assess how the changes would
specifically affect them.

Indicative of the attitude of most during the enforcement period was
that of veteran Connecticut State Chairman and former National Party
Chairman John Bailey. He wryly commented early in the proceedings that
he doubted whether his state's town committees would favor abdicating
their powers (especially those over intrastate delegate apportionment).
Unenthusiastically, he promised to do "as much as we are able to . . . by
1972."[5] The Maryland national committeeman, in opposing the reforms,
noted that the agents of the national committee "don't have as much of a
club over us as they think," which was true enough. The Illinois Democratic chairman took a different tack, saying, "I question the right of the
previous convention to set the rules of the 1972 Convention." This position was logically and legally indefensible. The Illinois leaders cared little
for the appropriateness of their objections. Eventually their party symbolized the pros and cons of the entire question of enforcement, and its
opposition provided the most sustained challenge to the movement.[6] Most
northern states followed a basic law of politics: say nothing, do little, see
how events work out.[7]

Other states, particularly some southern ones, were less restrained. The
most vocal of the early opponents saw themselves as the target of the
reform drive, and they resented it. The criticisms they raised covered
the full panoply of issues that could be brought to bear, and the medium
through which they voiced their discontent was publicity, the type of attack the national party feared the most. The redoubtable Lester Maddox,
governor of Georgia, threatened a law suit. The national Democrats, he

ventured, were "socialists" with "the platform of the Communist party" and had "almost lost the country."[8] For sheer flamboyance, Maddox cannot be topped. The warnings of South Carolina's governor, a respected member of the party orthodoxy, were weighed more seriously. The governor used a national party forum to accuse McGovern and his commission of renewing the divisions within the party by giving extremists a national television audience—strong words for a party trying to unite itself after a disastrous election year. The same themes were repeated by the governor in speeches in Tennessee and Georgia; had this initial attack persisted, the outcome of the reform effort undoubtedly would have been different.[9] But perhaps party members in Louisiana, a southern state with a Neanderthal political substructure, can stand as the most vocal and inflammatory of the first-wave critics. Their assault began early.

The commission had scheduled an early field hearing for New Orleans. Louisiana party leaders were irate. J. Marshall Brown, a national committeeman, wrote a pointed letter to the national chairman expressing his anger and giving an unintentional glimpse into some of the stultifying traditions that had accumulated over the generations that so irritated many party supporters. Brown notified the national party that the McGovern-Fraser Commission meeting seemed, to him, "to be in violation of every basic rule of party protocol." The reformers had scheduled their meeting "without having notified, let alone consulted with" the governor's office or either of the National Committee representatives, an action the state party found shocking. "I can assure you that none of us would officially enter another state without [such] prior discussion. . . . Neither [former] President Lyndon B. Johnson nor [former] Vice President Hubert H. Humphrey *ever entered Louisiana on a political mission without first notifying all three . . .* I find it very hard to understand Senator McGovern's motives, and even harder to justify his actions. If the party is now to be operated as a private club or an inner circle cloakroom committee, this action is understandable."[10] (Italics added.)

As with many such episodes, the ludicrous combined with the serious. Brown marked his letter to Harris "personal and confidential," and the thrust of the letter, which indicated the sharp displeasure of prominent state party leaders and the implicit threat to "perpetuate" the type of divisions that cost the party the presidential election, certainly raised touchy issues. However, the Louisiana national committeemen proceeded to circulate copies of the communication to hundreds of people, including former Presidents Truman and Johnson, Hubert Humphrey, Eugene McCarthy, Edmund Muskie, Edward Kennedy, the members of the National Committee's executive committee, Democratic state chairmen, governors, and representatives in the House and Senate, and, for unknown reasons, Republican Senator Howard Baker, Jr., of Tennessee. The exchange, of course, found its way into the newspapers. Several congressmen and state party leaders expressed sympathy, and Humphrey, backtracking from his warm support in January, acknowledged that he, too, had worries concerning the McGovern-Fraser Commission. Consequently, he had contacted Harris, his choice for national chairman, and had engaged in "a long discussion over the situation that prevails in our party and the activities of the McGovern Commission" (an incident possibly contributing to the growing wedge between the two men). "You may be assured," Humphrey told Brown, "that your concern is shared by others."[11]

The last sentence is ominous. Indications of a spreading grass-roots revolt could have crippled the reformers before they got under way. The commission's executive committee, which had originally routinely scheduled the New Orleans hearing, quickly met to rescind their decision. The regional hearing was transferred to Jackson, Mississippi. The executive committee then reinvited Louisiana's spokesmen to a Texas hearing. Robert W. Nelson, on behalf of the commission, wrote Brown a conciliatory letter, prodding him to "remember that I personally called you ahead of the hearing date to request your assistance, and we discussed the matter by telephone." He also stated (while not directly conceding the point on clearance) that the national chairman and the commission had "always made it clear . . . that advance notification of any of the Commission's regional hearings must be given to Democratic State Chairmen, National Committeemen and Committeewomen, Governors, Senators, and Congressmen and others." He concluded by assuring Brown that "it is not the policy or the practice of the Commission to inconvenience any official of any state."[12]

Flushed with success, Brown, meanwhile, had launched another probe. He wrote to his considerable mailing list that both reform commissions should suspend all activities until the Democratic National Committee met in September to define the scope of its work. This thrust was serious; the counterattack was in full flower. If the opponents succeeded at this juncture, reform would become the empty gesture many had hoped it would.

The commission, however, had begun a counteroffensive. The executive committee again met and, prodded by Fraser, reviewed exactly what had happened and its response. In attempting to conciliate the leaders of one state they had jeopardized their own independence. They voted to reschedule a meeting in New Orleans to replace the earlier cancellation and, rather than seeking "clearance," sent Nelson down to confer with Brown on arrangements (this was the first of many similar trips he made over the next few years). "We're working with state Democratic leaders, but not through them," a reform spokesman added, making a subtle but important distinction. This move effectively ended the immediate confrontation before it began.[13] The public session was held in New Orleans, but the problems with the state party were by no means resolved.

As time went on, Brown appeared before a Louisiana committee authorized to sort through the mess and come up with recommendations. Brown advised his state party to ignore the reform guidelines. "You've got the best method of selection now," he added. (The state committee selected the delegates, a process that in effect meant they accepted the governor's recommendations.) As to the charges of one state central committeeman that "we have silently, passively accepted the names [of prospective delegates] handed us," Brown contended that opening the system to popular participation amounted to "putting a price tag on the presidency."[14] These twin themes of contentment with procedures and fear of the cost of change recurred persistently. The state chairman, another ardent foe of change, repeatedly argued that the guidelines could be enacted only with legislative consent and would result in a "special election" at an estimated cost of $800,000.[15] One newspaper applauded the state party reaction, which it summed up as: "Take us the way we are and accept the delegates we send or lose our votes in the national elections."[16] An exasperated (and impolitic) party spokesman in Washington, in response to some of these charges, warned that it would be "shape up or ship out" at the 1972 convention.[17] Brown remained adamant to the end. Displaying his bombastic style, he managed publicly to call McGovern a "jerk" and a "knucklehead," and he reminded anyone who cared to listen that not one of the regulations was binding. All this occurred as Louisiana began to achieve the required changes.[18]

As it turned out, the state that had been in conflict with two-thirds of the commission recommendations and that in spirit represented the polar extreme of what the reformers sought managed an impressive turnabout. In late 1970 the tide had begun to turn with the appointment of a state-level reform commission, the initial step toward compliance. Selection by a closed committee of the party elite was replaced (without legislative action) by a state convention system fully in accord with the reform standards. In fact, Louisiana would have to stand as one of the commission's successes in terms of achieving the adoption of its rules despite concerted objections from the most powerful of political leaders within the state. The 1972 state delegation to the national convention was unusual for any southern state, and was a radical departure from previous Louisiana delegations. The change, drastic as it was, resulted from both the new rules, which favored those organized and knowledgeable about them and willing to work (in this case liberal McGovern supporters and black groups), and the ineptness of the regulars, most of whom ran as "uncommitted" delegates and lost. The state's governor adapted gracefully to the outcome, remarking that the success of "the black-McGovern coalition" (as he called it) indicated the power of "the new, the young, the idealistic—those who haven't been allowed to be involved in the past."[19]

Organized Opposition: The AFL-CIO

Along with state reluctance, manifested in many forms, to comply with the guidelines, was that of a number of groups of significance to the

Democratic party, which looked on the regulations with disfavor. The most prominent and the most influential of these was the AFL-CIO, represented by its president, George Meany, his chief lieutenant and the director of the Committee on Political Education (the principal political arm of organized labor), Al Barkan, and a number of presidents of affiliated unions, who sat on the AFL-CIO ruling council.[20] Curiously, the most vocal public critic of reform was the unusual alliance of federated labor and southern conservatives.

Organized labor was awarded positions on both reform committees, but the representatives of the AFL-CIO contributed little to the deliberations. I. W. Abel, the president of the Steelworkers and the AFL-CIO embassy to the McGovern-Fraser Commission, engaged in a well-publicized four-year boycott of the sessions (supposedly at Meany's request).[21] No federation spokesman appeared at commission hearings. While refusing to cooperate in any manner with the reformers, the AFL-CIO hierarchy was restrained in its early public opposition: "We are not against reform per se. But we do fear that the zeal of the reformers may throw out proven systems." The stand appeared to be reasonably moderate and simply cautionary.[22]

Perhaps the real objection of labor's biggest federation was voiced in the observation that the liberals might "not use the reform structure so wisely themselves."[23] Organized labor feared that reform was simply a device through which a new, and more liberal, faction would assume control of the party and its nominating procedures, threatening labor's power and even expelling it from its position of dominant influence within party ranks.[24] This position came far closer to labor's principal concern and accounts for its prolonged and bitter opposition: the AFL-CIO fought the reforms at every stage; it chose never to accommodate itself to the guidelines once they were adopted; it refused to accept or support the nominees of the Democratic convention (the fact that one of them was McGovern, the early reform leader and a politician personally disliked by Meany, did not help matters), who were chosen through the new procedures, thus giving latent support to Nixon, labor's arch rival for decades; and it led an assault on the new delegate selection regulations once the 1972 election year ended.

Even with a receptive party leadership[25] and a newly formed delegate selection reform commission more conscious of representing and pacifying the federation leadership, the AFL-CIO achieved only modest success. This lack of accomplishment, however, in no way muted the intensity of its antireform campaign. The federation's hostility was increased by its own ineptness. By avoiding the commission sessions, the labor leaders lost any opportunity to shape the final recommendations—a fact that did not embarrass them in attacking the guidelines as unrepresentative of the working man. Still smarting from the furious prenomination fights of 1968, they, like Talleyrand's Bourbon kings, had learned little four years later. They never bothered to master the content or spirit of the changes, yet they remained determined to increase their representation at the national convention. Employing the old ways, the aging federation leadership was deeply offended when its well-financed "uncommitted" slates repeatedly fell to delegates tied to specific nominees. It was infuriated when state officials insisted on running in support of one of the real contenders rather than cooperating in the old tactic of putting themselves forward as favorite-son candidates intended to insure the AFL-CIO a bloc of delegates to barter at the convention.

While openly backing Muskie, the front runner in many states, Meany felt no contradiction in publicly belittling him as "a cream puff."[26] The federation favored Henry Jackson of Washington State for the nomination, but the senator could excite little public support. Jackson was forced to drop out of the race prematurely; his main legacy was a bitter attack on McGovern in Ohio ("abortion, acid, amnesty"), little noticed at the time, but used with devastating effect by the Republicans in the 1972 general election. Labor backed the latecomer, Humphrey, and his California challenge before the convention, which effectively split the party. Still angered, Al Barkan reportedly shook his finger at a former United States senator from Maryland and criticized him for voting in favor of the McGovern position on the California challenge on the 1972 convention's opening night: "You so-called responsible leaders of this party seem to think the kids and the kooks and the Bella Abzugs can win you some elections. Well, we're going to let them try to do it for you this year."[27] True to his threat, the AFL-CIO, the single most important organizational supporter of Democratic nominees, sat out the 1972 presidential election.

Still unappeased, a fuming AFL-CIO began making the same noises immediately after the November election. "Gravel Gertie," an official of the federation announced to the press (referring to McGovern's choice of Jean Westwood as national chairperson and her throaty speaking style), "is going to go." Then, he continued, "The next thing we have to do is get rid of those damned quotas."[28] He was correct; within weeks Westwood had been replaced by the former national committee treasurer, Robert Strauss, a Texan sympathetic to labor's objections (who was supported by labor for the office), and a new commission had been established to review and possibly modify the McGovern-Fraser Commission standards. Still the AFL-CIO's troubles did not end, as they engaged in continual dogfights with the new commission, its leaders, and even the national chairman, all to little avail. With several modifications, the guidelines were retained.

The opposition of the AFL-CIO to the work of the McGovern-Fraser Commission presented the most serious challenge to fulfilling its objective of any group it encountered. The labor federation was well organized, a perennial power with the national and state parties, handsomely financed, and it had organizations at the state and local levels ready to do its bidding. Labor had full access to the media at all levels and knew how to exploit its advantage. Most elected Democratic officeholders of any consequence outside the South were in some manner obligated to organized labor and were sensitive to its objections. Yet, for all their power and the intensity of its opposition, they failed to keep the McGovern-Fraser Commission from realigning each of the state party processes, an extraordinarily difficult job even without federated labor's enmity. Why? The question is as hard to answer as the eventual outcome of the test of wills was unlikely. The AFL-CIO had other concerns during the period and, despite its bellicosity, devoted most of its energy to congressional legislation and union affairs. The ineptness of its antireform campaign, its unwillingness to move beyond public outbursts to the sustained hard work necessary to counter the changes underway,[29] its arrogance (which offended many even sympathetic people), and its total inability to understand what the reform effort was all about were all contributing factors to its humiliation. Its leadership was simply out of touch with events and too insensitive, apparently, to realize it.

Nonetheless, the antireform fever surged and abated over the years from 1970 to 1972, appearing in full force whenever a state or party leader suddenly realized the reformers were talking about him. Antagonists, those caught between the old and the new, and even friends at one point or another appeared critical of and disillusioned with the reform efforts. Ken Bode, McGovern-Fraser Commission research director during the drafting of the guideline, had resigned to head his own organization (the Center for Political Reform) for monitoring and assisting the reform efforts. Bode, a hard-liner on the reform, wrote that the enforcement was "faltering" in one widely circulated piece, and even predicted in mid-1971 that it would fail if the national party did not marshall its forces more effectively.[30] Party Treasurer Robert Strauss (who became national chairman in the post-1972 period) even managed to let himself appear in print intemperately condemning the "utter impracticality" of the reforms.[31] So the process went. The opposition to implementation was formidable. It would surface as the reforms began to impinge on areas of concern. Unified in some form, and combined with the natural and inbred resistance of party organizations to innovations of any type, it could have proved more than sufficient to neutralize the forces driving for change.

Major Events in the Chain of Reform

The proposed set of preliminary guidelines had, of course, been sent to the state parties for comments and guidance immediately after the September 1969 commission deliberations. The rules adopted at the November meeting were disseminated to the states during December, which constituted the first official notification of precisely what the commission desired each party to enact. No indication of exactly how the regulations would apply within the context of current state practices was included.

The culmination of a furious research effort led to the circulation, in early 1970, of intensive analyses of each state within the context of the fifteen required guidelines, signifying where a state was not in compliance with the new national rules and the type of action that would have to be initiated. The process had to occur quickly. The states that would need legislative changes (estimated to be eight at the time, although twenty states finally did initiate attempts at statutory modification) had to be identified, and the implications of the laws being required had to be made clear to potential sponsors. In a further affirmation of the hodgepodge that characterized American federalism, legislatures in some of these states met every other year, and in some, they regulated the entire length of the sessions (thirty to sixty days in some cases). A limited opportunity for action, combined with the normally cumbersome legislative process, placed a premium on early and thorough preparation of the changes that would be introduced.

After the dissemination of these analyses to the states, the commission staff engaged in extensive telephone and mail communication with each state, attempting to motivate party leaders to act and to guide them in introducing changes consistent with the intent of the regulations. The variability of state problems in this regard and the ingenuity of party officials in pushing modifications that met the letter (although not the spirit) of what the staff considered acceptable amounted to a continual test of wills between the national office and local operatives. It never ceased during the life of the commission, and it did lead to an early and climatic confrontation of major significance to the party.

The National Committee had never taken a stand on the proposed standards. The committee, basically a conservative and centrist assembly of professionals, would be unlikely to put its blessing on anything that stood to revise drastically what had become comfortably familiar operating procedures. Consequently, the commission went on its way, preferring to deal with the National Committee and its staff only when necessary. This independence proved hard to maintain as reports of state dissatisfaction and open revolt came back to party headquarters. As the state parties began to awaken to the full scope of demands being made upon them, the camaraderie that led to the early creation of "little McGovern" committees gave way to concern. If the McGovern-Fraser Commission staff was sympathetic but unbudging, perhaps a more favorable reception could be gained from the national chairman and the National Committee.

April 1970 saw the commission publish twenty-five thousand copies of *Mandate for Reform*, its major report recapitulating the guidelines, outlining the problems being treated, and giving the history of the group. The report went to all state and national party leaders, elected Democratic officials, media representatives, academicians, and anyone who might be interested in the commission's work. It remains the basic publication of the reformers. A proud moment for the commission, it nonetheless contributed little to the immediate easing of tensions.

A NEW NATIONAL CHAIRMAN

The increasing resistance of the state parties as the implications of the commission's work the previous year dawned on them coincided with a period of prolonged uncertainty in the national party headquarters. For a variety of reasons, Harris resigned as national chairman in the early part of 1970; after several false starts, the executive committee of the party prevailed on old pro Lawrence O'Brien to return. Certainly Larry O'Brien, a pragmatist and party realist to the core, would never favor the radical proposals being demanded of the states. At a minimum, O'Brien represented to the reformers a new face on the scene. His personal support and party position would be needed to make enforcement a success. Anything less, no matter how well intentioned, would constitute an accommodation of the state parties (which they badly wanted) leading to something considerably short of the full range of changes the commission demanded.

O'Brien, as is his custom, kept his own counsel. He said all the right things, giving general endorsements to the commission and its work while continuing to remain an arm's length from its operations. He lent a sympathetic ear to those with the strongest complaints, but he committed himself in explicit terms to little. Time passed. The May meeting of the National Committee was in the offing; pressures built. At this point, O'Brien called in the party's legal counsel, Joseph Califano, and asked for a formal opinion as to whether the guidelines were truly binding upon the state and national parties. Is this what the national convention, the party's supreme body, intended? And, more significantly, is it what they authorized? Was the commission simply exercising its legal powers as derived from the convention mandate, or was it in truth usurping powers to which it could make no justifiable claim?

The reformers were tense. They expected the worst. The simple fact that O'Brien had reopened the question signaled to some his misgivings about the ambitious program of implementation. Perhaps he sided with the opponents. If so, it was a clever move on which to begin an eventual counterattack. Certainly, the raising of the points clearly jeopardized the commission's legality. Everything now hinged on Califano's findings— although the commission had every intention of pushing ahead whatever the outcome. The going, though, would be most difficult without O'Brien's prestige behind it. It would be saddled with a report (if it came to this) denying their legitimacy and would be without a national party to back it—a group whose position would be badly exposed.

The Califano memorandum proved to be a masterful stroke that tore the ground out from under the critics. The legal counsel delivered his decision just prior to the May meeting. It said that the guidelines were indeed binding upon the states. Any state party not complying stood in jeopardy of losing its representatives at the next national convention. Califano's words are not as unequivocal as the construction placed upon them: "My view is that the Guidelines should be respected by the State Parties as their guide in assuring that the delegate selection processes within each state provide all Democrats with a fully meaningful and timely opportunity to participate; in line with the requests applicable to the 1972 Convention established by the 1964 and 1968 Conventions of the National Democratic Party. Those requests are the basic standards which must be met."[32] Califano stressed that the convention would retain the actual power of arbitration, but short of that, the commission's standards were indeed applicable to the states and should be adopted to avoid any possible complications during the presidential election year.

The pro-reform slant of the Califano memorandum received wide publicity within the party. It was circulated and read by all interested persons. Seemingly the basic questions as to the commission's authority had been laid to rest (although, of course, several states would choose not to accept this interpretation). What else could O'Brien do, then, but support the enforcement policy already in effect? As a good party man, this he did.

O'Brien still managed, however, to keep both reformers and their opponents guessing with his maneuvering. The ruling by the legal counsel that delighted the reformers was followed within days by a move that puzzled them and heartened their opponents. On the national chairman's recommendation, the party's executive committee appointed two committees from the membership of the National Committee, noted for their centrist position in the party, to help "implement" reform.[33] Were the committees needed? No. Why then were they appointed? O'Brien insisted he was only following the procedures demanded in the convention mandate. Yet why appoint two new committees except as a vehicle to pass on and modify commission recommendations before presenting them to the National Committee, a body whose role in the whole process continued to remain clouded? The chairman was keeping his options open, and the implicit threat of monitoring the substance of the recommendations (although this intent was denied by O'Brien) soundly irked both the McGovern-Fraser and O'Hara commissions.[34]

McGovern, adept at making the best of a bad situation, took the initiative. He pressured O'Brien into a private meeting in which the national chairman assured the commission's leaders that the new ad hoc committee intended to engineer the adoption of the McGovern Commission's standards and harbored no thought of revising them. The new group would "exhort, cajole and appease" local party barons cool to the reforms. O'Brien argued that such party regulars might encounter more success in their efforts to convince other regulars to acquiesce to the reforms than the commission could.[35] McGovern publicly called for his group's reform proposals to be written into the call for the upcoming convention. He welcomed the new ad hoc committee's assistance, denied its power to revise or abandon any guidelines, and emphasized that all of the rules should appear "intact" in the call. While not giving the proposals any "new legal sanction," such a move, he claimed, would help insure that they would be followed by the states.

A critical point had been passed in this episode with O'Brien. As the year progressed, the reformers concentrated on the worst of the hardcore state resisters while O'Brien continued to speak in strong pro-reform terms. He contended that implementation would require a sustained "national effort, comparable to a presidential campaign." Who would conduct it? "It's obvious to me we're going to have to do it," he said, pointing to himself. And he assured his listeners, "I'll get it done." By the year preceding the convention, O'Brien had become positively bullish on reform, predicting that the rules would "have a dramatic effect on the tone of the Convention" and, lest anyone mistake his appraisal as lukewarm, adding: "It's the greatest goddam change since [the advent of] the two-party system."[36]

It would appear that O'Brien's support was unequivocal. This raises questions as to why any state leaders chose to ignore the gathering clouds. In fairness, O'Brien was seldom this explicit, and his intentions were constantly questioned by the more ardent reformers. An image of equivocation stood closer to the one held of him by most regulars. Still, O'Brien has to be counted among the supporters of reform, and a goodly portion of credit for the successes achieved has to be given him. He remained basically cautious throughout (which is consistent with his political instincts), but came to regard the changes as "good politics" and in the best interests of the future of the party. By late 1971 and early 1972 his position had become strong: support for complete enactment. He took every opportunity to drive this home to the state leaders as well as to remind them of the consequences of any willful failure on their part to comply. Some continued to doubt and were enraged at his behavior up to and during the convention. He was to pay heavily for his support of reform and for his rulings on the California issue at the Democratic convention in particular. Many regulars and labor officials came to blame him, unwarrantedly, for whatever the reformers achieved and, more significantly, for the detested McGovern's nomination. McGovern, who was never close to O'Brien, dropped him from the party's chairmanship the day after the 1972 convention ended, one of the first of a series of gaffes that came to characterize the senator's general election campaign.[37]

The reform effort remained on course throughout the spring, summer, and fall, with concentration on the individual state parties and their difficulties (see figures 4.2 and 4.3). One pattern became increasingly clear. As the barrage of questions from the state parties began to descend on the Washington nucleus of the commission and the originality that could be applied in subverting the intent of the regulations became apparent, the staff took an increasingly hard-line position on what was permissible, sticking as much as possible to the letter of the rules and reducing the areas of maneuverability as far as possible. Self-preservation dictated the strategy, but it could have proved risky. The Califano memo and O'Brien's more open support added an authoritative voice to the efforts not previously encountered.

A CHANGE IN COMMISSION LEADERSHIP

The year 1971 proved the climactic one in the enactment drive. The year began with the resignation of George McGovern to pursue his presidential ambitions. Congressman Donald Fraser replaced him as chairman. McGovern had been an able chairman. He was politically astute, low-keyed, and eminently reasonable; through his leadership the reformers were able to get untracked, adopt moderate guidelines, and assert their authority over the states. McGovern guided the commission through its bleakest period, managing to dramatize (with an ability that was often underestimated) the changes required as the good and proper thing to do and to educate the public and the professionals to the dimensions of the problems facing the party. Approachable and nondogmatic, he alienated few who dealt with him personally, and he managed to carry the leadership of the party with him on the reform wave. His contribution cannot be minimized. He accepted a position he did not want and for which, in the opinions of many, he was not a prime choice (the regulars would have preferred someone more like themselves, and the early reformers touted Harold Hughes for the job), and he did an admirable job.

Fraser's rule would be different. His involvement with reform preceded even the creation of the committee he had been chosen to head. Quieter than McGovern and lacking his flair for publicity, the congressman nonetheless had a deep interest in the subject that transcended delegate selection procedures: he was committed to exploring ways of making parties truly representative institutions responsive to the public will. He believed that Americans have never enjoyed such a party system. A furious worker, Fraser, after a slow start, immersed himself in the details of the enforcement program and took a direct participatory role in overseeing the implementation of the guidelines during the next year and a half. Motivated, unperturbable, intelligent, highly knowledgeable, and, in his own quiet way, fearless, he proved the right choice for the tedious days that followed.

THE NATIONAL COMMITTEE ACTS

The first test (a most significant one) of the new regime came a month later, when the National Committee assembled to pass on the recommendations of the McGovern-Fraser Commission as conveyed to it by its ad hoc committee. Again the tension that accompanied so many of the key moments in the effort appeared. Skillful leadership would have to be provided. The National Committee could not be expected to be fully receptive to the guidelines. Each state had its difficulties, and the comfortable middle-aged men and women who theoretically represented their state's interests undoubtedly would want to raise substantive questions and to press matters relating to local enforcement, which was important to them. On a policy basis alone, with no political considerations attendant to the decisions, the National Committeemen would, at the best, be a reluctant ally of any serious reform. In the balance hung two years' hard work. While the commission bravely contended (somewhat successfully, as it turned out) that the National Committee had no legal powers over it, a cantankerous committee would prove embarrassing and, in the long run, would be fatal to its goals. Without question the National Committee had the power to issue the call to the upcoming convention. While downgrading the committee's significance, the reformers were bold enough to want it to incorporate their regulations into the call, thus making them the prescribed methods for selecting delegates to the convention. Such a victory would also establish them as incontrovertible party laws and as binding on the states (both of which the reformers claimed they had already achieved). Curiously, a docile committee did just as it was told. It issued an unusually early preliminary call to the 1972 convention and included each of the guidelines *without amendment*. The intent, the unnaturally cooperative committee announced, was to insure there would be no misunderstanding as to what would be accepted at the next convention.

The National Committee later rescinded, in part, its endorsement, allowing both outgoing and incoming (those elected in the convention year) national committeemen automatic (ex-officio) delegate status. The move represented an obvious violation of the guidelines, but was a healthy exercise of the fundamental principle of political self-interest. It served to reassure many political onlookers that everything had not changed. (Yielding to the pressure exerted by O'Brien and the reform cadre, and possibly feeling a bit guilty, the National Committee modified its stand at its next meeting—October 1971—voting to allow delegate positions only to national committeepersons elected in the convention year. The new position still constituted a break with the McGovern-Fraser rules, but not such a blatant one.)

The reformers were exuberant. The incorporation of the guidelines intact into the preliminary call to the national convention insured that there now was no question as to the acceptance of their objectives. The burden of proof shifted from the commission to the states whose parties would have to apply the regulations or be open to challenge before the convention on the grounds of violating the call to the convention. The weight the commission could exert now increased tenfold. Symbolically and legally the battle had been won. Politically, there remained the question of what might actually happen when a powerful state party (or parties) threatened open revolt or when the party's and the public's attention shifted from implementation to choosing a presidential candidate. Under either set of conditions the elaborate framework built over a period of several years might quickly perish. At this early point these possibilities were only suppressed nightmares, but they came to be—in fact, almost everything connected with the acceptance of the new regulations that could happen, did. The hope was to have the guidelines enacted before January 1972. After that date other concerns would dominate and everything would become unpredictable.

The success enjoyed at the 19 February meeting can be traced to a variety of sources. The commission and its chairman throughout were politically astute. They made their arguments and skillfully conducted their negotiations in private. At no point did they attempt to publicly humiliate or badger any foe. Their drive was professional and nonpersonal, an emphasis that greatly helped their cause. They also received O'Brien's full backing, which insured both a receptive hearing by the curious ad hoc committee he had created and the quiet backing of the party elders within the National Committee. The national chairman's open support of adoption of the guidelines meant that anyone opposing them had to do so on his own, making his arguments before the entire committee with little anticipation of the support that could be expected for his position. The opposition, in short, was effectively isolated. Antireformers were faced with attempting to build a coalition publicly, on short notice, and against the wishes of the party hierarchy. The odds were against their success. The pressure exerted on behalf of the reforms worked impressively. The only misstep came on the relatively unimportant issue of committeemen prerogatives at the convention.

One other point is of significance. There was a diversion of sorts at the February meeting that helped the McGovern-Fraser Commission proposals. The O'Hara Commission had belatedly (in comparison with its sister commission) begun its deliberations and had proposed some rules for incorporation into the proposed call. These seemingly less volatile recommendations had become a topic of hot debate, and they commanded most of the attention given to the preliminary call.[38] Most of the energy expended in the brief National Committee meeting went toward reshaping several of the Commission on Rules's most significant recommendations. These included a revision of the interstate apportionment formula for awarding delegate votes to each of the states and changes in the total number of delegates and votes awarded any state.

Good communication, hard work, strong leadership, and the realization that the McGovern-Fraser guidelines (unlike the O'Hara Commission's) were well into the implementation stage (thus insuring that any major revisions would be noticeably disruptive) all contributed to the commission's good fortune. The meeting of the National Committee in October would issue the final call. In doing so, it in effect ratified its earlier decision (with the only change involving the article providing uncontested delegate status for national committeemen if they were elected in the convention year).

The legitimacy of the commission's ultimate pursuits after the February 1971 National Committee meeting and the issuance of the preliminary call could no longer be called into question. The party had spoken in support of reform with a unified voice. What the state parties could challenge, however, in the best of political traditions, was the specific interpretation and application of the demands being placed on them. Several key sections of the guidelines continued to be debated in this manner. The staff had taken a no-compromise attitude on a number of sensitive issues, insisting that full compliance with the letter and spirit of the recommendations was the only means of avoiding challenge at the convention. Many state parties were unhappy. The voices of dissent were great enough for the commission to call another meeting to reconsider exactly what they could realistically expect of the states. The gathering, scheduled for 16 July 1971, would be the first full assemblage of the commission in twenty months—and the last.[39]

THE JULY MEETING

Tempers were short by the time of the meeting. Many professionals were tired of the talk of reform and wanted to move on to the "serious" business of finding a nominee and beginning the attack on the incumbent, Nixon. The ultrareformers were frustrated by what they believed to be the neglect of reform by the state parties and what they considered to be overly optimistic appraisals put forth by the commission and the National Committee.[40] What they feared most was exactly what the regulars anticipated—that the reform effort would be lost in the drive to select a presidential candidate. Between both positions was the majority of the commission and, of course, the staff, the latter charged with the day-to-day coordination of efforts to implement the guidelines. The pressures on everyone were great, and the events of the summer and the fall to follow had the effect of rekindling rather than soothing the anger of the various factions.

The regulars, as befitted their style and strategy, waited. Those pressuring for quicker adoption of the rules could not afford so comfortable a position—they pressed hard. An inevitable dispute broke out between the hardline reform wing and the staff. The fight was symbolized by Robert W. Nelson and his former associate, Ken Bode, who had previously served as the commission's research director. By the time of the July meeting, Bode was spokesman for his own watchdog organization, the Center for Political Reform (which he had founded), and codirector of an Americans for Democratic Action (ADA) task force established to monitor the reform effort. The tension between Nelson and Bode flared openly just prior to the July meeting. Bode was quoted in a number of publications assessing the progress the reforms had made one year before the national convention would meet. Bode was unenthusiastic. He questioned the vitality of the movement and its eventual success. He claimed, in an article widely read by the party cadre that followed reform activities, that the effort had stagnated, or, in his terms, gone "sour." He drew attention to the rates of implementation, which he found unimpressive, and particularly to the failure of the large industrial states (Ohio, New Jersey, Michigan, Pennsylvania, Texas, Illinois, New York, and California) to comply in any substantial degree with the guidelines. Bode's contentions were in turn challenged by Nelson and Fraser.[41]

In part, the different perspectives belie the objectives of the disputants. Bode and his group wanted to draw attention to the trouble spots and force, through intensified media and public attention, as much change as quickly as possible. Nelson wanted to nurture the idea of consistent progress and the inevitability of the whole process. The half-full, half-empty glass analogy partly applies. Both groups had the same objective. The fundamental differences between the two rested in the interpretation of the speed of the implementation efforts, whether goodwill efforts by the regulars could be expected at various levels of party operations, and the true significance of what had been accomplished to date.

Judging any process in midstream holds risks. For example, Bode pointed out that twenty-four states had not met the "timeliness" requirement, one of the most significant of the guidelines. Writing six weeks later, Fraser could note that the total had dropped to fifteen. In short, trying to stop a process in flux and evaluate its eventual achievements is extraordinarily difficult. Nonetheless, the confrontation served to dramatize the enforcement difficulties then being encountered by the commission and the laxness of a number of states.

If the major concern of the July meeting was to reassure one and all of the seriousness and progress of the compliance efforts, its second objective was to retest the willingness of the members to follow through on the course they had set. In the process, they were asked to refine what had been intended by "all feasible effort," the strictest criteria they applied to the states, and the precision with which they expected the quotas to be applied.

Quite clearly, there could be no retreating from the implementation tests. Some, however, would have liked to see the demands being made simplified, and a majority strongly felt there was a limit to what the commission should do. In particular, they demanded that the group not maneuver itself into a position of legal adversary to its own party. The commission position on "all feasible efforts" was tricky. The reformers expected a state party to incorporate the changes demanded or, if challenged, to be able to justify its failure. Where legislative or constitutional changes were required, the same burden was placed on the state party, regardless of whether the state legislature had a majority of Democrats or Republicans or which party held the governorship. All state units had to make a "genuine and demonstrable effort" to secure the statutory or constitutional modifications through "*all proper action* that . . . [would] not expose the party or its members to legal sanction."[42] (Italics added.)

In interpreting this last phrase, the July meeting showed that a majority of the commission and some of the staff had quite different conceptions as to its meaning. Should a state's procedures require legislative remedy, the state party was obligated to introduce legislation and secure the endorsements of all relevant party leaders (legislative leadership, governor, members of Congress, etc.) and actively campaign for passage of the relevant bill (through testimony at hearings, speeches on the floor, press releases, stories in the local press, letters to the proper state officials, newspapers, etc.). Everyone agreed on the interpretation of "all feasible efforts" to this point. From here on, though, views differed sharply.

The proposal before the commission, reflecting the views of Bode, Eli Segal (now with the aborted Hughes campaign for the presidential nomination), the New Democratic Coalition, and others, called for a state party to institute legal action when necessary and if legislative remedies should fail. The statement providing that state parties "should" begin legal proceedings to rectify failures to comply was changed to an unconvincing "could." The commission was precluded from entering suits as a litigant (in effect, an agency of the Democratic party suing the party), but it was allowed to submit amicus curiae briefs and to advise all "bona fide" elements of the party as requested in events related to legal actions or implementation more generally. This directive, of course, would apply to cooperation with the Credentials Committee of the 1972 convention.

Finally, the last section of the statement adopted by the commission demanded that state parties work within statutory limits to the extent possible to achieve their goals. When these could not be changed they suggested alternative or parallel structures if necessary (when a malapportioned convention could not be legally restructured, for example) to be employed with the intent of dispelling "the effect of any law which precludes total compliance with the Guidelines." The provision included a commitment, if all else failed, for the state committee to establish a totally new system that met commission requirements, an approach that suggested ignoring state statutory or constitutional requirements.[43] The proposal was struck from the final draft but should indicate, within the context of the total debate, how far the commission considered going to enforce its will.

In addition to clarifying the meaning of "all feasible effort," the July commission meeting was asked to specify what constituted effective compliance with the "quotas." The old enmities revived in the never-ending quotas debate, and positive action was stalemated. Given the ambiguous nature of the enterprise, effectively leaving the final decisions to the fears of the state as to Credentials Committee action and to the committee itself made for a reasonable political settlement of a problem that seriously and uncompromisingly divided the reformers. The proposal the commission deliberated repeated the content and agreed intent of guidelines A-1 and A-2 and explicitly applied these to primaries by stressing the need to bring them to the attention of slatemakers (a factor in the Chicago challenge of the following year). The provisions were to apply equally and separately to delegates and alternates, and the commission stand was not to be interpreted as precluding overrepresentation of the groups singled out for attention. Where the commission floundered in attempting to frame a common statement was in the effort to tie the "quotas" to some mathematical gauge of "reasonable representation" or to define acceptable limits of deviation from a norm. Conservatives on the question felt the reformers were going too far and were becoming impracticably rigid on the topic. Some liberals wanted a definition of the scope of the provision that the group would stand behind; others, and David Mixner was representative of these, felt any further clarifications issued by the group served to weaken and dilute what already had been accomplished. The proposals, consequently, were tabled.[44]

The July meeting refocused attention on the guidelines and the sincerity of the effort to fulfill the commission's early objectives. A number of loose ends were cleared up in one form or another, and with the group's adjournment a major phase of the implementation effort came to an end. A change in emphasis followed, with concern shifting now to the actual selection of the delegates and its effect on the convention just one year away.

The new thrust became clearer with the approach of the October meeting of the National Committee. The committee would endorse the final call to the convention and, as it turned out, make a minor concession to the reformers in revising the ex-officio provision and applying it only to newly elected National Committee representatives. But the significant battle took place over the National Committee's appointment of a temporary chairman for the convention's Credentials Committee. The two candidates were Harold Hughes, the commission vice-chairman and the choice of many reformers, and Patricia Roberts Harris, who was black, a lawyer, a former ambassador, briefly a law school dean, and the choice of the still-suspect O'Brien. The national chairman feared a Hughes victory would result in a too-stringent application of the guidelines to contested delegations. Party regulars fully shared O'Brien's apprehensions. The fact that O'Brien belatedly sought out an opponent to the then-uncontested Hughes candidacy did little to convince reformers of his good will. Harris, who had impeccable credentials and who was not active in any party battles, was a difficult choice to oppose. Nonetheless, the battle was loud, public, and as bitter as any that had preceded it. The outcome, however, was never in question. O'Brien marshalled the party's professionals, the AFL-CIO, the balance of the National Committee (which could be counted on to support his lead unquestioningly on most any subject), the Humphrey coalition, and anyone else who would help. Hughes lost badly (seventy-two to thirty-one).[45]

The failure of the commission to clarify its intent on guidelines A-1 and A-2 (the "quotas") continued to trouble the state parties. In mid-October the staff circulated to the states a memorandum outlining the types of steps that constituted "affirmative" efforts to increase representation. The commission, however, was still sidestepping the issue. Renewed pressure finally led to a policy statement by Fraser boldly presenting the commission's thinking. Fraser contended:

We believe that state parties should be on notice that whenever the proportion of women, minorities and young people in a delegation offered for seating in Miami is less than the proportion of these groups in the total population, and the delegation is challenged on the grounds that Guidelines A-1 and A-2 were not complied with, such a challenge will constitute a *prima facie* showing of violation of the Guidelines, and the state Democratic Party along with the challenged delegation has the burden of showing that the state party took full and affirmative action to achieve such representation.[46]

Strong words. Fraser's clarification, communicated to O'Brien in a letter of 29 November, was in turn circulated by the national chairman to all state party leaders with a letter of his own underscoring its significance. The minimal acceptable standard finally was quite clear and was certainly forceful enough to satisfy anyone who had fought for representation of the groups concerned.

Implementation proceeded, but as 1971 ended and the presidential election year began, attention was focused primarily on the convention and the actions it could be expected to take. O'Brien and Fraser had sent out their joint communication in December reemphasizing the national party's full support of the guidelines (and particularly A-1 and A-2) and asking for a report on each state's progress. Messages to this effect filled party publications, but attention was in the process of swinging to the gut issue of selecting a presidential nominee.

It was the highlights of the reform drive that provided the most excitement and quite naturally received the most attention: the flourishes provided by the National Committee meetings with their antiquated oratorical joustings, the July commission gathering and its disagreements, the sharp and unending infighting of the party factions, the continual reflections on O'Brien's sincerity, and so on. But the real work of enforcement is not so easily pinpointed. It consisted of the inglorious but persistent efforts on a day-to-day basis of the commission staff to answer questions, clarify points of interpretation, visit the provinces as necessary, keep a running tally of exactly where each state stood in complying with each guideline at a given time, insure that every party leader realized what his state needed, prepare background materials for party and press use, put out the innumerable brush fires as they arose, and keep up the momentum toward complete implementation. It was a tedious job, one demanding a sophistication in dealing with party professionals and an understanding of the problems they encountered, diplomacy in pressuring without alienating the leadership at all levels to accomplish the ends desired, and public-relations skill in keeping a skeptical press interested and abreast of developments and in answering without malice the charges and innuendoes that arose periodically from the states or various wings of the party. Overall the job was extraordinarily well done, the most significant single contribution to a successful compliance effort.

Scorecard

The progress of a state toward compliance can be traced by selecting a few significant checkpoints during the enforcement phase (January 1970 through 1 July 1972) and then assessing the position of the state at each point. Such a procedure nicely captures the broad movement toward implementation. It does not, however, give any feel of the problems of the particular states: the necessity of statutory change; the opposition or inertia of key party leaders; an inability to penetrate the wall of indifference in certain states until the closing stages of the effort; the stop-and-go spurts of activity that characterized most of the states; the byplay between opposing ideological or candidate factions or among different wings of the party (the gubernatorial and legislative, for example) that was a key feature in a large number of states; the early enthusiasm of vigorous state-level reform commissions (some of which did remarkable jobs) that later turned to apathy in a handful of state units; and the outright hostility or more clever dodges put forth without embarrassment by many state leaders and their parties. To gain insight into the fascinating struggle in each of the states would require fifty case studies, an effort well beyond the scope of this work. The broad sweep of the process can be captured, however, in relaying the progress of the states at significant stages of the commission's attempt to achieve full enforcement.

The point of departure is February 1970, when each state party received an impressively researched critique of its deficiencies and the exact nature of the changes needed to bring the party into full compliance with the commission regulations. The picture during this initial period was discouraging. Of the fifteen required guidelines, not one was met by all fifty states and the District of Columbia. Five of the guidelines found an incredible 87 to 98 percent of the state units in default, as close to a unanimous rejection as one was likely to come. Overall, there were 465 violations, or over 60 percent of the maximum. A quick gauge of the remarkable success of the enforcement can be seen two and a half years later, when the Democratic convention met in Miami Beach, and only 13 violations remained. By this standard the reform move was 97 percent effective. Table 4.1 provides an indication of the magnitude of the changes sought by the commission in 1970 and the changes brought about by 1972 by listing the fifteen requirements and the states out of compliance with each, both at the beginning and the conclusion of the process.

The checkpoints selected to monitor the process include early 1971, the end of the first full year of the effort to achieve compliance and the point at which the National Committee incorporated the commission rules into its preliminary call to the upcoming national convention; the summer of 1971, the time of the disputatious commission meeting and the publicity surrounding it (which brought all the old questions and fears back to the forefront of public attention); April 1972, not a truly significant date, but important in that it indicates where the states were in the middle of the delegate selection process and less than three months away from the opening of the convention; and, of course, the national convention in July, which marks the end of the implementation period and the expiration of the McGovern-Fraser Commission itself. Figure 1 graphically presents the swing toward near-total fulfillment of the commission's objectives.

The presentation illustrates that the movement took hold slowly, gathering noticeable momentum after the adoption of the preliminary call and had achieved its dominant successes by the end of the first quarter of the election year. Obviously the graph cannot provide insight into the progressive battles within the states that paved the way for reform. It does show that the most notable achievements occurred during the approximate year bounded by parts three and four and that the first half of 1971 reflected the first serious indication that the states were preparing to meet the commission's directives. Despite the commission staff's repeated thrusts, the first year of implementation was slow, not surprising given the lack of interest in national politics in the lull between conventions, the preoccupation with the off-year elections, and the professional tendency to wait and

Figure 1
Implementation of the McGovern-Fraser Commission
Guidelines at Five Check Points, 1968–72

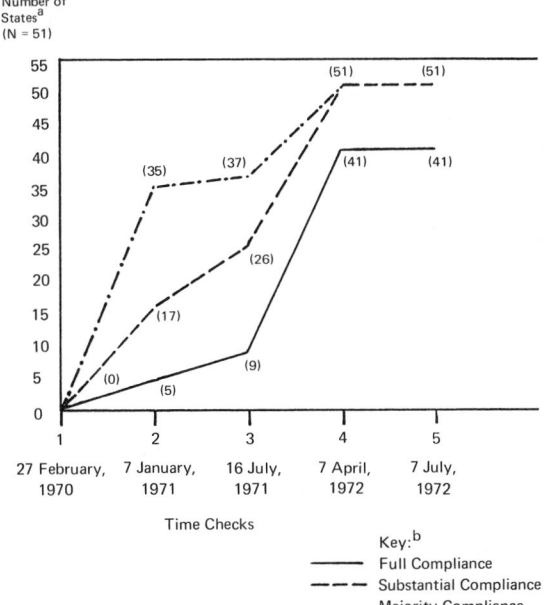

Number of
States[a]
(N = 51)

Time Checks

Key:[b]
——— Full Compliance
— — — Substantial Compliance
·—·—· Majority Compliance

[a]Total of 51 includes District of Columbia.
[b]Full compliance is defined as all guidelines satisfied; substantial compliance is defined as all but one or two (or parts of one or two) guidelines satisfied; and majority compliance is defined as over 50% of guidelines satisfied.

assess the amount of real support the national party and its leaders (especially O'Brien) would give to the reforms. By April of the presidential election year whatever was going to be accomplished had been. The last few months added no states to the list of those meeting reform standards.

Figure 2 provides a more explicit perspective on the events of 1970.[47] Seemingly major gains had been made in enacting guideline A-2, providing for the encouragement of the role of women and youth in party affairs. The gains were somewhat illusionary when the more specific question arose as to the exact proportion of a delegation to be filled by such representatives. But at this stage that difficulty was two years away. Fourteen states had acted on the unit rule ban, but the mandate of the convention (independently of the commission) should have given this added emphasis. More impressive are the gains in the number of states adjusting their rules on alternates, apportionment of convention votes, timeliness (a most significant guideline), public notice, and slatemaking. The quorum provision had already been met by a majority of states. The substantial movement in these areas contrasts with the absence of change on A-5 (the

Table 4.1
State Party Compliance with the Reform Guidelines, 1968 and 1972

Guidelines

State	A-1 Race	A-2 Sex, Youth	A-4 Costs, Fees	A-5 Party Rules	B-1 Proxy Voting	B-2 Clarity	B-3 Quorum	B-4 Alternates, Vacancies	B-5 Unit Rule	B-7 Delegate Apportionment	C-1 Public Notice	C-2 Automatic (Ex-Officio) Delegates	C-4 Timeliness	C-5 Committee Selection	C-6 Statemaking	Total
Alabama	○	○	○	○		○		○		○	○		○		○	10
Alaska	○	○		○				○		○				○	○	7
Arizona	○	○		○	○	○		○	○	○	○		○	○	○	12
Arkansas	○	○	N	○	○	○		○	○	○	○		○		○	12
California	○	○		○				○		○					○	6
Colorado	○	○		○	○			○		○					○	7
Connecticut	○	○	○	○	○	○		○	○	○	○		N		N	12
Delaware	○	○		○	○	○		○	○	○	○		○		○	11
District of Columbia	○	○		○				○		N					○	6
Florida	○	○		○	○			○		○		○	○		○	9
Georgia	○	○		○	○			○		○	○	○	○		○	10
Hawaii	○	○		○	○			○		○	N	○	○		○	10
Idaho	○	○		○	○	○		○	○	○	○		○		○	11
Illinois	○	○		○	○	○		○		○	○		○		○	10
Indiana	○	○		○	○			○		○	○		○		○	9
Iowa	○	○		○	○			○		○			○		○	8
Kansas	○	○		○	○	○		○		○	○		○		○	10
Kentucky	○	○		○				○		○					○	6
Louisiana	○	○		○	○	○		○		○	○		○		○	10
Maine	○	○		○	○			○		○			○	○		8
Maryland	○	○		○	○	○		○	○	N	○		○		○	11
Massachusetts	○	○		○	○	○		○	○	○	○		○		○	11
Michigan	○	○		○	○			○	○	○	○	○	○		○	11
Minnesota	○	○		○				○		○					○	6

128

Mississippi	C	C	C	C			C	C			C		C		C	7
Missouri	C	C	C	C	C		C		N		C		C		C	11
Montana	C	C	C			C		C			C		C			9
Nebraska	C	C	C				C	C					C			7
Nevada	C	C	C	C			C						C	C		8
New Hampshire	C	C	C				C						C			6
New Jersey	C	C	C	C	N		C						C	C		7
New Mexico	C	C	C				C						C			7
New York	C	C	C	C	C		C	C	C		C	C	C	C		13
North Carolina	C	C	C				C						C			6
North Dakota	C	C	C	C			C	C	C		C		C			11
Ohio	C	C	C		N		C			C			C			7
Oklahoma	C	C	C	C			C	C	C		C	C	C			11
Oregon	C	C	C				C						C			6
Pennsylvania	C	C	C	C	C		C	C	C		C	C	C		C	11
Rhode Island	C	C	C				C				C		C		C	8
South Carolina	C	C	C				C		C				C			6
South Dakota	C	C	C				C	C	C				C	C		9
Tennessee	C	C	C				C						C			6
Texas	C	C	C	C			C	C	N		C		C			8
Utah	C	C	C	C			C						C			7
Vermont	C	C	C	C	C		C	C	C		C		C			9
Virginia	C	C	C	C			C	C	C	N			C	C		9
Washington	C	C	C	C			C	C	C	C			C			7
West Virginia	C	C	C	C	C		C	C	C		C		C	C		11
Wisconsin	C	C	C	C	C	C	C	C	C		C		C	C		10
Wyoming	C	C	C	C			C	C					C			4
Canal Zone	C	C														5
Guam	C	C														
Puerto Rico																
Virgin Islands	C	C	C	C	C		C	C	C	C	C	C	C	C		11
Total, 1968:	49	49	54	37	17	1	52	31	48	22	10	33	11	40		466
Total, 1972:	0	4	0	0	0	0	0	0	2	5	0	1	0	1		13

NOTE: Listing includes territories and the District of Columbia.
C: State not in compliance with guideline in 1968; requirement met by mid-1972.
N: State not in compliance with guideline in 1968 or 1972.

Figure 2
State Movement in Satisfying Guidelines, 1970

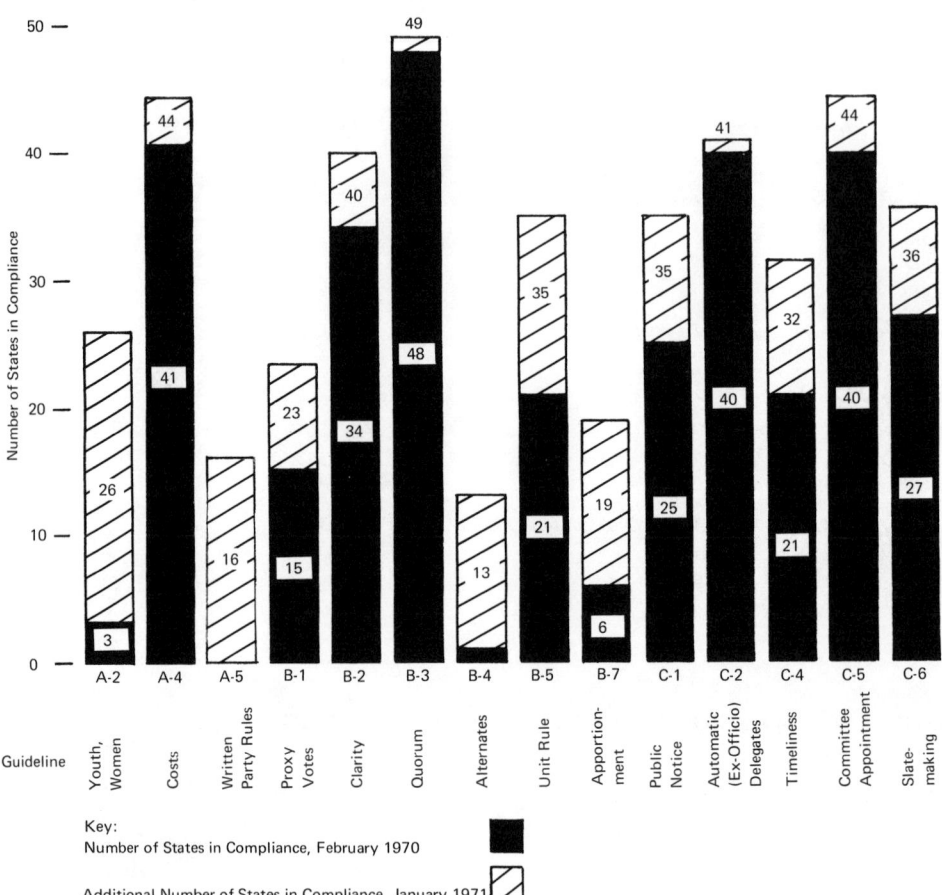

Key:
Number of States in Compliance, February 1970

Additional Number of States in Compliance, January 1971

publication of party rules, a sensitive issue in many state parties), ex-officio delegates (a provision to be fought), and the costs involved in seeking delegate positions (a murky requirement and one involving potential statutory revisions). Guideline A-1 received broad publicity, so any changes there would receive the most public attention. The short-term effects of action on this issue would be negligible, and the long-term consequence would depend on the will of the commission and whatever "clarifications" it might offer in future years. The matters of little public concern but on which party leaders could be expected to be sensitive (A-5, C-2) would be ignored as long as possible.

Perhaps a better indication of the progress on these key guidelines during the first year is found in figure 3. The base line in this figure is the number of states needing changing, and the compliance ratio consists of

Figure 3
Compliance Ratio: Proportion of State Change
on Guidelines, 1970[a]

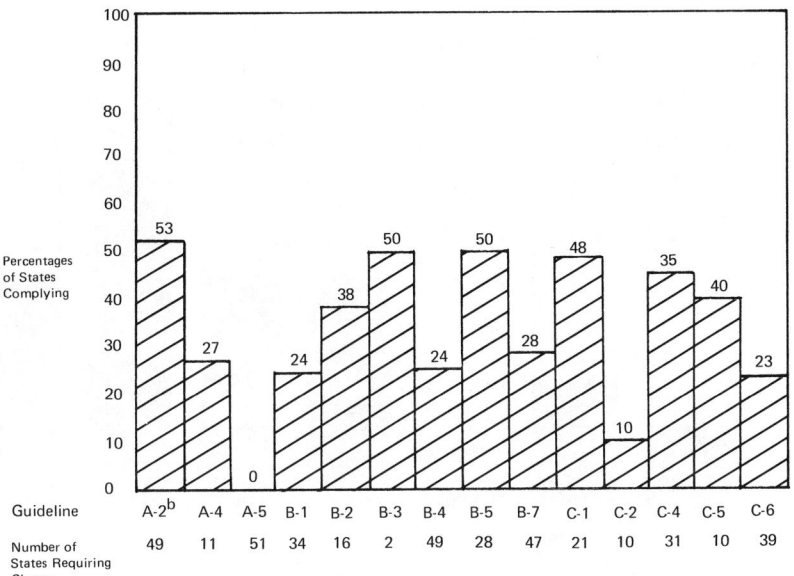

[a]Compliance ratio = No. of States Implementing Guidelines / No. of States Required to Make Change
[b]See Figure 2 for description of categories.

the proportion actually indicating they had made a positive contribution to meeting national party demands. The picture that emerges here clarifies the movement along the lines indicated. The compliance ratio can be expressed as

$$CR = \frac{C_A}{C_R}$$

where C_A = changes accomplished and C_R = changes required.

The basic gain in viewing figure 4.3 is an appreciation of how far the commission had to go to realize its goals of full compliance with the guidelines. Quite clearly the greatest gains had been made on regulation A-2 (female and youth representation), B-5 (the unit rule), C-1 (public notice), and C-5 (committee appointment), although the last involved changes in only ten states. Some of the guideline accomplishments that appear prominently in figure 4.2 (B-2 on clarity, C-2 on ex-officio delegates, A-5 on party rules where no newly affected state had completed its work) are based on past accomplishments, compliance with rules in effect prior to the reform drive. Figure 4.3 concentrates on the states needing reforms, and consequently presents a somewhat different picture. This

Figure 4
Compliance with Major Reforms, Summer 1971

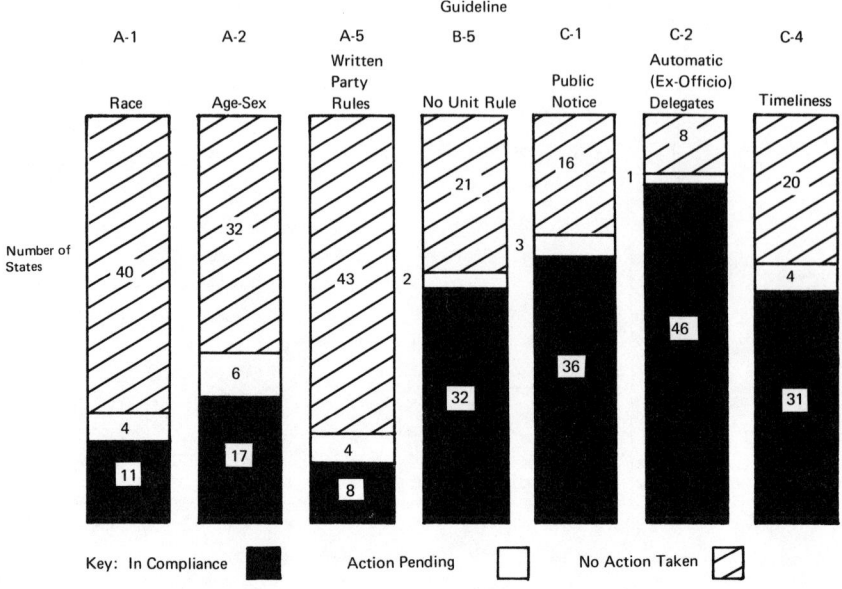

Source: Andrew J. Glass and Jonathin Cottin, "Democratic Reform Drive Falters as Spotlight Shifts to Presidential Race," *National Journal* 3, no. 25 (1971): 1302.

illustrates in large part the difficulty between hard-line reformers and the commission staff. One emphasizes the work to be done; the other the total number of states in compliance. Either approach is correct, although the interpretation as to what has been accomplished and where the reform movement is at any particular time can vary considerably.

The summer of 1971 was an eventful one for reform. A summary of state actions published by the *National Journal* and based on commission records showed that in seven vital areas the record was uneven (figure 4). Progress had been made on prohibiting ex-officio delegates and on the guidelines relating to adequate public notice, outlawing the unit rule, and the timeliness provision. Sixty to 90 percent of the states had complied with these four regulations. Less impressive were the accomplishments in the areas of acceptable written rules and the black/youth/female quotas, in part because the commission had tightened the limits of what was acceptable on each of these provisions. The nine most populous states had met less than one-third of the seven most vital requirements. Three of these states (Illinois, Michigan, and Pennsylvania) had been especially unresponsive, meeting only one (the ban on automatic delegates) of the seven guidelines. All three (as did five of the nine largest states) eventually required legislative action to satisfy the national party standards, although Illinois would fight the impositions of the rules on its convention delegation up to the convention floor. Only two of the largest states (New York and Pennsylvania) failed in the end to implement all the requirements. Both states were judged to be in "substantial" compliance with the guidelines, meaning they were usually negligent in only one area.[48]

Despite its soft spots, the process of enforcement was well along by mid-1971. All of the states had reform commissions, ranging from committees to survey their own laws, hold public hearings, and work for changes, to groups set up to help implement the changes legislated by the national party. In some states the work of these committees was perfunctory and in others the local reform groups existed only on paper. In a handful, however, the work of the state-level committees was extraordinary, tapping public interest, involving thousands in the consultations and, in some cases, backing a series of proposals that went far beyond the original nucleus of the McGovern-Fraser guidelines.[49] The creation of a state reform commission was more often than not a necessary step in evaluating what a state had to do in revising its party rules and the statutory requirements that controlled delegate selection for the national conventions.

By convention time, July 1972, the McGovern-Fraser Commission had gone as far as it could go. In its final analysis (see table 4.1), it could cite forty states and the District of Columbia as having totally complied with its guidelines and ten states as being in "substantial" compliance.[50] Of the ten states falling short of complete implementation, nine required legislative action. Although bills were introduced, the needed statutory changes were not forthcoming. These states would have to be judged, if the earlier commission grappling with appropriate standards was to be meaningful, by the "all feasible efforts" test that the reformers had molded so tortuously. The commission itself made no effort to apply the requirement, leaving it to the Credentials Committee of the 1972 convention.[51]

Summary

The success of the enforcement went well beyond anyone's expectations. Quite rightly, no party regular counted on the national party's dictation of changes in local rules to be enacted between national conventions. A "loyalty oath" at a national convention or a challenge by dissidents or, for southern delegations, a question as to racial representation were irritating, but they were in general acceptable exercises of authority by the national party. The presidential contenders could usually be counted on to take the edge off the battles and the Credentials Committee normally was composed of sympathetic regulars. The fact of the matter was that any delegation outside the South was seldom challenged, and even if one was disputed, the insurgents never won. The South had strayed in its party loyalties, and few regulars were overly sympathetic on ideological or practical grounds with its problems.

The McGovern-Fraser guidelines constituted a totally new departure, an active, persistent national party agency *demanding* change and, most significantly, getting it. The realization came slowly that all states would have to sacrifice in the name of national reform and that the changes required were to be explicit, specific regulations written into party laws. Generalities would not do. Appeals to youth or women to join party ranks did not satisfy guideline A-2. And the alterations would have to come in areas of core importance to party leaders as well as in the fringe elements that attracted most of the public attention. These discoveries hurt. The realization that due process would come to party meetings and that the influence of party insiders would be drastically and self-consciously reduced and that this would be done by the same people who stood to lose the most elicited bitter reactions. Much of the emotionalism and seemingly irrelevant oratory that surrounded the challenges that came before the convention can be explained in this vein. The extraordinary determination of regulars to see their positions defended until the last recourse had been exhausted—including the appeals made to the federal and state courts, normally the tool of outsiders and considered (for good reason) an anathema to regulars concerned with orderly party operations—can be seen as the backlash to four years of frustration in working to execute changes few of the regulars supported and many felt only harmed their position. Their feelings spilled over, in the last few months preceding the 1972 convention, into vituperative resistance to the reform standards. The unusual antagonism shown eventual party nominee McGovern, easily the most visible symbol of the reforms, was in large part a result of the same process.[52] Many regulars believed they had been dispossessed of *their* party at the national and local levels by the same militants who had marched in the streets of Chicago four years earlier. They fought back uncompromisingly, engaging in a war that ripped the party.

The explosion on the part of many of the state parties had been delayed. Although angered at various stages in the drive for enactment, all had complied eventually with most of the commission demands. Some of the local parties, however, had not seen fit to honor in practice the rules they had been forced to adopt. When officially challenged, their final reserve broke, and what followed was the most bitter series of credentials battles in memory. The Credentials Committee, however, stood with the reformers, successfully culminating two and a half difficult years of enforcement. Surprisingly, the new structures withstood the assault, an early indication that, come what may, after the convention they would be around for a long time.

A few additional observations on enforcement are in order. Early in the process (late 1969, the first part of 1970), the commission and its representatives were downplaying the number of states that would require statutory alterations. At that stage the commission's research indicated that the total would be less than ten. In reality, twenty state parties would seek legislative remedies (including nine of the ten that never reached full compliance), making for a process far more demanding than originally expected. If the full weight of what was being demanded of the state units and the seriousness with which it would be pursued had sunk in early, it is highly unlikely the movement would have progressed as far as it did. As it happened, the opposition, which was more formidable and far more potent than the reformers could ever be, was apathetic and disorganized. Each state was approached and worked on individually, so negative publicity emphasizing common problems in enforcement was avoided as far as was practical. By the time some of the state party chiefs had stirred themselves enough to organize an effective counterattack, they were put in the awkward position of opposing regulations already adopted by their own state parties. Consequently, the role of the Credentials Committee was not so much in enforcing the national requirements (although there was an aspect of this, particularly in the controversies over the acceptable number of women delegates in South Carolina and elsewhere), but in judging whether a state abided by its *own* rules in its selection procedures, a more comfortable position, closer to (although not identical to) the committee's traditional role.

The ten states that did not comply totally present a varied picture. Three (Georgia, Florida, Maryland) were southern or border states. Five (Connecticut, Indiana, Pennsylvania, West Virginia, New York) were known for their control by old-line party traditionalists. Only one (Oregon) would be considered a state with a noticeably progressive political tradition. Two states (Georgia and Maryland) failed to implement changes to acceptable delegate apportionment formulas, both preferring to employ congressional district allocations (and, given the evenness of district totals, basically a population distribution). Individual transgressions of guidelines C-5 (committee appointments) and C-6 (slatemaking) were recorded, but the most common failures occurred in meeting guidelines C-1 (adequate public notice) and A-4 (limited fees and petition requirements). Four states failed either to limit filing fees to ten dollars or less or to reduce petition requirements to one percent of the relevant population of Democrats. Connecticut, for example, still insisted in giving the party-endorsed slate preferential advantages (violating C-6). The state also required that insurgents pay a fee of fifteen dollars per challenger (which, as 1968 had shown, can amount to a considerable sum if the challenges are widespread) if they chose to contest the officially sanctioned slate. Those desiring to petition for a challenge primary within a Connecticut township (the basic political unit within the state) required 5 percent (rather than one percent) of the town Democrats in order to file, that is, required evidence of a substantial followership. Petition requirements in New York exceeded the one percent limit, and potential delegates or candidates for the state committee (which selected 10 percent of the convention representatives) were not allowed to indicate their presidential preference on the ballot. Oregon, on the other hand, was kept from full compliance by the most trivial of margins—the state's filing fee was five dollars more than the commission would accept.

The Quotas

"I never thought I'd see the day that middle-aged, white males would be our biggest minority."[53] So quipped an Arizona delegate-to-be with reference to the "quota" system his party was trying to enforce. The quotas raised some touchy political and theoretical problems. Women constituted over half of the adult population, but could claim only 13 percent of the representatives at the previous national convention. Youth, a subgroup given added emphasis by the introduction of the eighteen-year-old vote, now constituted 27 percent of the voting age population (it constituted only 4 percent of the pre-Twenty-sixth Amendment 1968 convention). And blacks, while making up 11 percent of the national population, had only 5.5 percent of the 1968 convention delegates. No one on the commission argued that an imbalance did not exist or that relief would not be beneficial. The members did differ heatedly on the remedies to be employed and the varying assumptions of democratic representation underlying each.

The politics of the situation were as clear as the imbalance in representation. The value of appealing to a woman's vote that amounted to 53 percent of the electorate needed no elaboration. The increased militancy of the women's organizations and their watchdog activities throughout the reform sessions, the selection of delegates, and the Credentials Committee hearings served to remind anyone who chose to forget of the newfound awareness and volatility of the women's groups' representatives.

Youth was a relative newcomer to serious national deliberations.[54] A number of politicians were uncomfortable about the youth vote, identifying it with the militancy of the antiwar protests and campus rebellions of the late sixties. The independence of young people, their strong issue-orientation, their affinity for insurgent candidates, and their seemingly personal distaste for professional politicians were all unsettling. Yet a major new bloc of votes was there for the parties to barter for.

Again the politics of the situation were irrefutable. In the eleven largest states, owners of 271 electoral votes (one more than needed to win the presidency), the newly eligible young voters (those eighteen to twenty-five years old who had not voted in any previous presidential election) accounted for between 15 and 20 percent of the electorate. In the six states (California, Illinois, Ohio, New Jersey, Florida, and Indiana) that Humphrey lost in 1968, the new voters could more than account for the difference. Quite obviously, youth—or virtually any other group but blacks

—is not going to cast its ballots entirely for one candidate. But when the new voters constituted anywhere from three to one hundred and twenty-five times the margin of difference between the two presidential candidates in the previous election and when the results in any of the twenty largest states could have been reversed by a strong appeal to the newly enfranchised element, politicians listened.[55] This type of arithmetic represents a powerful argument for inclusion in party decision-making. And the McGovern-Fraser Commission and the Credentials Committee after it recognized both the politics and the justice of the situation.

The struggle of blacks had deeper and more acrimonious roots than either of the other two. The battle had raged within the party for decades and had apparently been settled by the 1964 convention's creation of the Special Equal Rights Committee, which had done its most effective work under former New Jersey Governor Richard Hughes. The Democratic National Committee had adopted the Hughes Committee's "six basic elements," and the 1968 convention had supported the proposals. The McGovern-Fraser Commission incorporated the "elements" into its guideline A-1. It did strengthen them by requiring "affirmative steps" and by proposing a formula for convention representation reflecting the proportion of the black population within the state.

In terms of black support of the Democratic party's national candidates, the award of (on the average) 11 percent of the convention delegation appears paltry. Blacks voted overwhelmingly Democratic: from 85 to an incredible 95 percent supported Democratic presidential nominees. Proportionately, their relative share of the Democratic vote would thus be significantly higher than their representation in the population.

The politics of the matter again only reinforced the justice that entered in the argument. A fully mobilized black vote had the power (theoretically, at least) to provide the margin of victory in twenty of the thirty-seven states the Democrats had lost to the Republican or American Independent (George Wallace) parties in 1968. In the process 248 electoral votes would have been captured for Humphrey (which, when added to the 191 he had already controlled, assured him of a landslide electoral college victory).[56] It is not to deny the potency of the black vote and its particular significance to the Democrats to point out that arguments that implied this critical balance in prime states ignored the maximum support already given by blacks to Democrats. Nonetheless, the party had no intention of ignoring or jeopardizing the contribution. Politically, a non-quota "quota" made good sense.

The Credentials Committee and the "Quotas"

The morality of the representation of women, youth, and blacks may have been apparent. The political gains may have been equally clear. The only thing in doubt was the intent of the Credentials Committee. The hearing of the committee constituted more of a test of the "reasonable relationship" standard than the principle underlying the standards. Of eighty-two challenges from thirty-one states, those of six states and Puerto Rico were resolved amicably prior to Credentials Committee action. This action allowed twenty-two states, the District of Columbia, and four territories to be seated without further dispute (see table 4.2). Of the disputes in the other twenty-eight states, 80 percent dealt in some way with A-1 and A-2. The tough decisions were contested mainly on a political basis (what each presidential contender would gain or lose by varying resolutions). Concerning some states, the women's caucus, actively involved in the committee struggle, felt abandoned by their supporters and in particular by the McGovern staff and delegates.[57] Several of the controversies carried over into the convention and led to angry confrontations.[58]

In the final assessment, it would have to be said that the Credentials Committee was receptive to appeals based on A-1 and A-2. In fact, the committee increased the proportionate share of females (from 30 to 40 percent) and kept the levels of blacks, youths, and other minorities proportionate while increasing the convention membership from 3,099 to 3,194 (table 4.3). The most pronounced change of any standard took place in the controversies surrounding the Illinois delegation. The resolution of this battle alone (eventually decided by the convention) accounted for almost half of the women and youth and two-thirds of the limited number of blacks added to convention delegations.[59]

The battle over black representation had been settled before the McGovern-Fraser Commission ever met, although the fruits of the process were either not evident in many states or were embodied in the noticeable representation of hand-picked blacks distinguished primarily by their loyalty to the faction in power. Opening the nominating system changed the character of the representation and brought blacks up to their proportionate share. The question of whether blacks should receive equal consideration was not a factor.

With women, the game moved back to square one. The regulars felt women were quite adequately represented within the party, and they were slow to move on this proposal. The primary cause may have been generational as well as sexist. The increased militancy of the female organizations constituted a new and disquieting experience for many professionals. They underestimated the drive and seriousness of the women's movement and they were irritated by the watchdog activities of women's groups within their own states and at the national convention. With justification, they did not truly believe that the newly founded, politically aware women's organizations were perceived by the women at home as their policy representatives. An ingrained social bias, an inability to relate the national groups with their own constituencies, a failure to see any practical advantage in pursuing such a course too strongly, and a feeling that too great a receptivity to what had come to be called "women's issues" would only serve to weaken the party in the electorate and associate it with the vanguard of a new wave resulted in a strong reluctance by professionals to move expeditiously or in any depth in meeting women's requests.

The matter of youth was different. Youth was suspect: unstable in party support; unpredictable in behavior and fickle in loyalties; harboring often ferocious energy reserves; and capable of extraordinary moments of self-discipline and commitment that commanded respect. Youth represented a new political force open to persuasion by either party. The politics of the situation were irrefutable; the youth vote created by the Twenty-sixth Amendment was the most powerful single uncommitted force in American politics. Politicians could appreciate the implications of such a bloc and respond to them. And the Democrats, despite their reservations and a largely instinctive mistrust, responded rather well on this issue. If white, middle-aged males were not quite the minority the Arizona delegate claimed, the proportions of females, youth, and blacks had nonetheless increased decidedly in each of the states (table 4.4).

The McGovern-Fraser Commission attempted to provide a minimal set of guarantees in each state to all who participated in its presidential nomination selection process. To accomplish such a goal, the commission had to rescale a network of relationships. It required a unification of disparate state and local party enclaves in accepting basic assumptions and provisions as to how they would operate. It had attempted to remove from lower-level party discretion a number of areas never before challenged by or thought within the province of a national party. The commission was, in short, beginning the process of nationalizing the particularistic American parties. It is curious that this effort began in the more chaotic of the two major parties. The Democrats had always prided themselves on the looseness of their coalition, the diversity of its elements, and (in a perverse way) the rebelliousness that marked party gatherings. From the days of its founder, Thomas Jefferson, throughout most of its history, the Democratic party had emphasized the rights of the state parties to the disadvantage of the national party. This strain had remained through the New Deal and was present on the eve of the reform effort. Consequently the Democrats had little in the way of a national party apparatus and, beyond the evolving controversy over racial injustice and representation on convention delegations (and the related "loyalty oath" encounters), it made few demands on its state components. All this had dramatically changed with the proclamation of a set of national rules that were to be in effect by the next convention.

The commission and its staff in reality had little available to them to force state parties to do their bidding. They could cultivate public opinion. They could appeal to the long-term interests of the party and argue that

Table 4.2
Credentials Committee Action at the 1972 Democratic Convention

State	Credentials Challenge	Majority Report Challenge Withdrawn	Majority Report Seat as Elected	Majority Report Add	Majority Report Remove	Majority Report Both	Minority Report Seat as Elected	Minority Report Add	Minority Report Remove	Minority Report Both	Convention Action Majority Report	Convention Action Minority Report
Alabama	Yes	–	Yes	–	–	–	–	–	Yes	Yes	YES	Defeated
Alaska	Yes	–	–	Yes	–	–	–	–	–	–	YES	
Arizona	–	–	Yes	–	–	–	–	–	–	–	YES	
Arkansas	Yes	–	Yes	–	–	–	–	–	–	–	YES	
California	Yes	–	–	–	–	Yes	Yes	–	–	–	YES	YES
Colorado	–	–	Yes	–	–	–	–	–	–	–	YES	
Connecticut	Yes	–	Yes	–	–	–	–	Yes	–	–	YES	Withdrawn
Delaware	–	–	Yes	–	–	–	–	–	–	–	YES	
District of Columbia	–	–	Yes	–	–	–	–	–	–	–	YES	
Florida	Yes	–	Yes	–	–	–	–	–	–	–	YES	
Georgia	Yes	–	–	–	–	Yes	Yes	Yes	–	–	YES	YES (1)[a]
Hawaii	Yes	–	Yes	–	–	–	–	Yes	–	–	YES	Withdrawn
Idaho	–	–	Yes	–	–	–	–	–	–	–	YES	
Illinois	Yes (17th-23rd CD)	–	–	Yes	–	–	Yes	–	–	–	YES	Defeated
	(6th CD)	–	–	–	–	Yes	Yes	–	–	–	YES	Defeated
	(Cook County)	–	–	–	–	Yes	Yes	–	–	–	YES	Defeated
Indiana	Yes	Yes	Yes	–	–	–	–	–	–	–	YES	
Iowa	Yes	Yes	Yes	–	–	–	–	–	–	–	YES	
Kansas	–	–	Yes	–	–	–	–	–	–	–	YES	
Kentucky	Yes	–	Yes	–	–	–	–	–	–	–	YES	
Louisiana	Yes	–	–	Yes	–	–	–	–	–	Yes	YES	Withdrawn
Maine	Yes	–	Yes	–	–	–	–	–	–	–	YES	
Maryland	Yes	–	–	Yes	–	–	–	–	–	–	YES	
Massachusetts	–	–	Yes	–	–	–	–	–	–	–	YES	
Michigan	Yes (Humphrey)	–	–	Yes	–	–	–	–	–	–	YES	
	(17th CD)	–	Yes	–	–	–	–	–	–	–	YES	
Minnesota	–	–	–	–	–	Yes	Yes	–	–	–	YES	Withdrawn
Mississippi	Yes	–	Yes	–	–	–	Yes	–	–	–	YES	Withdrawn

State								Final	Status
Missouri	Yes	–	–	–	–	–	–	YES	
Montana	–	Yes	–	–	–	–	–	YES	
Nebraska	–	Yes	–	–	–	–	–	YES	
Nevada	Yes	Yes	–	–	–	–	–	YES	
New Hampshire	Yes	Yes	–	–	Yes	–	–	YES	
New Jersey	–	–	–	–	–	–	–	YES	
New Mexico	Yes	Yes	–	–	–	–	–	YES	
New York	Yes	Yes	–	–	–	–	–	YES	
North Carolina	Yes	Yes	–	–	–	–	–	YES	
North Dakota	–	Yes	–	–	–	–	–	YES	
Ohio	Yes	Yes	–	–	–	–	Yes	YES	Withdrawn
Oklahoma	–	–	Yes	–	–	–	–	YES	
Oregon	Yes	Yes	Yes	–	–	–	–	YES	
Pennsylvania	Yes	–	Yes	–	–	–	Yes	YES	Withdrawn
Rhode Island	Yes	–	Yes	Yes	–	–	–	YES	Defeated
South Carolina	–	Yes	–	–	–	–	–	YES	
South Dakota	Yes	Yes	–	–	–	–	–	YES	
Tennessee	Yes	Yes	–	–	–	–	Yes	YES	Withdrawn
Texas	–	Yes	–	–	–	–	–	YES	
Utah	Yes	Yes	–	–	–	–	–	YES	
Vermont	Yes	Yes	–	–	–	–	–	YES	
Virginia	Yes	–	Yes	–	–	Yes	–	YES	
Washington	Yes	–	–	–	Yes	–	Yes	YES	Withdrawn
West Virginia	–	Yes	–	–	–	–	–	YES	Withdrawn
Wisconsin	–	Yes	–	–	–	–	–	YES	
Wyoming	–	Yes	–	–	–	–	–	YES	
Canal Zone	–	Yes	–	–	–	–	–	YES	
Guam	–	Yes	–	–	–	–	–	YES	
Puerto Rico	Yes	Yes	–	–	–	–	–	YES	
Virgin Islands	–	Yes	–	–	–	–	–	YES	

NOTES: Dashes signify "No"; they have been used to facilitate reading.
Listing includes territories and the District of Columbia.
a Refers to Minority Report No. 1. See . . . of the people (Washington, D.C.: Democratic National Committee, 7 July 1972), p. 25.

141

Table 4.3

Credentials Committee and Democratic National Convention Action
on Delegation Challenges, 1972

Individual States

State	Delegates Added	Delegates Unseated	Net Gain	Change in delegate breakdown					
				Men	Women	Youth	Black	Latino	Indian
Alaska	1	—	1	+1	—	—	—	—	—
Georgia	6	—	6	+4	+2	—	+2	—	—
Illinois	85	61	24	-23	+47	+26	+12	+5	—
Louisiana	2	—	2	+2	—	—	—	—	—
Maryland	3	—	3	—	+3	—	+2	—	—
Michigan	13	3	10	+2	+8	—	+4	—	—
Missouri	12	—	12	—	+12	+5	—	—	—
New Jersey	8	1	7	-1	+8	+5	+4	+1	—
Oklahoma	2	—	2	+1	+1	—	—	—	+2
Pennsylvania	18	—	18	—	+18	—	—	—	—
Rhode Island	7	—	7	+7	—	—	+3	—	—
Virginia	3	—	3	+2	+1	+3	+3	—	—
Washington	2	2	0	-2	+2	—	—	—	—
Total	162	67	95	-7	+102	+39	+27	+6	+2

Overall Totals

	Delegates	Women	Youth[a]	Black	Latino	Indian
Preconvention	3,099	1,173(38%)	649(21%)	461(15%)	142(4.5%)	25(1%)
Additions	95	102	39	27	6	2
Total	3,194	1,275(40%)	688(21%)	488(15%)	148(4.6%)	27(1%)

SOURCE: Democratic National Committee, Office of the Party Secretary, Dorothy V. Bush; Sheila Hixson, Director.
a Defined as under 30.

142

Table 4.4
Proportion of Blacks, Youth, and Women at the 1968 and 1972 Democratic National Conventions

State	% Blacks[a] 1968	% Blacks[a] 1972	% State's Population Nonwhite (1970)	% Youth (Under 30) 1968	% Youth (Under 30) 1972	% State's Population "Young" (1970)	% Women[b] 1968	% Women[b] 1972
Alabama	4	27.0	26.4	8	10.8	19.2	14	19
Alaska	0	7.5	21.2	5	28.6	19.2	5	35
Arizona	3	12.0	9.4	0	44.0	19.7	21	32
Arkansas	2	18.5	18.6	2	18.5	18.1	22	44
California	5	20.3	11.0	5	34.7	20.9	14	48
Colorado	8	13.9	4.3	0	33.3	21.7	14	50
Connecticut	7	7.9	6.5	0	4.0	18.7	16	30
Delaware	5	15.0	14.9	0	10.0	19.8	9	45
District of Columbia	67	70.0	72.3	9	20.0	24.5	35	45
Florida	7	13.6	15.8	5	17.3	17.6	44	42
Georgia	26	34.0	26.1	9	20.0	21.4	19	32
Hawaii	0	0	61.2	4	20.0	23.3	8	20
Idaho	0	10.0	1.9	0	15.0	18.7	15	35
Illinois	6	35.1	13.6	1	18.6	19.0	8	12
Indiana	8	15.7	7.2	0	17.1	19.6	6	36
Iowa	2	9.0	1.5	4	15.2	18.0	17	41
Kansas	3	11.4	5.5	0	22.8	19.5	24	40
Kentucky	8	10.6	7.4	3	21.3	19.7	20	43
Louisiana	18	41.3	30.2	4	21.7	19.8	10	34
Maine	0	0	0.7	3	25.0	18.1	13	25
Maryland	6	16.0	18.5	0	16.0	20.6	8	23
Massachusetts	3	10.8	3.7	1	19.0	19.4	12	48
Michigan	20	21.1	11.7	1	20.4	19.5	19	41
Minnesota	5	9.4	1.8	3	18.6	19.1	18	47
Mississippi	50	56.0	37.2	7	32.0	18.7	7	44
Missouri	4	10.6	10.7	1	9.4	18.7	15	29
Montana	0	5.0	4.5	3	35.0	18.3	25	45
Nebraska	0	4.2	3.4	20	29.2	18.6	23	46
Nevada	7	10.0	8.3	10	30.0	20.0	17	40
New Hampshire	0	0	0.6	8	15.0	19.4	12	40
New Jersey	9	19.5	11.4	0	25.9	17.8	12	39
New Mexico	0	5.0	9.9	6	25.0	19.5	12	40
New York	6	12.6	13.2	1	25.2	18.8	9	49
North Carolina	6	20.3	23.2	1	7.8	21.4	10	47
North Dakota	0	5.0	3.0	4	25.0	18.4	28	40
Ohio	3	17.6	9.4	0	11.8	19.1	7	37
Oklahoma	9	10.3	10.9	5	9.7	19.3	21	41
Oregon	0	5.9	2.8	9	38.2	19.2	23	50
Pennsylvania	5	11.0	9.0	5	13.5	17.7	11	28
Rhode Island	3	6.9	3.4	0	37.9	20.3	12	41
South Carolina	13	34.4	30.7	0	16.0	21.6	5	25
South Dakota	0	0	5.3	4	35.3	17.6	23	41
Tennessee	11	32.7	16.1	0	30.6	20.0	9	49
Texas	4	9.2	13.2	1	22.3	20.4	12	30
Utah	0	0	2.6	0	15.8	21.5	23	37
Vermont	0	5.0	0.4	5	40.0	20.0	18	40
Virginia	6	23.6	19.1	2	35.7	21.7	11	38
Washington	0	7.7	4.6	7	13.5	20.7	14	35

Table 4.4 (*continued*)

State	% Blacks[a] 1968	% Blacks[a] 1972	% State's Population Nonwhite (1970)	% Youth (Under 30) 1968	% Youth (Under 30) 1972	% State's Population "Young" (1970)	% Women[b] 1968	% Women[b] 1972
West Virginia	2	0	4.1	11	5.7	17.9	5	6
Wisconsin	0	7.5	3.6	3	31.3	18.7	19	46
Wyoming	0	5.0	2.8	0	5.0	18.7	18	35
Mean Percentage	5.5	15.0	12.7	4	21.0	19.6	13	40

SOURCES: Commission on Party Structure and Delegate Selection, *Mandate for Reform* (Washington, D.C.: Democratic National Committee, 1970), p. 7; the New Delegate Selection Committee, "1972 Convention Delegates," mimeographed (Washington, D.C.: Democratic National Committee, 1973); and population breakdowns for the states are taken from available United States Census reports for 1970.
[a] "Other minorities" accounted for 5.5 per cent of the delegates in 1972. Comparable figures are not available for 1968.
[b] Fifty-one percent of the United States population in the 1970 census was female.

they were best served by adopting the course the commission advocated. They could bring to bear whatever informal pressure they could muster from national party leaders. They could threaten that the upcoming national convention and its Credentials Committee would punish offending delegations, possibly depriving them of their convention votes. Denying states a place in the convention, of course, represented a drastic action, unlikely to be invoked except in extreme circumstances. The convention could replace one delegation (or part of it) with another. It was a politically unpopular move to substitute the will of the national party for that of the state party, but this maneuver had been used with increasing frequency during the 1960s. Any severe disciplining of recalcitrant parties depended, however, on a convention membership substantially changed from previous meetings. The party regulars who had dominated earlier gatherings would not embarrass their own. Yet a reconstructed convention body relied, in turn, on the adoption of the very guidelines the committee was attempting to enforce. This threat was the reformers' principal weapon, but if any opponent had stopped to assess it based on previous experience, it would not have been impressive.

To an extent, the national party exists in a void. It provides precious few services to the state or local parties or directly to its membership. It is somewhat of a luxury; though useful to have a national-level party representative for publicity reasons and to provide a common frame of reference, in truth, it is far more dependent on its local components than they ever would be on it. The national party in America cannot give direction like a European party can. It does not have financial reserves to distribute. It is divorced from any national constituency and from the concerns of the community parties. It is considered a hostile entity, one competing for scarce financial resources with the congressional parties and often with presidential contenders. With feeble authority and a clouded legitimacy, it exists at the will of party leaders. It cannot afford to push their tolerance.

It should be clear, then, that the commission's approach in establishing national rules and requiring their enactment constituted a radical departure. The regulations themselves were not significantly obtrusive. They did not destroy the integrity of the reigning system. Rather, the guidelines were intended as minimal guarantees to people who wished to participate in delegate selection that safeguarded their rights. For this reason, they were difficult to oppose in principle. The assumptions behind the provisions, if not the exact specifications, were hard to discredit.

These factors gave the commission some room to maneuver. The individuality of the states alone makes it difficult for them to work together. The commission staff refused to allow itself to become a target for sustained attack by state party leaders, thus denying them what could have been a convenient symbol around which to coalesce the opposition. It was even difficult to argue against the most radical aspects of the commission report (i.e., that blacks, women, and youth should have more representation in party affairs), although much was to be heard concerning the controversial operationalization of the concept through mandatory quotas. No broad, solidified opposition appeared until the days preceding the 1972 convention, when the battle against implementation had already been lost. For this, much credit must be given to the commission staff, a clever newspaper and publicity campaign designed to embarrass local parties into acting, the adroit maneuvering of the national chairman and his staff, and, not to be forgotten, the goodwill and desire for improvement of hundreds of regulars and reformers who worked for change at the local levels of the party.

In framing its report and in executing its regulations, what the commission did not do is as relevant as what it did do. When faced with choices of any degree of difficulty, invariably the commission chose to simplify and compromise. Starting from an explicit statement of a problem and a proposed remedy and faced with the chaos of state practices and an expected sullenness of response, it consistently moved back toward a middle area, enunciating a standard and (usually) a permissively broad guideline. Its chief objective throughout was in realizing open and representative delegate selection processes. It did not desire, and it could not command, a surrender of state initiative. Politically, some type of compromise that did not violate the essence of the reforms was a necessity. A split in the commission over some aspect of the enforcement policy strong enough to bring factional rivalries into the open would discredit the entirety of its work. Instead of healing party wounds and stimulating productive change, the commission could have added to the divisiveness.

The commission and its staff recognized the tensions and acted accordingly. Their self-restraint, their effort to satisfy the need for a programmed move toward more explicitly democratic institutions while still protecting the individuality of the state parties, their tactfulness in handling disputes, and the willingness of commission members to resolve their own differences within the confines of the group and to abide by the decision of the majority, all served the party and the reform movement well. A sense of professionalism, a self-discipline, a sensitivity to the problems of others, and a commitment to the importance of its undertaking characterized the commission's enforcement and help account for the success it enjoyed.

There was little similarity or predictability in the response patterns of the state parties in moving to satisfy the criteria for open and responsive convention selection procedures. Competitive or one-party, southern or northern, influential in national party affairs or oblivious to them, rural or urban, much to change or little, the willingness to instigate reform and the speed of the process appeared dependent on internal factors peculiar to the state in question. With few exceptions, general patterns in the enforcement drive did not surface.

The big states moved slowly toward final compliance, although several had shown an early receptiveness to change. These larger states provided an implicit challenge to the commission that was not resolved until the commission had officially expired. Two were especially troublesome: Illinois, which did everything in its power to sabotage the results of the enforcement during the preconvention stretch of the 1972 presidential election year,[60] and California, which managed to hang on to its controversial "winner-take-all" primary through the deliberations of the Harold Hughes Ad Hoc Commission, the Rules and Credentials committees of the 1968 convention, and the McGovern-Fraser Commission. (The issue of the California primary was finally settled; the practice was outlawed by the 1972 convention after a disagreeable and costly bloodletting on the floor of the convention.)

It was expected that the states requiring legislative changes would have the most difficult time. To an extent, this was the case. States needing legislative changes that for one reason or another were not enacted accounted for better than 80 percent of those who failed to comply fully with the guidelines. Two states (Idaho and New Mexico), however, which also required statutory action, complied within the first year of their notification. In several states, as anticipated, the difficulty of legislative corrections was used as a dodge to frustrate change. Yet again, in some states that employed this tactic or sought legislative remedies belatedly (Illinois is an example here), their efforts proved successful. In characterizing the process in any one state, the total swirl of pro- and antireform forces and the events that surrounded implementation have to be considered to acquire any precise understanding of the outcome.

One general tendency was obvious. For many, the most direct means of providing open and representative process was to initiate some type of primary elective system. Consequently, the number of state-level primaries increased from sixteen to twenty-three (with Arkansas later choosing not to employ this option). Half of the delegates to the national convention were directly elected in primaries, a substantial increase over four years earlier. Conversely, the number selected through committee systems, a practice frowned on by the reformers, decreased by over 85 percent.[61] On the surface, the trend may look admirable. A fair argument can be made, however, that primaries tend to destroy party organizations. They can be expensive, physically exhausting, and prey to manipulation by strong party organizations; they can overrepresent minority candidacies, encourage irresponsible party behavior and even demagoguery, and attract unrepresentative electorates. These contentions should at least give pause to a tendency set in motion by the swift changes produced by the McGovern-Fraser Commission. There is much to be said for a state party retaining a viable convention system.

Finally, among the guidelines, the ones that appeared to prove the most difficult to enact included A-4 on petition and fee requirements and C-4, a significant reform providing for the timely election of delegates. Others also met with reluctant acquiesce (such as the stipulation for inclusive party rules), but once the party leaders supported a provision, enactment was relatively easy.

On the eve of the 1972 national convention the McGovern-Fraser Commission issued its final report on implementation.[62] Its leadership and the remains of its staff stayed active in the fight to salvage something from the joint effort of both reform commissions to create a party charter, but the commission itself, its work done, ceased to exist. Its accomplishments had been outstanding: it had framed a set of reasonable national regulations for delegate selection and, in the uncertain venture that is party politics, it had brought significant change to every state party. An incredible 97 percent of the guidelines had been enforced, an unequalled record of success.

FIVE

The O'Hara Commission: A Profile of Commission Operations

"THERE IS TOO MUCH HAIR and not enough cigars at this convention," said one labor representative at the 1972 Democratic National Convention. The case may be overstated but the impact of the reforms was apparent. Compared with any previous convention, he was right. In four years, things had changed remarkably.[1] The hair—youths, "ultra-liberals," and the rest—were now in the convention hall, including in their numbers two symbols of a far-off revolution, Abbie Hoffman and Jerry Rubin (allegedly the accredited press representatives for *Mad* magazine and *Popular Mechanics*), subdued and somewhat embarrassed by their newfound respectability. The McGovern-Fraser Commission, especially with its emphasis on the non-quota quotas, made an unquestioned contribution to the make-up of the new convention. The Commission on Rules, under the chairmanship of Michigan Congressman James O'Hara (who doubled, or tripled, as the 1972 convention's chairman of the Rules Committee and its parliamentarian), also made a substantial contribution, although more to changing the set of procedures than to recasting the mood.

The "hairy" young delegates (and many of the "non-hairy" ones as well) might well be attributed to the McGovern-Fraser Commission's emphasis on proportionate representation and the group's insistence on opening the delegate processes to all combatants. Less glamorous items, such as the number of delegates authorized to attend the convention, fell under the jurisdiction of the O'Hara Commission, the little-publicized companion of the flamboyant McGovern-Fraser Commission. The O'Hara Commission was the poorer relation of its better-publicized counterpart in a number of respects. It, too, had been created by mandate of the 1968 convention. It had first seen the light of day in February 1969, on the same day that marked the birth of the Commission on Party Structure and Delegate Selection, and, its mission accomplished, it expired at the same time. Its workload was considerably less interesting than that of its counterpart, consisting of remodeling the antiquated rules of operation for the national convention. It had no natural constituency—whether reformers, party professionals, or "hairy" youths. O'Hara's group had no direct contact with state or local parties and no spectacular enforcement process similar to its rival's. The McGovern-Fraser Commission, both through the nature of the problems it dealt with and its highly visible approach to its work, had preempted the field. By the time the O'Hara Commission came to grips with its areas of significant concern, few were interested enough to follow its deliberations. Nonetheless, a number of changes in the procedures of conventions can be traced to its recommendations.

The 1972 national convention was bigger (eventually containing 3,194 delegates) than ever before, a decision not applauded by those who blamed the size of the 1968 Chicago convention (2,622 delegate votes) for much of the disorder there. Yet the decision was of great significance in establishing reasonably accessible representation, and was one that spoke well for the independent judgment of the O'Hara Commission.

The delegates themselves were orderly, self-disciplined, and intensely concerned with the proceedings. Good humor on most occasions and a surprising display of amity and party unity characterized the meetings of at least two of the three convention committees as well as the convention's sessions itself, particularly in the closing days. The mood, the sense of order, the dedication to work, and the outcomes represented a polar extreme from the unhappiness that marked the gathering four years previously and, at least in part, represented a tribune to the implementation of recommendations put forth by the O'Hara Commission.

The nominating process underwent some welcome changes. The artificial "spontaneous" demonstrations for presidential candidates that had marked every convention since 1832 gave way to less synthetic outbursts of applause and circumscribed exhibitions of enthusiasm as each potential nominee's name was formally placed in consideration. The circus atmosphere did not entirely disappear, but it was at least less obtrusive during proceedings that were handled in an increasingly civilized manner. The presidential nominating speeches were cut in length, and the number of seconding speeches was reduced, resulting in a far more appetizing means of placing candidate names before the delegates.

The organization and management of the physical aspects of the convention were unusually well handled, an extraordinary departure from previous years and in particular from the ad hoc and still-secret manner in which such arrangements had been processed for the Chicago convention. The convention adopted itself more gracefully to the needs of the media, and especially television, without becoming its slave; it came closer to achieving the ticklish balance that Democrats (or Republicans) have yet to resolve satisfactorily. The endless number of resolutions honoring the work of the party's faithful was drastically reduced, although the convention leadership still managed to slip them in whenever a lull in the proceedings deserved a further emphasis.

A reduced number of convention committees ably processed the heaviest demands made on them in the history of the party. They did so with efficiency, while experimenting with new forms that reached out to states and communities in an effort to tap views or assess problems within a specific locale. And these committees were both more orderly in their procedures and more representative of the population and Democratic strength of the states than ever before.

The convention enacted another Commission on Rules recommendation by distributing to members the reports of the working committees prior to its opening, a factor contributing to the greater interest and more informed responses on the part of delegates.

The convention sessions were presided over by people knowledgeable in party affairs, people who were experienced politically and skilled in handling large gatherings (the main influences were National Chairman O'Brien, Parliamentarian O'Hara, and Joseph Califano, the party's legal counsel). The leadership held a broad commitment to fairness and was conversant with the new convention rules, the reform guidelines, and parliamentary demands. To those who recalled the bumblings of the presiding officer at the Chicago convention, the motions ruled in or out of order seemingly on whim, the inability of congressional officials out of touch with party affairs to provide direction to the proceedings, and the individual vignettes—Mayor Daley frantically signalling with a slashing movement across his throat to the convention chairman and succeeding in having him suspend deliberations (immediately after a similar motion from the floor had been denied)—Miami Beach provided a moderation and professionalism in the conduct of party gatherings that was appreciated.

The unit rule, a subject of acrimonious debate four years earlier and a fixture at Democratic conventions for 140 years, had been outlawed, and no one appeared inconvenienced by the omission.

A number of lesser changes were also noticeable. The aisles were wider, lessening the frustrations of moving from place to place and the number of confrontations between harassed delegates, press, and security people, which had been so marked during the Chicago meeting. Admittedly this was a small point in the order of things, but it is representative of the finer technicalities the party pols love to control. Wider aisles mean access to and communication among delegations. Small aisles create congestion, forcing people to rely more on the handful who are privy to information.

Security was tighter in Miami Beach, and considerably more efficient, yet those charged with this responsibility were courteous and usually tactful. The contrast between conventions in this respect was as marked as any. In Chicago, the Andy Frain ushers, backed by the combative city police, seemed menacing. In Miami Beach, the Frain organization employed pleasant young women and the authorities made every effort to keep personnel and police out of sight.

Delegations were seated on the convention floor and assigned hotel and working accommodations by lot, a new practice that removed one additional source of power from the convention leadership and made for one less arbitrary element in the convention's management.

Even the roll call underwent change. The southern accent of the party's secretary for thirty years, Dorothy Vandenburg Bush, still led the call of states (no totally automated votes yet), but instead of the familiar Alabama came California, in a new ordering chosen completely on a random basis—another break with a comfortable past unsettling to those who had come to depend on the ritualization of the roll call as one of the few safe harbors in an unpredictable world.

The O'Hara Commission had modernized the techniques employed for conducting a national convention. In the view of the party, expressed through a brochure intended to acquaint those concerned with their efforts, the Democrats would "show the nation and the world a simpler, fairer, more dignified method of nominating candidates for the presidency."[2] These goals they accomplished admirably.

All this is not to argue that the 1972 Democratic convention completely divorced itself from its predecessors. The essential strains of lineage were still apparent. The delegates were combative, and the battles on credentials, issue positions (defense, abortion, Israel, women's rights, busing), and nominations were intensely fought to the end.

The presidential nominations went well, *after* the eventual choice had demonstrated to everyone's satisfaction on opening night (through a series of votes on credentials contests) that he commanded more votes than needed to win. The vice-presidential nomination was a shambles, including votes for everyone from the momentary symbol of women's liberation to a television newscaster and a pop culture, antihero, professional television bigot, Archie Bunker. The party's presidential nominee was impatiently waiting to address a national television audience (he did not appear until 2:45 A.M. EST) to accept the party's endorsement and launch his campaign, yet, doggedly committed to showing that the convention was unbossed and independent minded, the delegates nominated seven candidates for the position, including one Stanley Arnold and one Clay Smothers (nominated by Clay Smothers). Eventually, of course, the choice of the presidential nominee won handily, only to be forced to relinquish the position seventeen days later, leading in turn to a "miniconvention" to select a replacement, the turning down of the position by a number of well-known Democrats, and the formation of still another reform commission to investigate better ways of choosing a running mate.[3] The event was hardly dignified or beneficial to the party. In fact, the shenanigans over the vice-presidential nomination became an outlet for the repressed tensions that marked the infighting underlying the week's deliberations.

But this episode was not the only one in which the revamped convention fell short. There were many inconsistencies and overly restrictive applications of the rules (for example, in limiting the access of nondelegate professional politicians to the convention floor), which bruised feelings. The convention sessions themselves lasted unnatural lengths of time. Originally designed to capture large viewing audiences during the prime television hours, they stretched well into the night and, in one case, ended after dawn.[4] Much of the convention's most critical business was decided well after midnight and was witnessed primarily by the dispossessed viewer of late-night movies. Exhaustion was the order of the day. The problem was partly procedural, partly a matter of arrangements, partly a result of an effort to be scrupulously fair, and partly a consequence of the nature of the business confronting a totally reconstructed institution.

Much of the new and a goodly amount of the old blended harmoniously in Miami Beach during the 1972 convention. An institution had undergone its most dramatic structural changes since its inception, had been remodeled in accordance with provisions set forth by the O'Hara Commission. What exactly was the O'Hara Commission? What had it attempted to accomplish? How successful had it been in achieving its objectives? How had it conducted its business? How did it achieve what it did?

A Quiet Beginning

The work of the Commission on Rules went largely unheralded. The efforts of the group were directed toward updating the procedures of the convention, a dry and thankless task, far removed from the concerns of the press and the average citizen. Progress was slow, seemingly unusually so as compared with that of its counterpart, and the outcome was less uncertain (being backed by the party hierarchy with no need for state-level acquiescence) and less significant, lacking the explosive potential of reforms directed toward changing each of the state parties. The limits on the commission were clearer, and the mischief it could do more restricted.

Its leadership was an unknown quantity. Congressman O'Hara, a representative for better than a decade of a blue-collar and heavily ethnic Detroit suburb, had a reputation as an able and progressive legislator, but he had little public visibility. He was known to be close to organized labor and a "comer" in the House, a second echelon leader of prominence who had the temperament and ability of a potential majority leader or Speaker. Further, he was a parliamentarian of skill in a body that rewarded such expertise, and he was known to be conversant (to the extent anyone was) with the shadowy rules that governed legislative and convention procedures.

Even with these commonly accepted characterizations, questions arose. Outside of expertise, why O'Hara? Especially, why O'Hara as chairman? What, if any, commitment did he have to reform? Exactly how close was he to federated labor? Were O'Hara and the Commission on Rules intended as conservative checks on the more aggressive McGovern-Fraser Commission? Was O'Hara the establishment's representative, the spokesman for a cautious House, a disapproving labor, and a skeptical party leadership?[5] These questions were not answered until the end of the commission's work, and they provided grounds for suspicion for those who expected the worse. Meanwhile, O'Hara proceeded in giving direction to the efforts for orderly change. In the process, the instinctively cautious chairman appeared to become mildly radicalized—at least to the extent of speaking more forcibly on the issues confronting his group and of defending commission decisions and prerogatives against critics.[6] Other of O'Hara's qualities became more evident as reform progressed. The congressman held a deep personal commitment to fair play and procedural guarantees and an abiding interest in providing a decision-making process open to those with a legitimate interest in the outcome. O'Hara's political realism, his fairness and respect for the rules, as well as his caution, guided the pace and substance of the commission's work over the four years of its existence.

The appointees to the Commission on Rules were uncertain of their precise roles (like the McGovern-Fraser Commission, they were to be defined by doing) and the powers they enjoyed. In addition, there was a question of accountability—to whom were they responsible?—that was to plague their efforts and eventually result in several serious problems. There was real concern with the overlap of jurisdiction between the two reform bodies (a problem that was never adequately resolved), and the knowledge that in several areas they would be dealing with issues on which the brash McGovern-Fraser Commission had already passed at least partial judgment caused consternation. Their painfully slow start, while justified by the fact that all their recommendations involved a convention four years away, did nothing to alleviate the skepticism with which the press and informed observers viewed their work. The McGovern-Fraser Commission had completed its guidelines and was in the process of enforcing them before O'Hara's committee even began the serious work of choosing among competing alternatives. Comparisons, which were unavoidable, hurt the group's credibility. This was unfortunate. The uneven progress of the two groups, forced to meet quite different sets of political problems, meant in effect that the accomplishments of the Commission on Rules were continually contrasted to those of the McGovern-Fraser Commission and, of necessity, were found wanting. As a practical matter, it also forced the committee to react to initiatives already taken by its counterpart, of which it was a little suspicious and more than a little jealous. Unclear objectives, confused responsibilities, a weak beginning, uncertain authority, conflicting jurisdictions, a restrained press reception, and an unenthused public all compounded the normal difficulties expected by both commissions as to funding and party backing and the reception to be accorded their final recommendations. The O'Hara Commission had a difficult time being accepted and cultivating a wide party following, liabilities that hurt it when it became involved in conflicts with the National Committee and its leadership (a problem the McGovern-Fraser Commission did not encounter).

The skepticism in which the O'Hara group was viewed was shared by politically sensitive people both on and off the committee. A sense of distrust prevailed as the commission began its deliberations; many members had little reason to be in sympathy with the presumed objectives of other representatives. As time moved on, however, an interest in the work and confidence in O'Hara's judicious leadership emerged that began molding the commissioners into a cohesive body. A process of attrition set in, also. The body, which met often once it began working in earnest, thinned down to those members with the most profound interest in the subject matter, those who cared enough about the outcome to do the actual work. Those who were less involved simply absented themselves from the proceedings, appearing only at intervals to pass comment on topics with which they were essentially out of touch. Although it is difficult to make a definitive judgment, it seems that the most involved of the liberal bloc, those who actively and consistently worked for change, were Donald Peterson, the Wisconsin delegation chairman who had commanded national attention at the 1968 convention; Liv Bjorlie, the national committeewoman from North Dakota; and Joseph Crangle, an early advocate of reform within the Rules Committee of the 1968 convention and Erie County and later Democratic Chairman of New York State. Less receptive to change, or at least more cautious in approaching it, were John Powers, the legendary national committeeman from Boston and the most outspoken of the group on most points (and uncontestably the most colorful); Carl Auerbach, a professor of law from the University of Minnesota who had a passion for legalistic detail; and, on several issues, the courtly and restrained Edward Breathitt, former governor of Kentucky. Fluctuating somewhere between these two groupings and continually active in the commission's deliberations were Irving Kaler, a good-natured attorney from Atlanta who contributed steadily to every aspect of the group's work; James Hunt, Jr., Democratic national committeeman from North Carolina; June Franklin, an Iowa state representative; Hodding Carter III, progressive Mississippi publisher and vice-chairman of the state party; David Harrison, a state legislator and Democratic state chairman from Massachusetts; Dorothy McDiarmid, a state representative from Virginia; Barbra Sylvester, national committeewoman from South Carolina; Benjamin Brown, a state legislator from Georgia; and Dennis O'Toole, a Harvard Law student and former vice-president of the National Student Association. Clear-cut distinctions between the member views were, for the most part, difficult to draw, depending a great deal on the issue under consideration and not surprisingly, given the history of the group, the stage of the commission's deliberations. As work progressed, and especially as the members began to fashion the final version of their report, their sense of rapport and pride of mutual accomplishment replaced the earlier uneasiness, insuring a cohesive effort in framing and then supporting their recommendations.

One factor that helped relationships among members was the realization that, despite the mild controversy surrounding its inception and the early doubts concerning its objectives, the vast majority of its membership and its chairman did want reform. Once the commitment of the members became clear, the bickering and maneuvering of earlier sessions gave way to a camaraderie and a spirit of accommodation that greatly eased tensions.[7]

The Commission at Work

The O'Hara Commission's approach to its responsibilities differed substantially from that of the McGovern-Fraser Commission, providing a contrast that serves as a convenient point of departure for understanding its contribution. The turtle and the hare analogy is not entirely appropriate in comparing the dissimilarities; in addition to being quick, the McGovern-Fraser Commission was also thorough, and it finished as emphatically as it had begun. Still, the image of a turtle-like advance does begin to convey the Commission on Rules's inching over each piece of ground unspectacularly and, for the most part, steadily moving to complete its work in time for the upcoming convention. The McGovern-Fraser Commission was forced to decide speedily on the guidelines it considered fair and then to publicize *and* implement them before the mid-1972 convocation. It had to apply immense public and official pressure and, most of all, it had to move quickly. The Commission on Party Structure and Delegate Selection expected controversy and, not to be disappointed, generated its fair share.

The O'Hara Commission was initially more fortunate. It had only to write the majority of its recommendations with an eye to enactment by the Rules Committee of the 1972 convention. As it turned out, the process of acceptance proved more difficult than generally anticipated, fulfilling the apprehensions of those who felt that the vagueness of the mandate would create troubles for the group in the later stages of its work. The National Committee and the national chairman acted as a rather forceful broker at the implementation stage, significantly altering several of the group's most important recommendations. The modification process feared by the McGovern-Fraser Commission only lightly touched its far more controversial guidelines, while taking full measure of key proposals of the Commission on Rules (as to the size of the convention and the allocation of delegate strength, for example). The O'Hara group's anxieties were fueled by its relatively harsh treatment by the National Committee, and its fears were not alleviated until it became clear that O'Hara would be appointed temporary (and, later, permanent) chairman of the convention's Rules Committee, thus insuring a full and sympathetic hearing for its recommendations and virtually guaranteeing their adoption.

THE APPROACH TO WORK

The differences between the manner in which the McGovern-Fraser and O'Hara commissions met their obligations were consistently and vividly brought home to observers. The McGovern-Fraser Commission ran somewhat like a national presidential campaign. The delegate selection committee took off running, attempted to gain as much publicity and press attention as possible, developed a specific schedule and held to it, clearly met its objectives and worked for them through consultation and pressure applied to the state parties, and ended as boisterously as it began. The approach of the O'Hara Commission was far more sedate and relaxed. It began slowly, a point O'Hara acknowledged in addressing a meeting of the McGovern-Fraser Commission,[8] and its scheduling and precise goals were both more specific (to rewrite the rules of the convention) and more ambiguous (to conform to what? In line with what standards?).[9] O'Hara kept the committee's long-range perspective basically to himself. He appeared to have a full appreciation of what needed to be done and the tempo at which the committee would conduct its affairs, but the knowledge was not widely shared. The schedule of the group's activities remained flexible. Rather than locking the body into any far-ranging commitments, the chairman usually preferred to plan no further than the date of the next meeting. O'Hara did make every effort to bring all members of the commission along with him at roughly the same pace, attempting to gain a near unanimity of views familiar in legislative committee processing that, while painfully tedious at many points, did ultimately succeed. Contentious issues were deliberately left unresolved, with action postponed to some vague future date. The approach strove for consensus and attempted to avoid any open or prolonged conflicts. It was modeled after the congressional mock-up sessions, on a piece of legislation that O'Hara felt comfortable with and obviously prized. The McGovern-Fraser Commission, in contrast, appeared willing to live with dissension and felt considerably more pressure to face and resolve its major problems expeditiously. Its emphasis was on articulating positions that were often antagonistic, reaching some types of agreement, and then moving to the next item on the agenda.

The members, split many ways by the issues brought before the group, had little of the energy or commitment needed to abstract principles sufficiently to form a consistent line of opposition or support based on how they believed a convention should perform. The multiplicity of problems that attracted review, the legalistic manner in which alternatives were phrased, and the seeming lack of relationship between topics made it extraordinarily difficult to weigh proposals with any sense of the fair operation of representative institutions in mind. The McGovern-Fraser Commission dealt in the specific on occasion (the disagreement over a 40 percent or 50 percent base for an acceptable quorum, for example), but mostly it tried to articulate principles that would assure open and meaningful selection processes and then encourage the states to adopt these in some form of its own peculiar circumstances. The O'Hara Commission approached the problem from a quite different perspective.

The O'Hara Commission depended far less on its staff, headed by a former legislative counsel and O'Hara intimate, than the McGovern-Fraser Commission did. Few staff people were employed: in addition to the counsel, usually no more than a secretary and, as need dictated, a part-time researcher, advance man for field hearings, or coordinator. The contrast to the large and involved staff (especially during the earlier days) and the bustle and openness that characterized the McGovern-Fraser back-up efforts was stark. The McGovern-Fraser Commission attempted a comprehensive review by the staff and consultants of all the problems that faced them, and developed some well-thought-out position papers arguing for alternative solutions. The O'Hara Commission opted for procedures whereby the commission members themselves debated the problem and actually worked out written solutions to the principal issues in full meetings. On some points staff work was adequate; on others it was nonexistent. The coordination of views and the complimentary phrasing of points raised were frequently left vague, at times heading parts of the commission forcibly, and unknowingly, in opposing directions. Failure of the commission to make specific records (transcripts or recordings) of each of the meetings left the reasoning for positions adopted difficult for them to reconstruct later. Neglect to maintain specific records meant that the precise compromise wordings on some issues escaped the staff when the time came to write its final recommendations. The approach to the problems explored insured that some areas would be overlooked accidentally (the proportion of women on convention committees was left out of committee drafts),[10] and others, by design. The role of the national party chairman in convention management, especially in the preconvention phase, was not clarified, for example. It remains a pivotal influence that is still basically unchecked. The responsibilities of the presiding officer at the convention and the limitations on his power were only touched on. Such omissions left major gaps in the final commission report.

An able staff would have provided the intensive research work and implicit direction needed to give unity and cohesiveness to the commission's efforts. The O'Hara group's staff was inexcusably deficient in this regard. Its membership was intentionally limited. Volunteers were not encouraged. Not surprisingly, these policies resulted in a small, closely controlled, and not very productive operation. The in-depth research and the perspective on past developments required to explore questions with any consistency or balance was missing.[11]

Another difficulty in the O'Hara Commission's operations was the manner in which questions were framed for group resolution. The approach was unswervingly legalistic. For example, the members of the staff would never ask what functions the committees of the convention should perform. Other questions were left unanswered. To what extent are these bodies an integral part of the convention proceedings? How can the performance of their duties be improved or in what ways should they be modified? Are the forms equal to the purposes they are designed to serve? And so on. Rather, the commission was far more likely to ask if there were duplications of effort among the convention committees. How could such an overlap be rectified? How many members should be on each committee? When should they report? And so on. These questions are not unimportant. But they are of a second order and would follow, as an illustration, some discussion of the relationship of the committees to the broader purposes of the convention and an evaluation of what would constitute adequate representation of delegate views on these decision-making bodies.

The McGovern-Fraser Commission approached its problems with a conception of the whole, an idea of the ultimate objectives it hoped to achieve: open, representative, and meaningful procedures for delegate selection. Alternative forms were then explored, and recommendations that fit the commission's conception of service to the broader goals were advanced. The O'Hara Commission chose instead to deal with the bits and pieces, hoping that somehow these would fit into a cohesive whole.

The Commission on Rules's intent was to facilitate convention operations. The group began with an assessment of convention committees because these were listed first in the convention mandate. A mechanical process of evaluation ensued. At no point did members choose to ask what functions they were designed to perform or what types of responsibilities they had assumed (or abandoned) over the generations. What types of jobs did they actually do and how democratically did they operate? What objectives should they have and how could these best be implemented? What should be the committee's relationship to the convention? There is a conservative institutional bias in such a legalistic perspective toward the status quo. There is a tendency to deal with those things that are observable as givens, never linking one to the other or to broader goals assigned the institution. Areas or procedures that do not fall into the obvious are omitted.[12]

It may well have been that a fundamental examination of the institution of the convention would have ended up with something fairly close in form, although more comprehensive and internally consistent, to the recommendations the O'Hara Commission finally made. The educational function of such an approach would have been helpful. An understanding of why we do what we do as well as an acceptance of it serves legitimizing functions for a political system increasingly in need of legitimization. A perspective that treated the convention as a coherent whole and built upon specified principles of representation could begin to deal with basic questions of powers, accountability, and democratic relationships. At a minimum, the final product would represent a more integrated, balanced, and understandable package of recommendations.

Overall, the approach of the Commission on Rules can best be compared to that of a legislative committee undergoing the process of drafting a bill. The committee does the work in a broadly consultative manner. A staff member sits in on the sessions but (depending on the chairman and his wishes) provides little direction or expertise. Every committee member is given an opportunity to express his or her views, and the majority prevails. The section under consideration is revised in committee, and the legislators move on to the next item.

The majority of decisions affecting principal issues within the bill have been made previously, or some type of compromise has been reached. More often than not, when a committee reaches the drafting stage the broad issues in question have been settled in some manner. Not so, of course, with the Commission on Rules. The committee forum was intended to be the means for resolving whatever problems or differing perspectives of the institution the members had.

Difficulties abound in such an approach. Congressmen on such a body, unlike lay party members, are experts on their subject matter. They come to the deliberations with knowledge, a point of view on the issue, and some type of objective they hope to accomplish. The legislators speak for concerned and articulate clientele groups to which they must report and defend their behavior. In this respect they are accountable. They serve on the committee because of their interest, their previous background, and/or the committee's relevance for their home constituency. Their legislative careers depend in part at least on their performance—their knowledge of the materials and their ability to achieve something approximating what they want. All legislators appreciate these unspoken rules governing committee behavior.

In addition, most legislators are lawyers with the developed skill of presenting their side of a case in the most favorable light. They also appreciate the symbolism of arguing through word placement and punctuation the larger issues involved in a question—who will receive preferential treatment, how actively an administrative department is likely to enforce a specific provision, and, most importantly, who has gained something and who has lost. They can also accept what is included in the final package

Table 5.1
A Comparison of Two Reform Commissions

Subject	McGovern-Fraser Commission	O'Hara Commission
Appointed	8 February 1969	8 February 1969
Early stages	Began quickly; by end of first year had held public hearings and formed guidelines.	Got underway slowly; regional hearings not held until 1970; working sessions October 1970 to July 1971.
Public hearings	Seventeen public sessions begun immediately (April) and completed in August; well publicized; large turnouts; drew on discontent from previous presidential year; generally successful.	Eight field hearings held almost a full year later than McGovern-Fraser Commission's; slow and uncertain in developing themes; poorly publicized; public and media confused by relationship between these hearings and earlier ones; basically uneventful.
Public relations	Excellent job; cultivated press attention and supplied media with accurate, up-to-date information; open, accessible, and informative stance of commission; staff director continually available to press or any interested person; press coverage good, consistent, and generally sympathetic.	Weak performance; chairman's briefings of press at meetings only consistent and integrative effort at developing media awareness; press not systematically cultivated and consequently often unaware of commission's work; media gave hearings and activities of commission sporadic attention; relationship between commissions confusing to press and public (and hurt media on O'Hara's or legal counsel's office, latter "second" commission more); decentralized focus for periodically not available.
Staff	Large, hard-working, dedicated; professional core with extensive volunteer help (especially in first phase of developing guidelines).	Small; legal counsel (staff director) and secretary normally only full-time employees; short-term consultants and workers taken on for specific assignments; volunteers discouraged; specific jobs on occasion assigned to trusted Washington lawyers.
Staff contribution	Staff work essential to commission's success; aggressive performance that gave direction to deliberations, especially in framing early questions for review and in promoting discussion of solutions favored by several pro-reform staff professionals; reduced staff in later stages in charge of overseeing enforcement; accomplished what it set out to do with minimum of acrimony.	Staff work generally weak; little back-up work or original exploration; handled limited number of inquiries; not in any sense initiators; mostly a holding operation.
Mood	Open, argumentative body; full commission consulted on all early decisions involving guidelines; staff critical to work; businesslike in approach; evangelical in spirit.	Cautious, slow, secretive to an extent; early background papers and proposals quietly solicited from knowledgeable people close to chairman; later work allocated to

160

extent by DNC); relations varied from tense and wary (like McGovern-Fraser) to poor;[a] at one point commission and DNC leadership angry opponents of each other; National Committee chose to modify several of its proposals (in one case the day after they were adopted); relations at end of process good.

Interpretation of mandate	Sweeping interpretation; ambitious program; wanted broad changes in delegate selection and planned to effect these *before* 1972 convention; worked early and hard to accomplish such an end.	Literal interpretation;[b] saw role as clarifying and specifying convention rules only; leisurely pace initially dictated by intent to report (through DNC) to Rules Committee of 1972 convention, the body that (it believed) would accept or reject its recommendations; 1972 national convention final arbiter.
Approach to work	Prepared, thorough, comprehensive investigation of all facets of problems; asked fundamental, hard questions; clear set of objectives—desired open political procedures and minority group representation in process.	Legalistic, legislative orientation; responded to and dealt with wording of rules, to the point that larger questions were often obscured; relations among aspects of institutions (convention committees and convention, delegate and his state delegation) never confronted; basic principles of participation (openness, etc.) or purpose, benefits, and priority functions of convention never established; chairman only one with clear conception of final product; since never proceeded from basic principles, serious conflicts in proposals entertained on occasion not recognized; sense of order and familiarity in progressing from one set of written rules to the next provided sense of security and progress that was deceptive; major questions often backed into.[e]
Chairman's role	McGovern forcefully articulated aims early in proceedings and gave strong leadership to early movement, although he was basically inactive in later phases of work; Fraser directed implementation and, in collaboration with staff director, kept daily pressure on state parties; quiet but effective.	O'Hara initially guided all aspects of work; oversaw staff operations; a fair, procedurally oriented chairman, he evolved good working unity on committee; less concerned than Fraser in final phases with joint effort of two groups to restructure national party; devoted energies to seeing his commission's recommendations adopted by 1972 Convention Rules Committee, of which he was chairman.
Overall assessment	Accomplished far more than could reasonably have been expected; area of concern broader, less known and more sensitive than that of Commission on Rules; extended procedural guarantees to entire delegate selection pro-	Its work resulted in a decided improvement in convention practices; basic contribution in establishing fair, commonly accepted rules of procedure; practices and responsibilities in some areas unaffected by commission

Table 5.1 (*continued*)

Subject	McGovern-Fraser Commission	O'Hara Commission
	cess, along with having auspicious impact on whole range of state party activities; realized goals in an area where national party's jurisdiction previously unclear.	work; innovations in committee processes for handling increased work load noteworthy.

[a] The incident is treated below. See O'Hara's conciliatory remarks on the subject to the commission on 30 July, 1971, and the letters of Liv Bjorlie and Donald O. Peterson to National Chairman Lawrence O'Brien, both dated 27 July 1971. The controversy was created by an article published by the syndicated columnists Rowland Evans and Robert Novak, "Fourth-Party Guerilla Wars," *Washington Post*, 23 July 1971, p. 23.

[b] The commission took its mission directly from the convention's mandate. The Rules Commission authorization was included in the Democratic National Convention's "Temporary Rules" of 26 August and as adopted in the "Final Rules" of 27 August 1968. As presented by Governor Samuel Shapiro, the Rules Committee chairman, and adopted by the National Convention, it is as follows:

The Chairman of the Democratic National Committee shall appoint a commission to be called the Rules Commission and consisting of members knowledgeable in matters of parliamentary procedures and familiar with convention procedure of the Democratic Party, and said Commission shall be charged with the duties of studying and evaluating and codifying the rules of past Democratic National Conventions, and investigating the advisability of rules changes, and the commission shall report its findings to the Democratic National Committee in a timely manner in order that the Democratic National Committee may submit said findings to the Rules Committee of the 1972 National Convention for acceptance, rejection, modification or amendment. (*Proceedings of the 1968 Democratic National Convention* [Washington, D.C.: Democratic National Committee, 1972], pp. 61–62.)

The mandate is not as clear as it first appears. In particular, the role and authority of the National Committee in the process is left unclear although the wording appears to state that its job was simply to store the Rules Commission's recommendations before it transmitted them to the National Convention.

[c] For example, at the 30 July 1971 meeting called to review the final draft of the recommendations, Liv Bjorlie, supported by Barbara Sylvester, Representative Patsy Mink, Irving Kaler, and O'Hara, drew attention to the fact that the rules omitted any reference to an equal distribution of men and women on convention committees. She pointed out that this was a regression from previous convention practices that divided convention seats equally among the sexes. Her proposed changes were not warmly received. Labor union leader Joseph Keenan argued that, on the contrary, "we're all grown up" and that "women can take care of themselves as far as being represented goes." He was against any changes in the commission draft for fear that old-timers would raise the devil and that an incurring split may mean losing the election in November. Kaler, a supporter of the Bjorlie motion, said he was for "equal representation as long as they [women] were not uppity," a remark that eased the tension. Others felt the convention would insure a basically equal representation of the sexes and minority groups on committees, an optimistic view as demonstrated by Illinois's and other states' later reluctance at the 1972 convention to divide their delegations proportionately even when required to do so. Representative Mink, with background materials supplied by the staff of the Center for Political Reform, demonstrated that the record of female participation on convention committees was deplorable prior to the adoption of the rule that the commission had accidentally rescinded. With this established, the commission proceeded to write in open session the provision needed, which was then endorsed by the 1972 National Convention.

During the debate, State Representative Benjamin Brown of Georgia proposed a motion requiring representation in delegations' leadership positions and on convention committees to be apportioned in relationship to race, age, and sex of delegates. The proposal was close to the McGovern-Fraser Commission's guidelines A-1 and A-2. These proposals incorporated major points of controversy (the nucleus of the whole "quota" debate) that curiously had never been considered by the O'Hara Commission.

After several attempts, the commission framed the following amendment to the rules which satisfied the majority of the committee's membership:

for simple purposes of symbolic reassurance to a given group, with the full knowledge that it will have little practical consequence. Such an approach assumes a certain level of expertise and sophistication among participants. It also centralizes power in the man who sets the agenda, guides the deliberations, supervises the staff, and produces the initial mock-up of the legislation: the committee chairman. These factors are recognized in Congress, and the process works with varying degrees of success on different committees.

How relevant such ground rules are for the operation of a party committee composed of a diverse set of organizational leaders and factional representatives is another matter. Few commission members could have been expected to have legislative experience or even legal training (although efforts were made to satisfy the latter criteria). Their lack of sensitivity to rules of the game totally foreign to a state party or private organization is understandable. The membership represented a diversity of views and talents and was approaching selective problems they had not considered in depth before. Not having a command of the area, they depended on staff work that was sporadic at best and over which they had no control, or, more realistically, they relied on their own inclinations. Consequently, they occasionally found equal merit in conflicting proposals or opted for an alternative that appeared reasonable on its face without having any sensitivity to the broader implications it concealed. As an example, in the confusing debate over the manner of apportioning delegates to national convention, one of the more progressive members persuasively argued for a system based on the state's Democratic vote for governor rather than on the electoral vote, a state's population, or presidential returns. It so happened that in the member's state the party's gubernatorial and presidential returns paralleled each other, with one significant exception: the gubernatorial vote appeared to be a truer index of party strength because it did not experience the rapid fluctuations to which the presidential results were subject. The important point, however, was that in many states the Democratic gubernatorial returns bore little relationship to the presidential vote; in effect, they represented quite different constituencies. This pattern was especially pronounced in the South. A Republican presidential candidate could carry the state while the Democratic gubernatorial candidate won easily. If national conventions are assemblages of the national party membership intended to select a viable presidential nominee representative in some part of the party base, then gubernatorial elections can constitute a misleading barometer of sentiments.

Commissioners with experience in only their own states who come upon a problem with little to guide them can be subject to whim. There is a need to find the correct wording in response to the document before them that would lead to some type of acceptable compromise. Such situations, especially in the absence of adequate staff preparation, are unlikely to lead to informed debate over the merits of contrasting proposals. In the example cited, the discussion was desultory and eventually lasted through several meetings. When initially proposed, the gubernatorial scheme did not receive strong opposition. It did not carry because of the lethargic discussion pro or con, the chairman's instinctive feeling that more should be known before a decision was made, and the decision to adjourn the debate for lunch. After recess, the group moved on to other matters, and it was weeks before it returned to the question of apportionment. When it did, the state vote formula had been forgotten.[13]

THE WORKADAY WORLD OF TWO COMMISSIONS

The deliberations of the McGovern-Fraser and O'Hara commissions were similar in one regard: their actions in deciding issues represented impressive exercises in participatory decision-making. They both were sensitive to public concern, they both made great efforts to be fair in their deliberative procedures and to be open to any and all influences they felt had something to contribute, and they both believed the work they were doing would contribute to a stronger party and a more representative political system.

Beyond this the commissions had little in common. In temperament, operating procedures, objectives, and problems encountered, the similarities between the two are hard to discern. Each went its own way. Beyond the sporadic progress reports to each other and the occasions on which they were thrown together (briefings to national committee representatives, fund-raising efforts), each pursued its own goals with little concern for the other. The normal relationship between the two was an unfocused tension: a fear that one might be laying claim to an area reserved for the other (in the unresolved debate over party structure, for example); an uneasiness as to whether the actions of one bound the other (on an apportionment formula, for example); and often simply an ignorance of what the other was doing. At the end, in the months immediately prior to the 1972 convention, they did join forces, hoping through a joint effort to address harmoniously the thorny problems involved in restructuring the national party. But the union was neither a profitable nor comfortable one.

Table 5.1 helps to highlight the differences in tempo and perspective of the two groups and provides a working assessment of the operations of them.

The First Year

The one thing left unspecified by the convention mandate was the exact influence of the National Committee on the deliberations of the Commission on Rules. A close reading of the proposal adopted by the national

Table 5.2
Chronology of the O'Hara Commission Meetings and Reports

Date	Event
1968	
26, 27 August	National convention adopts Rules Committee resolution; authorizes establishing committee for "investigating the advisability of convention rules changes."
1969	
14 January	Enabling resolution authorizing Commission on Rules to be appointed by national chairman and extending its jurisdiction to media problems adopted by National Committee.
8 February	National chairman appoints Commission on Rules with Congressman James G. O'Hara as chairman.
17 May	First meeting of full commission, organizational meeting; heard background reports on convention from four academicians.
26 July	Special meeting of commission to take testimony on problems of media.
19 September	Commission meets to hear select party officials discuss convention procedures and operations; approves draft of *Issues and Alternatives*.
October	*Issues and Alternatives*, a study guide that lists major problems to be explored by commission and principal alternative resolutions in outline form, published and distributed.
1970	
15 January	First of public hearings held in Minneapolis.
11 September	Last of eight public hearings held in Washington, D.C.
9 October	*Supplement to Issues and Alternatives* listing all new proposals from public hearings distributed.
16 October	First of eight working sessions to draft recommendations held.
1971	
17 February	Executive committee of Democratic National Committee met and modified Commission on Rules proposal on delegate apportionment (as adopted on 16 February).
19 February	Democratic National Committee adopts executive committee apportionment formula (with slight modification).
30 July	Last of eight working sessions of commission completes work on convention rules and issues final summation of proposed regulations.
13 October	Democratic National Committee adopts substance of O'Hara Commission proposals as temporary rules of upcoming convention; issues permanent call to 1972 convention incorporating new Commission on Rules procedures (as, for example, on credentials hearings).
19 November	Joint meeting of the McGovern-Fraser and O'Hara commissions to hear select witnesses on proposed changes in party structure.
1972	
19 May	A joint meeting of the O'Hara and McGovern-Fraser commissions issues party charter.
14 June	O'Hara Commission issues final report *Call To Order*.
22, 23, 24 June	Rules Committee of National Convention holds initial meeting to consider reform proposals as incorporated in temporary rules; committee report endorses new rules.
10 July	National convention opens.

convention suggests it intended the committee's role to be passive, a conveyor to the next convention of the final recommendations of the convention reformers.

In January 1969 the National Committee passed an enabling resolution authorizing the national chairman to establish both reform bodies. It added a qualification to those proposed by the convention, perhaps indicating early in the proceedings that it intended to play a more active role in the operations of this particular committee than many envisaged. The National Committee required that the group be composed of "representative Democrats, knowledgeable in communications, as well as those areas specified in the convention action."[14] The emphasis on the media's ("communications") role can be attributed to events that occurred during the convention but after the initial resolution on the Commission on Rules had passed. The contribution of television to the difficulties experienced by the Democrats had become a controversial issue. Finally, the National Committee required the Commission on Rules to report to it no later than at its first meeting of the presidential election year.

The O'Hara Commission was appointed shortly afterwards, but it did not hold its first meeting until well into the spring. O'Hara greeted his fellow commissioners by referring to the "jerry-built" nature of party procedures accumulated over a century or more of convention operations, and he promised a review of the "nuts and bolts" of convention practice.[15] The group began immediately. Four academicians briefly introduced the group to the evolution of convention practices.[16] The commission was then presented with a projected schedule of events prepared under O'Hara's supervision by one of his "marauders," a romantically named circle of friends (mostly Washington lawyers) who volunteered work on a scattering of proposals during the birth of the group. After modification the schedule was adopted, and it served as a broad outline for the agency's work over the next several years (see table 5.2).

The meeting's most important contribution was to authorize that an "issues" paper, which would outline the problems in the principal areas of concern and, briefly, the most logical alternative remedies, be prepared and distributed. The report—*Issues and Alternatives*—was ready by early fall and, following the policy employed by its companion reform commission, was distributed to party professionals, lawyers, academicians, the media, and anyone interested in reform or anyone who had the potential to contribute something to the effort. This one was the most widely circulated of the commission's reports, although it was followed by two others—a supplement distributed one year later intended to make available any new issue areas or alternative solutions that emerged from the eight public hearings held in the first nine months of 1970, and another report, published just before the 1972 convention, providing some perspective on the commission and the reasoning (to the extent it could be reconstructed) behind its proposals.[17] The agendas and proposals under consideration for each of the working sessions (see table 5.4) of the commission were also distributed at the conclusion of each meeting, insuring a process that was almost painfully consultative in certain respects.

The issues paper was intended to serve as an outline for the committee's work and as a vehicle around which to structure the anticipated regional hearings (see table 5.3).[18] It provided the key to the resolutions likely to receive the greatest attention and the basic format for deciding on the final recommendations.

The rest of the opening commission meeting was consumed by a lively discussion of problems members would like to see the group review (methods of improving vice-presidential nominations was an early topic of concern) and some of the anxieties members harbored (did they have any real authority to restructure the National Committee? To whom should they report and what was their relationship to the National Committee?). Several introduced agendas of their own, and virtually everyone had one or two issues they believed (and therefore felt the commission should believe) to be of paramount importance.

Only one other piece of business held any interest. On a nomination from a commission member, the group voted to adopt the rules of the House of Representatives to govern proceedings, a most curious action, and one taken without any deliberation. Given the small size of the group (twenty-six, down one from the original twenty-seven), the incredible ambiguity of these rules (understood by few), the availability and general acceptance of Robert's rules of order, and the enormous discretion the House rules vest in the presiding officer, they hardly constituted the best set of regulations for the job at hand. Fortunately, they were to play no significant role in the deliberations. The developing collegial atmosphere did not necessitate a reliance on anything so formal. On critical votes the procedures followed normal parliamentary lines. The episode can be seen as a further manifestation of O'Hara's inherent caution and his early uncertainty as to how matters would evolve. If scrupulously employed, the House rules would emphasize O'Hara's peculiar expertise at the expense of the other commissioners, as well as supplementing the already formidable power implicit in his role of chairman.

The summer meeting of the Commission on Rules, basically a hearing granted to proponents and critics of the media (especially television), was one of the best attended and most publicized of any of the group's activities. Television had emerged from the Chicago convention as the focal point of controversy. Many felt that the networks had created the difficulties the Democrats faced by their ambitious (some felt) broadcasting of the street demonstrations throughout the convention. Some believed television had provided the catalyst for the violence that followed, an effort to pay back Mayor Daley and the party for their unfriendly handling of network problems. Consequently, under the guise of regulating its role in the convention, television would have to be punished. The July meeting provided the first opportunity to hear the combatants, to assess the seriousness of the simmering controversy, the broad support for potential alternative proposals, and, most importantly, the receptiveness of the commission to various types of solutions.

The meeting, not unintentionally, proved something of a letdown, which helped to defuse emotions on the issue. Of the eleven witnesses, eight were media representatives and two were academicians with expertise in the area of communications. What followed was a somewhat dry description of the job of newscasting, the special problems faced by electronic journalism in particular, and the tensions implicit in the role of the communicator presenting an accurate and balanced picture of the news in progress.

The hearing gave broadcasters the opportunity to rebut the accusations made against them and to present their side of the argument, a curious service for a party committee to perform for a media under concerted attack at the time, not only from Democratic stalwarts because of Chicago, but from Congress more generally, on the issues of children's programming and violence, and, increasingly, from the Nixon-Agnew administration because of alleged bias in reporting. Yet the approach reflected O'Hara's restraint and his attempt to assess the unique problems television posed in a judicious manner. His concern was with an orderly convention rather than with singling the media out for punishment. Action on any relevant proposals was delayed until well into the reform process, over a year away.[19]

THE RULES OF CONVENTIONS PAST

The air cleared, the chairman and his staff could move on to a topic closer to their hearts. The convention mandate had singled out the problem as being of obvious concern: the codification of the rules of past conventions. The absence of such information suggests how arbitrarily these meetings could be run. Some felt that the convention intended this to be the commission's principal responsibility. The belief was that the Commission on Rules could review past regulations, eliminate the inconsistencies, codify and modernize the remainder, and petition for any new rules needed to replace those proven inadequate or to deal with problems not anticipated by the original provisions. The thinking of the convention (if it can be construed this narrowly) was quite logical, and barring any experience with former procedures, understandable. Unfortunately, it was incredibly far removed from the reality of Democratic conventions.

For those accustomed to a rule of law with established and impartial regulations, known and accepted by all, a Democratic convention can be an unnerving experience. A body of convention rules of sorts did exist: a hodgepodge of bits and pieces sewn together by succeeding bodies for almost a century and a half. The principal need proved not to be a facelifting synthesizing of past standards. The problem went far deeper. The Democrats required a coherent set of core rules to guide deliberations. The party had staggered through successive national meetings by adopting the rules that had governed the previous convention (with slight modifications, encompassing only the points in current political dispute—the unit rule, the two-thirds requirement, etc.), never stopping to question or review what these provisions might be. Incredible as it may seem, prior to the O'Hara Commission recommendations a set of permanent written rules to guide convention procedures had never existed, a point O'Hara was to make with increasing frequency as the work of his group progressed.

The rationalization and codification of existing rules, intended to be a principal and somewhat easy task of the commission, proved to be a highly frustrating experience. The contribution that could be made in this sphere was exhausted within the first few months of investigation.[20] After that point, the group directed its energies along different and more rewarding lines: the creation of an entirely new set of rules.

The practice of each convention adopting by reference (rather than enumeration) the rules of the preceding convention helped explain the notoriously brief sessions of the convention's Rules Committee. It also clarifies the heavy reliance on the cumbersome and antiquated House rules (understood, as O'Hara occasionally remarked, by very few people), supplemented when desired by the chair with *Robert's Rules of Order*. The system, deciding which of three sets of regulations (previous convention rules, House regulations, *Robert's Rules of Order*) were in effect and how they would be applied within the specific situation, lodged immense power in the presiding officer. When party regulars were in unchallenged control of events or when an authoritative figure like Speaker Sam Rayburn presided, the practice worked reasonably well. Under severe pressure and without a Rayburn-type figure to enforce order, difficulties were bound to arise. The 1964 convention suggested things to come. The raucous 1968 proceedings occasionally approached in intensity and disorder (if not in violence) the street scenes outside.

The commission salvaged what it could from past records, and then it moved on.[21] In a sense, the experience freed the group from tradition. Fear of contradiction of whatever recommendations it framed based on previous rules was minimal. Quite early in the proceedings it had become clear that the Commission on Rules would have to start at the beginning, constructing an entirely new set of procedures for the conduct of convention business. O'Hara had greeted his fellow reformers at the initial (17 May) meeting by telling them they had "the right and the duty to turn things upside down, around, or sideways" to insure the kind of convention they thought best.[22] What he omitted was the quality of necessity: they had little to build upon.

The completion of a scattering of position papers by O'Hara's twenty-five or so "marauders," the public visibility achieved by the commission's media hearing (although the substance and timing of the meeting had contributed little to committee deliberations), and the publication in the fall of the widely distributed outline of proposals, *Issues and Alternatives,* completed a leisurely but nonetheless moderately successful first year.

The Second Year

The second year witnessed two events of consequence: the initiation and completion of the public hearings and the beginning, in mid-fall, of the commission's working sessions, the cluster of meetings that did the real work of the group in drafting the final recommendations.

REGIONAL HEARINGS

The field hearings were modeled after the efforts of the McGovern-Fraser Commission, and were conducted along the same lines, although in practice they did not enjoy the clarity of focus or excite the interest of their predecessors. Several of the hearings (the ones in New York City or Salt Lake City, the latter held in conjunction with a regional party gathering) were successful by any standards. More commonly, though, disappointment resulted. Turnout was low and public interest lacking. Much of the sting of a national convention held two years earlier (an eternity in political circles) had been lost, siphoned off by time, the cathartic outlet provided by the delegate selection open hearings, and the transfer of attention by practicing politicians to the mid-term elections and (for some) the presidential nominations now only a couple years away. Many in the media and the party were perplexed by one set of hearings being followed within a year by another. The difference in focus between a reform committee that dealt with delegate selection to a national convention and one concerned with the rules governing procedures at a national convention is a subtle one, and it escaped most observers. One joint set of commission hearings actually would have been preferable. Most people had said what they intended (relevant or not to the commission conducting the session) the first time around. The confusion was not lessened by one commission announcing the reforms they hoped to see enacted and beginning to enforce these at the same time the other commission was taking to the states, ostensibly to find out what needed to be changed.[23]

Events conspired against the O'Hara Commission members. Witnesses seemed befuddled. Some spoke to the obvious convention abuses—high-handed parliamentary tactics, the size and disorder of the meetings, the costs of attending, the obtrusive role of television in bringing the chaos into the viewer's living room, and so on. Many had trouble focusing clearly on the committee's area of concern (a problem also familiar to the

McGovern-Fraser Commission), and drifted into discussions of any reforms they felt beneficial to the political system (from the direct election of the president to local party problems). The press coverage was not good, reflecting a general public apathy. Many who did contribute to the proceedings had done so earlier and could manage only a *pro forma* effort the second time around. The scheduling was not tight, and meetings were added on an ad hoc basis to suit the convenience of the commission rather than to explore nationally the dimensions of the problems to be encountered. The spark and vitality that marked the round of meetings the year before were absent.

Doggedly, the string was played out. The hearings stretched from January through the spring and summer, ending in Washington, D.C., as fall was about to begin (see table 5.3). The conclusion of the public sessions was followed within a month by the publication of a supplement within the format of the earlier report, intended to summarize the information gathered at the eight regional hearings and to draw attention to any new problem areas or proposals that required consideration. The preliminaries out of the way, the commission was prepared to begin its real work.

THE WORKING SESSIONS

Once the Commission on Rules entered the serious phase of its operations, it did an impressive job. In the ten months from fall 1970 to midsummer 1971, they met a total of eight times (see table 5.4) to give detailed consideration to the substance of the rules in the areas of major concern: convention size and the apportionment of delegates; convention arrangements; the standing committees of the convention; and the agenda of convention procedures. It was during this period in particular that the commission rose above its previous false starts and developed an identity of its own. The members who attended regularly evolved a rapport that contributed to a more accommodating atmosphere at the meetings and an acceleration of the work effort. As the group began to meet rebuffs from the National Committee in the winter of 1971 and some personalized criticisms during the generally difficult summer of 1971, a rise in spirits and a commitment to the recommendations it had so laboriously shaped became apparent, and these served the group well through the adoption of the recommendations by the 1972 convention. Had this cohesiveness and support for its emerging rules been more evident at earlier stages, the ability of the National Committee to reverse its decisions and mold its recommendations to suit its own will would have been lessened.

It was a select gathering that attended the working sessions. The frequency of the gatherings alone precluded many of the busiest and more prominently known from attending with any regularity.[24] The meetings (with one exception) lasted for a full day. Members were asked to evaluate either in preliminary or final form a set of rules concerning a given

Table 5.3
Public Hearings of the O'Hara Commission

Date (1970)	Place	Date (1970)	Place
15 January	Minneapolis	15 May	Boston
20 February	Atlanta	5 June	Detroit
3 April	Oklahoma City	14 August	New York City
17, 18 April	Salt Lake City	11 September	Washington, D.C.

topic (standing committees, logistics, etc.). Each grouping of rules underwent at least two readings at different committee sessions, and (with the exception of delegate apportionment and convention size, on which the National Committee had effectively stopped additional action in midstream) all rules were open to a final modification during the last series of meetings, in mid-summer 1971.

Once begun, the pace was strenuous. Additional pressure resulted from the intention of the National Committee to issue an unusually early preliminary call in February 1971 (the halfway mark in the commission's deliberations), which forced relatively quick action on the issues of apportionment and convention size and gave some early indication of the manner in which the committees of the convention would operate. Within three months of the final committee session the National Committee had again met to take final action on the recommendations and to issue its permanent call to the 1972 convention, a document that dealt extensively with the new procedures. Effectively, this meant that contributions of the O'Hara Commission were telescoped into a one-year period, beginning in fall 1970 and ending in fall 1971. The first year and a half of the commission's operations was an uncertain time, and the nine-month interlude between the National Committee's final action on its convention recommendations and the opening of the convention itself was a quiet one. During the later stage a disinterested commission provided moral support (through its leadership) to the McGovern-Fraser Commission's efforts to develop a party charter. Both commissions had fought for jurisdiction over this project for three years, but the convention task force (perhaps tired from the emotional investment a reform effort demanded) could mount little enthusiasm when the time approached to prepare recommendations.

The explicit procedures for introducing and adopting proposals left initial discretion with the chairman, but allowed for a thorough, democratic review of every proposal before it emerged as a commission recommendation. The initial draft on a topic would be prepared under O'Hara's supervision by the staff counsel or someone knowledgeable in the area who was chosen by the chairman. The full committee would then review the draft in excruciating detail—literally word for word—and introduce any revisions for which a majority could be mustered. The work, in O'Hara's own words, was "often boring," but given the nature of the approach, quite necessary. The modified draft was circulated widely to all interested

Table 5.4
Working Sessions of the O'Hara Commission

Date	*Event*
1970	
16 October	First working session. Initial discussion of proposals in standing committees of convention.
November	Draft proposals in standing committee distributed for comment.
13, 14 November	Initial discussion of logistical problems.
November	Draft proposals on logistics distributed for comment.
1971	
22 January	Initial discussion of apportionment of convention.
January	Draft proposals on apportionment distributed for comment.
16 February	Final recommendations on standing committees of convention and apportionment of delegates.
26 March	Final recommendations on logistical problems; initial discussion of procedural rules of convention.
April	Draft of procedural rules distributed for comment.
11 June	Final recommendations on rules of procedure.
29 June	Final recommendations on rules of procedure (con't.).
30 July	Final recommendations on rules of procedure; review of all proposals; completion of business.

groups and individuals and final action on the proposals was deferred. Unfortunately, the extraordinarily dry nature of the wording elicited little response from communicants. The subject matter was not intrinsically exciting. In addition, to assess the impact of a proposed rule, an individual would have to have some knowledge of convention operations and an appreciation of both the alternative possibilities and the consequences of different courses of action. Neither the understanding nor the motivation to act in response to the committee's proposals was widespread. Equally regrettable, what communications were returned were not automatically made available to the commission membership.

Another meeting would be devoted in part to reviewing the modified draft in detail, a repeat of the initial evaluation, although more speedily executed. If the proposal met with the commission's approval (or in the few cases where no further accommodations were forthcoming), a vote was called for, and if passed, the issue was considered resolved. Binding decisions were held over until the last series of committee meetings, although change at this point would come only under extraordinary circumstances, involving more often than not unintentional omissions (such as the question of equal female representation on the standing committees of the convention) rather than a redirection of policy. Once underway, the procedures worked admirably.

Implementation

The operations of the O'Hara and McGovern-Fraser commissions are a series of contrasts, and none is as clearly marked as that accompanying the process of enforcement. Seventy percent of the McGovern-Fraser Commission's efforts and time were consumed in persuading reluctant state parties to adopt procedures that, while fair, limited their own authority. Despite the grumblings and the more noticeable eruptions over the credentials hearings, the process was remarkably successful.

The O'Hara Commission had only to convince a hundred-member National Committee of the value of its proposals, but failed spectacularly on two of the earliest and most significant items. The implementation of the changes in delegate selection involved modifications of state statutes as well as party laws. The convention reform committee had no such problems. The McGovern-Fraser enforcement period stretched from the end of 1969 up to the 1972 convention. The O'Hara Commission's effort to gain acceptance for its proposals focused on three events: The two National Committee meetings in 1971 and the meeting of the Rules Committee of the 1972 convention. The enactment process on the convention recommendations began at the mid-point of the committee's deliberations and was over within a few months of the commission's final actions on its rules. All that remained was for the convention and its Rules Committee (chaired, as noted, by O'Hara) to provide their blessing, a perfunctory act, since a goodly number of the proposals had already been put into effect (including the most controversial) and the remainder excited few passions. The process was swift, drew little public attention, and bruised the feelings of few state party officials. Yet it was not an altogether happy experience for the convention reformers.

The first blow came shortly after the intensive work of the Commission on Rules had begun. Under pressure from national party leaders, the commission agreed to hold a meeting immediately prior to the National Committee session in February 1971 to conclude deliberations on the questions of convention size and delegate apportionment among the states. The timetable proposed was unusually ambitious given the committee's working procedures, but they acquiesced to the party leader's wishes in order to frame something for the anticipated preliminary call.

The McGovern-Fraser Commission, of course, had already acted on the problem of intrastate apportionment of delegates, adopting a complex formula giving equal weight to a presidential vote averaging and population. The Commission on Rules was aware of this, although the issue facing them—the distribution of delegates among the states—was considerably more politically sensitive and significant. The alternatives were the same: a division based on electoral vote, population, some measure of Democratic vote or party registration ("Democraticness"), or some type of combination of formulas. Briefly, the commission opted for assigning delegates on the basis of a state's population and its mean Democratic vote in the previous three presidential elections, a resolution identical to the McGovern-Fraser Commission's on intrastate apportionment. No state would receive less than sixteen votes under any conditions. The commission invited the National Committee to frame rules for alternates and for delegations from the territories (Guam, the Virgin Islands, and the Canal Zone), an abdication of its own responsibilities that only encouraged party leaders in what they were about to do. Finally, the convention membership was set at a giant-sized three thousand delegates.

Those actions took place at the 22 January meeting as reviewed on 16 February. Within a day of their last session, members realized how foolish they had been. O'Hara had been "invited" (requested) by O'Brien to report on two matters—the allocation of delegates to the states and the involved procedures for settling what were sure to be a record number of credentials challenges. It was felt that both items should appear in the preliminary call. The O'Hara Commission's recommendations on the matters were transmitted to the National Committee for incorporation in the early call. The McGovern-Fraser Commission approached this climactic meeting with reservations. It hoped for the best, but had already laid the essence of a defense should matters not proceed smoothly. The more trusting Commission on Rules was more casual in its approach, an attitude not justified if the willingness of the National Committee to expand the convention's mandate concerning the committee two years earlier was re-called. Throughout, the National Committee had been more aggressive in its approach to the O'Hara Commission, perhaps because of its inability to develop a national constituency similar to the one that supported delegate selection reform, the passivity of its early operations, and its failure to mold a strong group commitment to its initial recommendations (although this would come). And, of course, the McGovern-Fraser Commission had long since completed action on the substance of its guidelines, while the O'Hara Commission was only beginning to evolve its recommendations. Both commissions should have been alerted by the appointment of the two ad hoc committees by National Chairman O'Brien almost a year earlier. The appointed committees did little, but their presence should have indicated that the national party had not abdicated all hope of directly influ- encing the final reform proposals.[25]

At any rate, the worst came quickly. And the target, surprisingly, was the Commission on Rules rather than the more controversial McGovern-Fraser Commission. The National Committee chose to interpret the convention mandate authorizing the O'Hara Commission as delegating to it the power to pass on and revise recommendations before incorporating them in the call or transmitting them to the next convention. Additionally, it maintained that the authority to issue the call assured the national body power to approve everything that was included in it (thus permitting it to review the delegate selection rules should it desire). This interpretation of the O'Hara Commission's mandate is at best questionable. The assumption of authority over the content of the call, even when this involved revising judgments made by convention-authorized bodies, is arguable on either side. The issue had not been satisfactorily clarified. No matter, the controversy over National Committee authority quickly became academic, lost in the rush of immediate events.

The executive committee of the National Committee met on 17 February, and while endorsing without amendment the entire package of delegate selection guidelines, it severely remodeled the few proposals put forth by the O'Hara Commission. The meeting is a curious one by any standard. The ad hoc implementation committee established by O'Brien almost a year earlier made its only significant contribution to the reform process; unfortunately it was a negative one.[26] A docile executive committee then supported the new formula as a substitute for the distribution endorsed by the Commission on Rules. Speaking for the executive committee, party counsel Califano de-emphasized the significance of the changes (his reasoning, if correct, made the committee's decision less comprehensible). The O'Hara Commission proposal had the effect of giving 51 percent of the convention votes to the eight largest states (as against thirteen in 1968). The replacement put forward by the executive committee upped the number of states to nine, hardly a change worthy of risking a severe division within the party. The key, however, was in the weight thrown to the smaller states, a concession to party bodies built on federal principles of equal states. O'Hara had put his finger on the heart of the difficulty during his group's earlier consideration of alternative plans, when he cautioned that the "old system was weighted so heavily to the small states that any formula of 'one-man, one-vote' or 'one-Democrat, one-vote' is going to hurt more states than it benefits."[27] The convention reformers' allocation increased the representation of eighteen states but penalized the thirty-two others and the District of Columbia. Party leaders in the smallest states, hardest hit by the redistribution (see table 5.5), were angered, and they had influence in national party circles. Curiously, these same states, instrumental in forcing the commission proposal to be redrawn in their favor, have few electoral votes (it would take eight of these states to equal Michigan's electoral vote, twelve for either California's or New York's), and most rank among the least likely for a Democratic presidential nominee to carry (the seventeen smallest states accounted for 6 percent of the 1968 Democratic presidential nominee's total vote; the seventeen largest, 73 percent). A tension between the best short- and long-term interests of the party, a decision to place harmony above any potential future electoral or representative gains, and the power a poorly apportioned body (the National Committee) can yield in influencing fundamental policy all came to bear in the decision-making that ensued.

The executive committee formula was similar to one introduced in the Commission on Rules by Congresswoman Patsy Mink, a representative of a small state (Hawaii) that stood to lose by the commission's action. The Mink proposal was rejected by the reformers in an eight-to-six vote. The executive committee substituted electoral college for population in basing 53 percent of the delegate allocation on this and the remainder on the Democratic presidential vote in the three previous elections. The plan introduced a decided shift in the balance of power (table 5.5), rewarding the smallest states at the direct expense of the largest. The convention strength of the middle-sized states was basically unchanged in either scheme. The ten most populous states lost a total of 111 votes, and these were redistributed among the smallest twenty-five states. States ranking between tenth and twenty-fifth in size dropped only a total of 4 convention votes. The relative strength of the electorally most impotent states was enhanced further two days later, when the National Committee, after turbulent debate, endorsed (with slight remodification) the executive committee's plan, approving in the process a raising of the "floor" for the minimum number of delegates to twenty. Sixteen additional votes were distributed among the territories. The National Committee also accepted the invitation to provide for the election of alternates, and it permitted National Committee members to have full voting privileges at the convention, an honor denied them by the O'Hara Commission and a violation of the McGovern-Fraser Commission's ban on ex-officio delegates. To make matters worse, the leader, who introduced the motion in the National Committee against the ban (in both the O'Hara Commission's apportionment formula and the McGovern-Fraser Commission's prohibition against ex-officio delegates) against seating National Committee members automatically with full votes, turned out to be the O'Hara Commission's own Irish politician from Boston, John Powers. The Massachusetts national committeeman managed to call the proposed change before a committee caught up in an intense argument over delegate apportionment. Powers contended that the national committeemen "for four years . . . [had] kept the Party alive within their respective states," a gross overstatement but an appealing one for the committee members. He added, "I think until such time as the convention takes this right away from us, that we should not sit and preside over our own liquidation and our own demise, and this is exactly what we are going to do." Hardly the words of a reformer, hardly words calculated to make either commission comfortable. It became Powers's fate to utter the most memorable quote of the long battle (which continued from February through the October National Committee meeting): "Why should you be invited to my home, and then I refuse to let you sit down at the table?" While a befuddled committee struggled with that point, Powers managed to guide the proposal through the body without any further debate or anything more than a hasty voice vote (at least on the first and critical round).[28]

A numbed commission reacted slowly. Taken back by the unexpected action, O'Hara said initially that while he did not doubt the National Committee's right to make changes, it should do so "only in the face of the

Table. 5.5
Comparison of Delegate Apportionment Formulas for the Democratic National Convention
Prepared by the Executive Committee and the Commission on Rules.

State Ranked by Population, 1968	Numbers Proposed by DNC Executive Committee	Numbers Proposed by Commission on Rules	Differ- ence	Percentage of Democratic Presidential Vote, 1968[a]	Percentage of Electoral Vote, 1968[b]
1. California	271	294	−23	44.7	74
2. New York	278	301	−23	49.8	80
3. Pennsylvania	182	196	−14	47.6	54
4. Texas	130	139	−9	41.1	47
5. Illinois	170	181	−11	44.2	48
6. Ohio	153	163	−10	42.9	48
7. Michigan	132	140	−8	48.2	39
8. New Jersey	109	115	−6	43.4	32
9. Florida	81	83	−2	30.9	26
10. Massachusetts	102	107	−5	63.0	26
11. Indiana	76	79	−3	38.0	24
12. North Carolina	64	65	−1	29.2	22
13. Missouri	73	75	−2	43.7	22
14. Virginia	53	53	—	32.5	22
15. Georgia	53	52	+1	26.8	22
16. Wisconsin	67	69	−2	44.3	22
17. Tennessee	49	49	—	28.1	20
18. Maryland	53	54	−1	43.6	19
19. Minnesota	64	64	—	54.0	19
20. Louisiana	44	42	+2	28.2	19
21. Alabama	37	36	+1	18.7	19
22. Washington	52	53	−1	47.2	17
23. Kentucky	47	46	+1	37.6	17
24. Connecticut	51	51	—	49.5	15
25. Iowa	46	45	+1	40.8	17
26. South Carolina	32	28	+4	29.6	15
27. Oklahoma	39	35	+4	32.0	15
28. Kansas	35	32	+3	34.7	13
29. Mississippi	25	21	+4	23.0	13
30. Colorado	36	32	+4	41.4	11
31. Oregon	34	32	+2	43.8	11
32. Arkansas	27	24	+3	30.4	11
33. Arizona	25	21	+4	35.0	9
34. West Virginia	35	32	+3	49.6	13
35. Nebraska	24	21	+3	31.8	9
36. Utah	19	15	+4	37.1	7
37. New Mexico	18	14	+4	39.7	7
38. Maine	20	16	+4	55.3	7
39. Rhode Island	22	18	+4	64.0	7
40. Hawaii	17	11	+6	59.8	7
41. District of Columbia	15	12	+3	81.8	6
42. New Hampshire	18	12	+6	43.9	7
43. Idaho	17	10	+7	30.7	7
44. Montana	17	11	+6	41.6	7
45. South Dakota	17	11	+6	42.0	7
46. North Dakota	14	10	+4	38.2	7

Table 5.5 (*continued*)

State Ranked by Population, 1968	Numbers Proposed by DNC Executive Committee	Numbers Proposed by Commission on Rules	Differ- ence	Percentage of Democratic Presidential Vote, 1968[a]	Percentage of Electoral Vote, 1968[b]
47. Delaware	13	8	+5	41.6	6
48. Nevada	11	6	+5	39.3	6
49. Vermont	12	7	+5	43.5	6
50. Wyoming	11	5	+6	35.5	6
51. Alaska	10	4	+6	42.6	6

[a] National average for the 1968 Democratic presidential vote = 42.7%. The popular vote was divided as follows: Democrats, 42.7%; Republicans, 43.4%; and the American Independent Party (George Wallace as candidate), 13.9%.
[b] The total electoral vote comes to 538. In 1968, it was divided as follows: Democrats, 191; Republicans, 301; and American Independent Party (George Wallace as candidate), 46.

most compelling circumstances."[29] As his anger mounted, he labeled its behavior "imprudent" and "ill-advised" and argued that the National Committee did not have "any legitimate business tampering" with his group's recommendations.[30] Other commissioners were enraged. Irving Kahler found the executive committee's action "insolent."[31] Another member labeled it "foolish." Joseph Crangle felt the commission should close shop until its status had been clarified. One member charged the national party had "prostituted" itself to the interests of the smaller states.[32] In agonizing over this patently political act, the National Committee and its executive committee had not been able to scrutinize in detail or debate in any depth the complex array of McGovern-Fraser Commission recommendations (to which there was widespread latent opposition) or the tricky procedures established for resolving credentials controversies; these were proposals that marked a new departure for the party and that could have benefited from a public airing.

Such changes as were made were not looked on with the forgiveness that usually marks intrasquad clashes in the party. A sensitive chord had been touched. The reformers felt they had been badly undercut and did not understand why. The national party leadership believed it had been unusually generous to both reform commissions in funding them to the extent available and providing housing and staff services. It had also tolerated their activities—the incessant hearings, the turmoil, and the upheaval caused by efforts many state officials found threatening. Now, when it felt the need to meet the real worries of the smaller states (which the new apportionment formula and higher minimum allocation were intended to do), it expected the professionals on the convention reform committee to show restraint. The national party officeholders were stung by the ferocity of the counterattack and felt that the displeasure had been personalized and directed toward O'Brien, the chief architect of the changes. The tensions that lay beneath the surface were exposed by this incident. The

Commission on Rules was unwittingly to fall heir to the frustrations directed at both reform committees in the months to follow.

Neither side had heard the last of the quarrel. That much was clear. Two suits followed the National Committee actions from the ideological extremes of the party spectrum. A suit filed by Ken Bode and his Center for Political Reform and the Democratic party organizations of New York, California (the nation's two most populous states), and the District of Columbia sought to replace the electoral vote formula of the committee with a "one Democrat, one delegate" concept. As argued by the distinguished Washington attorney Joseph L. Rauh, Jr., the problem was one of representation, with the national convention designed to represent the party membership. An allocation based on electoral votes and especially solicitous of the smaller states favored the areas in which the Democratic party was weak and the South and ideologically tilted the convention to the right.

The other suit was brought by the state of Georgia. The state's attorney general argued that a formula based on the electoral college vote violated the principle of "one man, one vote," the assumption underlying the reapportionment decisions forced by the courts and the principle against which representative institutions were being measured.

The national party was worried, especially when the federal courts appeared sympathetic to the plaintiffs in the early going. Finally the court reverted to its traditional position, drawing a distinction between governmental institutions and party agencies and denying relief (in effect declining to intervene in the controversy) on the basis that the principles in question could not be applied by the judiciary to national conventions.

The court suits did not help soothe feelings. Tensions continued into the summer, when the quarreling again burst into public consciousness, this time centering on a nasty little attack leaked by an unidentified staff official at national headquarters to two willing journalists. The national syndicated report broke at the time the Commission on Rules was in the throes of completing its final report. Basically, the charges publicized by Rowland Evans and Robert Novak were that a "cabal" had formed to attack and personally discredit O'Brien as an enemy of reform. The "cabal" had launched a five-pronged guerilla offensive that included writing a set of final recommendations so outrageous that O'Brien could not accept them. The conspiracy extended to keeping the make-up of the Miami convention uncertain (the Bode et al. court suit). The objective was to "harass" the party for the entire year before the convention, debilitate its leadership, and, by implication, destroy its power to operate, thus paving the way for a fourth-party operation in the presidential election year (a specter many Democrats feared). The inference was that the "cabal" was working from within a Commission on Rules whose chairman was "in serious danger of losing control" of the group's activities.[33] In another report (from unnamed sources at national party headquarters), O'Hara was disparagingly referred to as "the Commission clerk, not the chairman," and the reforms to be proposed were supposedly viewed with "contempt."[34]

The incidents were ugly. The charges seemed paranoid, but many believed that reform was hurting the party and held everyone associated with it accountable, even if they did not believe the allegations themselves. Several members of the commission were forced to defend themselves (primarily Peterson and Bjorlie) within their states and to a national party constituency against someone's fantasies. There was one good result. The incident seemed to bring to a head the antipathy between national headquarters and the Commission on Rules, and the intensity of feelings displayed mildly shocked everyone concerned. The unanticipated blow-up exorcised the anger, and the commission went on in the next few days to complete work on its basically noncontroversial recommendations and prepare for the fall meeting of the National Committee.

At the biannual meeting the O'Hara Commission recommendations were no longer in question. The National Committee adopted them routinely—except for the continuing debate over the honors to be accorded national committeemen at the convention. Attention had shifted from O'Hara and his committee to the intense fight over the temporary chairmanship of the Credentials Committee. The O'Hara Commission's proposals benefited as much from the neglect as the McGovern-Fraser Commission's guidelines had half a year before.

When the Rules Committee of the 1972 convention convened under O'Hara's chairmanship (he was appointed by O'Brien with the consent of the National Committee, an indication of how much things had calmed down), the inclination was to accept the balance of the convention reform proposals not already incorporated in the call. At this point, prime attention focused on the latecomer to the halls of reform, the party charter (a marginal concern of the Commission on Rules—which now passed quietly out of existence).

SIX

The O'Hara Commission: The Substance of Convention Reform

THAT THE NATIONAL convention was badly in need of reform few disputed. From the most loyal of party stalwarts to the rankest newcomer, the wonder seemed to be that the institution had lasted as long as it had in the shape it was in. The bill of particulars directed against the arrangement varied widely, as did the types of problems different observers felt demanded the quickest attention. The Chicago convention had left deep scars and, as the Alabama state chairman had remarked, in a brief four days "virtually all of the weaknesses of our convention system had been highlighted."[1] It is a tribute to the contribution national conventions make to the party's and the nation's welfare that they were able to survive (and as it turned out, prosper) from a determined reevaluation.

The Democrats had a lot going for them before Chicago. "After the Republican Convention in 1968 it seemed inconceivable that the dull, colorless representatives of political mediocrity who had lulled us to sleep from Miami could ever win the mantle of national leadership. *After Chicago, however, boredom was a relief to the American public*"[2] (Italics added). These observations of a southern party regular have merit.

Congresswoman Shirley Chisholm, as usual, was more blunt. "The Convention," she claimed, "was so botched, that any change would have to be an improvement." "The whole purpose of reform," she added, "is to prevent another like the one in Chicago."[3] The range of specific objectives witnesses at the O'Hara Commission hearings raised against conventions was impressively wide. One party member, for example, felt that the party could no longer conduct its business in a "dignified, efficient and responsible manner" (if it ever had), a form of criticism raised by a crusty Dwight Eisenhower (once out of the presidency, of course), who likened the conventioneers to "a rioting mob of juvenile delinquents."[4] Others echoed the theme: the convention should not be "a fullfledged circus and side-show combination with unneeded parades, marches, New Year's Eve hats and loud gadgets and demonstrations";[5] the convention hall "sounded more like a large public market, or a multi-ring circus at Madison Square

Garden than a place where serious deliberations were afoot";[6] and the days of the "good-time Charlie" convention should be long past.[7] Entire delegations could not follow the proceedings. Individual delegates experienced a frustration and even a sense of alienation. "They are almost as far from the action as the man in the convention gallery or even the man observing events in front of the TV screen. The delegate senses momentous decisions being made all around him. He feels powerless to affect them. He is on the convention floor as a representative of tens of thousands of Democrats. His impotence is unnerving."[8] "At this point the Convention has become an every four year television special, consisting of 'other people, committees and decisions reached by unknown formulae'— in effect, the grand lady of the Democratic Party has become the loud lonesome voice of the painted carnival woman."[9] People had changed but not the convention institutions or the party's approach to them. Problems result, one southerner contended, from "using the systems of the '30s [or, it could be added, the 1880s or 1840s] on . . . [modern] population[s]. . . . the small, intimate houseparty reunions are gone for good. Today's delegate tends to be interested in issues, serious, feeling responsible and he/she resents feeling like a pawn in somebody else's game."[10]

Finally, a number of people commented on the "atmosphere of oppression," to use Paul O'Dwyer's phrase,[11] that they found to pervade the convention. A Mississippi delegate sounded a call many could respond to: "Let us never have to ride through streets lined with fenced slums, barbed wire and police at every corner like players in a dreadful documentary on life in a tinhorn dictatorship."[12]

Suffice it to say that a critic could be found for every convention practice. The overall picture of institutional laxity and inappropriate and democratically unjustifiable practices was impressive enough to invite the most broad-ranging reassessment of convention deliberations ever undertaken. The Commission on Rules tried to deal in some manner with the majority of objections put forward.

Getting There

An enormous amount of planning precedes the quadrennial national conventions. The Commission on Rules had to allow for this through provisions for a Site Committee and an Arrangements Committee. These two areas of influence are difficult to open to an accountable public, yet they contributed disproportionately to the serious misunderstanding at Chicago. There was the question of minimizing (or supplementing) delegate expenses to insure representation from all economic strata, a problem the O'Hara Commission was no more successful in mitigating then the McGovern-Fraser Commission had been. The reform committee also had to determine the size of the gathering and the allocation to the states of delegate votes, decisions, as mentioned, that the National Committee eventually appropriated to itself.

LOCATION

Why had the 1968 Democratic National Convention been held in Chicago? Many had wondered. The city was beset by transportation and communications strikes, there was a serious difficulty in providing the needed convention space on the dates required, political troubles and violent demonstrator-police encounters during the spring promised additional trouble, the television networks would save millions of dollars if both parties held their conventions in one place (preferably Miami Beach), and the depth of the controversies plaguing the Democrats would demand a sensitivity and broad-mindedness that no one accused Mayor Daley and his police officers of having. Sensing danger, party officials raised the same question: Why Chicago? The answer, of course, was that Daley wanted the convention there and Lyndon Johnson wanted to please the mayor. The more objections raised to the decision, the more it became a test of wills over who held the real power within the party, hence the more unthinkable a reconsideration became. The convention achieved the notoriety many had predicted for it.

SITE COMMITTEE

The Site Committee was a creature of the National Committee and therefore was open to national party directions. There was little the Commission on Rules could do about the practice. In fact there was no viable alternative; the National Committee presumed to be the representative continuing body of the party. The reformers did set the membership size—eleven—and standards and, more significantly, outlined the criteria to be assessed in evaluating potential locations: availability of inexpensive lodgings and food; adequate space near the convention floor for delegation caucuses and other meetings; adequate space accessible to the convention floor for presidential contenders; sufficient facilities and personnel; good communications facilities that permitted sending messages between delegates, the rostrum, and the media; and, to be practical, assurance that the host city was willing to help out on expenses. The last point need not have been listed; too often it was virtually the sole criteria applied.[13] The others begin to indicate how arbitrarily many felt the situation had been manipulated in the convention that led to reform. The National Committee, as it had in the past, would make the final decision after hearing from its Site Committee concerning its recommendations on each of the principal contenders.

LOGISTICS

The Arrangements Committee, another creature of the National Committee and one responsive to national party influence, had operated in mysterious ways in the past. Its decision-making was closed, and the favors promised and money transacted were never made public. Delegates became aware of the outcomes when they found hotel rooms not to their liking, accommodations far from the convention hotel or auditorium, insufficient seats for alternates, delegations placed in the corners of the hall unable to hear the proceedings, visitor tickets given only to favored politicians, security guards who manhandled delegates, poor or nonexistent communications facilities, and the thousand and one irksome details that everyone who went to a convention would experience in some form.

The O'Hara Commission sanctioned marginal improvements in the structure of the committee. It required a representative from each of the major contenders for the nomination to sit as a nonvoting member, hoping to provide a curb on excesses intended to promote one candidacy at the expense of another. It also scheduled the group to begin its work no later than the date of the first meeting of the National Committee during the election year. A longer time span provided the opportunity for an assessment of the committee's decisions and some feedback, factors previously missing in its deliberations. The Arrangements Committee would elect its own chairman, and its members did not need to sit as national committeemen. This was intended to provide a limited basis for some independence from national leaders.

The committee was given explicit authority over housing, communications, security (a matter of heated controversy in Chicago—the committee was awarded "sole authority" in this area), transportation, finances, and the arrangement of convention seating for delegates, each the focus of bitter misunderstanding at the 1968 convention in the continuing battle over authority between city officials and convention representatives. Unless specific exceptions were indicated in the rules, the committee had responsibility over all convention and preconvention operations. Security, in particular, would no longer be left to the whims of local officials. Further, in a novel departure that depressed some old-timers, roll calls for presidential and vice-presidential nominations and the awarding of choice and less desired seating, state delegation housing, and facilities for presidential contenders, would all be determined by lot. After generations of strenuous fights among contenders to secure the smallest advantage, it seemed ironic that entire matters would be left to chance. The move that grieved most was the substitution of a new order on roll calls. No longer would the calling of Alabama signal the beginning of the convention's most exciting business, no longer would there be the motivation to bring early pressure on small delegations like Wyoming or West Virginia, since no longer could their votes be decisive in early roll calls. No states could hold any undue advantage (Alabama by trading its number-one position to a candidate or state for the honor of being the first name placed in nomination; others because of their critical position in the balloting). All would be treated equally. Was nothing to be left unchanged?

Aisles were to be made wider, meaning better access and communication among delegations; seats for guests were to be divided equally among delegations (rather than, for example, being under the personal control of the national chairman or the mayor of the host city); presidential candidates were to be allocated equal numbers of floor passes and comparable space and facilities (again, no favoritism); each delegation would be furnished at least one microphone, one telephone (with directory, a convenient omission at the Chicago convention), and whatever other supporting facilities were needed; requests to the chair for recognition to speak were to be registered electronically in full public view, a provision that chipped away at the discretion of the presiding officer and one that the convention did not enact; and power to mediate floor access by the media and prohibit them from bringing bulky communications equipment onto the convention floor was given to the Arrangements Committee. While limiting congestion, the right of the media to full coverage was made clear. Finally, the National Committee was to issue an audited financial report by the first day of January following the convention and to permit public access to all convention and convention committee records, wildly open commitments in the secretive intrigues that shadow political conventions.

The records of each day's convention sessions were to be published and distributed to delegates on the following morning—again a noteworthy opening of information channels—and the journal of convention proceedings was to be published within a year of the convention's adjournment (rather than the four years common to both parties or a failure to circulate any journal at all).[14]

Authorization was made for a convention manager to be elected by the National Committee with proper public notice to work under the limitations established by the Arrangements Committee. In actuality, the position is a powerful one. This person has more to say concerning the effective operation of the sessions than any other and, like the discretion vested in the presiding officer, no significant effort was made (and none may be realistically possible) to democratize selection procedures or improve accountability.

The McGovern-Fraser Commission had not done well on the question of delegate expenses. The Commission on Rules did not improve matters substantially. The commission passed the burden on to the states, declaring that each of the state parties "shall take such steps as are necessary to assure that the cost of attending a Convention shall not preclude any duly elected delegates or alternates from attending." Should a state party have difficulty in meeting the assignment, it could petition the National Committee (already heavily in debt), which in turn was required to "make every effort" to help. Travel expenses and a per diem for members of standing committees convened prior to the convention were authorized, and the Arrangements Committee was directed to seek low-cost housing and eating substitutes. In truth, there may be little an impoverished national party can contribute.[15] The measures recommended obviously do not go beyond a recognition of the difficulty. Financial subsidies to delegates needing them are intended to insure representation from all economic strata. Judging by the occupational and income breakdown at the 1972 (or 1976) post-reform convention(s) it is still badly needed. The parties have yet to come to grips in a significant way with the obstacles faced by the less affluent.

THE NUMBER OF DELEGATES

One seemingly obvious villain held responsible for the Chicago disorders had an unique virtue: everyone—Daley-haters and -lovers, regulars and reformers, seasoned professionals and first-timers—could agree on it. This was that the convention was much too large. Whatever the other problems, much of the confusion in the Chicago Amphitheatre could be attributed to the extraordinarily large number of delegates, alternates, and supporting players present. The convention was the largest national gathering in the political history of the major parties. How could such a mob be expected to engage in any pretense of true deliberations?

The questions raised were not new; many had long engaged the attention of serious scholars. Periodically, arguments were made to the effect that conventions should be restricted in size to something approximating Congress (roughly five hundred delegates). Others believed that the traditional figure of about thirteen hundred (the size of Republican gatherings) was manageable and nicely balanced the need for order with the desire to represent directly as many party members as possible. Virtually everyone agreed that the Chicago assembly of 5,611 (2,622 delegates) exceeded reason.

Once the field hearings began the refrain was familiar. There were too many people at the national convention. Confusion reigned. Many found the marketplace atmosphere offensive. Deliberation was impossible. This was easily the most popular, most frequently repeated, and least considered proposal in the hearings.

The line of attack had a number of plusses. First, it was obvious, and on the surface it appeared to demand little thought. Consequently, it was incorporated among better-weighed proposals recommended by all observers. In party terms, as noted, it was conciliatory. It offended no one and, in fact, offered a cause for the troubles beyond the immediate control of any faction. It struck a common chord; no one treasured the feeling of depersonalization and insignificance that many (professionals and newcomers) had experienced. The change was easy to enact, and it gave the aura of reform, the sense of moving to correct an obvious evil.

Finally, there was no real tradition behind massive conventions. Large conventions were a recent phenomena (figure 5). The size of conventions had remained stable for decades, increasing only to accommodate the entrance of new states into the union. From 1900 to 1928, the years preceding the modern era of party politics (usually dated from 1932), the average size of Democratic conventions was 1,052, and Republican conventions, 1,018. The Democrats began to increase the size of their conventions during the 1960s: over 1,500 delegates in 1960; just under 2,300 in 1964; and 2,600 in 1968, history's largest to that point.

Political considerations (rather than any analysis of the institutional effect) lay behind the Democratic increases. From the early 1960s the goal had been assuring a Democratic reelection. The years 1964 and 1968 were years in which it was expected that a Democratic incumbent (whether it had been John Kennedy in 1964 or, as it was, Lyndon Johnson in 1964 and 1968) could be assured of easy renomination. The emphasis was thus placed on the campaign rally function of conventions, getting as many people involved as possible. With little real business to transact, the trip to the convention could serve as a reward for past service and as an incentive to a good campaign effort. The delegate apportionment formula, consequently, was continually amended in a jerry-built fashion to provide a base for an increased membership. By 1968 the delegate apportionment formula was as grotesquely bloated as some found the convention to be: each state was awarded three votes for each electoral college vote; an additional one vote for each 100,000 popular votes received by the Democratic presidential nominee four years earlier; a "victory bonus" of ten votes for each state that cast all its electoral votes for the Democratic candidate; and an additional two votes for its National Committee representatives. Few could resist such a deserving target.

The appealingly superficial question of size in reality masked sturdier questions. Is a convention a truly deliberative body? More importantly, should it be? If a representational body, one of its functions all agreed upon, were its representational qualities more critical than its deliberative aspects? If so, would not a large meeting serve representational tendencies better than a select gathering? Would not a larger body be more responsive to its constituencies and more open to newer influences than a smaller one? What was the convention's principal business: Nominating a presidential candidate? Establishing a policy agenda for the party? Legislating party affairs? Would it not follow that the greater the emphasis on the predominance of the nominating function, the stronger the argument for a large body of representative party members at conventions? Conversely, the greater the emphasis on policy issues (platform, rules governing party operations), the more valid a characterization of the institution as a deliberative one and the stronger the argument for a smaller number of delegates.

The answers to the questions seem apparent once one begins to isolate

Figure 5
Size of National Party Conventions, 1932–72

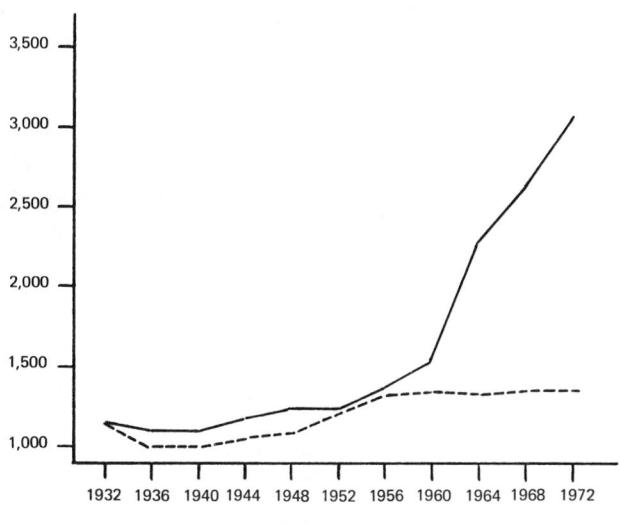

Key: Democrats ————— Republicans — — — —	Size by Year	Democrats	Republicans	Size by Year	Democrats	Republicans
	1932	1,154	1,154	1956	1,372	1,323
	1936	1,100	1,003	1960	1,521	1,331
	1940	1,100	1,000	1964	2,295	1,308
	1944	1,176	1,059	1968	2,622	1,333
	1948	1,234	1,094	1972	3,096	1,333
	1952	1,230	1,206			

and explore them in depth. To some, the point was already obvious. The testimony from a California witness, for example, anticipated the O'Hara Commission's own thinking: "The problem was not that there were too many delegates. The problem was that the facilities were totally inadequate. It would be far better in the future to hold conventions in locations which can accommodate the delegates rather than to eliminate delegates in order to enable us to utilize inadequate auditoriums."[16]

Large bodies of people are considered notoriously antidemocratic in operations, centralizing authority in a few people at the top. The Commission on Rules did not address this particular problem and did not attempt to build into its convention regulations means of making the convention leadership more responsive and accountable to the membership, a glaring omission in its work. The questions of whether size necessarily predetermines autocratic behavior and at what size (500? 1500? 3000?) a delegate loses any claim to meaningful rights were not explored. The O'Hara Commission did decide that a large convention (approximately three thousand people) best served the interests of the party, a decision that was welcomed by all factions within the party—a curious reaction given the testimony that had been received.

APPORTIONMENT OF DELEGATE VOTES

If the decision of the debate over the size of the convention membership provided a surprise, the outcome of the controversy surrounding the formula to be employed in dividing the convention votes among the states resulted in an unexpected twist of another sort. The political implications of the differing apportionment plans were clearly recognized. Also, there was a broader social basis for concern. The reapportionment struggles that had affected state legislatures during the early 1960s were giving signs of being carried over to party affairs. Everyone was clearly sensitive to the broad implications. Different formulas gave different weight to such considerations as population, Democratic strength, and the equality of the states within a federal structure (see table 6.1). In addition to the basic assumptions underlying the allocations, each formula rewarded some states handsomely while penalizing others. The strength of a third tier of states—the middle cluster—appeared relatively unphased by any decision on delegate apportionment. These political concerns were tricky, and eventually they proved the commission's undoing. Its job was to determine which vote distribution best served the present and future needs of the party, which made for the most representative convention, and which recommendation would command the most support and best enhance party unity. The demands may well be contradictory, but the failure of the convention reformers to settle on one formula and then to promote it as meeting such standards condemned their eventual choice to an acrimonious battle and a humiliating defeat.

As with everything, the commission began with a core area of agreement. Nobody could be found to defend the hodgepodge system of awarding convention votes employed at the previous convention. The formula met no standards of logic, political necessity, or convenience that anyone cared to see perpetuated. Change, then, would be welcomed. In question would be the nature of the revision and who would be thought to benefit the most from it.

Unfortunately the commission did not give the problem the time it deserved. Admittedly, it was under pressure to produce something by early 1971 on apportionment, size, and the complex procedures to be employed by convention committees in resolving disputes. These questions easily rank among the most difficult and significant the group was to encounter. Yet it did not begin to address them substantively until mid-October 1970. By the following February it was to report its conclusions to the National Committee, hardly a schedule to invite confidence in the thoroughness or judiciousness of its choices. The fact that it invited the National Committee to make its own determinations on alternates and the awarding of delegates to the territories emphasized the hastiness of the effort. The close votes in the commission on varying delegate apportionment alternatives suggested, in addition, no strong group consensus on the final distribution, and signaled to the national party leadership (under pressure from the states that stood to lose influence) that a firm hand could be applied with little chance of a strong reaction. The failure of the commission (perhaps an impossibility, given the time frame it worked under) to educate the party generally to the value of its decision meant that relatively few outside of the convention reformers knew of or supported what it had done in sufficient time to be of consequence—another factor, no doubt, in the party leadership's decision to intervene.

The allocation formula the reformers were determined to change had a long tradition behind it. The relationship between a state's electoral vote and its convention strength went back to the first Democratic convention in 1832. The first-time delegates sought a means for determining each state's relative weight in the deliberations, with the principal options presumably being some type of emphasis on equal states' rights or the more progressive electoral college division of the vote, which did give some weight to population. Without recorded opposition, the 1832 convention adopted four resolutions establishing the basic convention procedures for years to come.[17] Among these was the practice of allocating delegate votes in relation to a state's electoral strength.

The arguments favoring such a tack continued to be persuasive almost a century and a half later. An electoral college division of convention strength accurately reflected the peculiar structure of the electorate the party's candidate would have to contend with in the general election. Coincidentally, such a formula served to overrepresent the smaller states (inflating their proportionate impact as compared with a division of the vote in strict accordance with the population) and to underrepresent the larger states (see the first two columns of table 6.1).

Changes in convention practices over the years, particularly within the Democratic party, whose forms were more in need of rethinking, came painfully slow. A combination of elements—inertia, partisan advantage, and electoral logic—protected the electoral college distribution from any broad reevaluation. Modifications in the original did occur, though. The 1940 Democratic convention fell heir to an agreement reached four years earlier in which, in an attempt to mollify the South for the repeal of the two-thirds rule in presidential nominations (thus reducing the veto power of the region over candidacies), the convention had agreed to reward states that supported the Democratic national ticket with extra convention votes. The South, with its solid Democratic returns, stood to gain, and the two-party competitive and Republican-dominated states to lose from such an arrangement. Changes were not made frivolously and agreement proved hard to reach. The Rules Committee of the 1940 convention, in fact, could not settle on an acceptable compromise; in its original report it omitted any reference to the problem, thus leaving matters as they were.

This option was unacceptable. The convention forced the Rules Committee to submit a supplemental report that (in the best spirit of political indecision) called for further study of the problem. In the interim, it proposed that "such States as cast their electoral votes for the Democratic Presidential nominees for President and Vice President shall have two additional delegates-at-large to the Democratic National Convention."[18] The resolution passed by voice vote and was endorsed more emphatically by the 1944 convention, thus enshrining the practice of "bonus votes" within the delegate allocation formula for the next two decades.[19] Twenty years later the "bonus vote" concept had gained in sophistication. In addition to the assault on the basic integrity of the original formula by guaranteeing each of a state's two National Committee members a full vote at the convention, the bonus concept begat another bonus (one based on the votes received as well as whether the Democratic nominee carried the state). A fairly small state, Kentucky (3.2 million people in the 1970 census) could be represented by a total delegation (delegates and alternates) of over one hundred. New York's, the largest delegation, numbered over four hundred, an impressive display of growth compared with earlier conventions. Under the 1968 allocation, states carried by Lyndon Johnson four years earlier with large Democratic pluralities benefited handsomely. Texas, Ohio, Pennsylvania, and New York gained from seventeen to thirty-six convention seats; even smaller states, such as Rhode Island and West Virginia, that had voted "right" profitted from an additional twelve to thirteen convention votes.

The old apportionment formula as modified over time had lost its attractiveness. The distribution was built on negatives—if smaller states benefited from an electoral college division, then the larger ones should receive some compensation for size through a system of representation scaled closer to population (number of people voting Democratic); if the formulas adopted reflected nonpartisan standards (electoral vote, population), then a correction should be made for party effort and to better reflect the true party base (National Committee votes, the "victory bonus," extra votes for numbers of people supporting the Democratic ticket). The weighting had become grotesque. It satisfied few and it was susceptible to manipulation in its own interest by whatever party faction happened to control the National Committee when the call to the convention was issued.

The O'Hara Commission's first order of business was predictable; it voided the incorporation of bonus votes in all delegate apportionment distributions. Attempting to settle on an equitable apportionment formula satisfactory to a majority of party interests proved far more taxing. If no one supported the old hybrid system, few backed a pure electoral college distribution. There is an inherent logic in building into the convention the electorate the candidate eventually has to face to win office. The allocation was so severely biased against the largest and most important states and diverged so markedly when contrasted against measures built on population or "Democratic-ness" of the electorate that no commission member offered any serious arguments in its behalf (see table 6.1). This alone was surprising. As it turned out, it was also deceptive. The latent support that did exist, especially among the representatives of the smaller states, surfaced in the backing given the Mink proposal presented to the commission on 16 February (and defeated in an eight-to-six vote) and in the votes for the executive committee proposal (virtually identical to the Mink formula) in the National Committee.

The emphasis on "one man, one vote" found expression in an allocation based on population. Such a distribution has its attractive qualities. It ties the party to the electorate it must face at all levels of contest; it does not severely penalize any state or region (except in contrast to what they did have under the old formula); and it provides flexibility and the opportunity for growth to meet new demands of a changing electorate. It would probably meet any court challenges that might arise. It lost in a tie (nine-to-nine) vote within the commission.

The chief difficulty for some with a population index was that it did not provide for any gauge of Democratic strength. Basically the argument here was that the national convention was an assemblage of party members that should reflect the party base. Rather than an allocation based on "one man, one vote," many felt the catchwords should be "one Democrat, one vote." The distribution of convention votes should, therefore, respond to measures of party support. The McGovern-Fraser Commission had entertained identical choices. The difficulties that inhere with an allocation based on party strength include underrepresentation of some normally Republican states to the point of exclusion; severe fluctuations in the party's vote (for example, each set of two presidential elections from 1952 through 1972 witnessed a competitive election followed by a one-party landslide) that creates havoc with a state's representation from one convention to the next; and association of the party's base electoral support with past achievement, a dangerous commitment for any active group. Such a proposal was too stiff a departure for the commission, and while several of the basic assumptions as to the representation of the party's grass roots were attractive, a pure strategy founded on "Democratic-ness" commanded only modest support.

In reviewing the alternatives in relation to consequence (rather than underlying assumption), one is struck by the almost capricious variation in the influence of the various states under the succeeding plans, a reaffirmation of the gravity of the political stakes invoked in the decision. Alabama, the first state on the list, would receive forty-five to fifty-one votes if electoral college strength or population were employed as the criteria, but only nineteen if Democratic votes were used. Mississippi, Georgia, South Carolina, and Louisiana are in a similar position. Idaho could double its votes or better, as could Vermont, Wyoming, and Delaware, if the distribution were based on the electoral college rather than some other measure. Massachusetts could increase its proportion of convention seats two-fold if

Table 6.1
The Distribution of National Convention Votes among the States under Different Delegate Allocation Formulas

State	"Pure" Strategies of Distribution			Compromise Strategies of Distribution			
	By Electoral Vote	By Population	By Democratic[a] Vote	By 1968 Plan	By Mixed Formula[b]	By Commission on Rules Formula[c]	By DNC Formula[d]
Alabama	45	51	19	32	35	36	37
Alaska	15	4	3	22	7	4	10
Arizona	30	26	16	19	23	21	25
Arkansas	30	28	18	33	25	24	27
California	225	295	311	174	292	294	271
Colorado	35	33	32	35	34	32	36
Connecticut	40	45	59	44	52	51	51
Delaware	15	8	8	22	10	8	13
District of Columbia	15	11	13	23	14	12	15
Florida	85	100	65	63	81	83	81
Georgia	60	68	32	43	50	52	53
Hawaii	20	11	13	26	15	11	17
Idaho	20	10	8	25	12	10	17
Illinois	130	164	196	118	175	181	170
Indiana	65	76	76	63	76	79	76
Iowa	40	42	46	46	44	45	46
Kansas	35	33	29	38	33	32	35
Kentucky	45	48	38	46	44	46	47
Louisiana	50	54	30	36	42	42	44
Maine	20	15	21	27	20	16	20
Maryland	50	58	52	49	54	54	53
Massachusetts	70	84	141	72	111	107	102
Michigan	105	131	153	96	138	140	132

Minnesota	50	56	82	52	69	64	64
Mississippi	35	33	14	24	25	21	25
Missouri	60	69	76	60	72	75	73
Montana	20	10	11	26	14	11	17
Nebraska	25	22	16	30	21	21	24
Nevada	15	7	6	22	9	6	11
New Hampshire	20	11	13	26	15	12	18
New Jersey	85	106	121	82	111	115	109
New Mexico	20	15	13	26	16	14	18
New York	205	268	324	190	286	301	278
North Carolina	65	75	43	59	59	65	64
North Dakota	15	9	9	25	11	10	14
Ohio	125	157	163	115	156	163	153
Oklahoma	40	38	29	41	35	35	39
Oregon	30	31	34	35	33	32	34
Pennsylvania	135	174	217	130	190	196	182
Rhode Island	20	14	24	27	21	18	22
South Carolina	40	38	19	28	30	28	32
South Dakota	20	10	11	26	14	11	17
Tennessee	50	58	34	51	45	49	49
Texas	130	166	121	104	138	139	130
Utah	20	16	15	26	17	15	19
Vermont	15	7	7	22	9	7	12
Virginia	60	69	42	54	55	53	53
Washington	45	50	59	47	55	53	52
West Virginia	30	26	36	38	33	32	35
Wisconsin	55	65	72	59	68	69	67
Wyoming	15	5	4	22	6	5	11
Total:	2,690	3,000	2,994	2,622	3,000	3,000	3,000

[a] Average vote calculated in three previous presidential elections.
[b] The Mixed Formula is 50% of the Democratic vote, 25% of the Electoral vote, and 25% of the population index.
[c] The Commission on Rules Formula is 50% of the Democratic vote and 50% of the population index.
[d] The Democratic National Committee Formula is 53% of the Electoral vote and 47% of the Democratic vote.

195

a party loyalty index were consulted rather than one based on the electoral college. Similarly, New Jersey, Wisconsin, and Connecticut, along with California and the big industrial states of the North, would gain handsomely, if not as spectacularly, from such a decision. Florida would be hurt. Texas would benefit most from a simple index of population. Indiana has little incentive to choose between a division based on either population or Democratic vote but stands to profit if the electoral college standard is avoided. And so on, for each of the states. The influence of the myriad pressures ruled out any easy or quick resolution of the problems involved.

Through a process of elimination the Commission on Rules decided on a compromise: it combined the plans with the greatest popularity—those based on population and "Democratic-ness"—in a manner it hoped would alleviate the inconsistencies in the latter in particular while giving weight to the concept of a convention representative of its political base. The final vote in favor was eleven to six. The plan paralleled the one put forward by the McGovern-Fraser Commission for intrastate apportionment of convention delegates, thus assuring it had the combined weight of both reform groups behind it. The formula had several attractive qualities. The weakness of the approach was in the failure to dramatize these. The new apportionment departed severely from the old ways, and those who stood to lose the most had readied their appeal for another court.

Organizing a Convention

The chief vehicles for conducting the early work of the convention since its inception had been its standing committees: Permanent Organization, intended to choose the presiding officers for the meeting (keynote speaker, temporary and permanent chairman, vice-chairman, etc.); Rules, the group that adopted the regulations governing the convention sessions (and those applicable to the national party between conventions, as well); Resolutions (better known as Platform), the most glamorous and publicly visible of the four, charged with framing the party's stand on relevant policy issues; and Credentials, the body that decided membership qualifications and resolved challenges (subject to convention ratification of their decision) between competing claimants. Outside of the Platform Committee, whose sessions were usually well covered by the media, the public was not likely to hear much concerning the operation of the committees. Occasionally a credentials challenge of special significance would arise (as in 1948, 1964, and 1968), but even under these circumstances attention was likely to focus on the convention floor, where significant issues were finally resolved. All committee recommendations had to be reported to and ratified by the convention, the supreme governing body of the party.

The committees' general anonymity paralleled their status within the party. With the exception of the Platform Committee and occasionally the

Credentials Committee, assignment to the committees was not eagerly contested, and their contribution to the workings of the convention was minor. In a number of conventions, none of the committees met until well into the first or second day of the convention and then only to endorse proposals written by others. Their work done, they quickly adjourned. No one quarreled with the processes, an indication of the low expectation party members had of their performance.

The four committees had been established in 1832. They had evolved over the decades with a general appreciation of their areas of jurisdiction, little in the way of precedent or procedural rules, and a tendency to rely on the party leadership for their direction and to reflect its wishes on the occasional issues (beyond national policy) of consequence that arose for their consideration. Their membership, their performance, and their contributions to the convention were generally undistinguished. They had richly earned the apathy with which they were viewed.

COMMITTEE SPECIFICATIONS

The O'Hara Commission appraisals represented the first serious evaluation of the committees in their history. The convention reformers attempted to infuse a new life into a valuable set of agencies and to make them relevant to the demands of a modern convention. They sought also to give the committees some independence from the dictates of the national party leadership (not previously enjoyed) and to restructure them in a manner calculated to help them meet the enormous demands that would be placed upon them. The Commission on Rules succeeded admirably.

The first question considered by the O'Hara group in its deliberations was committee size. Originally each state delegation had been awarded one representative (increased to two with the advent of women's suffrage) on each of the four committees. The committee size had grown with the inclusion of new states in the union, stabilizing at 110 (2 members for each state, the District of Columbia, and the territories). Problems concerning the proper relationship between the committees and the convention they presumed to serve, the role of a member sitting on a committee and his responsibilities to his home delegation, and the discretionary power of committee chairmen and its limitations needed in-depth examination. Unfortunately, the Commission on Rules did not provide this. It did, however, take steps toward solving problems of size, jurisdiction, and procedures that made signal contributions to a revitalized national convention.

The O'Hara Commission required the election, when possible, of committee representatives by a state's delegation, which provided the rank and file some control over their actions. If this was impractical (some committees met before delegations were selected) an open party meeting held on the calendar year of the election could appoint temporary representatives (subject to replacement or ratification by the delegation). Committee chairmen were to be elected at the first meeting of the group at a date and time to be specified by the national chairman. Provision was made for the national chairman to appoint (with agreement of the majority of the National Committee) a temporary chairman of the Credentials Committee, where the work load was expected to begin early and be unusually heavy. No authority was granted the national chairman over the choice of acting chairmen for the Rules and Platform committees, although the party leader at the time (O'Brien) exercised the power.[20] All of the "temporary" appointments were confirmed by the full committees when they convened, making the 1972 convention little different from its predecessors in this respect.

State delegations electing committee representatives were cautioned (later interpreted as required) to divide the seats available from all committees proportionately among men and women; in individual committees, if there was more than one vacancy (often there was not) delegations were told to select "an equal or nearly equal [in the case of an odd number of appointments] number of men and women to each committee, giving due regard to the race and age of the men and women elected."[21] This was a belated addition to the recommendations, and although the sex division was strictly applied, was a far cry from the McGovern-Fraser Commission's "quotas."

Committee meetings were required to be open, another concession to participatory democracy, and all committees were required to meet prior to the convention. Further, the committees were to conclude their deliberations before the convention met and both the Rules and Platform committees were directed to mail their recommendations to the convention membership ten days before the opening session. The Credentials Committee, which might not begin its hearings until two weeks before the convention was scheduled, was required to make its report available to the public forty-eight hours before the initial convention session. These were seemingly small improvements. Yet for the first time delegates could have in their possession the results of the committees' actions. They would have the information and the time to think about it, could form any coalitions in favor of or opposing specific recommendations, and, at a minimum, could vote intelligently when the matter reached the convention floor. The 1972 convention would be, if nothing else, the most knowledgeable ever and the most participant oriented in its procedures.

Minority reports could be filed for convention action with the concurrence of 10 percent of a committee's membership, a reasonable threshold of support. Committee size was increased to 150, a compromise between some even larger and less manageable figures and the need to represent all states with at least one delegate. An attempt was also made to reflect a delegation's convention strength on committees. While weighted voting schemes were rejected with little real consideration, the surplus committee membership (95 positions) was apportioned among state delegations in relation to their size.[22] Each state, of course, retained at least one representative on each committee. In all, these were modest changes, perhaps, but they were decided improvements over previous practices.

A different order of reforms was proposed for the structuring and operational procedures of the original four committees.

PERMANENT ORGANIZATION

Among the historically dismal performances of the convention committees, the Committee on Permanent Organization had excelled. The worst of the worst, it had nothing to contribute and, most depressing for any political entity, lacked even the imagination to concoct a justification for its continued operation. The story is best told by Faye Broderick, the unusually candid chairperson of the committee at the Chicago convention.

Broderick appeared before an early and sparsely attended meeting (September 1969) of a select number of O'Hara Commission members intended to provide party officials the opportunity to acquaint the new body with the operation of a national convention. The meeting was perfunctory and, as often happens when party regulars congregate, a goodly amount of time was passed by members in congratulating each other for various achievements and in offering a few generalities on convention procedures. The bite, pointed exchanges, and determination evident in the McGovern-Fraser Commission meetings were absent at this early stage.

Broderick began conventionally enough, recounting how "deeply honored" she felt by her appointment from the national chairman to chair the committee. Then she outlined the group's functions and its organization:

The Committee on Permanent Organization is charged with the responsibility of recommending and nominating to the Convention a slate of permanent officers, such as the Chairman of the Convention, the Secretary, Sergeant at Arms and Parliamentarian, among many others. The Committee also nominates the Chairman of the Committees on Resolutions and Platform, Rules and Order of Business, Credentials, and Permanent Organization. The Permanent Organization Committee is an ad hoc committee whose authority and functions apparently terminate upon reporting to the Convention.[23]

Seemingly this was a moderately significant group. However, the committee's operations belie its functions. The National Committee recommended to the group a slate of temporary convention officers, including the chairmen of the other three committees of the convention. The Committee on Permanent Organization did not meet until the eve of the convention, a point at which the other committees had not only been in session but were concluding their operations.

Time and time again at our last Convention in Chicago, I was asked by members of the Committee—"Who selected the Chairmen of the four Committees?" "Why do we have to endorse the names submitted to us by you, Mrs. Chairman?" Time and time again I could only respond, "This is the way the system works." I was in effect telling this one hundred-ten member committee to sit down and don't make waves. One could only conclude that he or she had traveled hundred of miles to assist in affixing a rubber stamp to a predrafted slate of candidates. Can there be little wonder that the integrity of the system is now under attack. I tried to explain that the very nature of the Committees' functions—all four Committees—dictates that the Chairmen of the Committees be named well in advance of the Convention; that the keynote speaker, Chairman of the Convention, and all other permanent officers must, of necessity, have days, or even weeks, to prepare if they are to properly discharge their responsibilities. But the response was always the same—"Why then, the need for the Committee on Permanent Organization?"

Imagine if you will the confusion, indeed chaos, that would result if the Committee on Permanent Organization were to nominate and recommend to the convention its own choice for Chairman of the Platform Committee. . . . its own candidates for Keynote Speaker, Permanent Chairman, or for that matter any other permanent officer of the Convention. . . . *the present method of selection is so cut and dried that not a single officer of the 1968 Democratic National Convention appeared before the Committee on Permanent Organization* and only one biographical sketch was submitted to the Committee members. This, in my opinion, Mr. Chairman, is a form of deceit.[24] (Italics added.)

Broderick's conclusions are not hard to anticipate. She recommended the committee be abolished and its duties transferred to the executive committee of the Democratic National Committee, the body that already exercised the authority.

The listeners were stunned. Directness of this nature on a question of institutional arrangements was a new experience. The shock value of the Broderick statement left little to be said. The commission had asked for and received the views of the reigning authority on the subject. The commission eventually did the inevitable and abolished the committee, passing along some of its powers (the naming of the convention's chairman and permanent officers) to the Rules Committee.

RULES COMMITTEE

Excepting the Platform Committee, the committees of the convention receive little notice, and for good reason. Traditionally they have had little to do, although in fairness they do have their periodic moments of importance. The Rules Committee is as good as any in illustrating the syndrome. The committee ranks above the lowly (and former) Committee on Permanent Organization. It does have duties to perform in each convention: establishing the rules of procedure and the order of business for the convention. Any law pertaining to national party behavior or organization, special rules, or provisions for extraordinary commissions or investigative bodies (such as the reform commissions) would fall within its jurisdiction (although its power in this regard was not exclusionary). Such occurrences

—until recently—have been rare. On the few occasions when an issue of vital importance did face a convention (the threatened suspension of the two-thirds or unit rules, for example), a matter that would logically fall within the committee's authority (and in a formal and perfunctory sense did), agreement was normally reached among the interested parties outside of the committee's deliberations and, more often than not, over a period of several conventions. The Rules Committee then ratified the compromise and passed the needed resolution on to the convention for a final vote.

Its customary working schedule in recent times had been to meet for a brief period (one or two sessions in the days immediately before the convention's opening) and to sanction through reference (but not elaborate) the body of convention precedents, convention common law, and the general parliamentary rules of the United States House of Representatives to govern the conduct of convention proceedings. To the extent these provisions could be identified, they were made available in what came to be called "Cannon's Manual," which was actually published and distributed before the Rules Committee met.[25] Any specific new rules were spelled out and, its contribution made, the committee adjourned. Given the vagueness of the rules of conduct, *pro forma* sessions not given to intensive inquiry best served the needs of the party (although it is unlikely the brief meetings were thought of in this sense).

The 1968 Rules Committee sessions were unusual. When the committee assembled for what came to be a two-day meeting on the weekend preceding the Monday opening, there were as usual no clearly defined rules in existence to govern the operations (only the Credentials Committee, for which rules had been hastily contrived a few weeks before the convention because of what had become an extraordinary work load, had any), and the members' approach was as casual as it had been in the past. Things had changed, though. The reformers, and specifically Harold Hughes's Ad Hoc Commission, furiously at work for the preceding several weeks, had chosen the committee as its initial battlefield in seeking a reformed party. Thus the sessions proved more lively than usual. Proposals were debated, several witnesses made presentations, a minority report (eventually adopted by the convention) was put together, and the committee and its chairman even managed to squeeze out some media notice. The end result was a report that served as one basis for the reform commissions later appointed and the directives they received.

It is fair to say that at this convention the Rules Committee, somewhat unwillingly, came to assert the power inherent in its authorization (vague as it was) and to realize the value of its contribution to convention proceedings. Four years later it and Credentials (two of the lesser-known committees) were perceived to be of key significance by party regulars and reformers alike, who had come to appreciate fully their potential contribu-

tion. For some, mostly newcomers, the glamour of the Platform Committee still held a fascination. For others, the real power over party affairs lay
in Rules and Credentials.

The O'Hara Commission recommendations concerning the Rules Committee are not elaborate. As with each of the three remaining committees
of the convention, membership was established at 150, executive (closed)
sessions were prohibited, minority reports required the support of one-
tenth of the membership, reporting time was specified, and committee
members from the individual states had to be certified by the state chairman within three days of the end of the state's delegate selection process.
The committee was given "authority for recommending the Rules of the
Convention, the Convention's agenda, and resolutions providing for the
consideration of any other matter not provided for in the Rules of the Convention and not contained in the report of other Committees."[26] The
last grant is particularly broad and assures a committee of formidable
powers in future conventions.

The 1972 Rules Committee appeared to enjoy its newfound status. It
had jurisdiction over the O'Hara Commission recommendations (which it
looked on with favor), motions for new reform committees, proposals to
revise several party practices (most significantly the "winner-take-all"
primary, a change it and, later, the convention endorsed), and the complex
party charter framed by the combined McGovern-Fraser and O'Hara
commissions. The committee did manage to salvage from the latter plan a
proposal (also accepted by the convention) to enlarge and drastically
restructure the National Committee, the most significant reform in this
institution's history. All of these matters, of course, were in addition to its
principal objective of adopting the rules of procedure and setting the
agenda for the operation of the national convention. The committee even
managed to infuse life into an activity given it in the demise of the Committee on Permanent Organization, the recommendation of officials to
preside over the convention. A black female legislator, previously unknown nationally, almost unseated National Chairman O'Brien for the
post of convention chairman. On this score, the committee eventually
divided the posts between the national chairman and congresswoman-to-be
Yvonne Braithwaite Burke and required that in future conventions alternate sexes hold the position of presiding officer. Such frisky independence
may become less rare as the years pass.

RESOLUTIONS (PLATFORM) COMMITTEE

The best-known of the convention's standing committees was Resolutions or Platform, charged with molding a party stand on the outstanding
public issues of the day. The work of the committee was always important
and, on occasion, captured national attention because of the relevancy of
the debate on a question of immediate concern (and undetermined out-

come). For such circumstances an indication of the party's will on the matter could be significant in resolving the issue. The 1968 convention provided as good an illustration as any as to process in full operation. Obviously compromising on a policy statement so that most significant blocs of Democrats can support it is a difficult business. For this reason the party's platform favors generalities. Ordinarily the rule is that the more controversial and divisive the issue, the more generalized the wording. Consequently the platform has often been held up to ridicule. Critics point out that victories on policy questions within the committee are at best entirely symbolic; they are in no sense binding on party members, and they lack any legislative authority. Further, they need carry no weight with a legislative candidate. If the faction supporting an eventual presidential nominee loses in a Platform Committee battle, the candidate can "amend" the platform in practice to suit his own needs (although at the risk of some embarrassment; he is in effect denying the majority will of the party). One of the most famous instances of this sort was that concerning Al Smith, an ardent anti-Prohibition "wet" who ran on a 1928 platform supporting Prohibition. Opponents for many years derisively compared Franklin Roosevelt's bold legislative initiatives with the conservative party statement of principles on which he was initially elected in 1932.

The platform hearings provide a stage on which to publicize an incumbent president's program and/or to allow interest-group representatives with powerful constituencies the opportunity to gain national attention for their demands. The pledges in the platform indicate to groups and their leadership the extent of the party's commitment to their ends.

For some, platform battles are little more than self-indulgent party exercises of no particular significance. While lacking in authority—no one can be forced to support a policy position—the platform is nonetheless important. The pledges are symbolic and the wording of policy directions are clever and often indirect. Still, once a party has indicated its support of a particular stand it seldom retreats from the position. Further, there is a high degree of correlation between platform rhetoric and congressional action for both Democrats and Republicans, suggesting that the platform debates are part of the process of evolving a common party stand on issues. No other agency draws all elements of the party together to argue out issues and force some type of conclusion. The platform is a political party's one inclusive attempt at national policy-making. The extent to which the two major parties have differing principles and offer contrasting programs is found in the platform, although it may take a little training in semantics to divine the major philosophic differences.

The 1968 hearings of the Platform Committee serve as well as any in indicating the group's strengths and weaknesses. The failure of the committee (perhaps for reasons beyond its control) in this instance to reach a satisfactory compromise on a common stance toward the involvement in

Viet Nam postponed the decision until into the presidential campaign period, an act that hurt the Democrats' election hopes. The questions posed by the Viet Nam War badly divided both the party leadership and the rank and file. Some observers credited the issue with supplying the underlying tensions that eventually burst in the frenzy that was Chicago. The two insurgent candidates of that year (Eugene McCarthy and Robert Kennedy) entered the race primarily in reaction to the controversy, and Lyndon Johnson's withdrawal was influenced in large part by matters relating to the war and the insurgents' success in opposing it. By August attention focused on the effort to force the party and its eventual nominee, Hubert Humphrey, to indicate a course of action independent of the administration and favorable to a cessation of hostility. The Platform Committee provided the traditional arena for playing out the drama. The wording on the motions receiving the greatest attention was dissimilar enough to indicate different proposed future courses of action. An informed debate within the committee carried over onto the convention floor. Eventually the administration had the muscle to win. The majority resolution carried, but it failed to mute the criticism or unify the party behind its nominee, forcing him to reconsider and "clarify" his position a month later in favor of greater independence from past assumptions. The action came too late. Although the issue was too volatile to submit to resolution within the Platform Committee, the committee did provide for a neutral meeting ground in which both sides could argue their case, in the process educating the public and the party rank and file about their positions. The issue, as noted, was resolved in a more satisfactory manner under the pressure of an election deadline, but the resolution came too late to bestow its benefits on the Democrats during the campaign.

Unlike the other three convention committees, in the Platform Committee the O'Hara Commission was dealing with a viable agency that, although it had weaknesses, had performed satisfactorily. Rather than a major overhaul of procedures, modest improvements of operations were the rule. A committee of over one hundred members, it was thought, was too large to write the platform document. Therefore this critical work was done by a drafting subcommittee of fifteen, chosen by the party leadership and responsive to it. This was the critical step. Once the platform was written, it was difficult to muster a majority on short notice among the diverse state representatives to revise a position. The same was true of the convention floor. To democratize the procedure, the new rules provided that at their first meeting the delegates to the Platform Committee *elect* the drafting subcommittee and its chairman, the latter a sensitive post. The chairman of the Platform Committee, however, was permitted to offer nominations for the subcommittee and its chairman, a discretionary grant of power of some importance. Each presidential candidate was permitted to appoint a nonvoting representative to serve on the drafting subcommittee to argue his views and monitor the fairness of the proceedings, an action that serves to open the process considerably. Each presidential candidate also was invited to submit a list of recommendations to the committee at any point in its deliberations. Any other interested person could also submit written testimony and a request to be heard in person.

The O'Hara Commission endorsed one other change, which had the greatest visible effect on the 1972 meeetings. Enthused by the concept underlying its own and the McGovern-Fraser Commission's public meetings, the commission recommended a series of no less than eight regional hearings to take place throughout the country. The chairman of the Platform Committee had the responsibility for appointing the presiding panels, arranging for a representative list of witnesses, and handling the logistics of the meetings. The idea was to move platform hearings out of Washington or the convention city and to penetrate the concerns of people not ordinarily influential in party deliberations.

This departure from past behavior proved successful. The regional platform hearings served an educational function (as expected), publicizing social problems in several cases that had not been met by either party and incorporating in policy deliberations groups previously left unheard. The field hearings afforded the party an opportunity to showcase some of its prominent names and to dramatize issues in a manner not possible before. Senator Edward M. Kennedy held a conventional hearing in Pittsburgh during the day and a second session during evening hours in a firehouse in a working-class suburb. The turnout was excellent, and while the party did not always hear what it wanted, it did manage to tap a level of problems not often brought home to national decision-makers. A domestic worker in Atlanta pointed out the plight of those in positions with no tenure, no minimum wage, no health or safety standards, no set hours, no unions, no holidays, no national spokesmen—nothing, in short, that workers in other industries had come to take for granted. Other problem areas, less visible in Washington or Miami Beach, invited like attention.

The regional sessions had another unanticipated effect. They provided a balance and a corrective to the views being promoted by the party's major candidates for the presidential nomination as the ones concerning most of the people. The potential nominees invested a great deal of time exploring such topics as Viet Nam, national defense, the economy, welfare, busing, campaign financing, and governmental favoritism—an important but selective group of issues. As Boston Mayor Kevin White argued in the first of the regional hearings, one could assume that the cities' problems did not exist or were on their way to a satisfactory resolution. The mayor suggested more attention be given to urban dwellers and their problems: inner-city decay, satisfactory rapid transit, pollution, overcrowding, medical services, and the low levels of federal budgeting directed to meet such needs. The field hearings also captured media attention, an important consideration for an out-party that was millions of dollars in debt.

The Platform Committee did make one operating change in the O'Hara

Commission recommendations. The provision for an elected drafting sub-committee to complete the most critical single aspect of its work—writing the platform—smacked too much of the old ways. The committee rejected the idea. The platform was written by the full 150-member committee in open session, a feat considered an impossibility up to this point. Further, it managed to complete its work satisfactorily and harmoniously, which was possibly the most surprising aspect of the entire operation.

CREDENTIALS COMMITTEE

The procedures for credentials challenges were the most thoroughly revised and extended of any affecting the three remaining convention committees. Again, 1968 provides the point of departure. The Credentials Committee had been in existence since 1832. Formed initially to compile a list of authorized delegates, it found itself in the midst of a dilemma over the status of the delegation from the District of Columbia. Since then it has fallen heir to the task of determining membership qualifications and deciding among the claims of competing delegations. Potentially its decisions (as appealed to and sustained by the full convention) can determine the nomination (as in the 1972 Democratic convention's California challenges or, for the Republicans, the bitter credentials contests of 1912 and 1952).

In recent times the Democrats have been most absorbed with the problems of representation on southern delegations. The maneuverings over the problem go back generations. The southern contingent of states has been an uncomfortable ally in Democratic national politics, continuing in the party because of the historical antipathy to Republicans and the power it could wield under the two-thirds nomination rule. As these factors have changed and as the black vote has emerged as an electoral force of consequence, the old southern-national Democratic party alliance has come under strain. A number of southern states, angered by what they believed to be acts of previous conventions to dilute their influence and by the mild civil-rights commitments of the 1948 Democratic national convention, walked out. They formed their own party, presumably killing whatever slim hope the Democrats had of holding the presidency. An angry convention retaliated in 1952, requiring a "loyalty oath" of southern delegations, which pledged their support to the convention's nominees and their efforts to insure the party's ticket was represented on the state ballot. The move accentuated the relationship, and the struggle simmered up through the 1960 convention.[27]

After this point the issue changed, focusing more explicitly on black representation on delegations, but the target remained the southern states. This particular strain came to a head in the 1964 convention. The challenge of the Mississippi Freedom Democratic party to the delegation regulars was the only real controversy the delegates could hope to influence during the convention. The sympathetic party and media hearing given to the abuses suffered by blacks seeking representation alarmed many, and resulted in a settlement favoring the predominately black contingent. One aspect of this resolution was the creation of the Special Equal Rights Committee, which was charged with finding ways to insure an equitable black presence on future delegations. The endorsement of the special committee's work by the National Committee and the choice of Richard Hughes to head the 1968 Credentials Committee indicated that the party would treat harshly any state party accused of racial discrimination. While the signals were clear, later experience proved that the procedures were inadequate to fulfill the intent, leading to a resolution authorizing the creation of the McGovern-Fraser Commission.

Seemingly the party action in the four years preceding the convention had defused the one issue underlying most credentials challenges. This was not to be. A number of southern delegations chose to fight the battle one more time. More significantly, the 1968 Credentials Committee was inundated by challenges on a series of issues in a volume never before experienced: due process guarantees in delegate selection, proportional representation of a presidential candidate's strength within delegations, and closed selection systems in some states and localities.

Rather than black representation in the South, the majority of challenges dealt with problems of Democratic procedures that were national in scope and that affected all states. The Credentials Committee precedents and processes were singularly inappropriate to the burden placed upon them,[28] a point the chairman acknowledged in calling for new forms and new standards to be supplied by interim reform bodies.

An overview only begins to suggest the problems implicit in the operation. A glimpse of the inconvenience the process caused one state delegation (North Carolina) can be found in the testimony of the state chairman before the O'Hara Commission. He made the following claims, which do provide a perspective of the process:

1. There were no clear rules as to delegate selection and therefore no ample grounds for dispute.
2. The defense of its position cost the state party $17,500, an unusually large sum (which cannot be verified), required because of the National Committee's insistence that without a good defense it could be unseated.
3. The state party and its delegation did not receive even elementary courtesy from the convention in answering such questions as to the order in which disputes would be heard and when they should be prepared to defend themselves.
4. The state party was handicapped by actions taken by the state chairman's predecessor and for which the state chairman was held responsi-

ble, an ambiguous and potentially unfair judgment, given the absence of early and clear-cut rules.

5. The entire process of credentials evaluation put a strain on party unity, most evident in a pointed exchange between the state chairman and a committee member on the representation of blacks on their respective delegations.

His central contention that the process was unjust and that broad rules, determined well in advance of delegate selection, should be applied fairly and consistently to all concerned is difficult to argue with.[29] Applying ad hoc rules, no matter how laudable, or imprecise and often post facto standards to a state's delegate selection made for an uncomfortable and frustrating situation for all concerned. The problem would be resolved with the new reforms.

The McGovern-Fraser Commission determined the criteria for evaluating the fairness of delegate selection systems. The O'Hara Commission was to provide the new processes for the changeover. As a consequence, the resolution of seating disputes would evolve from an ad hoc series of political decisions made by party members sharing fundamentally the same political perspectives in a bureaucratized, highly structured, and inclusive quasi-legal arbitrative process with advocates and defendants, an impartial judge figure, findings of fact, a court of appeals, and a jury of one's peers to make the determinations. O'Hara had pledged, in the commission's initial organizational meeting, to commit the group to evolving a set of procedures that would exemplify the rule of law. Whether the commission achieved this or not, it did fashion a structure with all the trappings of a judicial hearing—a totally new experience for a casual party previously given to informal and flexible means of arbitrating disputes, and another concession to a modern age.

Under the new rules, severely tested by the incredible number of challenges in 1972, a challenger had to file within ten days of the close of the delegate selection process in the state a notice of an intent to challenge. This had to be followed within five days by the equivalent of a legal brief citing the defendants, the alleged violations, the proposed remedy (normally seating the petitioner), a list of witnesses and relevant documents, and a request for a hearing and for "findings of fact," an investigation to corroborate the abuses claimed. The state chairman had to answer the accusations in much the same format within ten days. The penalty for not doing so was unusually severe: "Failure to so respond in good faith shall automatically deem the challenger's alleged facts to be admitted as true." The provision was unnaturally harsh and conveniently forgotten once the process went into effect.

The recommendations then proceeded to introduce the most noteworthy innovation into the proceedings. A hearing officer, "known by reputation to be fair and impartial in the context of the challenge and . . . experienced in the law,"[30] would be appointed to hold an open (if requested by either group) hearing on the dispute and to submit a written "findings of fact" to the full Credentials Committee. The hearing officer's report was explicitly not to include recommendations concerning the seating of delegates, a power reserved for the committee. In practice, however, the hearing officers did make such judgments, and they were influential in the Credentials Committee's deliberations.

Each party to a dispute had the right to oral argument before the Credentials Committee and could, if it could muster 10 percent support within the group, appeal any unfavorable decision to the convention. Delegates under challenge could participate in committee proceedings but could not vote on their state's challenge, a practice that had permitted delegates who later were not seated in the convention to vote in the close decisions concerning other state delegations. In all, it was hoped the rules would provide "justice and fairness" to the combatants and, according to O'Hara's original charge to his commission; a conciliatory force within party councils. The last standard, judging from the first application of the procedures, may be more difficult to achieve.

Running a Convention

Past conventions have been known for their hoopla—the hired bands, odd hats, boisterous play, rhythmic thumping, and delegate marches—as much as anything else. The differences between this and the type of serious convention one could reasonably expect in nominating a presidential candidate may be substantial. Presidential nominating sessions appear on television to be little removed from the wild antics of a gathering of Lions, Shriners, or any other group out for a boisterous time. The image of irresponsible fun is not one politicians especially take pride in or one many feel accurately conveys the nature of national conventions. It is an image the O'Hara Commission intended to improve.

NOMINATIONS

The most notable event during the convention was the choice of a party nominee to seek the president's office. Names were placed before the convention for consideration in a lengthy process involving a series of speeches lauding each prospective nominee, from minor state governors and "favorite-son" senators to major candidates for the nomination. The initial speech on a candidate's behalf was followed by a prearranged "spontaneous" demonstration of banners, noise, marching, and enthusiasm intended to demonstrate the wide following an individual had and the joy his name evoked. Television commentators with nothing better to do would time the demonstrations, noting that candidate A had received an ovation of 16.5 minutes as against candidate B's 14.3, a point of apparent significance. The demonstration would be followed by more seconding speeches designed to show a widespread support for the nominee among all segments of the party. Once the presentations on behalf of one candidate subsided, the process began again with the next, and was not exhausted until anyone with any support had received his or her chance.

Obviously the system was open to abuse. The nominating speeches were long and the number of candidates excessive. A speech by Mississippi judge Tom Brady at the 1960 Democratic convention extolling the virtues of the state's hopelessly segregationist governor, Ross Barnett, and attacking every federal civil rights, fiscal, and social policy in decades droned on seemingly forever. Repeatedly interrupted by the presiding officer and requested to conclude, the imperturbable judge continued, insensitive to the annoyance of a convention determined to move on to its serious business. The lure of national television exposure proves too tempting for some candidates and states. The 1968 Republican convention suffered a long disquisition on the merits of Alaska as a place to live and play—twice the size of Texas, containing half the fish estuaries in the United States, etc. The delegates and a national television audience underwent this chamber of commerce boosterism for the sake of having Governor Walter Hickel's candidacy placed before a convention unalterably committed to Richard Nixon.

"Favorite-son" candidacies (a potential nominee put forth with support in only one state) added a further hindrance to the effective operation of the entire nominating system. "Favorite sons" were adopted by a state delegation to serve state party purposes: the presidential nomination process would honor a longstanding party member (former Republican Senator Leverett Saltonstall of Massachusetts, for example); a commonly accepted "local" nominee preserved party harmony and protected the state party from being cannibalized by the serious contenders (Democratic Governor Edmund "Pat" Brown and his California delegation in 1960); an "uncommitted" delegation (i.e., one pledged only to a favorite son) was free to barter its support for political advantage (Texas at the 1968 Democratic convention); a "favorite son" can exchange his votes for personal political gain such as the presidential (in a deadlocked convention) or vice-presidential nomination or a cabinet post (a strategy that could backfire disastrously, as it did for Governor Robert Meyner at the 1960 Democratic convention); and a "favorite son" can serve as a stand-in or stalking horse for a major contender with the hope of scaring any competitors away (Governor Roger Branigan of Indiana and Attorney General Thomas Lynch of California, both in 1968 Democratic primaries). The "favorite-son" strategy represented an anachronism from the age of the boss. It denied voters a direct choice among real presidential contenders. It excluded a contender from building coalitions from all available party voters and it denied a contender the opportunity to travel within a state and acquaint himself with its people, leaders, and problems. The tactic is also risky. A "favorite son" can hold his delegation too long (as Alben Barkley did in 1952, as Meyner did in 1960, or as Ohio Governor James Rhodes did at the 1968 Republican convention); he can deliver his votes to the wrong candidate (as Oklahoma Democratic Senator Robert Kerr did in 1952); or he can lose control of his delegation (as Governors Brown and Meyner did in 1960), to the detriment of himself and his state party. The national convention should be concerned with the serious candidates in an open elective process (at least this is what the O'Hara Commission believed), while still attempting to provide mechanisms for a flexible process of choice.

The Commission on Rules streamlined the nominating ceremony by further institutionalizing and delimiting the process. Nominations had to be submitted by the close of the business day (6:00 P.M.) preceding the actual roll call. Petitions required the written approval of the prospective nominee (to avoid unnecessary coyness or unauthorized maneuvering) and between 50 and 200 signatures, with no more than 20 coming from any one state. The intention of forcing a candidate to attract firm support in a minimum of three states represented a new departure, although a mild one, in an effort to prohibit "favorite-son" candidacies.

The order of nomination was to be determined by lot, and each candidate received a maximum of fifteen minutes for one nominating and two seconding speeches, to run without interruption from the time of initial recognition. All demonstrations on behalf of a candidate were banned, and the onus was placed on the candidate's nominator to quell any that arose: demonstration time came out of the candidate's grant for nomination.

The procedure for the vice-presidential nomination was much the same, with two exceptions. A twelve-hour interval had to elapse between the nomination of the presidential candidate and beginning of the process for the second place on the ticket, a waiting period intended to allow for some reflection on the choice. Second, requests to nominate were accepted until three hours before the scheduled presentation of the nominating speeches. Delegates were also allowed to vote for individuals not formally placed in nomination.

The procedures as applied in 1972 did discourage "favorite-son" efforts to tie up state delegations and, in combination with the McGovern-Fraser guidelines, decreased the volume of "uncommitted" delegates and, more than likely, the number pledged to minor candidates. In truth, the total impact of the reform movement had more to do with this than the mild O'Hara Commission rules on nominations. The number of nominations, however, was not severely reduced. The place of the local notables, so visible in previous conventions, was taken by candidates with demonstrably broader constituencies. These included candidates with regional overtones (Wallace, Sanford) or those appealing to national-level interest groups within the party (Jackson, labor, New Deal Democrats; Chisholm, blacks, liberals).[31] The quality of the oratory, if not improved, was mercifully briefer. Denied the luxury of time, the speeches were more pointed than those of previous years. A Viet Nam prisoner of war's wife, for example, gave an emotional seconding speech for McGovern, and I. W. Abel, president of the Steelworkers, AFL-CIO spokesman, and erstwhile reformer (a nonparticipating member of the McGovern-Fraser Commission) managed in a brief talk on behalf of the Jackson candidacy to convey the depths of federated labor's displeasure with the entire proceedings.

The weaknesses of the new procedures—or, better, their inability to improve materially the old ways—was best evidenced in the nominations and balloting for the vice-presidential slot on the convention's last night. The process was a shambles, ending in a display of irresponsibility that substantially hurt the party's chances in the November election. Orderly procedures should offer protection against mindless disruptions or frivolous byplay. Nonetheless, it is important to understand the mood of the convention. The delegates were exhausted. Many were angry. The major business of the convention had been completed. There was no question that McGovern's choice for a companion on the presidential ticket would prevail. All of substance that was left was for the two nominees to make their remarks and launch the campaign.

Many delegates were disillusioned. Most had been campaigning since January, and some, for over two years. Organized labor and its considerable army of sympathizers felt that somehow the party had been taken from them. Regular Democrats believed they had been orphaned by strange new processes they failed to understand. Proponents of the women's movement were angered over their treatment on the South Carolina challenge. Wallacites felt they had not been heard during critical moments in the floor debate. Liberals were frustrated by the convention's unwillingness to permit a vote on the party charter. The supporters of the losing candidates were bitter for a variety of reasons, and some of McGovern's delegates were equally upset by what they believed to be the unprincipled tactics of their opponents once the nomination had been won. All of these feelings, overlaid by a week-long fatigue, exploded into a series of frivolous nominations: Stanley Arnold, unknown; Clay Smothers, unknown; Endicott Peabody, former Massachusetts governor distinguished only by his active national campaign for the office, a new phenomenon; Senator Mike Gravel of Alaska, who gained attention through his insistence on seconding his own nomination (a tactic favored by Smothers also); Frances ("Cissy") Farenthold, the women's movement candidate; and, in addition to the eventual nominee Eagleton, a New Jersey "favorite son," Representative Peter Rodino, who later gained fame as the chairman of the House Judiciary Committee that considered the Nixon impeachment. If the nominations were out of hand, the vote (in which a delegate was not restricted to choosing among the nominees) taxed the imagination: George A. Dowdy, Phil Burton, Eleanor McGovern, Cesar Chavez, Joseph Montoya, John DeCarlo, Edward Kennedy, Fred Seaman, Daniel Berrigan—the great and the obscure received their tributes while the delegates proceeded to have their fun. Lost in all of this was the tragedy of a choice that the presidential nominee would replace within weeks: twelve hours was insufficient time to make a decision of such consequence, a point a review of the nominees of both parties over the last two decades should have made clear.

A new reform commission would have to be appointed to attempt a solution. Under the leadership of Senator Hubert Humphrey, the committee, which met after the 1972 election, proposed a longer waiting period (twenty-four hours) between nominations, or that the job be done in a "miniconvention," a special meeting of the National Committee called for the specific purpose of selecting a vice-presidential nominee sometime after the national convention. The proposals did not go to the heart of the problem.

The O'Hara Commission recommendations on nominations tidied up the procedures. They did not accomplish several of their main objectives, such as limiting consideration to the serious contenders and eliminating the nuisance candidacies. The reforms may well be along the right lines, but the provisions need considerable tightening.

TELEVISION

Everyone's favorite scapegoat for the Chicago convention—and for that matter for all of the disturbances that plagued the sixties and early seventies—was television. It was not the event that was the problem, but the medium that brought the action into the home that was to blame. Television did this more graphically and for a wider audience than any other source of news. It was a powerful instrument, and its influence and role were resented. Mayor Daley made the point in an interview preceding the convention's last session:

For weeks and months the press and radio and television across the nation have revealed the tactics and strategy that was to be carried on in Chicago during the convention week by groups of terrorists. The intention of these terrorists was openly displayed. They repeatedly stated they had come to Chicago to disrupt a national political convention and to paralyze our city. They came here equipped with plastic [*sic*], with helmets, and with their own brigade of medics. They had maps locating the hotels and routes of buses for the guidance of terrorists from out of town. To protect the delegates and the people of Chicago from this planned violence the city worked with the Secret Service, the Federal Bureau of Investigation, the Department of Justice, and other agencies directly involved in the maintenance of law and order. . . . It was also pointed out they would attempt to assault, harass and taunt the police in reacting before television cameras. Fifty-one policemen have been injured. Sixty percent of those arrested did not live in Illinois, and 70 percent did not live in Chicago. In the last two days we have seen the strategy of these announced plans carried on in full, and the whole purpose of the city and law enforcement agencies distorted and twisted. One can understand how those who deeply believe in their cause concerning Vietnam would be deeply disappointed, but to vent their disappointment on the city and law enforcement agencies, that these dissenting groups and television should be used as a tool for their purpose of calculated disruption and rioting is inexcusable.[32]

Daley stated what for many was to become dogma: terrorists planned to sabotage the convention and, if possible, the city and the political system. Through the gullibility or actual connivance of the television networks, which were angered by the party's and the city's failure to cooperate in meeting their needs, the insurrectionists were largely successful in discrediting the party, the city, and the Democratic presidential nominee. The events were planned well in advance—in fact the city administration, through the local prosecuting attorneys, later charged in the courts that a conspiracy had existed. But it could not have reached millions of Americans in the spontaneous manner it did without the active intervention of television. There was a feeling that television had to be punished and its role in future conventions severely restricted. Although no one went this far publicly, there were forces in both major parties that firmly believed television should be a tool of the parties and their candidates rather than a vehicle for embarrassment or opposition. The question that was centered in the O'Hara Commission's deliberations was how far the movement would go.

A shrewd politician, Daley, of course, was not alone in either his opposition or his particular line of attack. John Criswell, the quickly forgotten convention manager in 1968 and Johnson loyalist, said, "I consider the major networks to have been grossly unfair. They promised us in advance we could expect a hard time from their newsmen—and I must admit they kept their promises."[33] Humphrey, the man who lost most in the bloody encounters, was alternately stunned, furious, defeated, and embittered. Humphrey yelled at a television set that had interposed shots of his nomination with the street riots, "I'm going to be President someday. I'm going to appoint the FCC—we're going to look into all this!" Later, reminiscing, he said, "I was the victim of that convention . . . I felt that when we left that convention we were in an impossible situation. . . . Chicago was a catastrophe. My wife and I went home heart-broken, battered and beaten."[34]

Unfortunately, as Humphrey and the Democrats knew, the national convention was the key event in the election year. One-third of the November voters had made their decision prior to the conventions. Another third did so during or immediately after the conventions on the strength of what television and the other media told them of the candidate and his views and depending on the extent to which the event reinforced their party ties. By the end of the national conventions two-thirds to three-fourths of the electorate (depending on whether one or both nominees were new) had made their choice. The general election campaign would seek to persuade the remainder.

Television was in a curiously ambivalent position. It was a powerful weapon, unquestionably the most awesome a candidate or a party could engage in their behalf. Ninety-eight million television sets reaching 95 percent of American homes constitute the type of statistics politicians savor. Still, the medium was vulnerable to political pressure. The Federal Communications Commission controlled the networks' access to the air waves and, as Humphrey indicated, the president appointed the FCC. In short, the FCC was a blatantly political body with enormous power.

Humphrey, of course, did not win the presidency, and it was left to Richard Nixon to do what he would with the regulatory agencies. The Democrats' major hopes rested with the O'Hara Commission. Corporate television knew its own weakness. It feared repercussions and the turnout of network brass whenever the Commission on Rules considered matters relevant to television coverage was mute testimony to its concerns.

O'Hara handled the problem with tact. His chief weapon was delay, intended to allow tempers to cool and to permit an unemotional reevaluation of the role of television and the other media in reporting the convention. The commission's first public hearing concerned the problems of television and the media, but from the perspective of the newscaster, it served as a stage for relaying the difficulties he encountered and for making suggestions for improvements.[35] With the exception of a later hearing (December 1969), called under pressure from congressional leaders angered by network programming (and essentially irrelevant to the commission's work), the group did not consider proposals governing the conduct of television reporting for two years, and did not make its final decision on its recommendations until the swirl of meetings that concluded its deliberations.

The problems posed by television are complex under the best of circumstances. Television has proved to be a mixed blessing, as the Chicago convention illustrated on a grand scale. But more mundane difficulties have always persisted. The problem is that there are significant dividing lines between creating a convention for television viewers and operating one to accomplish the convention's business, which television simply records and transmits to the viewer. The extent to which the industry attempted to create interest (through, for example, provocative interviews) rather than just report the happenings blurs the event and begins to transform the institution. Television reporters on the floor of the convention became star attractions in their own right—actors center stage in a national drama, better known and far greater attractions than the delegates they were supposed to cover.

Conventions can be, and normally are, dull affairs. Action is concentrated in a few roll call votes, with the rest of the time being filled by unexceptional speeches, routine committee reports, controversies over rules, and passage of resolutions. These events are unexciting to watch, but they are important to the party. Television demands action, excitement, confrontation. Consequently, conventions bear witness to the spectacle of an army of television newscasters with little to do, earnestly bidding to run down every rumor, all conceivable interpretations of any action (no matter how insignificant), and any political figure of celebrity value. The competition among television reporters is fierce, on occasion interfering with the matters at hand. Conventions are serious business. Television treats them as entertainment, with good guys and bad guys, personal and political confrontations, and endless intrigues, both real and imagined.

The charges stemming from the Chicago convention were of course more serious. The implication of some critics was that television was responsible for fomenting much of the disorder. And the networks supposedly had done it for revenge. They had grievances with the city of Chicago. The telephone strike hampered their communications. They had trouble installing their equipment in the convention hall. Taxi and transit strikes made movement difficult. Their mobile units were restricted in their movements and harassed by police and city authorities. A number of newsmen were caught in the crush of violence. Several were seriously hurt and some charged that the police deliberately sought out those with media badges to punish, or at best ignored their credentials in impartially clubbing onlookers. Two CBS television reporters, Mike Wallace and Dan Rather, were assaulted by security people within the convention hall. Obviously there were ample grounds for ill will, and as the convention week ended, a prolonged controversy over the role of the media, and especially television, erupted.

The O'Hara Commission had inherited the squabble. The media was given its day, as were its critics. All were asked to suggest changes that could improve the proceedings and minimize the difficulties the media, and especially television, presented. Possibly even the job of reporting could somehow be made easier. The remedies favored by the broadcast industry (such as the popular wider aisles and fewer delegates) did not deal with the difficulty. Other industry spokesmen suggested means for facilitating television reporting or shortening the sessions (possibly to two hours) and abandoning the less important, routine business, steps to heighten the "entertainment value" of conventions that were not well received by the commissioners.

Several provoked commission members and a goodly number of witnesses, stung by the reactions to the national convention and holding television accountable for the party's deficiencies, angrily and repeatedly stressed a limited role for media representatives. Critics argued for the banning of all television cameras and, as some would have it, all reporters from the convention floor. The objective would be to provide broadcast booths and interview areas off the floor where a willing delegate, upon being notified by a messenger, could go to be interviewed. A number of party regulars (not on the commission) wanted harsher measures applied in restricting access to convention figures and delegates, although the implementation of such procedures appeared unmanageable.

The lifeblood of the party was in its ability to communicate, a point the balance of the commission recognized. Unnecessary harassment of newsmen was firmly opposed, and the committee, under O'Hara's deliberate leadership, focused on the problem over which it had jurisdiction—improving convention performance. Tempers cooled and the matter was compromised. Something was given to everyone while theoretically and practically the work of the convention was expedited. Television cameras were banned from the floor (except for the pool of cameras mounted on platforms strategically placed around the convention hall), and television newscasters and interviewers were allowed limited access to the floor. Places for television interviews were provided off the convention floor. Interviews with delegates on the floor were permitted if the cameras picked up the scene from distant locations (the platforms or television booths). The printed media were allowed a restricted supply of twenty-minute floor passes on the assumption that they would contact a predetermined delegate about a specific matter and then leave. All media representatives were forced to receive accreditation from the convention manager's office, a process intended to restrict sessions to the working press and to limit the passes given to any one newspaper or network to a reasonable number. The provisions were mild, serving to defuse a potentially ugly confrontation and at the same time expedite the operation of the convention.

CONVENTION CHAIRMEN

The presiding officer of the convention wields enormous powers. The O'Hara Commission spelled these out in greater detail than before and enunciated their limits, but did little to change their substance. While a convention is in progress its chairman is singularly the most awesome individual within the party. He recognizes individuals to speak, controls the pace and timing as well as the agenda (within broad limits) of the daily sessions, has the power to maintain proper order in the convention hall, can call for and must interpret voice votes as well as "sense of the convention" motions, schedules roll call votes (or, alternatively, these can be forced by 20 percent of the delegates), can place limits on debates, decides when to shut off the vote switching that follows roll call, appoints lower-level convention officials as needed, controls the communications between the chair and delegations (through a telephone and microphone system he regulates), can send representatives to poll a delegation, can make available to the media at his discretion official vote tallies and records of proceedings, decides when a quorum is present and business can proceed, determines (subject to appeal and a majority vote) the interpretation and application of rules, decides when appeals are "clearly dilatory" and therefore deserving of no further consideration by the convention (as O'Brien did on at least one occasion in 1972), has limited discretion in entertaining adjournment motions (and, depending on their contents, can set the time to reconvene), supervises the convention debates and overall proceedings, and has the liberty of rearranging the schedule (within bounds) as he deems necessary. His formal duties are impressive. Informally, his influence can be even greater: he is the catalyst that makes the convention go.

The power implicit in the office can be illustrated with one example drawn from the postreform convention of 1972. O'Brien, as presiding officer, had to decide who voted on questions of credentials challenge within a delegation and what would constitute a convention majority under such circumstances. The problem was extraordinarily sticky and, worse, the presidential nomination quite clearly rested on the outcome. After painful soul-searching, O'Brien, in consultation with O'Hara, the convention's parliamentarian, determined that members of a delegation not under challenge could vote on questions concerning those delegation members being challenged. Further, a majority of those eligible to vote would constitute the necessary margin of victory, a total that would clearly shift depending on the individual state challenge under evaluation. The decisions were critical to the maneuvering on the California challenge, and were believed to benefit the McGovern forces, creating problems for both O'Brien and O'Hara with supporters of the other leading contenders and with federated labor in particular.

The greatest limit on the actions of the chair is the spirit of the rules and the office; he is presumed to be objective in his interpretations and fair in his conduct of the office. It is expected that he will look to the party's long-term interests rather than the advantages to be gained by a candidate or faction. There are appeals to the decisions of the chair, but marshaling a majority vote on such issues is difficult. The rules also can be suspended, but the two-thirds majority requirement in effect nullifies this option for controversial items. To the extent a presiding officer violates the unwritten rules of impartiality, he damages his own credibility. Still, the limited nature of the available remedies places greater emphasis on initially choosing a respected and knowledgeable party figure for the post.

Given the natural power that accrues to a chairman and the limited restrictions on his conduct of the office, one curious loophole was inserted in the reform provisions without debate or objection. It constituted a carry-over from less-enlightened, earlier convention practices. "In interpreting these rules," the final draft of the O'Hara Commission reforms read, "the Chair may have recourse to the rulings of Chairmen of previous Demo-cratic National Conventions, to the precedents of the United States House of Representatives and to general parliamentary law." It seemed the movement for convention reform had begun at this point. If the investiga-tions that followed demonstrated anything, it was the leeway such a provi-sion granted a presiding official and the absence of definition inherent in the sources identified.

CONVENTION RECORDS

As benefits the bizarre events of Chicago, the records of the convention have never been uncovered. When a new convention manager was ap-pointed to arrange the 1972 convention he made the point that everyone already knew; there was absolutely nothing to go on. The practice in the National Committee (at least for Democrats) has long been that when an individual leaves he takes his files with him. The justification for the tradi-tion varies. Some contend that the files are basically their own personal business, a strange position for officials of an agency that is assumed to be public. Others argue that they take the files so as to preserve them, that if they are left with the National Committee they will be thrown out in the normal course of housekeeping. The latter contention has past experience to support it.

Whatever the reasons, the end result is the same. The convention as an organization has no collective memory. Regardless of the event's impor-tance (and preparing for the convention is by far the biggest project under-taken by the National Committee) or how public the matters involved, nothing is available to guide decisions. The same ground is covered and mistakes repeated at potentially great cost in time, energy, and organiza-tional resources.

The Democrats had an additional problem. For several years after the 1968 convention they were paying off debts incurred in relation to the event for which they had little background information on the reasons for the obligations or the authenticity of the charges. To an extent, they re-mained at the mercy of creditors.

The practical difficulties are severe. The loss to serious observers inter-ested in the evaluation of a party's operations are even greater. Once these records disappear, any analysis of the process by academicians or others is rendered moot, a point those who remove their "personal files" are not unaware of.

These arguments were made before the O'Hara Commission by, among others, Paul David, the group's primary consultant and a man interested in convention procedures. The presentations received a sympathetic hearing, and the commission's recommendations, as adopted by the convention, provided that all records of business and correspondence of the National Committee as it related to the convention be collected and maintained at the party's Washington headquarters. The files were to be open to the public and available for copying at the individual's expense. Further, a journal of every day's proceedings at the convention was to be made available the following day to all delegates, and the full transcript of the official proceedings was to be published and distributed by the National Committee within a year of the convention.

The intent of the provisions is clear enough. Unfortunately, politics is concerned with the present and sometimes the future, but seldom the past. Convention records fall into the category of completed business. The retrieval and protection of convention records has not been stressed. As an example, the 1972 convention's Credentials Committee and its staff disbanded immediately at the conclusion of the convention's proceedings. The records of debates, votes, and decisions of these significant hearings were stored for a short time in the law offices of the former chairperson, Patricia Roberts Harris, and made available at expense by her as a public service. Eventually returned to the National Committee, they were stored until someone could find something appropriate to do with them or until they were discarded. The records of the Rules and Platform committees came to a similar end. The preservation of past records serves the party's interest. It is a step beyond the secretive arrangement of the past. The haphazard institutionalization of the National Committee unfortunately hinders the implementation of any fundamental change.

Overall, the O'Hara Commission accomplished a considerable amount. It contributed to the significant gains made in modernizing an institution basically unchanged from the party's earliest days. Its recommendations did not constitute fundamental changes in the same way that those of the McGovern-Fraser Commission did, nor are they likely to have the same prolonged impact. What they did do was remold the convention to better serve the party's need for a gigantic common meeting of party members to conduct the business of selecting party nominees and running a national and uniquely original organization.

Within a short time some of the deficiencies in the commission's recommendations have become clear. The nominating procedures need an overhaul. The control of the National Committee and the national chairman and his staff over the earlier phases of convention planning need a review they did not receive from the Commission on Rules. The reformers did no violence to the historic role of the presiding officer, leaving his powers intact and his discretionary authority only slightly diminished. The extraordinary nature of the position limits what types of changes can be instituted. Simple acts such as relying on the commonly used *Robert's*

Rules of Order would open the proceedings further, lessen the chairman's control of the proceedings, and remove some of the potential discretionary abuses from the process.

The O'Hara Commission did not enumerate the rights of the individual delegate, the resources at his disposal, and the power he has over events. This possibly was the commission's largest omission. A set of due process guarantees for the individual delegate would begin to achieve a truly revolutionary reform, the shifting of real power from a small elite of convention officers to the mass of the membership. The O'Hara Commission has undoubtedly begun the process. Such an addition would accelerate it substantially.

SEVEN

The Reaction
and a Reassessment

A TIDAL WAVE of protest engulfed the Democratic party in the bitter aftermath of the 1972 presidential defeat. Everyone was disillusioned and angry. The reforms became the natural scapegoat for the failures of the party and its presidential nominee. Change was in the wind, and the likelihood was a return to the pre-1968 system or something closely approximating it. The reforms were in trouble.

George McGovern was both the Democratic party's presidential nominee and the man most closely associated both among the public and among party members with the reforms. McGovern had run a hopelessly inadequate campaign against a strong opponent at the height of his powers. George Meany and the AFL-CIO had officially remained "neutral" for Nixon. Many party regulars and state organizations never really took the national ticket seriously, preferring to concentrate on local races of more immediate significance to themselves. The McGovern campaign was poorly organized and poorly led. The candidate was continuously on the defensive. His bungling over the welfare question in the final California primary simply anticipated a series of crucial mishaps: the floundering before settling on a new national chairman; the creation of a three-headed campaign organization; the Eagleton affair and the manner in which it and the choice of a successor were handled; the failure to educate the public to the implications of the emerging Watergate scandal; the inability to come to terms with labor, to establish a clear and definite campaign strategy for the few months before November, or even to settle on the dominant themes and issues of the campaign, all presaged the overwhelming defeat that followed.

The outcome of the election was predictable. From the beginning the Democratic nominee—whoever he was—would be the underdog. The Democrats would lose. But what stunned party members was the magnitude of the defeat. The party had been humiliated, and party members were angry. The party became wracked by dissension. And the scapegoat for the party's frustrations became the reforms. The reforms had "created" McGovern, and McGovern's ineptitude had caused the election debacle. Or so the dominant argument ran.

The reasoning was predictable and had actually been anticipated by the threats from some of the antireformers before the election. The reform movement spoke to much broader concerns than the McGovern candidacy, but the reaction had set in and the early betting was that the reforms would be dumped. The party regulars, the Meany wing of organized labor, the party's financial backers, party and elected officials, and policy conservatives had, of course, all opposed them from the beginning. More disturbingly, many of the reformers themselves had been thrown into self-doubt. Seemingly, the very worst predicted by the critics had come to pass. Maybe a return to something approaching the old ways was called for. The experiment in participatory democracy, it would seem, had failed. Substantial change appeared to be imminent.

The Initial Response

The post-1972 years began in a manner similar to those of the post-1968 campaign. Hubert Humphrey (now United States senator from Minnesota) appeared before a party meeting in the aftermath of the election to warn Democrats again (and they seemed to need it) against the corrosive effects of "back-alley brawling." Humphrey cautioned his fellow party members on the need for unity and, seemingly unnecessarily for a political group, the value of winning elections.[1] It seemed, then, that few gains had resulted from the institutional convulsions that had marked the four years since Humphrey, then the defeated party nominee, had made a similar appearance to perform the same duty.

If anything, and if appearances could be counted, matters had worsened. McGovern had captured the party's nomination from his chief rivals, Humphrey and Senator Edmund Muskie. Both were party centrists. Some claimed McGovern had won by capitalizing on the rules he helped promote. The presidential vote in 1968 had at least been close. The presidential election in 1972 resulted in the most decisive defeat for the party in recent memory and one of the worst in its history. To compound the mood of defection, McGovern himself, the symbol of reform to supporter and opponent alike, appeared before the same meeting Humphrey addressed (the initial gathering of the Charter Commission) to urge reform of the reforms. Poetically, he described them as "an innovation, a voyage in an uncharted sea." "In many respects," he told the mildly startled assemblage, "the reforms worked better than our best expectations"; but he added, "they can be improved."[2]

Specifically, McGovern counseled abandonment of the quota concept, the most visible of the issues in the enforcement struggle; a healthier representation of senior party leaders at national conventions; the modification of requirements covering slatemaking, the abuse of which led to the party-splitting ouster of the Daley faction from Miami Beach; and the return of ex-officio voting status at the convention to national committeemen. Had McGovern advocated such changes earlier, or even been less intent on the full implementation of the reforms, much of the controversy surrounding enforcement may have been avoided. Recommending these changes now seemed to some extraordinary poor timing and to others the first wave of the predicted mass assault on the newly enacted regulations. Change was assured. The questions to be answered centered on the direction the reformulation would take (McGovern had provided clues here) and its extensiveness.

The Guidelines Reconsidered

"We need not pretend that the reforms were written in stone," McGovern had told his listeners.[3] The party had no misconceptions along these lines. A mood of revolt had surfaced and the object of its ire was clear.

The 1972 convention had provided for a new body to reassess the controversial rules put into effect during the prenomination period (as well as a second commission to fulfill the obligations as to "party structure" left hanging with the defeat of the unfortunate "party charter"). The New Delegate Selection Commission,[4] eventually referred to as the Mikulski Commission (after its chairwoman, Barbara Mikulski, a city councilwoman from Baltimore), had an unusually rocky tenure. Even for Democrats at their worst, the constant bickering, institutional maneuverings, and shortsighted yet intense personality clashes that dotted its two brief years of existence were unusually petty. Despite it all, the group—before its unnatural early demise—performed admirably. Little would be gained from a detailed recounting of its deliberations, the options before it, its continual political trials, or even its intricate and somewhat chancy decision-making procedures. It should be sufficient to point out what it had going against it and what (in cooperation with others) it managed to achieve.

First, a look at the factors working against it. Most impressive of these was the already noted ugly mood of the party after the presidential election fiasco. The feeling against reform was broadly shared throughout most of the party. Discontent ran deep. The expectation was that the regulars and centrists partial to Jackson, Humphrey, and (to a lesser extent) Muskie would extract their revenge. Alternately, the belief was held that the newcomers represented at the 1972 convention primarily as a consequence of the McGovern campaign would return to their apolitical suburban pursuits, leaving politics to the old-line professionals (and hence the anti-reformers). McGovern's early concessions were taken as evidence that a reform constituency no longer remained viable. Few in the party were eager to make a determined stand for regulations many had come to associate with political suicide.

AFL-CIO

Major groups within the party could, in fact, barely wait to election day to begin the overhaul. Foremost among them was the AFL-CIO. The leadership of the federated organization had sat out the presidential election (although more labor representatives than ever had attended the Democratic convention). The decision had been fatal to McGovern's already shaky underdog candidacy. The AFL-CIO's antipathy was well known, and the Meany-Barkan leadership, eager to show its strength, actively intervened in the first postelection meeting of the party. The newly constituted National Committee convened one month after the election to select a new national chairman. The AFL-CIO had been strident in its opposition to the presidential nominee's choice, Jean Westwood of Utah, installed as national chairwoman the day after the national convention ended. With the unflattering battle cry of "Gravel Gertie must go!" the AFL-CIO threw its support behind Robert Strauss, a Texas conservative and personal friend of one of the state's former governors, John Connally.

Strauss was known as an adept fund-raiser with strong ties to the financial world and to party conservatives, particularly those from his native Texas. He had served a distinguished term as party treasurer, and during his tenure the enormous debt, a holdover in large part from the 1968 presidential campaign, had been systematically reduced and the day-to-day financing of National Committee activities put on the most regulated basis in the party's history. Strauss was considered close to the "fat cats" in the party (understandably), the regulars, and elective and party office-holders—in short, those whom he considered—and proclaimed publicly on repeated occasions—to represent the true interests of the party. He was not sympathetic to the reform movement, with which he had had little contact. He was acceptable to federated labor and, in fact, he was its candidate for the party leader's post.

The National Committee had been newly constituted and enlarged on the last day of the 1972 national convention. The restructuring of the National Committee, the creation of a Charter Commission to review and recommend changes in party structure, and the granting of permission to hold a 1974 midterm convention represented the extensions of the reform thrust approved by the national convention. The first duty of the new National Committee would be to elect its leadership, the incoming national chairman. The meeting was called for the month following the election and the battle lines were drawn.

In an impressive ceremony closely resembling the national convention's for nominating a presidential candidate and, as far as anyone knew, the first truly open election process in the party's history, Strauss narrowly prevailed in a crowded field. Surely now federated labor would have its way. Strauss, who wanted above all a unified party reflective of what he called "people with constituencies," tried to appease it. He failed. A basically decent and fair-minded man (despite the continual zig-zags in his policy executions), he attempted to put the broad interests of the party, as he saw them, first. His independence was not appreciated. Within eighteen months an infuriated Barkan had begun to protest that Strauss represented "the worst political mistake" COPE's director had ever made.[5]

Coalition for a Democratic Majority (CDM)

Another, less-conventional, group emerged from the postelection debris. One of its founders was Ben J. Wattenberg. Wattenberg had been a supporter of and campaign manager for Washington State Senator Henry Jackson, and he was coauthor (with Richard Scammon) of the politically controversial *The Real Majority*.[6] Spurred by Wattenberg and other likeminded individuals, the new organization sought to combine centrist to rightist Democratic politicians with academicians (notably political scientists) in an alliance intended to accomplish three goals: help institute substantial modifications in replacing the McGovern-Fraser rules (its most pressing objective); return the Democratic party to the Roosevelt coalitional base, the New Deal-Fair Deal combination of groups (unions, workers, ethnics, small farmers) and issues (economic, defense) reputedly endangered by the reform movement and the McGovern candidacy; and, so it was rumored, provide a base for a Jackson candidacy in 1976 by helping to structure a party atmosphere receptive to the type of views the senator held.

Somewhat akin to the "citizen's lobby" Common Cause, the group campaigned through paid advertisements in major newspapers to attract a selective group of quality members. Its appeal proved moderately successful. Congressman James O'Hara, scarred by a narrow election victory and himself a recent appointee to the Charter Commission, agreed to serve as cochairman. Austin Ranney, late of the McGovern-Fraser Commission, served on the executive board, as did Wattenberg and Penn Kemble, author, journalist, and academician, who doubled as executive director. The reports circulated by the coalition were unusually able; before it began to concentrate attention on policy concerns of more immediate political significance, they provided the most sustained and thoughtful critique of the reform guidelines available.[7]

A reading of *The Real Majority* best serves to reveal the group's intellectual convictions, many in marked contrast to those (had they been as clearly developed) of the reformers. The organization's goals and fears (the unraveling of the politically successful Roosevelt coalition) have been commented on. Wattenberg and his coauthor Richard Scammon, an election analyst of unusual distinction, stated the underlying apprehension of those who eventually came to support the CDM in an assessment of the reform drive within the precepts of *The Real Majority*. The authors placed their faith in the "center":

A political party in the United States operates effectively between the two 35-yard lines of the political football field wholly aware that there is a major substantive difference between one 35-yard line and the other, aware too that heading starkly for the end zone leads to a political fumble. A political party must keep itself aware that compromise and coalition are the essential tools of political action. It must be aware that it must listen as well as lead and that elite theorizing will only allow [the opposition] to govern the nation.[8]

But the "new politics," the politics of reform, the authors saw as "elitist," divorced from and scornful of the traditional social roots that distinguished the Democratic party:

For many years of Liberal Democratic hegemony, it was the Republican Party that was perceived as the party of the elitist: the banker, the broker, the doctor. And it was the Democratic Party that was seen as the party of the little man.

That was the taproot of Democratic power. For the man who chooses the Presidents of this country is the man who bowls on Thursday nights. He is the man in his blue work shirt who is perfectly content to watch the greenies don the beads while he presides over . . . the blueing of America. He is a man who is decidedly turned off as he watches the Democrats-of-Despair hand out the campaign buttons of the New Politics, buttons that read MEA CULPA.[9]

The reformers, in short, had begun a holy movement "convinced that there is but one shining truth that all right-thinking men must accept." These reformers entertained two options: "harass, disrupt and coerce the party and the party's candidate towards its own views," and, if this failed, "consider acting upon their threat to start a new party—in fact, to institutionalize the movement."[10]

The political repercussions of these tactics could be enormous: "The Democratic party's militants' hard work can win them a state primary when 30 percent of the voters turn up; their hard work, occasionally, can dominate a national convention; but it can never dominate a national general election when 80 million Americans go to the polls to choose their President. And if the party's candidate is either the handpicked choice of the militants or if he is seen as snug and cozy with the militants, that candidate and his party, by transference, can be severely hurt at the polls."[11]

The charges were harsh and the feelings running through them deep-felt and sincere. Further, and more significantly, the views spoke for a large constituency of disgruntled Democrats. The results of the presidential election seemed to fulfill their ominous predictions and in turn lent impetus to the move to form a national organization to channel the post-November discontent along lines compatible with their own thinking.

The association's views, reflecting the bias of the antireformers, require elaboration. The coalition accepted as valuable the standardizing influence the guidelines imposed on the unregulated growth of local practices. The application of democratic concepts to the process of delegate selection was accepted in principle. The CDM did reject what it believed to be the assumptions behind several of the guidelines, especially the imposition of what it referred to as "pre-set standards" to the outcome of political processes. Consequently, it fought the quotas ("arbitrary biological categories"), which it maintained had no intrinsic relationship to effective representation.[12]

The coalition took exception to the favoritism shown "participatory" as against "representative" leadership they found in the rules. Translated, this meant (in its eyes) that elective officeholders, party chieftains, and interest-group representatives were discriminated against in a process that stressed active participation as a condition of selection. It held that the national convention that resulted from the enactment of these procedures did not reflect "mainstream" Democrats, thus contributing to the choice of an unrepresentative candidate and a predictably decisive electoral defeat. The association's single hypothesis explanation created too great a burden for the reform guidelines to carry, but, as it was quick to remark, its objections were not significantly different from those advanced by the repentant McGovern.

The CDM specifically lobbied for a repeal of guidelines A-1 and A-2 (the "quotas"), although it felt a continuation and strengthening of the Special Equal Rights Committee's "six basic elements" advisable. It called for the abolition of C-6 (curbing slatemaking) while emphasizing the value of A-4 and the 1972 convention's rule that any candidate pledged to a presidential contender be a bona fide supporter of the prospective nominee. It would also permit a modified proxy usage, confined to instances where a certified delegate had to leave a meeting. As a rejoinder to the elitism it found in the "New Politics," it would rewrite C-2 to "require" at-large seats for all Democratic governors and United States senators and congressmen, and C-4, to allow officeholders elected more than a year before the convention to serve as ex-officio delegates. To represent "those on whom the Party relies for continuing support and who must be its active supporters if national campaigns are to succeed . . . —Democratic mayors, state legislative leaders, state Party officials, fund-raisers, and labor, minority and community leaders," it argued that C-5 should be modified to authorize state committees to appoint one-fifth of the national delegation.[13] The coalition, at least, was explicit in identifying those whom it believed should be accorded preferential treatment, inaugurating its own nonelective quota for public and party officeholders. These revisions, it was contended, would introduce a balance and a professionalism to conventions absent in 1972, a meeting the CDM scorned as a gathering of amateurs, 83 percent of whom were attending their first national convention.

The group went beyond specifying these modifications of the original guidelines to recommend a series of what were for the most part minor housekeeping improvements. As to party caucuses, they advised meetings held on the same day statewide with adequate public notice (certainly in line with the intent of the original reforms); for newcomers, thirty-to-sixty-day prior party registration as a precondition for participation in party affairs, a restriction intended to help insure the presence of only "bona fide" Democrats; no meetings unless "someone duly authorized by the State Committee is present *with a list of all voters who are eligible to participate*" (italics added),[14] a provision that not only would be extraordinarily difficult to enforce, but one that would invite gross abuse; and several lesser suggestions for such things as adequate rooms for gatherings, simplified voting procedures (left unspecified), and the conclusion of meetings at a reasonable hour.

As to primaries, the association of like-thinking Democrats endorsed the national convention's actions in adopting rules limiting these elections to party members only (eliminating the "cross-over" vote) and outlawing the divisive "winner-take-all" primary. The convention had charged the New Delegate Selection Commission with devising a formula for the equitable division of the convention votes among contenders in a primary. CDM members recommended 10 percent of the vote as a minimum prerequisite for receiving a proportionate share of the state's delegation, although they would not apply this rule to nonbinding primaries (these were the people sympathetic to the Humphrey position on the California challenge) or to committee-selected ex-officio delegates, and their (and later Strauss's) feeling was that it should not be enforced on gatherings below the congressional-district level. Opportunism and principle, not surprisingly, walked hand in hand.

Finally, and quite correctly, the CDM encouraged the investigation of ways to implement the 1972 convention provision that an elected representative of a prospective presidential nominee be a bona fide supporter of that contender. The intent was to eliminate situations in which an individual ran on the ticket of the candidate most likely to sweep the district simply as a means of attending the convention. Through this stratagem and other, more systematic, perversions of the nominating system, delegates appeared at Miami Beach who gave a presidential candidate the required nomination vote but who supported the positions of other contenders (their real choices) on credentials challenges or Platform or Rules Committee issues.

In general, the coalition was supportive of the balance of the guidelines.

Most of these rules dealt with less contentious procedural matters. The differences the CDM chose to emphasize are significant, and directly reflect the belief that the reformers entertained a prescribed and limited sense of democratic performance, an antiprofessional bias, and an elitism that shortchanged the common man—the blue-collar worker, the ethnic, the elderly, and anyone else not included among the economically and educationally favored middle classes.

The bland wording of the CDM proposals and the seeming restraint that underlay their presentation belies the intensity of feeling associated with the antireform mood. The stakes were high—the future base of the party and the nature of its potential nominees—and there were few misconceptions on either side this time around. The contours of the battlefield had changed dramatically, though. Opponents and supporters were now arguing from a reform base. There was no question that the national structure instituted under the supervision of the McGovern-Fraser Commission would be retained; more than likely it also would be expanded into other areas of party operations. Both camps were conceding that reform had become an accepted fact of life. In effect, the more significant battle was not only over, it never took place. The questions debated were on the content of the rules, not their existence, and the groups that would be hurt or would benefit from their application, in itself an honored and conventional framework for political disagreements.

The CDM provided the most thoughtful and fully documented attack on the reform guidelines. It articulated nicely its own beliefs and forced into open debate the intellectual and political confusion behind several reform premises. While the McGovern-Fraser Commission had been considerably more conscientious in developing its basic value positions than, for example, the O'Hara Commission or the Republican party's DO Committee (which never tried), significant questions went begging: To whom would the system be opened? Whom, in fact, should it represent equitably or be biased toward? What constitutes a truly representative process? And what effect would the changes contemplated have on the party and its future success? The coalition brought these questions more pronouncedly into public discussion and, of course, in the process advanced its own answers.

The CDM served another function for the antireformers. It constituted a semipermanent body with financing, an able staff, political expertise, and access to party organs and the media, which could work continually to realize the antireform objectives. No such organization had existed in the early days of the reform movement. The antireformers had learned from their adversaries. Like the early reformers, they were in the position of attempting to force change in operational standards. They had to assume and maintain the initiative. Although conditions were favorable, this meant hard work, carefully developed arguments, a coordinated assault, and a day-to-day monitoring of events, functions that the new group pursued admirably. The CDM came, in time, to serve as a reference point for all of the interests—federated labor, party professionals, reform conservatives, unhappy academicians, and those with their eye on the forthcoming presidential nomination—disenchanted for varying reasons with the McGovern-Fraser guidelines. It would have its impact, although it was not to be as influential in reversing the direction of the reform emphasis as one might have expected early in the proceedings.

The New Delegate Selection (Mikulski) Commission

The New Delegate Selection Commission was associated with controversy from its birth to its premature death. No one questioned the need for a successor to the McGovern-Fraser Commission—there had simply been too much dispute and confusion associated with the original guidelines to leave them unattended—but virtually everyone envisioned different aims for the group. The national convention, without dissent, authorized the creation of the new reform committee, adding the curious proviso that it be appointed within sixty days of the close of the convention's deliberations (or while the McGovern forces still held power). As the dimensions of the McGovern defeat began to become apparent, attention within the party shifted to the naming of the new commission. Here the next major drama in the reform battle was to be played out.

The new national chairwoman, Jean M. Westwood, wasted little time. Almost concurrently with the official opening of the general election campaign (the end of the first week in September), she appointed the new group. Her thoughts, and those of many others, already were drifting toward the inevitable postelection repercussions. The committee was representative of all party elements, including articulate national spokesmen for the reform perspective. Leonard Woodcock, president of the sympathetic United Auto Workers, was designated chairman, and Baltimore City Councilwoman Barbara Mikulski, a mid-thirtyish former social worker expected to have a strong ethnic (especially Polish) identification, cochairperson. Woodcock soon requested a less time-consuming position, citing the press of union business. He and Mikulski then switched jobs.

The arrangement held only until August 1973, when Woodcock felt it necessary to withdraw entirely from the group's deliberations to devote his full time to the negotiations with the automobile manufacturers then underway. In the interim federated labor had become disenchanted with Mikulski, feeling her too sympathetic to the "New Politics" they detested. AFL-CIO spokesman Al Barkan proposed a commission member, Chicago lawyer and Daley lieutenant, Alex R. Seith, as not cochairman with a vice-chairman's responsibilities, but as cochairman with power over the staff and the commission commensurate with Mikulski's. Seith's most notable accomplishment to that point had been to serve as chairman of the

Cook County Zoning Board of Appeals. It was an audacious move. Predictably, an angry Mikulski objected. Then the controversy began to spread. Illinois Governor Dan Walker, a Democrat with national ambitions and an opponent of Daley's, announced his opposition to Seith's appointment (although Seith had supported Walker and other liberal candidates), and attempted to rally fellow governors around an alternative candidate, Richard Hatcher, the black mayor of Gary, Indiana. Another unwanted fight had erupted.

Daley, although not a prime mover in the affair, now felt challenged. Still smarting over his rejection at Miami Beach, he decided to display his strength within the national party and decided that Seith must carry as vice-chairman (not equal to Mikulski) despite Walker's objections. In effect Daley was pushing a compromise (although it was not advertised as such) in a fight he was now determined to win. In truth Daley cared little for what a national party committee might do, but he was concerned that his Illinois party opponent, Walker, not accumulate any unnecessary power or good press. On behalf of the AFL-CIO, Barkan reluctantly accepted Daley's position, but not before accusing Strauss and the national party of a double cross for not acceding to his wishes. The reformers found the arrangement acceptable although Mikulski seemed befuddled: "I don't know whether Strauss had the authority to make the appointment. All this has come about very quickly, with no real consultation with me. I never even got a letter of resignation from Woodcock."[15] To conclude the incident, within a few weeks the September commission meeting added Hatcher as a second vice-chairman. The inherent weaknesses of the party had been again demonstrated, and the bitter remnants of the earlier fights reinforced. All of this took place within months after the first commission meeting, a year after the convention that created it, and a year before its early demise.

The abbreviated history of the group was continually marred by such petty squabbles. Many felt that National Chairwoman Westwood had rushed in naming the committee to insure a liberal representation. Pressure was placed on Strauss, once elected chairman, to repudiate the commission or enlarge it, naming reform conservatives to the new posts. The AFL-CIO was particularly adamant in this regard. Strauss wavered, finally naming twenty-one new commissioners (supposedly to insure representation from all the states) for a super-sized final total of eighty-one members. The initial Strauss appointees did not offend most of the party, and the final committee had a fair degree of ideological balance.

THE MIKULSKI COMMISSION IN ACTION

The new group began its work with a get-acquainted meeting in late April 1973. The ambitious two-day gathering reviewed the regulations in effect, discussed prospective changes, defined the limits of the staff's authority (a decision forced by several of the more liberal reformers, curiously, who had been instrumental in providing the McGovern-Fraser Commission staff's impetus), and set the agenda for its activities. The now-mandatory regional public hearings were held in Milwaukee, Boston, San Francisco, Denver, Atlanta, and Baltimore, attended, it was claimed, by over two thousand, with three hundred persons submitting written testimony. An essentially pro-reform seventeen-member drafting subcommittee was created (endorsed by the 21 and 22 September commission meeting), which sequestered itself over two weekends to prepare the report that formed the basis for the full commission's proposals, adopted on 27 October 1973.[16]

The group's staff was built around a nucleus of six professionals (although it was to undergo violent paroxysms during its short life), originally led by Gerald Cassidy, a McGovern in-law and former general counsel to the Senate Select Committee on Nutrition and Human Needs, and including Carol Casey, a holdover from the McGovern-Fraser Commission staff who was the most knowledgeable member of the new group and the one who was conversant with the original commission's accomplishments.

The policy toward such problems as "unfaithful delegates," "crossover" voting, and "winner-take-all" primaries had already been decided by the 1972 convention, although the new reform group was to implement it. These actions initially left the Mikulski Commission free to grapple with the major unresolved issues. The committee's evaluation included all aspects of the "democratization" provisions, but tended to center on the problems associated with the most controversial of these: the quota concept, a proper definition of the roles of election and party officials in conventions, practical guidelines as to the representation of a presidential contender's strength at succeeding levels of the delegate selection process, and a review of the procedures instituted by the Credentials Committee (as stipulated by the O'Hara Commission) to adjudicate challenges.

In many respects the last item is the most interesting, especially when seen from the perspective of the long-term institutionalization of party processes.[17] The commission fully appreciated the cause of many of the difficulties faced by the party in its attempt to resolve credentials challenges. Essentially, the reformers had striven to enunciate fair standards to guide an open selection process. They had, in effect, attempted to impose a rule of law concept on an essentially political series of events. As the commission noted, the Democrats were moving toward the institution of a body of national party law although, outside of the recent work of the O'Hara Commission, they had given little thought to the need of a vehicle to enforce fairly and without prejudice the regulations being drawn up.

For party laws to be meaningful, they must be enforced in a manner which all recognize to be uniform, predictable, evenhanded and politically neutral. Systems of law enforcement generally strive toward fair application of laws through the promulgation of laws that are clear, unambiguous and concise, and through the establishment of an impartial judiciary, free from the political pressures of the moment. To achieve the latter, an impartial judiciary, in the context of National Convention delegate selection rules requires a "depoliticization" of the credentials certification process. In 1972, the most obvious weakness of the McGovern-Fraser Commission Rules was the inherent conflict between Judicial functions assigned to the Credentials Committee and the political nature of its selection, composition and primary role, i.e., acting as delegates for a particular nominee, at the Convention. Accordingly, the Committee's decisions are unavoidably influenced by the political ramifications of a challenge, rather than the merits of the dispute.[18]

The Charter Commission had met the same problem with a recommendation for a within-party judicial structure similar to an appellate court system. The Mikulski Commission took a different road, advising the creation of a Compliance Review Commission to act as a "preliminary Credentials Committee." The proposed new national-level group would monitor the delegate selection process in each of the states, implicitly enforcing the national party rules but also operating as an arbitrator in challenges to state practices, and, it was hoped, resolving these well before the national convention. The intent of both commissions was to keep such matters from the federal courts, in the belief that the increasing tendency to draw the court system into party disputes would eventually destroy what little authority the political parties retained. The objective also, of course, was to lessen political misunderstanding and its attendant frictions wherever possible.

Conservatives had wanted Strauss and the Democratic National Committee staff, sympathetic to the party's regulars, to oversee compliance. At a breakfast meeting on 13 October attended by Strauss, Hatcher, and Ohio Governor Gilligan, among others (although not Mikulski), the compromise had been decided upon. It was presented to the drafting subcommittee, which, by account of Robert Vance, the Alabama State Democratic Chairman and an opponent of Wallace who was generally supportive of the reforms, found it "pretty good." According to Vance, "Both sides are suspicious and neither can control it. So it must be fair!"[19]

Mikulski then campaigned for the chairmanship of the proposed committee, implicitly accepting the logic of the argument that her commission was meant only to form the substance of the reforms but not enforce them, and thus allowing her body to die a quick death. Strauss opposed her candidacy on the valid grounds that someone of more national stature was needed (and, it can be assumed, someone more acceptable to the party regulars and federated labor), someone who was less identified with the substance of the measures to be enforced. Strauss favored former Mayor Robert F. Wagner of New York, a choice well received by almost all party elements.

Mikulski and Strauss then engaged in a cat-and-mouse game as to their respective appointments to the new committee (each had five)[20] that consumed a good deal of energy through the winter months. In the final analysis both the Mikulski and Strauss lists strived for an ideologically balanced and representative party slate. Without such moderation, the Compliance Review Commission had little chance.

On other matters the Mikulski Commission's actions drew a reaction less hostile than anticipated. Party conservatives specifically wanted an end to implied quotas and the prohibitions against closed slatemaking, proxy voting, and ex-officio delegates. The remaining reformers opposed these concessions and in turn sought proportional representation of a presidential candidate's strength down to the precinct level and a commitment that all prospective delegates would have to declare their preference as a guide for voters.[21]

With reformers willing to compromise some and party regulars accepting the concept of national party rules guaranteeing fair and broad access to selection procedures, the two sides were not as far apart as their rhetoric might indicate. The Coalition for a Democratic Majority, for example, opposed proportional representation at all levels in non-primary states (while favoring it for binding primaries), but its opposition to the institution of the practice was less intense for races at the congressional district and above in any state. The grounds for compromise thus existed on this and other issues. The resolution of this problem centered more on assessing what was practicable and, in its final form, cut across any clearly drawn ideological lines.

The 10 percent "fair reflection" (proportional representation) rule was initially applied to all stages of the delegate selection process. On other questions, the National Committee was "urged" to extend "privileges" (although not voting rights) to Democratic governors, United States senators, congressmen, and members of the National Committee; in truth this was a tactful rejection of the ex-officio argument, although it built into the convention a potential role for party officials. Closed slatemaking was approved as long as no slate received the "official" party designation or preferential treatment by the party or through state law and all slates met identical qualifying requirements for appearing on the ballot, a realistic solution more in line with the original objectives behind the criticisms directed against closed selection processes. The committee went on to permit proxy voting under specified conditions. A state party could (but was not required to) allow a duly accredited participant in a meeting, once he or she appeared and established his or her identity, to leave a proxy with another individual if no bona fide alternate was present. A person was permitted to hold up to three proxies, a resolution that appeared to meet the practical objections to the total ban and still avoid the abuses associated with the practice.

The quota idea gave way begrudgingly. The party wished to free itself from the incubus of mandatory categorical representation but it was also sensitive to charges that it blinded itself to the reality of state-level discriminatory actions. To accomplish its ends it reaffirmed its commitment to the "six basic elements" that grew out of the 1964 convention. It prohibited discrimination based on "race, sex, age, color, national origin, religion, ethnic identity, or economic status." To encourage full participation of, in particular, "minority groups, Native Americans [ethnics], women, and youth" in delegate selection and all party affairs (seemingly a purview beyond its immediate powers), the commission mandated that the state parties adopt and implement alternative action programs.[22] These programs were to be submitted for approval to the Compliance Review Commission by mid-December 1974 with implementation to begin by mid-March of the following year.

The participation of the target groups within the party was to be judged against "their presence in the Democratic electorate,"[23] a standard (if enforced) much tougher than the previous reliance on their proportionate representation in a state's population and technically one harder to implement. Explicitly, however, mandatory quotas were not to be used to reach the objective, and composition of a state's convention delegation would not alone constitute a prima facie case of discrimination. The burden of proof in such challenges shifted from the state party (where it had been under the McGovern-Fraser rules) to the challenger, a situation more in keeping with traditional party practice but historically one that challengers had a difficult time meeting. Finally, and notwithstanding any other requirements, an equal division of party positions between men and women was not prohibited. Provision was made for local groups to review a state's affirmative action program and later, if needed, to challenge its implementation. Effectively the quota concept had been killed. To what extent the party would revert to its prereform apathy on the question remained unclear, but any total abdication of the duty to represent such groups was unlikely given their increasing political savvy.

Beyond its decisions in these areas, the commission effectively implemented the policies adopted by the 1972 convention. "Cross-over" voting was abolished ("State parties must take all feasible steps to restrict participation in the delegate selection process to Democratic voters only")[24] and through a clarification of the wording on the unit rule and the requirements on proportional representation of candidate strength, the ban on the "winner-take-all" primary was endorsed. A presidential candidate was given the right to approve all delegates offering themselves for election in his name and to require them to sign a statement of support; no delegate, in turn, could be forced to vote against his or her stated presidential preference—requirements it was hoped would prove an antidote to the "unfaithful" delegate problem.

Having accomplished its major objectives, the commission proceeded to clarify in more specific terms each of the provisions it required, allowing the state parties less leeway and intending to avoid the interpretative conflicts that arose in abundance during the previous presidential nomination contests. The commission elaborated the content of party rules to be made available at no cost ninety days prior to the start of the initial delegate selection actions and in no case later than 1 January of the election year: a failure to pay a cost or fee could not exclude a person from any stage of delegate selection; meetings were to begin at reasonable hours on (with some exceptions) uniform dates within a state; the 40 percent quorum provision was not applied to the first level of delegate selection, a stage at which accurate membership figures are elusive; four formulas were proposed (equal weighting of population and the Democratic presidential vote in the previous two elections; equal weighting of the Democratic presidential and gubernatorial vote in the most recent election; party registration combined with the measure of presidential strength; or a compromise giving one-third value to each "pure" standard) for the intrastate apportionment of national convention delegates, and each body prominent in the selection process had to be apportioned in relation to some measure of population and/or Democratic strength. Reformers managed to keep the requirement that all potential delegates formally identify their presidential preference (or absence thereof), but regulars succeeded in hiking the proportion of delegates a state committee could appoint to 25 percent (up from 10 percent and a substantial concession), provided the state committee was selected openly in full compliance with specific commission regulations. A delegate who resigned was permitted to select his or her replacement (where feasible) from among the elected alternates, choosing someone of the same political preference and, if possible, someone from the same political subdivision. In case of a delegate's death, the delegation would fill the position giving weight to the same considerations required of the original delegate.[25]

After some indecision and the usual debate, the executive committee made two mild changes in the Mikulski Commission's rules, modifications that were accepted by National Chairman Strauss and the National Committee. The 10 percent base requiring delegate representation was raised to 15 percent, and the membership of the Compliance Review Commission was increased from the original seventeen to twenty-five. According to a principal supporter in the actions before the National Committee, the final adoption was anticlimactic. On the day the National Committee met, she reported, "He [Strauss] came up to me and said, 'Billie, what is it you want?' I told him we wanted the Delegate Selection Commission report adopted as it was. He told me he only wanted two changes. I told him we could probably live with the fifteen percent on proportional representation but that I'd like to know who the twenty-five members of the C.R.C. would be. He turned to an aide and said, 'Give her a list.' I took it to our caucus and we went over it and decided it was fair." She concluded, "We got eighty-five percent of what we wanted."[26] Neither side did badly in the complex bundle of compromises that emerged from the Mikulski Commission's deliberations. The overall impact was to make the reforms more palatable to all party segments without seriously compromising their integrity.

THE AFTERMATH OF THE MIKULSKI COMMISSION

The period of reevaluation ended when the Mikulski Commission disbanded. The Compliance Review Commission added little of substance to the process. It met sporadically to review proposals and regulations submitted from varying states and to clarify the nature of the demands being made upon the state parties.

The body had no real power to compel the state parties to do anything and no particular desire to do so. Its chairman, former New York Mayor Wagner, was known as a compromiser and a conciliator. He was a party regular and his tenure was expected to be uneventful. The commission's staff was controlled by the National Committee and in reality was an extension of it. This had not been the case with the McGovern-Fraser, O'Hara, and Mikulski commissions, which had preceded it. The new development signaled several things. The creative reform period begun in the wake of the 1968 fiasco had ended. This fact was recognized by reformer and regular alike. The demise of the Mikulski Commission effectively ended this aspect, easily the most important one, of the reform drive.

Second, the regulars and conservatives, through their control of the national party offices, the sources of funding, and the timing and agenda of future meetings would, in their way, effect something of a comeback. As events unfolded they would be given the opportunity to rewrite the content of reform provisions and to oversee their enforcement. They would take advantage of the opportunity. But few would care.

Once a reform is introduced and, in its way, accepted, it is virtually impossible to turn back the clock. Once delegate selection had been opened to the party base, once the concept of a fair regulation of the proceedings had been implanted and rules governing these written and accepted, once the new reforms had been experienced, there was little of a fundamental nature the party's right wing could accomplish. The battle had been fought and the outcome was established. The regulars and conservatives would rewrite some of the rules and they would be more assertive in appointing and staffing future reform committees, but the fight was over. The basic principles of the reform movement were established and, in truth, it mattered relatively little what the regulars did. The party had been opened. It could not afford serious disagreement or fundamental conflict over rules, and it would go to extremes to avoid it.

If the foregoing is an accurate assessment of the period from 1969 to

1974, what, then, was left for the Compliance Review Commission and its successor, the Winograd Commission, to do, and on what basis could they be expected to decide the issues that would come before them? The application of the new rules to the states formed the substance of the CRC's deliberations. Predictably, with the basic substance of the issues not in contention, meetings became focused on controversies over political advantage, a type of concern professional politicians are far more comfortable with. Issues that came before the CRC were often decided by votes projected on the basis of which potential presidential contender would be likely to benefit the most (for example, the liberal Udall or the more conservative Jackson, the expected front runners at the time). Such a calculus is risky under any conditions, and the events of 1976, including the success of Jimmy Carter, the greatest long shot and the most pronounced outsider in the field, proved how futile an exercise it can be.

The CRC received little media or public attention. Its public-relations value for the party (and that of its successor, the Winograd Commission) was minimal. Everyone had about had their fill of the reform controversies. The national press, in particular, quickly grew tired of the petty bickering and tedium that characterized the CRC meetings. Even the National Committee, which through its staff effectively controlled the CRC, experienced some reservations. In its October 1975 meeting, the National Committee directed the CRC to pass only on the substance of affirmative action programs submitted by the states. The CRC's powers had been severely reduced and its role restricted to the one area on which there was close to universal agreement in the party.

The prohibition was possibly unnecessary, and under any conditions was virtually impossible to enforce. The CRC meandered on its uneventful way, a cluttered addition to the long reform drive.

The Credentials Committee and the 1976 Convention

The CRC submitted its preliminary report on 26 June to the convention's Credentials Committee. It had found two states, North Dakota and Utah, in partial noncompliance with the national party's rules on delegate selection. The issues raised were hardly momentous. North Dakota had a qualification in the right of a presidential candidate to approve delegates who ran on his behalf that the CDC found unacceptable, and the Utah party was found wanting in its method of selecting alternate delegates and deciding delegate succession and in a ban of public and party officials from seeking convention seats at the congressional district level.

In marked contrast to the Credentials committees of the conventions of 1964, 1968, and 1972, that of the 1976 national convention had no serious business to come before it. It met for three days rather than the two weeks set aside for some of its predecessors, and it adjourned each session early. The committee was scheduled to hear fifty challenges. By the time it met, all but seven had been resolved. It did not concern itself with the minor transgressions of the North Dakota and Utah parties. In the only challenges of any possible note, some delegates from Florida who did not have presidential candidate Jimmy Carter's specific approval (but were for him nonetheless) were amicably replaced by some who did and, in an affirmative action dispute, two white at-large delegates from Pennsylvania were quietly replaced by blacks. The noisiest challenge to come before the group was one involving two warring party factions from Puerto Rico. The dispute grew out of internal party strife on the island. It had nothing to do with the reforms. The Credentials Committee submitted no minority report to the convention. It had little to do and nothing to argue about, a result of the general acceptance of the reforms and an appreciation (absent from years earlier) of how they worked.

Also, there was no political capital to be gained through reform challenges (unlike the acrimonious debate by the Humphrey and McGovern factions over the California delegation in 1972). Jimmy Carter had laid undisputed claim to the party's nomination well before the Credentials Committee met. By the time of the national convention, Carter had no viable opponents, making any challenge over the rules for whatever purpose somewhat pointless.

The Charter (Sanford) Commission

The last unfinished business from the reform wave of the late sixties and early seventies involved the attempt to furnish a national party constitution and through it a codified national body of law relevant to all party structures.[27] What had been the stepchild of the reform movement from the beginning assumed new importance after the 1972 convention. Seemingly embarrassed by the belated joint effort of the two earlier reform commissions to create an acceptable party charter, all sides at the convention appeared determined to smuggle the issue by the delegates with a minimum of discussion. The convention did enlarge the National Committee from 110 to 303 members and did make it more generally representative of the party base, and it did authorize a new commission (eventually chaired by Terry Sanford, a former North Carolina governor, a 1972 darkhorse presidential aspirant, and a southern moderate and party regular in good standing with all elements of the party). To some the effort to formulate a national constitution for the party represented the one real opportunity to institutionalize a party and in the process make it more representative of its base and more effective in executing its duties as broker between its supporters and their elected officials in Washington. To others the new Charter Commission was another unwelcome irritant, a threat to the old ways whose one virtue might be the chance to deal a lasting blow to the entire reform syndrome.

Controversy was assured. In mandating the reform group the convention also authorized a midterm convention, to be held in 1974, the first of its kind and a vehicle reformers since the nineteenth century had sought as a means to update the party platform and to articulate the views of the party membership in the interim between national conventions. Party regulars, of course, abhorred the idea. Officeholders and the AFL-CIO leadership felt it intruded on their concerns, and they did all in their power to influence the national chairman to schedule it after the midterm elections (so as not to complicate these contests), which he did, and to deny it the right to discuss policy issues, a position with which he sympathized.[28]

The Sanford Commission had two pressing immediate concerns. First, it had to devise an equitable means of selecting delegates to some type of representative off-year national convocation. Second, it had to frame, prior to arriving in Kansas City (the site chosen for the meeting) in December 1974, a reasonably attractive party constitution that would appeal to most party groups. Neither job proved easy.

The commission set the size of the upcoming convention at a healthy 2,035. Eschewing the work of both previous delegate selection committees, the group devoted a great deal of time to framing its own procedures and rules for the selection of the convention membership. Ex-officio delegates were permitted; in fact, 337 seats were reserved primarily for Democratic governors and United States senators and congressmen. In a number of states, one-fourth to one-third of the delegation was reserved for non-elected (as delegates) ex-officio members (who, of course, had full delegate rights). The commission chose to permit a state option system for delegate selection, in effect allowing the state parties (controlled by the regulars) to fashion selection plans they found comfortable and from which no doubt they would benefit the most. The state parties did not miss their opportunity on this round, some creating elaborate multitiered certification and election procedures fathomable only to the professionals who designed them. The Sanford group did require that the state practices not be in violation of the McGovern-Fraser and Mikulski guidelines and it did provide a limited appeal process. A special party committee, composed of the executive committee of the Democratic National Committee and the chairmen of the two reform commissions (Sanford and Mikulski), was empowered to pass on the challenges that arose. Appeals to the convention floor were prohibited.

Delegate selection took place primarily during the first nine months of 1974. It aroused little media or public attention. Under the best of conditions, a convention devoted to assessing a technical document such as a party charter, devoid of the glamour of candidate selection or policy debate and protected by a complicated selection process, could expect to attract little notice. In competition with the unfolding Watergate scandal and the Nixon resignation, the entire process went unnoticed. Public involvement was minimal. Where they were so inclined, the party regulars easily dominated the proceedings.

The charter itself proved more interesting. Molded in four hard-working but basically uneventful sessions, it held some surprises.[29] Its presentation to the August 1974 meeting of the commission, the one intended to adopt the final wording to be presented to the December convention, provoked an unanticipatedly ferocious backlash. It compared to the worst of the encounters between reformers and party conservatives in the previous six years. The issues raised far transcended the structural proposals contained in the proposed constitution. Nonetheless, it was over these seemingly innocuous provisions that the storm broke.

The charter built upon the ideas contained in the original McGovern-Fraser/O'Hara Commission document, although it went well beyond the original. The products of a period of more intensive thought and labored compromises, the inclusions seemingly had the support of most of the party elements concerned with them (excepting, of course, the always truculent AFL-CIO leadership).

Article I, a preamble of sorts, listed the functions of the invigorated party the reformers sought. Several were culled from the previous by-laws of the National Committee (which were still in force at this point). More interestingly, the priorities had been reordered, giving added weight to policy articulation and educational functions as well as procedural guarantees of fair and unbiased treatment in a more open and responsive party organization. The phraseology was strikingly reminiscent of the McGovern-Fraser era, although the perspective was considerably more broad: The Democratic party should, it said, "establish standards and rules of procedure . . . to afford all members full, timely and equal opportunities to participate in decisions concerning candidates, party policy, and the conduct of party affairs without prejudice . . . and to promote fair campaign practice and the fair adjudication of disputes."[30] The charter went on to relegate state party rules and state laws to an inferior position, recognizing their force only when they did not conflict with the new constitution and national party by-laws (a move that effectively raised to a national policy level the actions of the McGovern-Fraser Commission during its enforcement period). The assumptions underlying the reform delegate selection rules were reiterated, again indisputably establishing their claim to national party supremacy. A midterm national party conference was authorized, although some wished to change the "shall hold" in the draft to the permissive but not mandatory "may hold." The membership, size, duties, and structure of the National Committee were spelled out in detail and were substantially similar to those already in effect. A minor disagreement over the national chairman's tenure led to a majority resolution that attempted a feeble distinction between a chairman appointed by the presidential contender for the campaign period and one who signed on for the duration between conventions. In all cases, a chairman could be removed (and elected) by a majority vote of the committee, a factor that bridged the gap between the proposals. Of more significance, Article VII established a Judicial Council, a revolutionary departure for the organizationally moribund American parties, and Article VIII created a National Education and Training Council, a more ambiguous body whose activities critics likened to those of the more settled European Social Democratic parties.

Explicitly, the Judicial Council was established "to decide challenges to procedures for the selection of delegates to National Conventions" and, if later authorized in party by-laws or by the National Committee (or, implicitly, the national convention, the supreme governing body of the party), "other disputes." The Democrats wanted no more of the efforts, so prevalent in 1972, of state parties as well as challengers turning to federal and state courts in attempts to win battles lost on the political fields. The members of the Charter Commission were well aware that, even as they met, the Daley faction, unseated by the 1972 convention, was keeping alive several court cases, including one pending before the Supreme Court that questioned the authority of any national party to establish its own rules and determine its own membership.[31] The charter itself was an effort to create an acceptable case of party law. The Judicial Council would rule on this body of law as it applied specifically to delegate selection, incrementally building a set of precedents that, through even-handed application, would eventually minimize conflicts over procedural questions and eliminate a reliance on outside agencies such as courts.

The nine members of the Judicial Council (intentionally analogous to the Supreme Court) were to be elected by a two-thirds vote of the National Committee for four-year terms. Candidates for the position should be "distinguished for their ability to act in a fair and impartial manner in party disputes." They could not include those who held other party offices or who were active in support of a presidential candidate. Next to the conception of the council itself, it was this effort to instill impartiality to which the leaders of federated labor and many party regulars most objected. The membership of the new court determined its own structure and operating procedures, although these could be amended by the National Committee.

Article VII had been adopted by a majority vote of the commission. A strong minority, over 40 percent of the membership, opposed it enough to include an alternative proposal in the draft charter, calling for the rejection of the entire idea. The dispute insured that the item would be a central topic of debate at the midterm convention.

The National Education and Training Council had an independence somewhat akin to the party court. Its nine members were appointed by the executive committee, under whose supervision it operated, and its ranks included the national chairman. Possibly its most interesting feature was a budget that was to be approved at least one year in advance of expenditures, thus legislating a thoughtfulness and continuity into anticipated operations not found in other party activities.

The charter also called for the National Committee to publish a fair campaign practices code, although enforcement provisions were left unspecified. Other features of the proposed constitution were now familiar: an affirmative action program; a national finance council much like the one in existence to fund party groups; an annual financial report available to the public; the use of *Robert's Rules of Order* at all meetings lacking other provisions; open party meetings for all committees and groups unless a majority of the membership voted otherwise; and a provision for regional organizations whose form and duties were left to future deliberation. A two-thirds vote of the National Committee or the midterm conference was needed to amend the party constitution once it was adopted.

The document was straightforward. It attempted to avoid the detail as to structure or selection procedures found in the earlier draft proposed by Fraser and O'Hara on behalf of their commissions. Intellectually it drew heavily from this earlier work. Its emphasis on broad principles was roughly similar to what the framers of the American Constitution attempted. Flexibility and growth potential were permitted through general statements of intent that left the spelling out in more appropriate detail to the principals of future committees or conferences.

Another Effort at Repeal

The issues still pending at the mid-August gathering of the Charter Commission included the word "shall" as against "may" hold, authorizing a permanent midterm conference; the Judicial Council; and the manner of specifying the national chairman's tenure. None of these issues was of sufficient concern to trigger the blowup that ensued. In fact, of themselves, they stimulated little passion in either reformers or party conservatives.[32] What did arouse the feelings of the delegates was the efforts of the AFL-CIO Meany-Barkan leadership, working through sympathetic commission spokesmen and Strauss and several of his lieutenants, to employ the meeting as a vehicle through which to scuttle not only the party charter but also the delegate selection reforms and the list of party innovations that, as some saw it, reached back through the McGovern-Fraser and O'Hara commissions[33] and Richard Hughes's Special Equal Rights Committee clear to the 1964 national convention. A decade of solid work, dictated by the troubles experienced by a fragmented party attempting to reconstitute itself, appeared open to revision. This perspective, at least, was shared by most of the 40 percent or so of the commission members who felt their only recourse was to walk out of the acrimonious meeting, denying the chair a quorum and forcing the issues before the December conference for resolution.

The background maneuvering leading to the commission meeting indicated trouble. Barkan, on behalf of the AFL-CIO, and Strauss, although they needed each other, had an acrimonious, tense, and unpredictable official relationship. Piqued at the substance of the Mikulski recommendations, Meany and Barkan followed the course they had two years earlier and broke off relations with the national party. Strauss, eager to regain the financial and organizational resources that COPE in particular made available to the party, decided to mobilize support for the more conservative of the alternatives at the upcoming August session of the Sanford Commission. Ironically, without any concerted organizational drive to pressure them, the moderate to conservative majority on the commission stood likely to adopt the less revolutionary measures on their merits. Either the party leaders were unwilling to chance this acceptance or they felt it was not enough. Thus the intrigue began. In June Strauss proposed that congressmen who served on the commission be permitted proxies. A suspicious Democratic National Committee executive committee, exercising an independence undreamt of in the pre-1972 era, rejected the plan, fearing an abuse of the practice that would serve to swing the Sanford Commission farther to the right. As the summer wore on Strauss and his agents systematically identified commissioners unlikely to attend and encouraged others, through intermediaries, to resign. Strauss then mobilized support for conservative replacements.

After several false starts the national chairman convened a bare majority of the executive committee on short notice to certify the replacements. Events were growing more nasty. Fraser, a member of both the Charter Commission and the National Committee's executive committee, registered alarm: "There has been a concerted effort to get people to resign . . . I think that it is bad politics. . . . In my twenty years in our state party in Minnesota, I've never seen an operation conducted like this. We don't go around trying to stock commissions at the last minute . . . it's an unnecessarily high cost to pay for the national party . . . there will be considerable hostility and bitterness."[34]

Strauss was unmoved. He brushed aside the criticism, calling the actions "routine" and indicating that "nothing controversial is coming up at Kansas City [the site of the meeting] anyways."[35] Nothing could be further from what actually transpired. The Democrats' penchant for self-destruction was about to evidence itself again, with a vengeance. It is worthwhile remarking at this point on the relative positions of the two parties during the period. The Republicans were saddled with the Watergate episode—a president undergoing the televised impeachment hearings of the House

Judiciary Committee, the collapse of his congressional support, and eventual resignation. The new president had a government to reconstruct and roaring inflation to curb. The Democrats looked impregnable in the November elections. The one possible nuisance seen by the regulars was the unpredictable midterm convention that was to be held in December. Their best strategy lay in keeping quiet and resolving any differences as expeditiously as possible. The December convention could then serve as a celebration of the party's openness, fairness, and unity, as well as its new political muscle (assuming the November elections turned out as expected). Instead, the influential AFL-CIO, with the party leaders' blessing (initially), managed to ignite what had been destined to be a lethargic summer meeting.

The regulars at the meeting were coordinated by a Barkan assistant (working on some of the earlier issues with a National Committee staff member) and led on the floor by Washington State Representative Thomas Foley, a Jackson supporter. The conservative position prevailed quickly and easily on the three points in the charter in question. Then the underlying tensions that had gnawed at the AFL-CIO leadership exploded. Clearly it had control of the convention. Federated labor[36] took out after the conservatives' bugaboo, the shadow of the old quota concept they managed to find in the charter. They moved to strike from the constitution the section on affirmative action programs that defined the objective of these state party programs to be "to encourage participation by all Democrats as indicated by their presence in the Democratic electorate in delegate selection processes and in all party affairs." The same paragraph states that the goal should not be achieved "directly or indirectly by the imposition of mandatory quotas." This assurance was not enough. Federated labor's representatives believed the provision established "implied quotas," and these, they argued, were no less pernicious than "mandatory quotas."[37]

The reformers were furious. Blacks in particular felt betrayed. They had compromised on the issue repeatedly in the name of party harmony, even agreeing to the critical substitution "encourage participation" for the far stronger "insure participation." Overdramatically, they and their supporters referred to the Foley-sponsored amendment as the "final rape" of the charter that was intended to drive blacks and women from the party. Alarmed by the angry debate, the warring groups attempted several compromises and finally agreed to carry the issue over to the December convention, with each side proposing two alternatives.

The seeming reprieve was only temporary. The delegates directly responding to the AFL-CIO initiatives (perhaps three dozen in all) went back to their prepared agenda and managed to have the commission kill (by a seventy-to-forty-six vote, a margin indicative of their overall strength at the meeting) the section of the charter permitting the national party to establish criteria for participation in primaries and other party affairs. One of the recently appointed substitute delegates (the wife of an AFL-CIO official)[38] took the floor to propose the delegates strip from the charter the ban on the unit rule, the prohibition on "winner-take-all" delegate selection, and the effort to insure proportional representation of a presidential candidate's strength. She also moved to permit delegate selection activities to begin earlier than 1 January of the presidential election year.

It is difficult to determine what possessed the conservatives at this juncture. They had pushed too far and, belatedly, they realized it. They attempted to modify their position on the unit rule, but the damage had been done. The blacks walked out, followed in short order by the balance of the liberal forces and some moderates, forcing adjournment of the meeting for want of a quorum. The issues were carried over to the December assembly.

The normally unflappable Sanford, viewing the wreckage of his once-peaceful commission, lamented the "error of judgment" he attributed to Strauss and the "inappropriate" behavior of Strauss's aides he held responsible for the disaster. Hodding Carter III, a young Mississippi publisher and early reformer, accused the conservatives of turning the charter into a "sham." "You're killing ten years of reform and eighteen months of work by this Commission," he protested. Rhetorically, Fraser asked "why anyone would want to revive the discredited unit rule unless they are so obsessed with turning back the clock they've lost sight of everything else." Perhaps the key to some type of understanding lies in these words. A national political correspondent reporting on the scene suggested that Meany and Barkan did not "want conciliation; they wanted control of *their* party back from those who, in their view, usurped its franchise when they nominated George McGovern in 1972" (italics added).[39] The columnist quoted old-time labor minions as comparing the battle to the purging of communists from the unions decades earlier; if they were not purged, they would subvert the organization.

Surely the labor representatives had overstated the nature of the confrontation. Nonetheless the analogy provides some idea of the intensity of the feeling underlying the entire reform struggle, and it gives some clue to the seeming irrationality and destructiveness of the eleventh hour attempt at repudiation.

The Midterm Convention

The charter debate at the midterm convention, as well as the convention itself, turned out to be something of an anticlimax. Perhaps in comparison to the volatile August session almost any meeting would have appeared tame. There were fireworks to be sure—triggered, as expected, by AFL-

CIO emissaries—which resulted in some angry floor clashes, but for the most part the meeting was harmonious and, at least as surprising, successful for almost all factions of the party.

Much had changed during the fall. Strauss had begun to realize that the situation as it stood after the August blowup verged on getting out of control, that the unity he had worked for above all else was about to evaporate. Party moderates began to seek the national chairman out. Had not the antireformers gone too far? Why alienate the blacks so? Why reopen reform issues seemingly successfully concluded? And of most immediate concern, why detract from the Republican party's problems by redirecting attention to questions that split the party along the disastrous lines of 1968?

The most effective group in heading off the impending disaster proved to be the Democratic governors. The governors met in November, after the midterm elections, and chose to place emphasis on the electoral success the party had enjoyed. They pointed with particular pride to the party's convincing victories in the off-year congressional races (due in large part to the Watergate backlash and a deteriorating economic situation). The party's bright future prospects intrigued them. The governors, mostly moderates themselves, believed that both the party's integrity and its electoral viability were best served by the compromises already reached by the Mikulski Commission on affirmative action and by the basically centrist positions on the other issues facing the Sanford Commission. They felt a middle-of-the-road course on the controversies facing the reform group to be most appropriate for guiding the party through its current difficulties. The delegates to the midterm convention, mostly centrists themselves, agreed. This resolution was not as conciliatory as it may appear. In effect, this decision meant a rejection of the AFL-CIO position.

Strauss had been moving, during the fall, in the same direction as the Democratic governors. By late November (with their prodding) he had come to embrace a centrist position on reform: retain the basically moderate compromises found in the original charter; avoid reopening fundamental reform issues not vital to the debate over the charter; appease as best he could the party's regulars while not alienating outright the reformers and blacks; sidetrack all emotional issues that might split the party; and, above all, come out of a quiet December meeting with a unified and harmonious party, strategically placed to battle effectively for the presidency two years hence.

It is probable that Strauss saw the December convention as the last real hurdle along the road to reform. The national chairman never favored reform; his background and his values carried him in quite another direction. He did desire party unity, though, and he did want the Democratic party to win the presidency in 1976. He also knew that his tenure as national chairman would be judged by criteria of electoral success (especially in relation to the presidency), and not by the contents of an arcane document of interest to only a few party members. If only the December confrontation could be rechanneled along constructive and harmonious lines, then Strauss was within view of achieving his objectives.

PRELIMINARIES TO THE MIDTERM CONVENTION

Strauss put his considerable energies into controlling every possible aspect of the midterm convention. His intention, of course, was to insure the outcome he sought. The national chairman had earlier, persuasively, pushed for delegate selection procedures left to the discretion of the state parties. Strauss and his staff effectively controlled the watered-down appeals process on delegate selection instituted for the midterm convention. At the convention itself he chaired the committee, supposedly representative of the midterm convention membership, that met immediately prior to the convention and passed on the substance of the proposals in the charter to be put before the full body. His assumption of such a position was most unusual. Strauss then ran the daily sessions of the midterm convention, relinquishing the gavel only to the authorized chairperson, for ceremonial functions, and to Sanford, for presiding over the substance of the technical debate on the charter itself.

The exercise was hardly a lesson in enlightened democratic procedures, but it worked. Strauss orchestrated something of a Democratic party love-in—in fact, at one point he rushed from the podium to plant a kiss on the cheek of a startled Richard J. Daley. The incident delighted photographers and discomfitted the jowly mayor. Daley had received the unwanted reward for agreeing at a crucial spot in the deliberations to sponsor a compromise that effectively terminated the controversy among party factions over the charter.

Not everyone, of course, was happy. The party regulars, centrists, pro-charter reformers, blacks, and others had found a new equilibrium, but federated labor was still unappeased. In the most explosive episode of the convention, an angry AFL-CIO representative took the floor to castigate Strauss personally and to warn both him and the party he represented to either stand with the Meany-Barkan faction or face defeat in the presidential election two years hence. Federated labor remained unreconciled to the end. But the party had made its choice.

THE CHARTER

Basically the adopted charter, or new party constitution, reverted to what it had been before the disruptive August meeting. The McGovern-Fraser rules as modified by the 1972 convention and the Mikulski Commission were endorsed as binding party regulations. The National Committee was further enlarged, this time to 350 members, and minimal procedural safeguards were introduced for the selection of National Committee representatives and for the conduct of National Committee meetings. All party gatherings were opened to the public. Annual written reports by the national party were required, and written rules of procedures for all state parties were mandated.[40]

On the more contentious issues, the midterm convention did vote to create a National Education and Training Council and a Judicial Council, although their operations and eventual impact remained hazy. It extended "affirmative action" programs to all party affairs. And it made provision for future midterm conventions (in effect making them optional) with specific arrangements left to the National Committee.

Its work completed, the midterm convention adjourned in a blaze of good fellowship. The last unfinished business of reform had been completed. Attention now turned to the choice of a presidential nominee. Many prospective candidates had actively sought the delegates' support during the convention, and the upcoming presidential election was less than two years away.

Yet Another Reform Group: The Winograd Commission

As the dog days of the Compliance Review Commission dragged on, Strauss and his assistants decided to create yet another body to consider reform questions. The new group, initially called the Commission on the Role and Future of Presidential Primaries, was specifically directed to look into one of the unexpected results of the earlier reform efforts—the unprecedented growth in number and importance of primaries in the presidential nominating process. The new commission also would give regulars one more chance to fashion whatever rules they could bring before their body in a manner more accommodating to their own interests.

The new reform commission, unlike its predecessors, was created and given its mandate in the fall of 1975 by the national chairman. This was unusual. All of the other major reform groups had been created by direct action of the national convention. The group was legitimatized by a largely disinterested national convention a year later and, by order of the convention, its name was changed to the Commission on Presidential Nominations and Party Structure. The new title helped bring under its jurisdiction, if it were so inclined, the broad substance of all of the previous reform bodies.

The commission's potential powers were enormous, but the group excited little interest. The public, the media, and the party at-large were clearly disinterested. The commission began slowly, accomplishing little in its first year. Its schedule of gatherings was episodic, and the meetings themselves were desultory and poorly attended. Most of its staff activities centered on acquiring information for potential commission deliberations on the projected impact of primaries on delegate selection, the national convention, and state and local party structure.

The reform fever had been spent. The ultimate impact of the new group seemed to be in giving the more persistent of the regulars an opportunity to nudge the party more along the lines of the closed party, with more stringent delegate selection procedures and built-in rewards to the regulars. One thing, however, was noticeably different.

Jimmy Carter, the rankest outsider of them all, was now in the White House. His choice, former Maine Governor Kenneth Curtis, was national chairman, and several White House underlings were placed in the commission to safeguard the president's interests. Carter had won the Democratic presidential nomination courtesy of the new rules. Under the old system, the former Georgia governor would not even have emerged as a serious regional threat. Yet the interests of a Carter in the White House were quite different from those of a Georgia farmer. Carter sided with the regulars; in fact, his people led the fight to tighten the requirements and close the system, the better to sidetrack any potential opposition to his renomination in 1980. The new talk centered on such things as encouraging "cohesion" and "consensus" within the party, encouraging "leadership" and rewarding "experience," long the concern of the regulars and reform conservatives. The most tangible form of the new push came in the proposal by the Carter emissaries to raise the division of the vote from 15 to 25 percent before contenders in, for example, primaries held at the state or congressional district level could claim any national convention delegate votes. The game continued long after just about everyone had lost interest.

The creation of the Winograd Commission bore witness to several things. First, reform activities were now accorded respectability, and the public and the party membership were willing to accept and even look with favor on new reform bodies. At the same time, the mass of party followers and state party leaders remained thoroughly disinterested in the proceedings and their implications. Both the reform mood and its emotional backlash had long since passed.

Secondly, the Winograd Commission demonstrated the persistent desire of some of the party regulars at the national level and the ideological conservatives (on party matters) within the party to have another crack at the post-1968 rules.

And, finally, commissions such as the Winograd body may be created with regularity in order to afford incumbents and the faction controlling the national party at any given time the opportunity to fashion delegate selection procedures in the manner most amenable to their own success. The rules of the decade that began in 1968 are not in danger of being repealed. But they can be modified and reshaped to favor one group or individual or another. The lesson is that this, one of the oldest political battlegrounds, will be a constant draw for those inclined to do battle. The curious thing is that now such attacks can be cloaked in the respectable ideology of ever new "reforms."

The early part of the period from 1972 to 1976 was generally one of reacting to the changes initiated by the McGovern-Fraser Commission. The consequences of the standards of delegate selection adopted between 1969 and 1972 had, for the first time, become strikingly clear. The extraordinary revolution in the process of choosing a presidential nominee and the extent to which this represented a departure from previously accepted ways had finally sunk in. The seventies, which initially had appeared to promise a dismantling of the new forms, gave way in short order to a consolidation.

The work of the Mikulski Commission is notable for two things: First, the final acceptance by the party of procedures a few years earlier many had felt approximated a new-left coup. The value and necessity of modernized and more open methods of selecting presidential nominees came to be appreciated by most factions within the party. The anticipated gutting of the reforms never took place. Secondly, the Mikulski Commission made the McGovern-Fraser rules more livable and more acceptable to most (again, the AFL-CIO is the consistent exception) within the party. The initial guidelines were experimental, although, of course, they were enforced with a vengeance. The outcome of the Mikulski Commission deliberations made the rules more functional and more in line with the needs and power distributions with the party's confederation. This was a signal contribution.

The one new reform thrust during the four years beginning in 1972 came with the codification and then endorsement of the party charter. Even this action was not totally new. It built on the work of the McGovern-Fraser and O'Hara commissions and completed the one piece of business they had left unattended. The charter adopted in December 1974 closely resembled that proposed in May 1972 as a virtual afterthought by the two combined earlier commissions, a document that the turbulent 1972 national convention did not have the energy to consider.

The new party charter could represent a significant shift in the practice of American politics. Power and responsibility could gravitate markedly to the national level and, for the first time, the United States would have a reasonably unified and coordinated party structure with a clear sense of priorities, a strong infrastructure, and a programmed and systematic approach to its duties. Certainly, the powers to develop such a combat-effective and policy-oriented party vehicle are locked within the charter. An early assessment, however, is that the potential for new departures within the party organization will have to await future developments. The party charter's early contributions suggest only marginal differences in the way the national party is operating. The state delegates to the National Committee appear more independent of the national chairman, and the newly constituted executive committee appears willing to dispute with him occasionally, but neither has exercised any significant control over the national chairman, his staff, or the commitments they make in the name of the party as a whole.

The natural end to the reform era came in 1974 with the demise of the Mikulski and Sanford commissions. The period following this represents a refining of procedures previously endorsed and a battle for minor concessions that could result in projected political advantages for a prospective presidential candidate or a party faction. These years, and maneuverings, constitute a cluttered ending to an emotionally and historically significant period. Yet the period was one that presaged the future: "reform" committees, created and subtly controlled by party professionals, will continue as a fact of political life. Such committees appear to be looked on with general approval by the public and by party members. At a minimum they could provide a modest public-relations yield, an important consideration for a national party. On a different level, however, their intent will be to provide those who create them an opportunity to forward their own interests by modifying rules in ways that will best promote their own ends. The reform movement has long since spent itself; reform could become subject to the interests of a few, dealing in esoterica, beyond the scrutiny or real concern of the public, the media, or the party membership.

EIGHT

Further Considerations on Reform

THE REFORMS INTRODUCED a remarkable era to American politics. More was attempted, and accomplished, than can truthfully be said to have been envisioned in the decades since the Progressive movement of the early 1900s. Remarkably, the reforms had been initiated and executed by a political party that perceived itself to be in trouble. In contrast to earlier attempts at political change, the intent was to strengthen and preserve an institution of incomparable value to the American political system rather than to destroy or replace it.

The changes introduced were many. The traditional priorities of American party structure had been reversed. The national party units had attempted, with some success, to establish a code of fair and decent behavior and to have it prevail in the conduct of party business. A sense of rationality had been introduced into an incredibly complex system, and an aura of openness and equity had begun to prevail in several areas— changes in the presidential nominating process, the most significant of the national parties' duties, appeared to be an excellent foreboding of future changes in all aspects of party operations. A series of organizational structures and institutional values, little changed since the formation of the political parties over a century and a quarter earlier, were giving way to a new sense of national purpose and, it was hoped, a relevancy and responsiveness to constituent pressures, responsibilities neither party had acquitted impressively over the years.

The political implications of what the reformers were attempting to accomplish were never far from mind. The work of the reformers would effectively open the party in two regards. First, it would permit new groups to enter and make their views as to policy or candidates felt without depending on the goodwill or sponsorship of party elders whose favor they would have had to curry. Second, it would develop the foundation for establishing a permanent set of rules that would treat all with an impartiality previously unknown in party circles. It is too much to argue that such

objectives were achieved by the first, and more than likely the most decisive, of the reform bursts, but a substantial beginning had been made.

Party processes were given a new legitimacy at a time when parties had
begun to appear increasingly irrelevant to the solution of the main problems besetting American life and when both the party and the political
system more broadly needed whatever support they could muster. In these
terms then—and they are impressive—the reform movement, and most
significantly the achievements of the McGovern-Fraser Commission, had
accomplished a good deal. In its own way the reform era constituted a
revolution in party operations, notable as much for its impact on traditional modes of thinking as on the structures it placed in question. One
would be hard pressed to find comparable moments of achievement in the
long history of political parties in this nation.

What Reform Accomplished: The Long-Run Implications

The ramifications of the reform period were many. A listing of the
accomplishments and their broader implications would include the following.

Opening the Party

The party was opened and, in the process, made more responsive to and
representative of its rank and file. The new openness was meant to extend
to all aspects of the party organization. The effort was made, for example,
by the Sanford Commission, to extend procedural guarantees of fair play
to party organizations from the local to the national levels. The party
charter set standards and established guidelines for all manner of party
deliberations. The Sanford Commission, in conjunction with the
McGovern-Fraser, O'Hara, and, to a lesser extent, Mikulski commissions,
attempted to restructure party institutions to make them more responsive
to grass-roots sentiments.

The most notable success in opening the party to influence from the
rank and file was the transformation of the presidential nominating process. The work of the McGovern-Fraser Commission, of course, was responsible for turning a relatively closed nominating process, controlled
primarily by the party regulars, into one directly reflective of the concerns
of those party members who chose to participate in delegate selection.

Rearranging Power Distributions within the Party

In the process of opening presidential nominations, the power relationships within the Democratic party were rearranged. Gaining increased
influence were the party activitists and candidate supporters who worked

during presidential election years to advance a cause, an issue, or a presidential contender with whom they identified. For the most part, these tended to be the professional people—lawyers, businessmen, teachers— and the young persons, blacks, housewives, and minority groups attracted to the party during the significant prenominating races. Losing influence were the power-wielders of the pre-1972 period: the party regulars, elected officials (governors, congressmen, senators, mayors, state legislators), party organizational personnel (state chairmen, national committee representatives, county chairmen), and the "fat cats," as they were called, of the business world who sought influence in politics by bankrolling candidates and campaigns and on whom the party had been heavily dependent.[1] Also losing power in the new alignment favored by the reform procedures were the southern states and their parties, which were experiencing transformations, and the old-line factions and interest groups at the state and national levels, which had at least been consulted on nominations. These latter groups had held, in many cases, a negative veto over both candidates for the presidential nomination and the issues treated in the party platform.

The most dramatic example of the last category would have to be the labor unions and, in particular, the Meany-Barkan group dominant in the AFL-CIO federation. Organized labor had provided much of the money and resources for many campaigns and had underwritten a number of party activities. Labor represented the most powerful single interest group within the national Democratic party's coalition. However, by 1976, quarrels that had eventually spilled over into arguments with normally sympathetic regulars, such as organized labor's intransigence on reform questions, its repeated efforts to roll back reform initiatives, and its personal antagonism to many of the reform leaders, had led to the undermining of its influence within the party. The AFL-CIO continued to be a significant contributor to the congressional campaigns of Democratic candidates, but its concern with the national party affairs lessened. The opposition of the Meany leadership to the reforms helped dramatize the split within labor ranks between the more conservative building trades unions and other unions with younger and more aggressive leadership. The latter did not want to break openly with George Meany. They were, however, amenable to the reforms and more attuned to the social currents and political tides at work in the nation. During the reform period of 1968– 1976, the divisions within labor's ranks became more noticeable. The United Auto Workers, under Leonard Woodcock and his successor, Douglas Fraser (no relation to Donald Fraser of the McGovern-Fraser Commission), continued their independent ways, and other union leaders (such as Jerry Wurf of the American Federation of State, County, and Municipal Employees) began, quietly at first but then with more assurance as the years progressed, to chart their own initiatives on political and reform questions.

The challenge of the AFL-CIO's power within the national party was but one example of the reshuffling of political priorities that resulted from the turmoil caused by the reforms. Enough traditional interests within the Democratic party had been abruptly displaced and their influence over party affairs proportionately reduced to insure that the issues raised by the reforms would not be completely settled for years to come.

The Nationalization of the Party

The reform movement altered the power distributions within the Democratic party in an even more fundamental way. The historic relationship between the national party and its local and state units was altered, and before reform had run its course, dramatically reversed. Traditionally, the national party exercised little real power in party matters. This role was reserved for the state and local units, the party agencies presumed to be closest to the voter. The national party appendages were relatively inactive. They occasionally provided skilled services to state and local parties in such areas as registration, polling, and getting-out-the-vote campaigns, but their contributions seldom went beyond the level of rudimentary back-up support. The national parties, of course, did hold their semiannual national committee meetings, but these were uneventful gatherings of no particular significance to the parties at any level. The national party also supervised the arrangements for the quadrennial national convention. Here the power over the convention scheduling and agenda could be significant to the faction controlling the national chairmanship at the time. The national party, however, had little concern over such basic practices as delegate apportionment formulas, settled by tradition, or the delegate selection practices within the states, controlled by the state parties and influenced by local political customs and power arrangements.

All of this changed abruptly, and more than anyone could ever have predicted, because of the McGovern-Fraser Commission. Building on the precedent established by the (Richard) Hughes Special Equal Rights Committee, the McGovern-Fraser Commission required the state parties to enact changes demanded by itself, the offspring of the national party. The basic argument was that the national conventions could deny representation to any state party not enacting the reform proposals. The assumption, of course, was that the national party had such authority and that in the areas delineated, its authority was supreme. The argument was boldly put by the McGovern-Fraser Commission and its staff, but, to a large extent, it was a bluff. The previous practice and politics of national conventions provided little encouragement to any reform commission to depend on the convention to discipline state parties and to enact extensive change. The national conventions are in reality gatherings of the state parties, and had enough of the state parties appreciated the extent of the reforms, they could have easily banded together to neutralize any potential national convention sanctions.

The state parties were very slow to realize the ramifications of the demands. For the most part, the resistance to the reform pressures was sporadic, uncoordinated, and isolated. Not until well into the prenomination candidate selection process in the early spring of 1972 did many states come to realize the severity of the requirements—rigorous compared with previous practices at least—and the seriousness of the implementation. The states raised challenges through the normal processes available to them that were heard at the national convention. However, at this point, they were asking the balance of state parties, most of whom had now met the reform standards, and a presidential candidate with the balance of votes at the convention, who was also most closely identified with the reforms, to make exceptions for them. In most instances, the cases put forward by the reneging states were not strong. Their arguments rested mostly on political considerations in a convention weighted in the other direction, and they evoked little sympathy.

The most severe test of the new national party supremacy doctrine came in the challenge from the Chicago delegation to the 1972 Democratic National Convention.[2] The challenge was noteworthy on two levels: political and judicial.

The Chicago Democratic party was the best organized and most powerful single party unit within either of the two national parties. Its leader, Mayor Richard J. Daley, had been a dominant influence in Democratic party politics at least since the 1960 presidential election, when he was considered instrumental in delivering, first, the Democratic nomination and, second, the state of Illinois to John Kennedy. The Illinois vote in the general election was crucial to Kennedy's victory.

The Mayor paid little attention to the evolving reform efforts. He had been a principal—a negative symbol, perhaps—in the events that had set the reform chain in action, and he had little sympathy with the reformers, their problems, or their proposed solutions.

Daley ran the Chicago delegation in his usual style in 1972, and when challenged on failing to comply with the newly enacted reform guidelines, he appeared little concerned.[3] He reasoned, as did many others, that the Democratic National Convention could not afford to incur the displeasure of, much less to discipline, so powerful a political figure or an organization whose electoral strength was vital to the party's success. As matters turned out, of course, the convention voted to unseat the Chicago delegation, an outcome as startling and unprecedented as any during the reform years.[4]

The Chicago Democrats were embittered by the rejection. Frustrated and angry, they began a series of court actions intended to challenge the national party's authority, to reverse its decisions and, if possible, to penalize the insurgents who had unseated them and those who had supported them. The cases were to drag on in the courts for years. The most significant, *Cousins* v. *Wigoda*, was decided by the United States Supreme Court in January of 1975. The outcome and the Court's decisiveness in handling the issues were to affect national party and local party relationships more than most expected.

THE SUPREME COURT ACTS

The Daley Democrats believed their legal case was as strong as their political one. They argued that they had been legally elected in the March 1972 primary and therefore should have been seated by the national convention. These elections met all the requirements of the Illinois statutes. The insurgents who had attempted to unseat them had not been elected in the primary in which over 700,000 voters had participated. If the act of the national convention were sustained it would place party rules over state laws; void the results of the primary election, thus negating the decision of the voters; and run counter to previous court decisions on related questions. The argument had a great deal of merit. The Illinois Appellate Court, in fact, found for the Daley Democrats. This decision was appealed to the Supreme Court for final adjudication.

The Appellate Court agreed that the Daley delegation had been chosen in violation of party rules, which had been contended by the Democratic party, the 1972 Credentials Committee, and the 1972 Democratic National Convention. It went on to maintain, however, that "[t]he right to sit as a delegate representing Illinois at the national nominating convention is governed exclusively by the Illinois Election Code" and that "the purposes and guidelines for reform adopted by the Democratic National Party in its Call for the 1972 Democratic National Convention . . . in no way take precedence in the State of Illinois over the Election Code."[5] The Appellate Court made its position very clear. It declared that "[t]he law of the state is supreme and party rules to the contrary are of no effect . . . ;" "the interest of the state in protecting the effective right to participate in primaries is superior to whatever other interests the party itself might wish to protect . . . ;" and "since . . . [the Daley Democrats] were admittedly elected to the position of delegates to the 1972 Democratic National Convention by operation of the Election Code, an Illinois Statute, this court finds . . . [that a lower courts decision upholding the Daley Democrats' position] did not abrogate . . . [the insurgents'] fundamental constitutional rights of free political association. . . ."[6]

The weight of precedent favored the Appellate Court's decision. The Supreme Court, however, did not. It reversed the decision on appeal and ruled on behalf of the insurgents. The arguments underlying its ruling hold important implications for the parties.

The Supreme Court began by stating that the "National Democratic Party and its adherents enjoy a constitutionally protected right of political association."[7] No one would argue with this. More debatable was the Court's next assumption. First, it pointed out that the election in question was a primary election within the Democratic party and not a general election. It then went on to state, "Consideration of the special function of delegates to such a Convention [the Democratic National Convention] militates persuasively against the conclusion that the asserted interest constitutes a compelling state interest."[8] It contended that "delegates perform a task of supreme importance to every citizen of the Nation regardless of the State of residence."[9] In performing this duty, the nomination of the presidential and vice-presidential candidates, the Court argued that the delegates and the national party executed a party function of national concern. Therefore, it concluded, "the Convention serves the pervasive national interest in selection of candidates for national office, and this national interest is greater than any interest of an individual State."[10] The national party rules in the area of delegate selection to the national convention thus took precedence over state law.

The Supreme Court ruled in favor of the reforms. In the process, they went against legal precedent and opened a broad, new avenue for the potential development of national party powers. The decision was a bold one. Its implications, as tested and refined over the years, are likely to be sweeping.

The Supreme Court's decision stands, of course, as the law of the land. Most observers were taken aback by the breadth and boldness of the decision in affirming the new and dominant status of the national party's authority in the areas specified. The accumulation of power by the national party and its move toward dominating party affairs would have to rank as the most significant and far-reaching outcome of the entire reform era. Unwittingly, this gain in power resulted from the push generated after the 1968 Chicago convention and the all-out resistance of the Chicago machine to the reforms that emerged in the 1968–1972 period, a battle that ended in the legal codification of the newly enumerated national party powers.

MOVES TOWARD NATIONAL PARTY SUPREMACY

The efforts to promote national party dominance can be found in other aspects of the reform movement. The party charter attempted to restructure national party organs and make them more relevant to a political party in the twentieth century. The charter also attempted to prescribe standards for local and state party operations and, in effect, to extend the procedural safeguards and rationale behind the McGovern-Fraser Commission's guidelines for presidential delegate selection to party affairs at all levels. The outcome of this particular aspect of reform remains in doubt. Whatever its ultimate achievements, however, it would have to rank second in importance to the McGovern-Fraser Commission's initiatives and their ramifications.

Extending the Rule of Law to Party Affairs

Implicit in the proposals throughout the reform period was the effort to protect the interests of the individual party member and to extend and safeguard his influence in party deliberations. The intention was to remove, insofar as was possible, control over participation from the whim and caprice of individuals who happened to be in authority in a given place at a particular time. To a large extent, such an effort ran counter to the customary political efforts of using every available instrument to gain a political edge, however small, and certainly counter to the experience of the Democratic party. Traditionally, the party had resolved differences in a political give-and-take between contending party factions or candidates in any manner the combatants might devise. Manipulating rules or enforcing selective by-laws was among the many stratagems a party faction might use to gain its ends.

This effort to abolish the regulars' control over participation was not good enough for the reformers. They not only wanted an inclusiveness and an intraparty democracy in political decision-making, but they also sought an impartiality in party rules and procedures that was foreign to the historic practices of the Democrats.

The emphasis can be seen in all aspects of the reform movement. The McGovern-Fraser Commission's rules attempted to establish a model of fairness and openness in delegate selection that set the tone for future developments. The O'Hara Commission created elaborate procedures for resolving credentials committee challenges that assured clear standards of performance impartially assessed through a series of mechanisms similar to those employed by the courts. There would be briefs and counterbriefs, set times and dates for the selection meetings and for the various steps involved in adjudicating any disagreements, hearings of facts by qualified officers, and appeals made to a credentials committee and, potentially at least, to the national convention. The Credentials Review Commission carried the process a step further by attempting to provide a continuing assessment of the applicability and relevance of state party rules to the national party's reform guidelines.

Less successfully, the O'Hara Commission made efforts to open the flow of information to the individual delegates and to advance their control over presiding officials within the convention. Most dramatic of all, the Charter Commission wrote a party constitution for party affairs and established a judicial council, modeled after the Supreme Court, to codify and apply party rulings in all disputes brought before it. The Charter Commission's actions are perhaps the ultimate steps, if they prove to be feasible, in instituting the rule of law within party councils.

Reform as a Continuing Problem

One other result of the reform movement may be less obvious. The reformers extensively reviewed party processes and then rewrote the rules of behavior for the totality of national party activities. As a consequence, the reform era opened questions, once presumed settled either for better or worse or at least removed from immediate political debate, to continual reassessment. The sucess of the reformers in overhauling party procedures within a very few years invites others to try. The public and the party membership have now been conditioned to such reassessments. Such activity is accepted as a legitimate national party function and the authority of the party to engage in such exercises—including the enforced implementation of its directives—is no longer a subject of contention. There is much to be gained by a restructuring of procedure by any party faction that might control the national party apparatus, a national convention, or simply a reform commission. The process invites attempts at duplication. In fact, because the impressive changes brought by the McGovern-Fraser Commission serve as a model of what could be accomplished, repeated attempts to introduce new reforms (in these situations, changes intended to favor one faction or candidate) may be difficult to avoid.

For the most part, the original review of procedures and the changes introduced by the reformers were badly needed. The presidential nominating process had evolved over generations, with little rationale or logic underlying the diverse procedures utilized in the states. The reformers contended that the process was closed and arbitrary and that it gave unfair advantage to the party regulars who controlled the processes. In this broad sense, the reformers' claims were not contested by the regulars (although, of course, the measures proposed by the reformers were less well received).[11]

No particular rules governed the operations of the national convention and its management, and the procedures were open to gross abuse. The bylaws applying to local, state, and national party organs were complex, often unrecorded, and openly manipulated by those in power. Such problems demanded some type of ordering. The reform movement attempted to accomplish this task.

The work of the McGovern-Fraser Commission and, in the wake of the post-1972 election, the Mikulski and Compliance Review commissions, indicates that no area of presidential selection can remain off limits to reevaluation and potential modification.

Presidential primaries and nominating procedures, national convention operations, and the selection of vice-presidential candidates as problems in democratic representation have all stimulated their own reform commissions. More "reform" commissions are likely to follow. The political implications of such maneuvering are enormous, and the potential for abuse is great. It is conceivable that the faction controlling the national chairmanship—or the White House, should there be a Democratic president—could attempt to rewrite the party rules governing presidential selection (or, for that matter, any other aspect of party business) under the guise of added "reforms" in order to further its own immediate political ends. A president could recast the rules so as to effectively close the nominating process to all but the most adventuresome potential contenders, thus going far to reassure his own renomination. The danger is real. Under such conditions, centrist candidates or candidates with national constituencies and future ambitions to occupy the White House, would be the ones most likely to shun a rigged nominating contest. Such candidates would suffer the most from the embarrassment of a poor showing. If the rules are cast in such a manner, thereby promoting an incumbent's already formidable advantage in seeking renomination, the potential contenders with the least to gain from an indecisive or weak challenge would be precisely those candidates who, under less disadvantageous circumstances, would provide the most formidable opposition to the incumbent. The field might be left open to the long-shot or the fringe candidate with little to lose by such a race.

In fact, the continual reexamination of the party rules after each presidential election virtually insures efforts to recast them before the next election in the manner best suited to the interests of the party faction conducting the review. If a commission is intentionally leavened with a working majority favorable to one candidate or party faction, if a commission chairman is less than impartial, or if the media and party rank and file pay little attention to the proceedings (and it is only under the most extraordinary conditions that a broad public interest can be kindled), then such perversions of the "reform" process are likely to occur.

The consequences of such opportunism are enormous. Instead of an open process, there would be one skewed to the interests of one party group. Instead of a wide array of candidates identified with most of the party's major interests contending for the nomination, the field could be reduced to an incumbent (or one major candidate) and several contenders with, perhaps, unusual constituencies and limited appeals. For the Democrats, this could mean that the majority of the nation's party members and sympathizers would be given little real choice among representative contenders for the nomination. Once again, the process would effectively be closed and the voice of the party rank and file muted at perhaps the most critical stage in the entire election process and the only stage in which the voter has a wide choice of potential nominees.

The purpose of this discussion is not to argue that the reform period accomplished all its goals or that other objectives are not worth pursuing. Much work remains to be done to insure that the parties will be vibrant and democratic instruments of the popular will. My purpose is to argue that "reform" can cover many things and that it is open to abuse.

TWO EXAMPLES

The efforts of the Compliance Review Commission (CRC) and of the Winograd Commission illustrate the potential difficulties. The Compliance Review Commission was formed to monitor the progress of the states in meeting the Mikulski Commission's guidelines and to assist the state parties in their efforts to comply with them. The operation was relatively small. The commission's work was technical, and it received little attention in the press or from party members. But the CRC was effectively controlled by National Chairman Robert Strauss and his staff. Their intention was to insure that the state parties would be given a good deal of leeway in what they were permitted to do and that the interpretation of the rules would be softened (and, in some cases, the standards of what constituted compliance redrawn) to avoid controversy. The effort was quite successful. Largely through the intervention of Strauss and his staff, the Credentials Committee for the 1976 Democratic National Convention entertained few challenges, and it made no minority reports to the convention, an unusual occurrence. If the goal of reform is party unity at any cost and a peaceful convention, such efforts are to be applauded. If, however, the reforms are meant to assure open processes and a significant role for the rank-and-file participants, a more conscientious application of the rules might be encouraged.

The Winograd Commission was ostensibly established by National Chairman Strauss in 1975 to assess the ramifications of the spread of presidential primaries (up to thirty for the 1976 election year.) Primaries had been instituted by a number of state parties in the belief that they constituted the best means of meeting guidelines intended to establish fair and inclusive nominating procedures. Many persons, reformers and regulars alike, thought that primaries weakened party organizations by encouraging participation in presidential nominations through channels almost completely divorced from party control and other party concerns. These critics argued that the spread of primaries had to be curbed and that an emphasis on a caucus-state convention system could meet the objectives of the reform standards while serving other party interests better. Hence, the Winograd Commission was formed.

The commission did little its first year. Its mandate was broadened by the 1976 National Convention, which was effectively controlled by the Carter forces, to include all aspects of presidential nominations and party procedures.

After Jimmy Carter's election, the commission membership was expanded, giving the new administration roughly a two-to-one majority. The commission then set out, with little public attention, to rewrite the nominating rules for 1980. In its report, the commission endorsed a number of proposals that came from the White House and had the objective of closing the delegate selection process and minimizing competition for the nomination. The intention, it was claimed, was to build "consensus" within the party, reduce the influence of the media in the delegate selection process, and increase the power of the party regulars over nominations. Among the proposals endorsed by the commission was one to reduce the nominating season from six to three months; a shortened campaign season normally favors an incumbent. A second proposal reserved 10 percent of all delegations for party professionals and elective officeholders. A third increased the "floor," or minimum level of support all candidates had to meet before they could receive any national convention delegate votes in a state primary, caucus, or convention. A minimum vote of 15 percent would be needed in the early primaries and caucuses (10 percent or 15 percent had been the level used in 1976), 20 percent in the midseason ones, and 25 percent in the late ones (when almost 60 percent of the national convention delegates had been selected in 1976.) Candidates who did well in the early primaries (as Jimmy Carter did in 1976) could expect to do well in the later primaries. In a race against an incumbent, for example, the burden would be on a newcomer to generate enough publicity and support *before* the delegate selection season began in order to run a respectable race in the early primaries. This would be extremely difficult. And if a contender stumbled in the early tests, his chances for the nominations would be severely diminished. He could not expect to build support over a relatively long nominating season against others in an open field. Such proposals favor the incumbent and those with organizational and financial resources and media access.

The Winograd Commission recommended advancing the closing date for candidate entry into state nominating processes to fifty-five days before the start of the state's delegate selection process. This change would assure that no late filings or potential new contenders would materialize if a front-runner, or the early contenders, demonstrated little appeal. Such a premature closing of a process, already restricted to ninety days, would have gone a long way toward eliminating such candidacies as Senator Robert Kennedy in 1968, Senator Hubert Humphrey in 1972, and Senator Frank Church and California Governor Edmund Brown, Jr., and others, in 1976.

There was one exception to the compacted nominating schedule. The rules were written so that New Hampshire, a state in which then-candidate Carter had done well in 1976 and the one, in fact, that had launched him as a serious candidate, was permitted to hold its primary outside of the specified three-month period and before the nominating processes had begun in the other states.[12]

The new rules obviously favored the incumbent president. There had been no controversy of note over the nominating standards in effect in 1976, nor over their application. Because the reform guidelines had not been in effect for long (and thus had no weight of tradition) and because few persons followed or understood the post-1976 maneuverings over party rules, it was relatively easy for the incumbent president to influence party councils and to dictate the adoption of nominating procedures most conducive to his own renomination. The prospect of minimizing competition may well prove as attractive to others over the years, and they are also likely to exercise the option of reshaping the rules to advance their own objectives. "Reform" can serve many masters and disparate, even contradictory, ends.

The Immediate Reaction to Reform

The reforms following the 1968 National Convention stimulated a strong critical reaction. To the extent that reform questions were debated in the media and among party groups, it was the shortcomings of the movement that received attention. The debate focused on who would get hurt. The reaction was natural.[13] The reformers attempted to change established patterns of behavior, and in doing so, in recasting the rules as to who would be rewarded and for what types of achievement, they aroused the strongest reaction from the people who had the most to lose. The response was based, quite rightly, on practical political considerations. In the continuing debate over the attractiveness of reform objectives, this should not be forgotten. A glance at some of the most commonly heard arguments should be enough to convey their flavor.

The range of criticisms and their critical depth varied. Among the more familiar points raised in the media and by those opposed to the new rules were the following. The old system was not so bad. It resulted in the nominations of Franklin Roosevelt, Harry Truman, and John Kennedy. The 1968 national convention itself was better than it looked. Its problems were simply reflective of the times and the social divisions that were ripping the country apart. It did debate the war in Southeast Asia (the main point of contention among the party's various factions), and it did nominate Hubert Humphrey. Its worst problems were caused by radicals and dissidents who were well outside the party's fold and who had no stake in its future. Those dissidents were acute but short-term problems for the Democratic party, the administration, and the city of Chicago and its mayor. They had nothing constructive to contribute. Some party leaders (and notably Mayor Daley) saw the virulent rowdyism of the convention week as a conspiracy directed against the nation and its leaders.

Humphrey did well. If it had not been for the disruptive convention he may well have beaten Richard Nixon. If the purpose of a national convention is to pick a winner, as the regulars unequivocally contend it is, then Humphrey, the near victor, fulfilled this goal far better than McGovern, the nominee of the "reformed" 1972 convention. McGovern ran an inept campaign and lost overwhelmingly to the same Richard Nixon in one of the worst defeats in American political history.

Humphrey was a representative Democratic presidential nominee, drawn from the same tradition as Johnson, Kennedy, Stevenson, and the rest. He was an established and experienced liberal leader who was in touch with the party's roots and traditions and who had strong ties to its major factions (blacks, organized labor, state party leaders, and liberals). Humphrey had been a spokesman for the liberal wing of the Democratic party for a quarter of a century and he had led the fight for civil rights at personal political risk well before such battles were popular. Humphrey, in short, was an able and seasoned representative of the best the Democratic party had to offer. These points were usually raised to contrast Humphrey to McGovern, to the former's advantage. Many believed McGovern had led the fight for the new rules so he could win the nomination. Otherwise, they contended, he would have had no chance for the position.

There were other criticisms, and these went beyond the personalities involved and the 1968 and 1972 conventions and campaigns. Some contended that primaries and caucuses were unrepresentative of the party and its best interests. These events draw a small percentage of the party faithful and, most commonly, those most motivated to participate on ideological grounds. They hardly speak for the mass of Democratic voters. Therefore it was felt that their role in a given election year should be reduced. The power to decide presidential nominations should be restored to the party's established leaders—the governors, state chairmen, congressmen, mayors, and the like—who would be more likely to pick a strong contender who was also in line with the party's best interests. In short, the mechanism designed to include the party's rank and file in the deliberations over a presidential nominee should be changed so this base would be in a position corresponding to its more traditional (or pre-1972) role. Discretion over convention choices would then be returned to the powerbrokers who had been dominant in national conventions until 1972, those with the greatest practical experience in politics, those who could be presumed to look out for the party's vital concerns.

The reform movement was an effort to destroy the Democratic party. The new rules were concocted by the New Left, a general coalition of the young, radicals, antiwar-types, and apolitical ideologues, whose real intent was to disable the Democratic party. Its real goal was a third or fourth party, possibly along the lines of those that renegade Democrat McCarthy formed in 1972 and 1976.

The quotas were considered unrepresentative, undemocratic, and fool-ish. Why not quotas for old people, ethnics, the poor, and so on? There were at least as many arguments as there were critics. Yet despite their variety, they had several things in common. They were emotional. The reactions to the reformers were angry. The criticisms tended toward the bitter and the personal. Many built upon the divisions of the period from 1964 to 1968 and the chaotic 1968 election year and the splits within the party it engendered. They served to open old wounds and to inflict a few new ones, insuring that the battle would not be soon forgotten.

Debating the Merits

The controveries created by the reforms are not likely to abate. The reform movement raised fundamental questions about American political parties that are not easily answered and that go to the very essence of what political parties in the United States are, or should be, about. What is a political party for? Whom does it serve? What does (or should) it stand for? Whom should it represent (and *how* should these groups, interests, and individuals be represented?) Implicit in the controversy is the question of the adaptability and adequacy of political parties—institutions devel-oped in another age—in dealing with the pressures and problems of late-twentieth-century American life. Are political parties relevant to the major concerns of contemporary American Society? If not, can they be made relevant?

THE RESPONSE OF THE REGULARS

The answers that the Democratic party regulars and reformers would give to these questions should be clear enough at this juncture. The party regulars would contend that political parties are quite adequate to the demands made upon them.[14] They would say that 1968 and its problems were exceptions to the long and basically successful exercise of party authority. If a little care is taken, the problems of that election year need not be repeated.

Political parties are electoral coalitions intended for winning elections. The achievement of this end is, by all odds, their most significant function, and all other obligations are secondary at best. The regulars would con-tend that a party should, of course, represent the best interests of its members, but they would go on to argue that the most effective way to do this is by winning elections. The way to pick the candidates most likely to be victorious is to give the decisive role in party affairs (including presi-dential nomination contests) to party and elective officeholders. These individuals have the greatest stake in the party's success as well as the knowledge and experience necessary to select the most formidable nomi-nees representative of the party's long-run interests.

THE RESPONSE OF THE REFORMERS

Reformers would be more skeptical of the claims made on behalf of the political party. They would argue that the party has not served its membership well, that its procedures are out-dated and discriminatory, and that it has not adapted to a changing electorate and an evolving society. Their perception of the 1968 election year and its attendant difficulties would be quite different from that of the regulars. They would see that election year and the Democratic prenomination difficulties and national convention as symbolic of the internal decay that has been spreading within the party system. The 1968 election year was simply a manifestation of how serious the problems have become.

The reformers have little faith in the party regulars. They openly question the breadth of the regulars' concerns and the extent to which they accurately reflect, or possibly even consider, the sentiments of the party rank and file. Reformers differ with the party regulars on where a party's major obligations lie, and they contest the wisdom, competence, and representativeness of the party regulars. They see no particular value in entrusting the fate of the national party or control over its presidential decision-making process to an elite with which they have so little in common and which they believe to be out of touch with its constituency and with national political currents.

The reformers would argue that the grass-roots party members should be represented in all party bodies and should, to the furthest extent possible, control their deliberations. To enlarge upon this belief, reformers feel that party members who participated in the presidential primaries and caucuses should have a controlling voice in the concerns of the process. The reformers believe in a participant-oriented party, accessible to those who cared to identify with it and take part in its activities, and open to influence from below. And they seek a party that would best represent and implement as precisely as possible the views and wishes of its membership.

The conception of an open, participant-oriented party responsive to and dependent on the goodwill of its rank and file is at odds with the regulars' view of a quasi-closed organization led by a somewhat inaccessible and self-perpetuating elite that would look out for the party's best interests. In fact, an open party that entrusts ultimate power over, for example, the choice of a presidential nominee to the individual party member acting in a primary or a caucus at the local level makes the need for indirect representation through local or state party organizations or elected officeholders extraneous. The reformers want a direct correspondence between the individual party member and national-level decisions, a relationship that deemphasizes the role and contributions of any intermediate agencies.

The reformers would also reject winning office as the sole end of a political party. Instead, they would contend that a party serves many functions and that perhaps its most important is adequately to represent the views of its members and to funnel these into governmental decision-making. Unless a political party responsively addresses its members' concerns about pressing social issues, its victories will be hollow. They believed that a political party has to be in direct touch with, and representative of, its grass-roots sentiments. Anything less means that the political party is not fulfilling its obligations.

The reformers would emphasize a broader set of party goals and activities (witness the party charter) than the regulars. They would argue that a party should attempt to fulfill a number of functions, from educating its membership on the issues of the day to campaigning for office, and that it should have permanent organizations active throughout the year with full-time professional staffs to serve the needs of its members. These party organizations should be open to direction from the rank and file.

While they favor a more ambitious program and a more highly institutionalized (and open) party structure, the reformers would be more skeptical of the party's operations and the adequacy of its contributions to contemporary society. They would want the party to engage in more activities while at the same time being more demanding in their assessments of the relevance and value of what the party undertakes. And they would insist (as they did) that to reach any of these goals, the Democratic party would have to be thoroughly restructured. The regulars, of course, would disagree on each and every point.

TWO MODELS OF REPRESENTATION

The two sides in the reform issues are operating from different models of political behavior. They are applying different standards of acceptable political conduct and accountability. The two models have little in common. The party regulars are advocating "a taking care of" (to borrow Hanna Pitkin's terminology)[15] concept of representation that sees party regulars and the established interest group leaders within the Democratic coalition as the best conservators of the interests of the party and its members.

The argument is familiar in political theory. It can take many forms, from Edmund Burke's conception of "virtual representation" to such characterizations as a "trustee" or "guardian" relationship between the representative and his constituent. The representative is given considerable leeway (justified by his position, expertise, and experience) to provide for the needs of the nation, organization, or constituent. The representative, for example, is only responsible to the voter on a periodic basis. At this point, if the representative has not done a satisfactory job of safeguarding his constituents' interests, he can be replaced. At all other times, the constituent is in a dependency relationship in which he exercises little power or self-direction over or responsibility for his own fate. As seen by the party regulars, a form of indirect representation in which they are given considerable discretion in executing the party's business would best serve the party's continuing interests.

The reformers, obviously, favor a quite different concept of party organization and of those who should control its deliberations. They see few distinctions in terms of ability, wisdom, or experience between themselves, on the one hand, and party regulars and party officials, on the other, that would better qualify the regulars to tend the party business. Not trusting the party regulars to represent their interest, they believe that they, and every party member, should be given the opportunity to directly represent themselves in party matters. They trust their own judgments and abilities to operate within structural outlines that give no particular advantage to any group. Under such conditions, they are confident they can advance their own, and their party's, best interests. They consider themselves perfectly able to express their interests, and they feel they should be given every opportunity to do so.

The reformers would argue that a system that directly reflects rank-and-file-views and allows the grass-roots participants control over party decisions, particularly over the critical choice of a presidential nominee, is not only preferable but is the only type of procedure that will meet their concept of democratic accountability.

To the extent that direct control over party decision-making is not feasible, the reformers would opt for an "agent" theory of representation. The representative chosen by the individual party members would be given limited independence. On the major issues facing the party, he would be carefully instructed on how to perform in order to best fulfill his sponsor's wishes.

The two conceptions of representation have little in common. The issues raised, both in theoretical and practical terms, are fundamental to one's definition of a political party and the relevance of its contributions to a society. They deal with the nature of the party and its continued existence. Add to these concerns the groups displaced by the turmoil caused by the reforms and the stakes being contested in the fight for control of a national party and its nominating processes, and it is not difficult to see why the debate over reforms has continued.

The reformers won the initial battle and much of what they accomplished cannot be reversed. Nonetheless, the basic differences between the competing conceptions of what a political party is (or should be) and the manner in which it should fulfill its obligations are essentially irreconcilable. At a minimum however, political parties in the future may be judged by stricter standards of performance than in the past. Political parties should be continually called upon to prove their relevance and justify their contribution by a public that is increasingly skeptical of their value.

The reform movement accomplished a great deal in a short period of time. It managed to breathe new life into moribund party structures and to center debate on the operation of these agencies. Political parties are seldom the focus of public concern. They have grown episodically over the last century and a half to fill immediate political needs. They are of immense concern quadrennially, when the various presidential contenders and their supporters attempt to bend them to their will. Between presidential elections a short-term interest is replaced by a more customary apathy. It can be argued that during the interim between elections the hulking organizational monster that constitutes the remnants of the national party only fitfully serves any function of consequence to the electorate.

The reform movement attempted to resurrect an interest in party activities per se and to revitalize party structures and adapt them to modern concerns. Two questions require answering before any proper understanding or assessment of the conflux of problems and forces that took shape during the reform period can be made: Why did the reform movement arise at this particular time? And how successful was it?

The first question is relatively easy to answer. The second may be impossible without the testimony of future decades. Political parties had changed little in form or activity since their inception. One factor, however, had become increasingly clear: they had become spiritually exhausted and increasingly less relevant functionally to the operation of a modern democracy. The demand for organizations adequately executing the duties the parties are supposed to perform cannot be quarreled with. Critical concerns of any democratic nation include the mobilization of voters behind representative candidacies of similar policy persuasion; the selection and promotion of the most able within its ranks to positions of public responsibility; the effective representation of the views of its members; the day-to-day scrutiny of the acts of those in office; and the provision of sensible policy and candidate alternatives to an electorate it educated to the implications of official behavior. Both parties performed these functions with increasingly less ability.

In truth the parties had become fractious, warring tribes, divorced from their bases of support and slavishly dependent on a president chosen from their ranks. They responded more to organized pressures and financial strength than they did to the mass of their membership. A review of party history during the last few troubled decades would make it appear that the party supporters were an inconvenience to be suffered and catered to only during national election campaigns.

Such foreboding might never have arisen above the level of irrelevant speculation had it not been for 1968. The fury unleashed by the obvious abuse of official party machinery and the ugly picture of party operations that resulted convinced most people within and without the Democratic party that change was overdue. The forces that would propel reform had been set in motion, but the events of that election year proved the catalyst. Beyond a doubt, the immediate need for remedial action had been demonstrated. Change was required; the need had been dramatized in a manner that would create the necessary reform constituency, and people were available and willing to devote themselves to the effort. So began the attempt to democratize one of the nation's oldest and most significant political institutions. The remedies advanced and the nature of the support for differing kinds of changes varied. This is what this book has been about: an analysis of what is potentially the most vital series of changes to be introduced into the modern party structure.

These observations lead in turn to the second question: How successful has the movement been? Clearly some notable results have emerged. It is unlikely that these can be reversed to any significant extent. The real question in this regard centers less on the substance of the reforms or who got what and why than on to what extent the parties (and more realistically the Democratic party, the repository for the plurality of Americans' political affiliations) have been made equal to the present-day demands made upon them. To what extent does the party now reflect its base in the citizenry? What measure of control do party supporters exercise over party actions? How effective has the party become as a representative instrument in advancing the needs of its constituents? In what measure does it compliment and strengthen the operation of other democratic structures? Obviously the party has a long way to go in these regards. Will the intelligent beginning that has been made in the period under discussion be accepted, consolidated, and then expanded in the years to come? Will change come quickly enough to insure that political parties will continue to perform—with increasing skill—the fundamentally critical role within democratic society that they have, with varying degrees of success, in the past?

The reform movement treated in this book constitutes but a beginning. Where the parties go from here and what their future contributions will be to a democratic nation sorely in need of their services depends on them. It is safe to predict that in the near future the insightfulness of party leaders as well as the parties' commitment to democratic values in their own operations, their willingness to respond to an evolving electorate, and their determination to voluntarily execute the troublesome changes needed to protect and solidify their position as vital agents of popular representation will be severely tested.

Chapter One

1. Statement of Eugene McCarthy before the Commission on Rules, Washington, D.C., Hearing, 19 September 1969.

2. Two opposing views of what happened in Chicago and the stimuli that provoked events are the reports prepared for the Eisenhower Commission (the so-called Walker Report, named after the Task Force's chairman and later Illinois governor, Daniel Walker) and the one issued by the city of Chicago (the city also presented a one-hour television version of its arguments). The reports mentioned are *Rights in Conflict*, a report prepared for the National Commission on the Causes and Prevention of Violence (Washington, D.C.: U.S. Government Printing Office, 1968), and *The Strategy of Conflict* (Chicago: The City of Chicago, 1968).

3. The proceedings are concisely summarized in the report by Congressional Quarterly, *The Presidential Nominating Conventions, 1968* (Washington, D.C.: Congressional Quarterly, 1968), pp. 115 ff.

The confrontations and demonstrations of the convention period produced a public reaction decidedly unsympathetic to the protestors and supportive of the police and other authorities. See John P. Robinson, "Public Reaction to Political Protest: Chicago, 1968," *Public Opinion Quarterly* 34 (Spring 1970): 1–9.

4. Democratic National Committee, *Proceedings of the 1968 Democratic National Convention*, transcript (Washington, D.C., 1968), p. 248.

5. Ibid., p. 250.

6. Anne Wexler to William Sueppee, 23 July 1968.

7. Statement of Harold Hughes to the press on 4 August 1968, the official date signifying the creation of the Ad Hoc Commission. This section is based on interviews with the materials provided by Thomas P. Alder, Eli Segal, Donald M. Fraser, Anne Wexler, and others involved in the work, in addition to published reports.

In addition to Hughes, the commission included Vice-Chairman, United States Representative Donald M. Fraser of Minnesota, a Humphrey supporter destined to head the Democratic party's Commission on Party Structure and Delegate Selection; Harry Ashmore, Executive Editor of the *Arkansas Gazette* and a coordinator of the Center for the Study of Democratic Institutions; Professor Alexander Bickel of the Yale University Law School; Julian Bond, a state representative from Georgia; Frederick G. Dutton, a lawyer and former State Department official who had supported Robert Kennedy; and Doris Fleeson Kimball, who had that year relinquished her nationally syndicated newspaper column.

8. *The Democratic Choice* (New York: The Commission on the Democratic Selection of Presidential Nominees, 1968).

9. Ibid., p. 2.

10. The Ad Hoc Commission refused to take a stand on the "winner-take-all" provision (such as the one in California's regulations). In part this resulted from the

advocacy of Frederick Dutton, a commission member from California. Dutton, later a member of the McGovern-Fraser Commission, repeated his arguments in favor of California's "winner-take-all" primary. Neither commission took an explicit position on the issue. The two other areas in which the commission had the greatest difficulty were in determining the formulas for proportionate representation of minority political views and the allocation of convention committee votes to a state delegation. The first two items also caused the McGovern-Fraser Commission great difficulty.

11. *Democratic Choice*, p. 16.

12. The room had a capacity of one hundred eighty. One hundred ten delegates held seats on the committee, leaving seventy places for staff, representatives of the candidates, party onlookers, newspaper and television reporters, and the public.

13. The unit rule was not the only matter considered by the Rules Committee, although it was by far the most explosive. It symbolized the combination of forces and pressures that swirled around the reform efforts in the convention and, in a different mixture, during later years. Basically, most of the Ad Hoc Commission report constituted legitimate grounds for committee deliberations, as Shapiro noted.

14. *Presidential Nominating Conventions, 1968*, p. 118.

15. The text of the statements and the background debate can be found in the relevant party records. A summary of what occurred, with supporting documentation, can be found in the Congressional Quarterly's *Presidential Nominating Conventions, 1968*.

16. The charge to what was to become the O'Hara Commission was more explicit than that given the McGovern-Fraser Commission. Quite clearly, the O'Hara Commission had no powers of implementation. Those rested with the Rules Committee of the 1972 convention, with, of course, appeal to the full convention. What was left unclear, and what came to trouble their work, was the ambiguous role of the National Committee. The O'Hara Commission was to "report its findings" to the National Committee in "a timely manner" so that the National Committee could submit these to the 1972 convention's Rules Committee: Did this arrangement permit the National Committee the power to vote on, modify, or reject the O'Hara Commission proposals before submitting them to the convention's Rules Committee? The grant gives the National Committee no such explicit authority. Yet the National Commitee chose to exercise it, much to the discomfort and eventual anger of the O'Hara Commission. The ambiguity in the statement turned out to be an important aspect of what constituted the final recommendations to the convenion. The O'Hara Commission had been denied the power to include their recommendations in the call to the 1972 convention; this in effect meant that the National Committee, the group that framed the call, could exercise its judgment as to which of the O'Hara Commission proposals, in what form, it wished to include in the call. The National Committee's veto power could be cast over all preconvention aspects of the recommendations (e.g., size of the convention, apportionment of votes, authority and operating procedures of the committees of the convention). On the other hand, the ambiguity of the implementation phase of the McGovern-Fraser mandate gave this body the opening for claiming powers of enforcing full compliance.

17. *Proceedings*, pp. 244–51.

18. Ibid., p. 269. Anne Wexler's discussion of the background of the Crangle motion and its relationship to the full Rules Committee report as given before the McGovern-Fraser Commission on 1 March 1969 is helpful in understanding the intentions and thinking of the reformers. Anne Wexler et al., "Minority Report of the 1968 Rules Committee," mimeographed (Washington, D.C.: McGovern-Fraser Commissions, 1969).

19. Both of the reform groups, but especially the more aggressive McGovern-Fraser Commission, called on other party actions for legitimacy. During the period from 1964 to 1968 the Special Equal Rights Committee of Richard Hughes served as the unquestionable spiritual forefather of the reform movement. One act involving the Special Equal Rights Committee had particular meaning for the initial stages of the reform effort. On 24 August 1968, immediately preceeding the convention opening, the Democratic National Committee formally adopted the report of the Special Equal Rights Committee, which contained the passage: "That a Commission on Party Structure should be voted to study the relationship petween the National Democratic Party and

its constituent State Democratic Parties, in order that full participation of all Democrats, regardless of race, color, creed or national origin, may be facilitated by uniform standards for structure and operation." This represented one of the root influences for the McGovern-Fraser Commission and explains half of the body's title of "Commission on Party Structure and Delegate Selection." This particular thrust of their work was never satisfactorily concluded, and, in fact, led to difficulties with the O'Hara Commission.

20. Unintentional humor marked some of the disarray. Carl Albert, the frustrated convention chairman, proposed the interruption of the roll call by remarking that, "Under the rules of the convention and of the House of Representatives, nothing but a point of order can interrupt a roll call until the roll call is finished, and it would be a bad precedent not to follow that rule." He then, of course, proposed they do just that: suspend the rules by unanimous consent. When the consent was not totally unanimous, he announced that "the Chair cannot interpret that kind of sound" and introduced the speakers on the next resolution (*Proceedings*).

When Albert later was asked whether he would serve in 1972 as the convention's permanent chairman he vigorously declined, and recommended National Chairman Lawrence O'Brien, the man who had given him the job in the first place.

Chapter Two

1. The election results were: Republican Richard M. Nixon, 43.4 percent, Democrat Hubert H. Humphrey, 42.7 percent, George C. Wallace (the third party candidate of the American Independent Party), 13.5 percent, and a mixed bag of "other" candidates, .6 percent. Nixon held a decisive edge in the electoral vote total, 301 to Humphrey's 191 and Wallace's 46. The popular vote difference between the two principal candidates was 0.68 percent, or less than one percent of the total votes cast, a closeness never imagined during the campaign.

2. Harris's populist philosophy is best summed up in his *The New Populism* (New York: Saturday Review Press, 1973) and *Now Is the Time: A New Populist Call to Action* (New York: McGraw-Hill, 1971). The problems Harris encountered and some indication of the thrust of this administration of the party are included in a radio interview with Gene Gibbons, 25 February 1969, syndicated by the Democratic National Committee. Harris proved too liberal for his state. He did not seek reelection to his United States Senate seat, although he did conduct a short-lived campaign for the Democratic presidential nomination in late 1971 and early 1972 (and later in 1976).

3. Humphrey compared the Democratic party's state to the little boy who was "good about attending Sunday school. He learned all the religious verities. So the local preacher was going to show him off and he said to the little boy 'Now you have been attending Sunday school regularly, and so you know the truth.'

"He said, 'Who made you?'

"And the little boy said, after hesitating a moment, . . . 'I don't know. I am not done yet.' "

In Democratic National Committee, *Proceedings of the January 14, 1969, Meeting of the Democratic National Committee* (Washington, D.C., 1969).

4. See resolution numbers 11 and 12 and the discussion of these in ibid.

5. These questions were put forward by Marshall Brown, national committeeman from Louisiana, a strong and vocal foe of any reform attempts. See ibid., p. 162.

6. Harris had taken a fair amount of time in announcing the membership of the two commissions, bringing some to charge that he and the party were not seriously entertaining the prospects of any fundamental change. Harris's own version is that he carefully screened the prospective appointees in accord with the standards he established and that he sought a consensus among party leaders before announcing his selections which is creditable. He was placed in the unwelcome position of balancing conflicting pressures—the need for change against the sensibilities of those power-brokers who had yet to recover from the aftereffects of a bitterly divisive campaign and for whom party reform held at best a low priority. The latter's positions were already well established and would gain little from the modifications of normal party

practices. The reform constituency, on the other hand, was clearly suspicious, and for a long period (many through to the end) continued to be suspicious, of any actions initiated by the party. This schizophrenia dogged the entire reform effort.

Harris cleared the nominations with Humphrey and O'Brien, who later made it a point to note their role in the process. Their action, in effect, endorsed the choices or vetoed those considered unacceptable, which gave the new committee membership a sense of legitimacy and some acceptance by party regulars and, of course, made it suspect to the insurgents.

The press was also wary of the reform movement, both at its inception and throughout its history. The inclination at the beginning was to reserve judgment. Later there appeared to be an inclination to believe the worst. Two of the more thoughtful commentaries at the early stage follow.

Paul Hope (*Washington Star*, 16 February 1969, p. 1) wrote:

> Democratic National Chairman Fred R. Harris named the committees and their chairmen [the McGovern-Fraser and O'Hara Commissions] a few days ago. But opinion within this party is divided as to what might come out of the exercise. Some see it as an opportunity to revolutionize the party—to make it more truly reflect the voices from the grass roots. Others see it as amounting to very little.
>
> One committee is to study the selection of delegates to the national conventions to try to inject more of the "participatory politics" that Sen. Eugene McCarthy and the late Sen. Robert F. Kennedy talked about last year.
>
> The other [the O'Hara Commission]—which most party leaders seem to think is of lesser importance—is to codify and perhaps suggest new rules for the actual running of the convention.
>
> Born in controversy, the reform committees, at least the delegate-selection committee, still are surrounded by argument. McCarthy supporters claim *the committee on delegates has been stacked against reform*. Some of the younger Kennedy men are of the same opinion. (Italics added.)

Jules Witcover, in an assessment in *The Progressive* 33, no. 2 (April 1969): 22–25, offered some cautionary observations. Witcover observed the early work of the McGovern-Fraser Commission and warned that "the Democrats may not grasp the scope of the job ahead." Their attempt, as he saw it, would be to unite the "Old Politics" of the Humphrey coalition with the "New Politics" of the McCarthy-Kennedy movement, youth, and the affluent issue-oriented suburbs. The effort, he thought, might exacerbate the "divisiveness" inherent in a deeply split political party. Witcover felt the party should expect serious opposition to change from the power centers of both the North and the South.

7. McGovern's opinion on the matter, stated after he resigned the commission's chair, appears as a frank summation of Harris's and O'Hara's role: "Both Fred Harris and Larry O'Brien, as Democratic national chairmen, did better than I had expected they would. They didn't give us very much money, but it was because they didn't have it. What they did give us was vocal support. They did indicate to the party apparatus across the country that reform was a serious business." In early 1972 McGovern expected reform, with party backing, to be implemented in most of the states. "McGovern Discusses the Issues," *ADA World* 27, no. 2 (Washington, D.C.: Americans for Democratic Action, February 1972): 1ff.

8. See Paul Hope's account, "Party Reform Hearings Slated by Democrats," in the *Washington Star*, 6 April 1969, p. 8, and David Broder's in-depth review, "Democrats Get a New Breath of Life," in the *Washington Post*, 23 March 1969, p. C-1. The latter in particular captures the mood of Harris and his associates in embarking on their course of action.

9. The outgoing party treasurer, Robert Short, had announced at the January 1969 meeting of the National Committee that the National Committee had agreed to assume all the campaign debts of the Democratic presidential contenders during the 1968 presidential election year (except those of Eugene McCarthy, who preferred to pay his own). This was an extraordinarily bold move for a National Committee that was already in debt and that had no viable accounting of what it owed, no assurance at that

point of exactly what these new obligations would amount to, and no independent sources of income (the Democrats and especially their National Committee were notoriously inept at fund-raising), besides being the national committee for a party that was out of power. The assumption of the debts was sprung on a startled but slow-to-react party. Coupled with the committee's own financial obligations, the total debt eventually came to $9.3 million, and the Democrats made little headway in retiring it until Robert Strauss, national chairman in the post-1972 period, took over as party treasurer in early 1970. Short, a Minnesota businessman (trucking, hotels) and long-time Humphrey supporter, retired from the party post to oversee his varied business interests, including the ownership of the Washington Senators, a baseball team (which he eventually moved to Arlington, Texas).

10. In his initial announcement establishing the reform commissions (press release of 8 February 1969, on file at the Democratic National Committee headquarters), Harris called on the Republican party and its then-national chairman, Ray Bliss, to join him in an effort at modernizing party rules, which could have led to the appointment of a mutually agreed-upon, nonpartisan panel of experts (national leaders, academicians, and lawyers) that would survey the operations of the entire electoral process and recommend changes suited to the public interest. It was hoped that such a body would receive independent foundation funding. In addition, Harris called attention to the need for a rationalization of the costs of politics. After a back-and-forth exchange made difficult by the tenuous position of Bliss in the new Nixon Administration (he was, in fact, replaced in April 1969 by Rogers Morton) and fueled by the suspicions and mistrust of, on the one hand, a party in power with no visible organizational or financial woes, and on the other, a party badly divided and deeply in debt, the effort died a-borning. After some indecision, Morton appointed his own reform commission in June 1969, the DO Committee (Delegates and Organizations), under the chairmanship of Rosemary Ginn, the Republican National Committeewoman from Missouri. Harris then proceeded to appoint two new commissions or task forces. The Freedom to Vote Task Force was appointed in July 1969 with former Attorney General Ramsey Clark as chairman and Mildred Robbins, Honorary President of the National Council of Women as vice-chairman. This task force was charged with exploring the reasons people failed to vote and recommending ways to deal with the problem. The task force's reports include *That All May Vote* (Washington, D.C.: Democratic National Committee, 1969) and *Registration and Voting in the United States* (Washington, D.C.: Democratic National Committee, 1970). Their work eventually led to congressional efforts to reform registration practices, including the adoption of a post-card registration system and universal voter enrollment.

The Freedom to Run Task Force was also appointed. This task force did relatively little, deciding instead to concentrate whatever energies and resources that were available on the introduction and promotion of specific bills before the Congress. These included efforts to equalize access to television and put limits on campaign spending, a full disclosure act, and a check-off plan for presidential election and federal campaign financing, some of which later became law. Another task force, on youth, never operated. For Harris's earlier statement on reform and reform commissions see his press release of 14 January 1969. On the aborted negotiations between the two national committees for a joint effort at evaluating the needs of the electoral process in their entirety, Harris's press release of 1 March 1969 is helpful.

11. Broder, "New Breath of Life."

12. Statement of 8 February 1969.

13. Ibid.

14. McGovern was not a willing recruit. He accepted only when given some assurances as to financial and other kinds of support from Harris and when Humphrey vetoed the choice of Harold Hughes, a prime contender for the position, but a man he distrusted. McGovern was aware of the difficulties and the sensitive nature of the job. He addressed some of the aspects surrounding his appointment in opening remarks to the organizational meeting of the full commission, noting at the time that he had been urged to accept the responsibility by Humphrey, Muskie, McCarthy, Kennedy, and Hughes. Hughes was named vice-chairman. (See McGovern's opening statement of 1 March 1969, delivered at the meeting of the Commission on Party Structure and

Delegate Selection, Washington, D.C., and Hope, "Party Reform Hearings.") Mc-Govern's private attitude at the time (revealed later) and his public optimism contrasted sharply: "When I took on the chairmanship of that [the McGovern-Fraser] reform commission I really had a lurking fear that the whole thing would be a disaster. I didn't really think you could reform the Democratic party to the extent that we are [*sic*] asked to do it" ("McGovern Discusses").

15. Hughes had presented, among other things, the major nominating speech for McCarthy at the Chicago convention. Of the original seven members on the Ad Hoc Commission, Hughes, Fraser, and Dutton, as noted, were appointed to the Commission on Party Structure and Delegate Selection, and a fourth, Alexander Bickel, was made a consultant.

16. Originally twenty-five, one dropped out shortly after being appointed.

17. See Hope's observations in the *Washington Star* of 16 February 1969.

18. Nelson had extensive experience in procedural politics, having worked in earlier McGovern campaigns, in South Dakota. He was a journalist, editor, and public-relations man, specializing in agricultural matters. For four years he had served as administrative assistant to McGovern and for the eight years immediately prior to his appointment he had been deputy assistant secretary for water and power in the Department of the Interior. Segal, who was from New York and who was a graduate of the University of Michigan Law School, had been administrative assistant to New York Congressman Joseph Resnick (Democrat) and a consultant to the Urban Coalition. Joan Scott, the executive assistant, had previous experience as an executive secretary in both the Department of Housing and Urban Development and the Department of the Interior. Bode, who had a doctorate in political science from the University of North Carolina at Chapel Hill, had taught at both Michigan State University and the State University of New York at Binghamton, and had worked in McGovern's brief campaign for the nomination in 1968. Also active in the early campaign were Carol Casey, Ted Tschudy, Yvonne Alston, Richard Norling, Joseph Gebhard, William McDonald, and Marcia Goodman. At its largest the permanent and volunteer staff numbered about fifty. A list of most of the members can be found in the Commission on Party Structure and Delegate Selection, *Mandate for Reform* (Washington, D.C.: Democratic National Committee, 1970), p. 4.

19. Statement of 8 February 1969.

20. See the McGovern "Opening Statement" of 1 March 1969.

21. See the statement by Anne Wexler of 1 March 1969 before the Commission on Party Structure and Delegate Selection. Wexler's expertise rested on her service as coauthor of the "Minority Report of the 1968 Rules Committee." Hughes's remarks also relied heavily on the Ad Hoc Committee's work, which was brought to fruition in the "Minority Report." Curiously, and as a continuing testimonial to the imprecision of politics (even when conducted by lawyers), the convention's adoption of the "Minority Report" was the only one of the three convention resolutions McGovern chose not to trace the ancestry of his commission through. Yet the principals behind this resolution provided the argument for the clarification of the convention's intentions as regards the commission mandate and, more specifically, its enforcement responsibilities. The "Minority Report of the Rules Committee" of the 1968 convention is the strongest statement of reform implementation and the one Wexler developed in detail. The overlap among the three convention resolutions is considerable (and McGovern's confusion is justified), and it created an ambiguity that the McGovern-Fraser Commission capitalized on in extending its powers. The limits on the O'Hara Commission were much clearer.

The "Official Summary of (the) March 1, 1969, Meeting," prepared by the commission staff, if anything, adopted a stronger tone and left little room for vagueness. The relevant part reads: "The Commission adopted Mrs. Wexler's interpretations as its official guidelines: 'all feasible efforts,' according to her interpretation, applies only to State parties in which both State laws must be changed and the legislature is Republican-controlled; otherwise, *there is an absolute requirement that procedures must be changed in the States now out of conformity.*" (Italics in the original.)

22. Hughes's comments followed McGovern's and reiterated the themes of reasonableness and dedication to change. Hughes went on to delve in more detail into

substantive issues and to articulate one of the hidden assumptions on which the Mc-Govern-Fraser (as well as the earlier Ad Hoc) Commission operated: namely, that the national convention had intrinsic value as a device for conducting party business. "There is nothing inherently undemocratic about a national convention, . . . its weaknesses are the product of inertia and indifference, rather than structure, . . . with meaningful reform, it is a contribution well worth preserving." *Proceedings of the 1 March 1969 Meeting of the Commission on Party Structure and Delegate Selection,* on tape. For this reason, more exotic or revolutionary ideas, such as a national presidential primary (although an evaluation of the merits of such a proposal was suggested by one commission member, former Utah Governor Calvin Rampton), received no serious attention. The focus was on improving and opening existing institutions, not replacing them.

23. The full debate can be found in the official tapes of the meeting. The most vocal opponents of the majority will included Davis, George Mitchell, national committeeman from Maine, and Carmen Warschaw, national committeewoman from California, although the informal group added and dropped members depending on the issue being discussed. Among the most consistent supporters of the McGovern-Hughes-Wexler position were David Mixner, Aaron Henry, and William Dodd, in particular, although a majority of the rest obviously identified with the interpretation.

24. The national conventions have the power to pass on the qualifications of their own members through the device of the credentials committees. They are reluctant to exercise such authority. Basically the sanction was a negative one, applied primarily in cases of blatant racial discrimination in which the party was embarrassed into taking a stand. The National Committee also has power of judgment as to membership powers, although it has been restricted to judging the qualifications of contestants for seats claimed by several people. Historically it has been even more reluctant to exercise its judgment on such matters (it normally does not maintain a permanent committee analogous to the Credentials Committee, for example, preferring to appoint an ad hoc body as the need arises), although during the 1950s it did exclude a national committeeman from Texas who had serious difficulties with the then-National Chairman Stephen Mitchell, ostensibly for the state's failure to meet a financial quota to defray national headquarter staff expenses, a basis on which the representatives of most state parties could be excluded. This incident and related ones are treated in Cornelius P. Cotter and Bernard C. Hennessy, *Politics Without Power: The National Party Committees* (New York: Atherton Press, 1964).

25. The executive committee consisted of McGovern (chairman), Hughes (vicechairman), LeRoy Collins, William Dodd, Frederick G. Dutton, Donald Fraser, Aaron Henry, David Mixner, Katherine Peden, and Adlai Stevenson.

26. In fact, the presentation of the proposals was handled in an unusual way (especially at the September 1969 meeting). Segal and Bode sat at a table in front of the commission and introduced and then defended in depth each recommendation, answering the commission members' questions as best they could. Then the commission members debated the merits of each proposed guideline.

27. The principal staff members involved in this phase of the work were Nelson and Casey, who acted as research director and coordinator of the state efforts, with help from Alston and Tschudy.

28. The membership of the three initial committees was as follows. Delegate selection: Fraser (chairman), Abel, Bayh, Christopher, English, Garcia, Hooker, Peden, and Ranney; grass-roots participation: Stevenson (chairman), Dodds, Graves, Martin, Mauzy, Mixner, Pena, and Warschaw; and party structure: Collins (chairman, succeeded by Fraser when Collins resigned and Fraser's subcommittee on delegate selection became extinct), Beer, Bennett, Davis, Dutton, Henry, Knox, Mitchell, and Rampton. A full list of commission members with identifying commentaries can be found in *Mandate for Reform,* p. 3.

29. See the agenda and working papers prepared for the first meeting of the subcommittee on grass-roots participation (22 March 1969) to acquire some idea of the scope of the work and the activist role envisioned for this group.

30. The Youth Participation Subcommittee was composed of McGovern (chairman), Hughes (vice-chairman), Bayh, Dodds, Dutton, Fraser, Graves, Knox, and

Mixner. Its public meeting was held on 22 July 1970, and received testimony from former Attorney General Ramsey Clark, Senators Edward Kennedy and Edmund Muskie, and elections expert Richard Scammon, among others.

31. See, for example, Fraser's letter of 19 March 1969 to McGovern, in the files of the Commission on Party Structure and Delegate Selection.

32. See *Prospectus: Subcommittee on Party Structure* (Washington, D.C.: Commission on Party Structure and Delegate Selection, 1969), p. 13. The early work of this group was promising despite the problems raised by the overlap with the O'Hara Commission.

33. The meeting announcing the charter took place on 19 May 1972. The charter is well worth reading and may constitute the parameters of the debate on the questions raised. It can be found in the Commission on Rules' *Call To Order* (Washington, D.C.: Democratic National Committee, 1972), pp. 133–43.

34. McGovern's acceptance speech and those immediately preceding it (Eagleton's and Edward Kennedy's) were intensely emotional, constituting the highlights of the convention. Unfortunately for McGovern, these appeared on television screens between 2:00 and 4:00 A.M. in most of the nation. They had been pushed back by the fight over the party charter and the lengthy nominations preceding Eagleton's selection as vice-presidential nominee.

35. Both Fraser and O'Hara were appointed to the new Charter Commission, which began operations under Sanford in 1973.

36. "Purpose of the Hearings," staff memo to commission members (Washington, D.C.: Commission on Party Structure and Delegate Selection, 27 May 1969).

37. The examples and quotations used here can be found in the transcripts of the relevant hearing on file with the Commission on Party Structure and Delegate Selection.

38. Seventy-three percent of the Florida population lives in eleven counties represented by only twenty-two members (16 percent) of the 134-member state executive committee. See *Atlanta Hearing* of the Commission on Party Structure and Delegate Selection, transcript (Washington, D.C., 1969).

39. The Maddox delegation was the one led by Georgia's segregationist governor, Lester Maddox. It was challenged by an integrated delegation led by black state legislator Julian Bond. The convention eventually split the seats between the two, which angered Maddox enough to make him pull out of the convention, and most of his delegation followed.

The testimony recounts both the subtle and less subtle ways in which dissidents were kept in line and in which candidates not representative of the state party leaders' views were severely underrepresented on a delegation. On Florida, see the *Atlanta Hearing* and James Minter, "Florida Rebel Resisted HHH Backers," *Miami Herald*, 30 August 1968, p. A-32.

40. The example was given of Missouri's Boone County. Here two-thirds of the voters lived in one city (Columbia), yet only one-third of the County Committee came from that city, a malapportionment ratio some felt excluded adequate representation.

41. The laws can be specific and mischievous, assigning seemingly arbitrarily different quotas of committeemen to electoral districts and giving them varying terms of office.

42. Ten percent of Missouri's population and a far higher percentage of its Democratic vote had been awarded two out of sixty delegate positions.

43. Mayor Daley's usual practice was not to hold press conferences except to issue announcements. He then stalked from the room, either to preclude questions or because of a hostile question. The door from the press room to his office was a few feet immediately behind the podium, so the tactic effectively concluded the conference.

44. Illinois' twenty-three-month registration law (a prospective primary voter had to register in the party twenty-three months prior to the primary) was suspended by court action in 1972 (a decision later upheld by the United States Supreme Court). The 1972 primary thus allowed new and "cross-over" voters to participate in the Democratic primary. In this election the candidate backed by Daley for the gubernatorial nomination lost to an insurgent Democrat (Daniel Walker of "Walker Report"

fame from 1968). The commission backed a closed party primary under reasonable tests of party membership, but did not "require" compliance. Daley did open slate-making sessions to the public and media in 1973 (in preparation for the 1974 elections). The press was allowed to witness the prospective candidates presenting their qualifications. When the time came to make choices among the candidates, Daley closed the sessions; no votes were made publicly. The net result of the mayor's largess was the gain of free television time for the party.

45. This statement and the ones immediately prior to it give an indication of why the reform battle in Chicago and the later controversy over Chicago delegate selection practices, which came before the 1972 National convention, proved to be so acrimonious.

46. The League of Women Voters pointed out that in 1968 Illinois had 118 votes at the Democratic National Convention divided among 138 delegates, only 48 of whom were elected. The difficulty involved in binding or instructing even these 48 delegates left the voter powerless within the process.

47. The speaker, "the only one of the eighty [committeemen] elected against the wishes of the leadership of the regular Organization of Cook County," related the following incident: "During the 1964 election campaign one of the suburban committeemen at a meeting called by the Cook County Chairman rose to his feet to say that he feared we were not giving sufficient attention to the election of the president of the County Board. He said that he had been in a contest for election as committeeman, that he had spent $25,000 of his organization's money and $22,000 of his own money to be elected. 'How am I going to get that back,' he asked, 'if we lose the presidency of the County Board?' And how does he get it back if we win?"

See *Chicago Hearing* of the Commission on Party Structure and Delegate Selection, transcript (Washington, D.C., 1969).

48. See *Jackson* (Miss.) *Hearing* of the Commission on Party Structure and Delegate Selection, transcript (Washington, D.C., 1969).

49. Vance's statement and that of the treasurer of his faction, George L'Maistre (as well, of course, as Cashin's), are worth reading as an introduction to the morass of Alabama politics. These can be found in the transcript of the Mississippi hearings. The views presented here do not represent the extremes. Both groups are trying to work with the national party. Individuals and organizations with different objectives and the Wallace supporters did not attend the hearing.

50. "Purpose of the Hearings."

51. Ibid.

52. The hearings so impressed some of the states that they held their own, including sectional open hearings within the state. North Carolina was one of the earliest to follow this procedure, which proved successful there. National Chairman Fred R. Harris had requested every state to appoint its own reform commissions and, in effect, to institute its own reform movement. By the end of August twenty-six states had established their own "little McGovern" commissions. Eventually every state in some form met this request (which was actually considered an informal guideline by the commission, and a necessary sign of good faith during implementation).

The only two members of the commission who did not attend any of the public hearings were the Steelworker's I. W. Abel and Texas State Senator Oscar Mauzy.

Chapter Three

1. Convention mandate as found in the convention records or as excerpted in the Commission on Party Structure and Delegate Selection's *Mandate for Reform* (Washington, D.C.: Democratic National Committee, 1970), pp. 52–53.

2. See especially the first memo ("Nature of the Commission Mandate"), which was sent out with a letter from McGovern in the Files of the Commission on Party Structure and Delegate Selection.

3. These same items had been seriously questioned in the executive committee meetings that first reviewed the prospective guidelines in August and September. See the minutes of these meetings and McGovern's memo to commission members of early

September, "Proposed Guidelines, 'Full, Meaningful and Timely Opportunity to Participate' in the Delegate Selection Process" (Washington, D.C.: Commission on Party Structure and Delegate Selection, September 1969). When the proposed guidelines were distributed to all interested groups and individuals by the commission after its September action, these two issues were explored in consultants' memos prepared by Alexander Bickel of the Yale Law School and Richard Wade of New York University.

4. See McGovern's opening statement of 23 September 1969.

5. The genuine effort of the commission to engage broader consultation bore fruit. The prospective guidelines and accompanying reports were sent to national committeemen, state chairmen, governors, United States congressmen and senators, former party officials, luminaries without portfolio in the party, elected officeholders, labor unions, lawyers, youth, women, minority groups, media representatives, academicians, and anyone who indicated an interest or who could be identified as having an interest in the outcome. Over one hundred twenty-four responses were received, most commenting in detail on the proposals. Most were well received. The return is about 4 percent of the total mailed, which is not bad considering the request being made of the recipient. Most seemed to agree that the wording of the proposals needed clarification. Awkward phrasing bedeviled the guidelines until the end. The responses can be evaluated in the commission files. A short overview can be found in the commission memo of 12 November 1969.

6. The vote on the proposal was eight to eight, with McGovern (a probable supporter) absent due to the debate in the Senate floor on the food stamp bill, an issue on which he had a deep interest and a piece of legislation for which he was the floor manager. Quite clearly, the intensity of one side made up for the general lack of feeling on the other—the commission was divided evenly.

7. The transcript or tapes of the hearings on these points are worth reviewing. The staff of the Credentials Committee of the 1972 convention examined them for some indication of the legislative history and background on these matters. The Credentials Committee, while supportive of the reforms, did settle most challenges on these issues based on the politics of the situation involved, a not unreasonable approach.

8. From the transcript of the meeting of the Commission on Party Structure and Delegate Selection, 24 September 1969. In communications following the meetings, the staff clarified this phrasing to mean that "call upon" carried the full authority of the commission to obtain the stated purpose. "Recommend" was to be used when the commission did not demand the change desired. The terms were still ambiguous and the problem of definition arose again at the November meeting.

9. Minutes of the 28 August 1969 executive committee meeting.

10. Warren Weaver, Jr., "Democratic Reform Commission Asks Full Party Participation for Youths," *New York Times*, 25 September 1969, p. 27; and Weaver, "Democrats Split on Party Reform," *New York Times*, 24 September 1969, p. 16.

11. In addition to Weaver's, commentaries include Robert Walters, "Democratic Panel Maps Broad Reform Program," *Washington Star*, 23 September 1969, p. 1; William Greider, "McGovern Unit Divided over Delegate Issue," *Washington Post*, 24 September 1969, p. 2; "McGovern Panel Stymied in Effort to Reform Party," *Washington Star*, 24 September 1969, p. 12; and "Democrats Urged to Accept 18-year Olds," *Washington Post*, 25 September 1969, p. 26.

12. William Greider, "Democrats Complicate Party Reform," *Washington Post*, 30 November 1969.

13. R. W. Apple, Jr., "Democrats Bar Delegate Order," *New York Times*, 20 November 1969, p. 21.

14. Harold Hughes's remark prior to the vote on the Bayh amendment ("it is contributing to the total confusion of what we're doing") proved to be not far off the mark. This aspect of the controversy is captured in the Associated Press report of 19 November 1969, published in the *Philadelphia Inquirer*, 20 November 1969, as "Democratic Panel Votes to Broaden Convention Setup." It should be noted that this debate took place before the eighteen-year-old vote was made constitutional.

Dutton's assessment was that the requirements indicated "goals to be sought—moral standards, not quotas." Hughes's contention was that "no matter what we may have said we have, in fact, established something which you might call a quota system." At this meeting the commission in effect endorsed the idea without "requiring" compliance, but in the long run Hughes's assessment was closer to the reality of the situation. See William Greider, "Democrats Widen Delegations," *Washington Post*, 20 November 1969, p. 6.

15. The practice was outlawed at the 1972 Democratic National Convention. The reference is to the bitter fight between Hubert Humphrey and George McGovern. McGovern won a narrow primary victory over Humphrey in the California primary (although the expectation had been for a decisive McGovern edge, an outcome similar to that in the primary between Robert Kennedy and Eugene McCarthy four years earlier). Humphrey then challenged—after the fact—the "winner-take-all" primary as being inconsistent with the reform guidelines (although before the election he had publicly vowed not to follow such a course). The challenge, of course, was strictly political. McGovern narrowly lost the vote in the Credentials Committee but won decisively on the convention floor after a rough fight. McGovern's victory on this issue at the opening of the convention determined the party's presidential nomination, and Humphrey, Muskie, and the other principal contenders quickly withdrew. Neither the party nor its candidate, however, ever recovered from the devisive fight. Even without the other problems McGovern encountered, he had little chance against the Republican incumbent, Richard Nixon.

16. The McGovern-Fraser Commission, in effect, adopted this strategy. The commission brought to the attention of the O'Hara Commission at the appropriate time its own resolution of the apportionment problem and suggested, indirectly, that the issue had been decided. To give cumulative weight and consistency to the reform proposals, the Commission on Rules (it was tactfully suggested) should endorse the earlier decision of the McGovern-Fraser Commission by adopting its formula. The O'Hara Commission was unimpressed. Several years later, under Terry Sanford, the new Charter Commission (which was created by the 1972 Democratic National Convention to deal with the unfinished business of party structural reform), after considerable deliberation, adopted a complex formula of its own for delegate selection to the 1974 off-year convention.

17. Later modified to include the last three presidential elections in order to avoid, or average out, the precipitous swings in the vote from any one presidential election to the next.

18. The ban on National Committee members serving as ex-officio delegates was incorporated in the guideline C-4 prohibition against all ex-officio delegates. The original C-5 guideline, a rambling discussion of National Committee elections, tenure, and appointment that contained matters on the fringe of the commission's authority (if not beyond it) was dropped. This reduced the original nineteen guidelines to the eighteen that were eventually promulgated. The original subject matter of the excluded regulation dealt more with party structure items, which fell between the jurisdiction of the McGovern-Fraser and O'Hara commissions.

19. Although McGovern's contention that the "favorite son candidacies have been abolished for all times" was an overstatement, as was later made clear by a close inspection of the rules (and events), the work of the McGovern-Fraser and the O'Hara commissions did make such candidacies more difficult, and it reduced their number and influence in national conventions. (*Proceedings of November 19 and 20, 1969, Meeting of the Commission on Party Structure and Delegate Selection*, in commission files.)

20. Robert Walters, "Democratic Reform Falters," *Washington Star*, 21 November 1969, p. 8.

21. *Washington Post*, 21 November 1969, p. 2.

22. Ibid.

23. Ibid.; and "Democrats under Urban Influence," *New York Times*, 21 November 1969, p. 21.

24. David Broder gave a basically supportive interpretation to events in his column in the *Washington Post*, 25 November 1969, p. 21.

25. *Washington Post*, 21 November 1969, p. 2.

26. "Democrats under Urban Influence," p. 21.

27. At one point (17 June 1972) 43 percent of the delegates chosen were under challenge.

28. Guidelines A-3 on voter registration, B-6 on the representation of "minority"

political views (which played a significant post-1972 role in the deliberations of the Mikulski or New Delegates Selection Commission), and C-3 on "open and closed" selection methods have been excluded. These provisions deal with actions "urged" on the state parties, which, therefore, were not binding or mandatory. They represent issue areas in which the commission failed to take a final stand acceptable to the majority as to what should be demanded of the states. Portions of guidelines A-4 on costs and C-5 on the role of party committees "urging" or "recommending" changes also have been omitted. These can be found in *Mandate for Reform*, pp. 39–48.

29. This is the word used by the Special Equal Rights Committee. The "elements" are listed in *Mandate for Reform*, p. 39, n 1. The history and work of this committee can be taken from the records of the 1964 Democratic National Convention, the proceedings of the Democratic National Committee (especially the meeting of January 1968) and what remains of the Special Committee's files.

30. This changed drastically in the 1972 Democratic National Convention (see below).

31. In the two presidential elections of the 1950s 70 percent of blacks supported the Democratic presidential nominee. This rose to 82.3 percent for the three presidential elections of the 1960s. (Gallup Opinion Index, "Votes by Groups in Presidential Elections [1952–1968]," report no. 49 [Princeton, N.J.: Gallup International, Inc., July 1969], p. 29.)

32. Testimony of H. A. Glickstein, Acting Staff Director, United States Commission on Civil Rights, before subcommittee no. 5 of the House Judiciary Committee, 14 May 1969, p. 12.

33. Ibid., p. 14.

34. The court decisions relating to the example are: *Smith* v. *Paris*, 257 F. supp. 901 (M.D. Ala. 1966), *aff'd* 386 F. 2d 979 (1967) and *The United States* v. *Democratic Executive Committee of Barbour County Ala.*, civil no. 2685-N (M.D. Ala., 24 July 1968). The examples and testimony used here and in the following (unless explicitly noted) are taken from materials supplied to the McGovern-Fraser Commission and are therefore relevant to the decisions the committee made. In this case, the redistribution was done on patently racial grounds. The action was overturned by a federal court, which had grown increasingly critical of racial incidents of this sort.

35. The ten southern states were: Alabama, Arkansas, Florida, Georgia, Louisiana, Mississippi, North Carolina, South Carolina, Tennessee, and Virginia. The courts have been reluctant to intrude into party affairs (for example, in applying the "one man, one vote" apportionment concept to party bodies). For a discussion of the broader questions involved in party representation, see Paul T. David, "Reform Efforts Continue on State Party Structures," *National Civic Review* 61, no. 5 (New York: National Municipal League, May 1972): 226–31.

Of the seven states whose delegations were challenged before the Credentials Committee of the 1968 convention, five had no blacks on their executive committees. In all, 18 of 725 positions were filled by blacks. Unfortunately, the figures for the rest of the South and the border state of Kentucky are no better.

1998 Democratic Party, State Executive Committee

State (South)	Number of Positions	Number Held by Blacks
Alabama	72	0
Georgia	200	6
Louisiana	117	0
Mississippi	15	0
North Carolina	220	12
Tennessee	36	0
Texas	65	0
State (Border States)		
Arkansas	72	0
Florida	134	0
Kentucky	35	1
South Carolina	51	0
Virginia	20	0

36. These materials may be found in the relevant hearings for Los Angeles and Philadelphia and in the presentations in New York City by Herman Badillo and Percy Sutton. The registration figures produced in New York lend weight to the accusations. Another incident, in Ohio, lends perspective to the black difficulties in some areas. A "miniconvention" was called in late summer of 1972 to select a Democratic vice-presidential nominee to replace Senator Thomas Eagleton after he resigned from the party's ticket. The national convention, of course, had been a bitter setback for the party regulars. Frank King, the Ohio AFL-CIO leader and delegation chairman, jumped over a black delegate, who was next-in-line, to pick Congressman Wayne Hays for a "miniconvention" position. Some charged racial discrimination; King claimed he was trying to meet the quotas, in this case, providing sufficient white representation. The commission explicitly permitted "oversubscription" to its "quotas," which were considered minimal guarantees. The Ohio flare-up probably had as much to do with intrastate party divisions as anything else, but it did stir up a goodly amount of adverse national criticism.

37. There are many materials of direct consequence to this guideline. Worth reviewing are the transcript of the extensive commission debates on the concept implicit in the quotas, prepared by Monica Borkowski for the Credentials Committee of the 1972 Democratic National Committee—or the tapes of the commission hearings themselves; United States Commission on Civil Rights, *Political Participation* (Washington, D.C.: U.S. Government Printing Office, 1968); "Discrimination on the Basis of Race, Color, Creed or National Origin" (Washington, D.C.: Commission on Party Structure and Delegate Selection, 1969) (the consideration of ethnic influence was omitted early, and constituted one of the major deficiences for which the commission report was attacked); "Comments on Guideline A-1" (Washington, D.C.: Commission on Party Structure and Delegate Selection, 1969); Statement of Frankie M. Freeman, United States Commission on Civil Rights, before Subcommittee on Constitutional Rights, United States Senate Judiciary Committee, 9 July 1969; United States Commission on Civil Rights, "Analysis of S. 2507, a bill to Amend the Voting Rights Act of 1965," mimeographed (8 July 1969); and Testimony of H. A. Glickstein.

38. Richard Childs calls these "dupli-kates" (duplicate women) in his review of party organization in the one hundred state parties. Richard S. Childs, *State Party Structures and Procedures: A State-by-State Compendium* (New York: National Municipal League, 1967), pp. 4–5. Matters had not improved much by 1972.

39. This broad social issue went well beyond the party. Twenty-one as the age of majority had been taken over by tradition from England to the colonies. The social ferment for change was great, and much had been written on the subject. Despite some clear indications that voters aged twenty-one and over were not in favor of the eighteen-year-old vote when it was put to them, the national mood seemed more receptive to change. According to Gallup, support for such a measure had increased progressively from 17 percent of the American public in 1939 (when the first poll was taken) to 64 percent in 1967. *Congressional Quarterly* (Washington, D. C.: Congressional Quarterly Service, 10 May 1968), p. 1050. Once enacted (through the Twenty-sixth Amendment in 1971), the issue died quickly.

40. These states usually have an additional escape clause, which states that a candidate ignored by the official agent can still appear on the ballot (as, for example, in Wisconsin) by submitting a specified number of signatures from each of the state's congressional districts. The problem centers more on the responsible body being overinclusive rather than overrestrictive, guided by a desire to give the citizens of the state a choice from the full range of presidential candidates. The law usually provides that any recognized candidate or potential candidate should be entered. Not all candidates prefer to contest in every primary or in any given state. Some presidential contenders chose to be considered noncandidates ("dark horses"), unblemished by a decisive defeat in a primary from a front runner. Such aspirants wait for the national convention to begin their public drives for the nomination. The full regulations can be found in the state statutes and state and national party rules. A sketch of those in effect in 1968 can be found in *Human Events* (3 February 1968), and a comprehensive presentation and review for 1972 can be found in William J. Crotty, *Presidential Nominating Procedures* (New York: National Municipal League, 1974).

41. Indiana has a tradition of kickbacks from those appointed by the party to public office or state jobs. The "Two Per Cent Club" in the state has gained a certain level of notoriety. The name refers to a practice whereby appointed patronage workers turn over to the party 2 percent of their annual salaries. See John Kifner, "Kickbacks Still Thrive in Indiana," *New York Times*, 11 July 1972, p. 42.

42. See Kevin L. McKeogh and John L. Bibby, *The Costs of Political Participation: A Study of National Convention Delegates* (Princeton, N.J.: Citizen's Research Foundation, 1968); Paul T. David, Malcolm Moos, and Ralph Goldman, *Presidential Nominating Politics in 1952*, 5 vols. (Washington, D.C.: The Brookings Institution, 1954); Paul T. David, Malcolm Moos, and Richard C. Bain, *The Politics of National Party Conventions* (Washington, D.C.: The Brookings Institution, 1960); and the survey study codirected by William Crotty, Jeane Kirkpatrick, Warren Miller, and Elizabeth Douvan on the 1972 national conventions, available from the Inter-University Consortium for Political Research, University of Michigan, Ann Arbor, Michigan.

43. See the comments by Ken Morrell, "McGovern Group Seeks Convention Expenses," *Nashville* (Tenn.) *Banner*, 18 October 1969, p. 39.

44. In an earlier memo prepared by the commission staff, a system in which all presidential contenders (regardless of their wishes) were placed on the ballot was endorsed. The committee backed away from this stand in its final report, however.

The Supreme Court, in *Moore* v. *Ogilvie* (1972) invalidated an Illinois statue that required a minor party to collect 200 signatures in at least fifty counties in order to be placed on the ballot. The geographical dispersion aspects of the Illinois law are not uncommon in such statutes. They are intended to force a party to demonstrate support in areas where an urban-based or sectional party might not command a following (thus excluding them from the ballot). In *Moore* v. *Ogilvie*, the Court declared that the provision unjustly discriminated against the populous urban areas. It is likely that future court actions will build upon this case, opening the representative processes to other than the party coalitions dominant at any one time.

45. "Comments on Guideline A-5."

46. "Comments on Guideline A-5: Party Rules, Uniform Dates, etc."

47. Weighted voting, of which proxy voting is a form, has been declared illegal in deliberative and legislative bodies by the Supreme Court. It is considered a violation of full and equal representation under the Fourteenth Amendment. The argument has yet to be applied to party agencies. See *Morris* v. *Board of Supervisors of Herkimer County*, 50 Misc. 2d 929 (Sup. Ct., 1966).

48. For a review of these practices during the 1960 presidential election year, see Richard S. Childs, "The Presidential Primary Ballot of 1960" (New York: National Municipal League, 1960).

49. The provision was basically unenforceable, and was unlikely to have any major effect on the conduct of party meetings. It was a minor point in a broader attack. In truth, there is even a legitimate question as to what type of meetings the requirement applied. A member of the Michigan Reform Commission commented, "Given this requirement, my own county committee could not have transacted one item of business during the past two years." "Comments on Guideline B-3." It is likely that a large number of other party committees would encounter the same difficulty.

50. See "Comments on Guideline B-4," and especially the evaluation of Professor Clarence Berdahl of the University of Illinois in his communication to the Commission of 21 October 1969 (excerpted in the official "Comments").

51. A partial list of states with some form of unit rule (broadly interpreted) includes: Maryland, where one-fourth of the national convention delegation is chosen by the state convention and bound to the winner of the state's presidential preference primary: California, Florida, and South Dakota, with "winner-take-all" primaries; Indiana and Massachusetts, with primaries that bind delegates for one ballot, and Oregon, with a primary that binds for two; Connecticut, where several town committees voted to impose the unit rule on delegations to the state convention (which had a direct role in national convention delegate selection); Texas, where 224 of 254 county conventions employed the unit rule (it was also used in precinct caucuses and by the national convention delegation); and in some form (although the application could be lax and easily avoided, and, in some cases, was not sanctioned by party law),

Alaska, North Carolina, the District of Columbia, Tennessee, and North Dakota. In Oregon, although a prospective delegate ran pledged to a given presidential candidate, if elected he was bound by the district or at-large primary results. At least five states (Iowa, Minnesota, Kentucky, Michigan, and Minnesota) explicitly banned the unit rule.

The typical wording on the abbreviated reference to the abolition of the unit rule, reaffirming the convention decision on the matter, masks some bitter infighting, both in the 1968 convention and the commission, as to its precise meaning and scope (what specific areas of delegate selection and party policy it could reasonably be applied to).

The executive committee of the commission wrestled with the difficulties raised at one of their earliest meetings (11 September 1969). In one form or another, the problems raised as to the intent of the prohibition continued up to the 1972 convention, culminating in the most serious challenge to the then-front runner for the nomination, Senator McGovern, in the form of a decisive California challenge.

The legislative history of the prohibition in the unit rule can be quickly summarized. The unit rule, which allows a majority of a delegation to cast a state's whole vote on any question that comes before the convention regardless of the views or wishes of those opposed in the delegation, is entirely a creature of the Democratic party. From their first convention in 1856, the Republicans have emphasized the right of the individual delegate to cast the vote he or she chooses. (Carl Becker, "The Unit Rule in National Nominating Conventions," *American Historical Review* 5 [1899]: 64–82.) The unit rule persisted from a rudimentary start in the first Democratic convention in 1832. In that initial year, one of the convention rules adopted stated that "the majority of the delegates from each state designate the person by whom the votes that state shall be given." The earliest conventions did not compel unanimity, but the practice gradually evolved. By 1860 the national convention explicitly permitted a state convention to bind the votes of its convention delegation, although it allowed members not instructed at the state level to vote their conscience (as it was called). The rule was always troublesome. Theoretically it magnified the importance of a state by forcing all its caucus votes to be cast as a bloc for the candidate who won majority support. In practice it achieved its intended end, but it also denied minority representation, transformed delegates into ciphers during the convention, and emphasized the power of the political boss—as was its objective. (In fact, Becker reports that the Republican party bosses of Illinois, New York, and Pennsylvania so envied the power of the unit rule given to their Democratic counterparts that they attempted to have the 1880 Republican National Convention adopt the practice. The convention ended by reaffirming past policy.)

The politics of the tradition are easy to appreciate; the unrepresentativeness of the practice, however, is hard to justify. From 1872 to 1896 the Democratic Delegation Chairman was allowed to cast the entire state vote with no provision made for a challenge as to its accuracy by any member of the delegation or convention. The unit rule came under sustained attack at succeeding conventions, second in intensity only to the two-thirds rule for nominations. The 1896 convention reversed earlier practice and allowed a delegation to be polled as to its intent if the vote cast by its chairman was challenged by a delegation member. The rule itself was left untouched. The 1912 Democratic convention faced a question not dissimilar to that confronting the reformers six decades later. The advent of the primary added a confounding factor. Could delegates elected in primary elections at a congressional district level (as provided by state law) be bound by a state party convention? The Democrats tried. The convention came down on both sides of the issue, finally adopting by a modest margin a change in the rules prohibiting a state convention from binding delegates elected in primaries not under state party control. (Curiously, at this time the unit rule was justified in Democratic conventions as an extension of the rights of the states, supposedly a contrast to the Republican emphasis in placing final controls on the federal level.)

The unit rule continued to be contentious until the 1968 convention. As part of the politics that divided this convention, both while it was in session and while the delegation selection processes were taking place in the states, the unit rule became an odious symbol of the less defensible aspects of nomination procedures.

It should be recalled at this point that the Ad Hoc Commission chaired by Harold

Hughes that met prior to the 1968 convention faced the same question. It hedged, declaring that the question needed serious investigation. Frederick Dutton, one member of the six-man Ad Hoc Commission, argued strenuously that, for example, a "winner-take-all" primary held unusual advantage in publicity and dramatic value that served to increase both interest and turnout. The fragile unity of the Ad Hoc Commission was kept by sidestepping the question.

The problem facing the McGovern-Fraser Commission was more explicit. The convention had ruled. Furthermore, it had referred to primary elections in its sweeping requirements. The question before the commission was to signify which primary systems violated the intent of the convention. The application was new. The job was difficult. And the commission was unsure of itself in this area. (When the alternatives were posed to the executive commitee of the commission on 11 September 1969, four members believed that the unit rule ban applied to all states and forms of delegate selection, including primaries; one felt that the prohibition applied only to non-primary states, a more traditional application; and two members abstained from voting. See the "Background Paper on the Unit Rule" prepared for the commission meeting of 23 September 1969, in commission files.)

At one point the commission tried to fathom the precise meaning of the unit rule prohibition. Did the 1968 convention oppose the purpose of the unit rule (maximizing a state's impact at a convention through a bloc vote), or did it intend to protect against the effects of the unit rule (an individual being forced by a majority vote to cast a ballot for a candidate he did not support)? Virtually all of the arguments in the Rules Committee and on the floor of the 1968 convention dealt with the last point. The argument went as follows. If the interpretation of the effects of the unit rule was correct, then would not a primary that permitted a winning presidential contender to choose his delegates after the primary vote (as the California primary was to arrange) be technically permissible? The variations being argued were subtle indeed. California and her representatives on the commission felt strongly about the issue. Many others were trying to do justice to the objectives of the convention mandate; others were confused; and still other commissioners were conscious of the human dynamics of the situation and the possible implications of the dispute for attempting to reach a consensus on numerous other thorny points. Under any circumstances, a twenty-eight-member body operating under public scrutiny is not the best forum for arguing such a delicate matter. In its final statement, the commission elected to take a conservative course of action, shunting the major outstanding issues. The wording does not make clear whether the unit rule was forbidden in party rules that applied to all manner of party business (a reasonable position given the manner in which the commission ended its edict), or whether the unit rule was banned only in party activities directly related to delegate selection (the commissioners' actual jurisdiction). Further, the wording carefully tiptoes around the California question, but quite obviously, and intentionally, does not explicitly ban an exercise such as the primary winner choosing delegates committed to him after the primary. The commission left it to its staff and the upcoming convention to settle any ambiguities implicit in its stand.

52. Actually the 1968 convention adopted two resolutions on the matter. While differences exist in the language, the second basically extends the earlier prohibition to the call to the 1972 convention and expands it to all stages of the delegate nomination process. See *Proceedings.*

53. Favorite-son candidacies do create difficulties for a party, the convention, and a voter trying to influence directly access to the presidential nomination. These and related points are treated in the chapters discussing the O'Hara Commission and its recommendations.

54. The staff took this position and tried to implement a ban on "winner-take-all" primaries, but with little success. It negotiated over a period of two years with the California Democrats, but was unable to persuade them to change to a proportional representation primary. The commission had considered applying such a sweeping prohibition (note 52 to chapter three), but had not adopted it. In fact, the California party was correct in arguing that such primaries as theirs had not been outlawed. They made few concessions on the issue, ending with almost the structure they had wanted at the beginning.

55. Guideline B-6 concerning "proportionality," the representation of the propor-

tionate strength of presidential contenders at all levels of delegate selection (another aspect of the unit-rule controversy), one of the thorniest to beset the reformers, is omitted because the problems presented were never adequately resolved. The commission devoted as much time to this issue and to intrastate apportionment of delegates in its first year as to any others. The commission then simply commented on the difficulties and "urged" the state parties to represent fully minority candidate strength at all levels of delegate selection. The recommendations are extremely broad and lack any punch. The committee suggested that state parties could divide their at-large delegates among presidential contenders in relation to the latter's strength (and most states tended to follow this fair-share strategy), a provision that, if required, would have effectively dealt with "winner-take-all" primaries (rather than tucking the issue as an afterthought into B-5, where it does not fit). In truth, the issue of such primaries was fully discussed in regard to the guideline, and could not be resolved. The reformers also suggested choosing delegates from "fairly apportioned districts no larger than congressional," a provision rendered unnecessary by the explicit requirements along these lines in B-7 (apportionment of convention votes). Finally, admitting its ineffectualness, the group called for public discussions on the issue. Given its resolution, the problems encountered would have been better raised in an introduction, and the unnecessary guideline avoided.

The commission forfeited another opportunity in its failure to reach a compromise on these matters. A draft "Bill of Rights" for the delegate had been prepared, which would have given the individual specified protections as well as clear standards against which to measure party performance. It was scuttled in the general retreat from the issues raised. This represents one of the largest single omissions in the reform effort. The "Bill of Rights" was unquestionably years ahead of its time (it may yet come). The McGovern-Fraser Commission reforms opened institutions and provided prospective presidential contenders with some protections in attempting to win delegates. The O'Hara Commission changes helped modernize an old institution (the national convention). The exact rights and protections afforded the delegate (or prospective delegate) were never clearly spelled out or guaranteed in either commission.

Although it was left unresolved, a good deal of time and effort was devoted to the issue, as the numerous staff papers and research reports attest (including consultant Alexander Bickel's memo, distributed to the commission and all interested parties after the meeting of September 1969 failed to reach agreement on the matter). It was left to the Mikulski Commission, the post-1972 successor to the McGovern-Fraser Commission to deal with the problem in more specific terms.

56. For example, Arizona, Connecticut, and Missouri employ the gubernatorial vote as the base; Idaho uses congressional returns; and Indiana calculates on the basis of the outcome in the state's secretary's race. At least fourteen states used the congressional district for their division of votes. Interstate apportionment of delegates to the national convention came under the jurisdiction of the O'Hara Commission, which was not to act on the problem for another two years. There was a serious question of potential conflict (as well as jurisdiction) here, which the McGovern-Fraser Commission resolved by simply plunging ahead. See "Jurisdiction over State-by-State Delegate Apportionment Formulas," Commission memo.

57. "Comments on Guideline B-7: Apportionment." There are many examples of the difficulties that arose. One Arkansas party member, in reviewing the options before the committee, argued that there was "no reliable index of Democratic strength in Arkansas." He went on to say that "people who consider themselves Democrats have not voted for our last two gubernatorial nominees." Communication to commission of 13 October 1969, excerpted in "Comments." Congressional districts in Colorado witnessed a discrepancy of fifty thousand or more votes in 1968 between the Democratic United States Senate contenders and presidential nominees.

Another factor in using any gauge of voting (or party registration) is ascertaining who is *not* being represented. Alabama, as an example, had an average turnout in their presidential elections of the 1960s of 39 percent. The 1966 off-year election in Texas drew only 21 percent of the eligible electorate in a year in which better than one-half (twenty-six) of the states attracted turnouts of less than 50 percent of their voting populations.

58. Taken from Richard Wade's memo of 20 October 1969, as distributed to com-

mission members and other interested parties before the November 1969 commission meeting.

59. The state executive committees determined the allocation and division of delegates between at-large and congressional districts in Idaho, Massachusetts, Kentucky, Minnesota, New Hampshire, New Jersey, North Carolina, Ohio, and Pennsylvania. Minnesota, North Carolina, and Pennsylvania chose to employ these powers arbitrarily, to reduce the delegate strength of the maverick McCarthy forces in 1968. Abuses can and do occur. Louisiana's 1968 national convention delegation was chosen after a week of closed conferences. The Indiana party retains the discretion to allot delegates even after the primary had been held. In 1964 Alabama Governor George Wallace carried one congressional district. The state committee determined after the votes were in that all delegates would be at-large, thus negating the Wallace achievement. Governor Carl Sanders of Georgia, a state that concentrated total powers in the governor and state chairman, allowed each congressional district party committee in 1964 to name one delegate and one alternate. Georgia has a history of overrepresenting rural areas at the expense of the burgeoning urban centers.

60. Most states did well by their major party officials. Indiana, Illinois, Missouri, New York, Ohio, and Pennsylvania (states controlling most of the large delegation votes) particularly distinguished themselves in this regard, generously providing in various combinations for the governor, congressmen, United States senators, state chairmen, committeemen, state legislators, party wheel horses, and political cronies of every description.

61. The call to 1972 Democratic convention issued by the October 1971 National Committee meeting did, of course, authorize National Committee members elected during the 1972 presidential year to sit as ex-officio delegates with full floor and voting privileges.

62. The possibility of giving such people honorific delegate status but not votes was one solution briefly discussed. The objections to (and arguments in favor of) this plan were basically the same used against the ex-officio concept in general.

63. Communication from Congressman Jim Wright (Texas) in commission files.

64. Guideline C-3 concerning the effort to prescribe an "open" process of delegate selection was not resolved and is therefore omitted. The commission "urged" a party registration that left the door open for non-Democrats to become party members but limited delegate selection to party members. Perhaps the best example of the problems that can occur with a too-restrictive or too-lenient (thus encouraging a "cross-over" vote from the Republican party as well as an inclusion of a large number of Independents) enrollment system is provided by Illinois. Prior to 1972 the state permitted only those who had registered as party members twenty-three months before the party primary to participate. This requirement is excessively restrictive, and denies many newer party members an opportunity to vote. Consequently, the courts voided the provision immediately before the 1972 primary. With an "open" Democratic primary and no major contests in the Republican party, an unusual event occurred—the organization-backed candidate for the Democratic gubernatorial nomination was defeated by a narrow margin by an "Independent Democrat," a stunning upset for the machine. The margin of victory was provided by areas that were normally Republican. With a meaningful primary, the Republican gubernatorial primary vote in 1968 came to 684,112. In 1972 it fell to 574,307. The "closed" Democratic primary of 1968 drew 617,780 gubernatorial votes. With an "open" primary in 1972 and a contest for the gubernatorial nomination, the Democratic gubernatorial vote better than doubled, to 1,401,133 (a 227 percent increase). The organization candidate lost by only 45,475 votes, or 3 percent of the total.

Illinois' twenty-three-month law is one extreme. The diversity of American politics never fails to impress. What is sacred in one area is anathema in another. Party primaries in the South are as open as the general election and, in fact, have often substituted for it. Hawaii's Democratic party forces prospective members to fill out an official registration declaration and obtain the endorsement of a party member (seemingly similar to requirements for entering a private club). Even then the newcomer must wait forty-five days before being allowed to vote in precinct caucuses. Connecticut will not permit Independents to join the party after the campaign starts (they must declare before late January), while New Hampshire provides for someone to establish party membership on polling day. Texas, Indiana, Missouri, Alabama, Wisconsin, and Vermont have no registration laws whatsoever. Seventeen states do not require voters to register by party affiliation, four states do not report total registration statistics, and another four report only approximations. Twenty-two states and the District of Columbia do provide registration by party.

Texas illustrates how complex registration practices (or their substitutes) can become. The Democratic party in that state allows anyone who shows up at the polls to vote in the party primary. An election judge then stamps the person's party affiliation on his registration card, decided by which of the primaries he has chosen to vote in. He needs this card as proper endorsement if he intends to participate in the party precinct conventions held on the same day as the primary election (hence, while there is no registration for the primary, there is registration for the precinct meetings). The justification for the absence of registration laws varies by state. Wisconsin has a classic law, a by-product of the strong influence of the antiparty Progressive movement on the state. The statute provides that "each voter shall be given the ballots of all the parties participating in the presidential preference vote, but may vote on one ballot [thus in one primary] only." The Missouri (a state with far different political traditions from Wisconsin's) Democratic State Chairman defended his party's practice this way at the St. Louis commission hearing: "For my part, if a man says he is a Democrat, I want him in my meeting and welcome him and I don't want to set any rules that says who is a Democrat and who isn't." (*St. Louis Hearing* of the Commission on Party Structure and Delegate Selection, transcript [Washington, D.C., 1969].) The Georgia Democrats apparently were even more open. In advertising their party's state convention, they invited all "Democrats, Republicans or Independents" to attend. (*Atlanta Constitution*, 11 October, 1966, p. 12.) In 1969 the Georgia state chairman still opposed party registration, preferring to keep the amorphous coalition of state's rights, liberal Democrats, corporate interests, blacks, rural areas, and what in other states would be suburban Republicans that characterized the Democrat's support. (See communication of 2 November 1969, excerpted in "Comments on Guideline C-3: Open and Closed Processes.")

Given this background, the commission's non-position on the issue may appear more intelligible. The group's report "urged" rather than required state parties to provide for a party registration that allowed non-Democrats to become party members and that provided easy access and frequent opportunity for unaffiliated voters to become Democrats.

The breadth of wording makes the provision inapplicable. The preliminary report offered a workable alternative. In an effort to map the indefinite zone between unregulated and highly restrictive party identification measures, the memo provided that any voter not affiliated with another party could become a Democrat up until the beginning of the delegate selection process. Secondly, it endorsed a clear means for identifying the party membership of each participant in delegate selection. The approach makes a beginning toward a realistic attempt to resolve the issue. The full commission, however, chose not to be this concrete. Happily for the convention, which would have had to judge any actions taken, the regulation was not mandatory, and the state parties decided to concentrate on other matters.

65. Commission on Party Structure and Delegate Selection, *Mandate for Reform*, p. 30.

66. The breakdown is as follows: the first step in national convention delegate selection takes place before the calendar year of the convention in Arizona, Connecticut, Georgia, Idaho, Iowa, Louisiana, Michigan, Minnesota, Pennsylvania, and North Dakota; delegates are apportioned by an "untimely" committee in Alabama, Arizona, Colorado, Indiana, Iowa, Massachusetts, Kentucky, Missouri, New Hampshire, North Carolina, Ohio, Pennsylvania, and West Virginia; delegates (or slates) are endorsed by an "untimely" committee in Connecticut, Indiana, and Massachusetts; vacancies are filled by an untimely committee in Rhode Island, Connecticut, and Massachusetts; and selection of some or all delegates by a committee or individual elected in an "untimely" (i.e., in a year other than the calendar year of the convention) takes place in North Carolina, Georgia, Rhode Island, and Louisiana. The list is not exhaustive. In addition,

virtually all states that permitted ex-officio delegates violated the "timeliness" guideline (the public or party official—governor or national committeeman, for example—was elected prior to the convention year).

67. A specific review of the states affected, their processes, and their problems can be found in "Untimely Delegate Selection: A Report of the Staff of the Commission on Party Structure and Delegate Selection" (Washington, D.C.: Commission on Party Structure and Delegate Selection, 1969).

68. Well, it was almost uniformly looked down upon. The Washington state chairman, as an example of the opposition, did not agree that anything was amiss. He wrote to McGovern, "It has become clearly discernible to me that . . . a rule, carelessly passed at a national convention or by a commission such as the one you chair, may not help the democratic process and may be a punishment to a Democratic organization, because of conflicting state statutes. *I refer specifically to the rules which state that the delegate selection process must begin in the year of the convention.*" (Italics in original.) (Communication of 20 October 1969, excerpted in "Comments on Guideline C-5: Timeliness.")

69. *Proceedings.*

70. The Harold Hughes Ad Hoc Committee recommended that all delegate selection be confined to the six months immediately preceding the national convention. The commission toyed with a similar idea, stating in an earlier draft of its report that "it is possible that . . . the first stage of the delegate selection process may begin within the calendar year of the National Convention but *so early in the year that presidential candidates are not know and meaningful participation is excluded.*" (Emphasis added.) ("Draft: Premature Delegate Selection [Timeliness]," Commission memo.)

The commission could do no better than ask the states to "keep this possibility in mind," thus insuring that even if adopted the resolution would have no impact. Arguments on behalf of such a proposal are occasionally put forth, and legislation to confine the nominating process to as little as two months have been introduced into Congress. Any truly abbreviated period would introduce a momentous change into American politics, increasing the advantages of the incumbents and not permitting the field of candidates to properly filter down to the two or three with the most popular support.

71. The commission flirted with the idea of arguing that committee abuses were so gross as to be out of compliance with the call to the 1972 convention. Such a bold position would have been difficult to enact. "Draft: Committee Selection Processes," Commission memo.

As usual, the recommendation encountered some interesting (and confused) commentaries. From Pennsylvania came a reinforcement of the McGovern-Fraser Commission's suspicions: "In Pennsylvania, the committee selection process has been notorious for producing unrepresentative convention delegations and has caused much bitter division among Democrats." From Louisiana came a rejection of the commission's position by the League of Women Voters: "You may find it of interest that in a 1964 study, local leagues of Louisiana indicated that they wanted delegates chosen by the party committee." See "Comments on Guidelines C-5: Committee Selection Processes."

72. The status of some states in this category is questionable, although listing them here is probably more representative of their actual behavior than listing them in the other two categories would be. In Georgia, Rhode Island, and Louisiana, the governor and state chairman played dominant roles, sometimes with little or no formal check from any other agency.

Beyond the fact that it makes a gross number of delegates dependent on a committee selection process in whole or in part, the procedure can violate the integrity of the entire system. An enormous range of abuses can then be introduced. Georgia and Louisana gave no pretense of being open or representative of anything beyond the governor's feelings. The governor and state chairman in both states, of course, are elected well before the convention year. Arkansas left the choice of convention delegate to the incumbent Democratic governor or United States senator with approval needed only from a compliant, two-year-old state committee. In Kentucky a state executive committee chosen one year early had the power to apportion the delegates, which they used to redistribute drastically the number allotted to congressional districts and for at-large purposes. Oklahoma selected its congressional district committees one year prior to the convention. Those committees in turn elected half of the national convention delegations, and state party rules failed to require any precinct or county elections prior to the state convention that selected the remaining half. Vermont gave the power to organize and restructure the entire process from caucus convention to a committee elected one year before the national convention. In Maryland the local central committees (which constituted the state executive committee and were delegates to the state convention, and which selected roughly one-fourth of the national convention delegates) were elected two years before the presidential nominations took place. Similarly, Hawaii awarded delegate status to central executive committee members elected two years earlier. And the National Committee members who became delegates were automatically selected, in most cases, four years before the convention.

73. New York, Pennsylvania, Maryland, Oklahoma, Massachusetts, Wisconsin, and Missouri.

74. Connecticut, Idaho, North Dakota, Wyoming, Tennessee, and Illinois.

75. The number of primaries did increase from fourteen to twenty-three in the period from 1969 to 1972. The idea of a national primary was given passing attention in some of the commission meetings and was mentioned as a possible reform by some witnesses at the regional hearings. It would require national legislation. On its merits alone, however, it is not a good idea. It would be expensive, exhaustive of a candidate's resources, and it would encourage demagogues possibly and more than likely help destroy what is left of party organization. The idea did not receive serious attention or support within the commission.

76. A New York spokesman was unusually candid about the qualifications his state's committee smiled upon: "By and large the controlling factors in appointments of at-large delegates have not changed. The telling factor is: What have you done for me lately? . . . We must have leaders—call them bosses if you will—I've talked to three or four McCarthy adherents; none of them contributed $250 to the party. I respect their intelligence, integrity, and sincerity, but you can't run a campaign on that." *New York Times*, 20 July 1969.

77. "Open" slatemaking procedures can be tricky. A glimpse into the "open" processes used by McCarthy supporters in California shows how complicated these can be. See the memo of Gerald N. Hill to Eli Segal et al. of 25 July 1969. The example provided by the insurgents in the Chicago challenge to the 1972 convention is also instructive. The effort to mold such a process represented the weakest link in their challenge.

78. William Greider, "Democrats Complicate Party Reform."

Chapter Four

1. R. W. Apple, Jr., "Texas Proves That the New Delegate Guidelines Work," *New York Times*, 16 June 1972, p. 22. See also Apple, "Texas Yields Boon to McGovern," and Martin Waldron, "Texas Delegates Allotted; Wallace is Victor with 42," in the *New York Times*, 15 June 1972, p. 44; Apple, "Texas Convention Still Big, But All Else Is Different," and Waldron, "Texas Leaders Lose in Delegate Selection," in the *New York Times*, 14 June 1972, p. 36; and Jon Ford, "Texas Democrats Grumbling: McGovern Commission Calls for Reform," *San Angelo* (Tex.) *Standard-Times*, 21 December 1969.

2. For example, the nationally syndicated columnists Rowland Evans and Robert Novak could be expected to interpret events in the worst light. See their column, "McGovern-Daley Clash Spotlights Civil War Ranging among Democrats," *Washington Post*, 11 June 1969, p. 27.

3. *Transcript of McGovern-Fraser Commission Meeting*, 1 March 1969, commission files.

4. Not to all however. A senior Democrat in Congress, asked to comment on an early draft of the proposed reforms in the fall of 1969, wrote McGovern: "Dear George: Only one thing—keep out of my state. Sincerely, ———.''

5. *Congressional Quarterly* (Washington, D.C.: Congressional Quarterly, 27 March 1970), p. 872.

6. Andrew J. Glass and Jonathan Cottin, "Democratic Reform Drive Falters as Spotlight Shifts to Presidential Race," *National Journal,* 19 June 1971, pp. 1293–1304.

7. A handful of states acted early and for the most part effectively on reform. They established reform commissions of their own and moved to make the needed changes, sometimes going well beyond what the McGovern-Fraser Commission required. Among these were North Carolina, Michigan, Minnesota, Alabama, New York, Florida, Maryland, and Delaware. The initial enthusiasm displayed wavered for several of these states, however, and, like Delaware, they became progressively more obstinate as the reform process evolved. *Congressional Quarterly,* p. 872.

8. David N. Ordan, "Maddox Suit on Party to Overturn Rules Reform," *Atlanta Journal,* 14 Decembr 1969, p. 1.

9. *Washington Star,* 22 September 1969, p. 69; and *Congressional Quarterly,* 27 March 1970, p. 872.

10. Brown to Senator Fred R. Harris, chairman, Democratic National Committee, 13 May 1969. The meeting had been scheduled for New Orleans on 22 May. Brown also accused McGovern of using the commission to further his own presidential aspirations. See also the UPI dispatch of 23 May 1969 and Evans and Novak, "McGovern-Daley Clash."

11. Evans and Novak, "McGovern-Daley Clash." Humphrey's ardor seemed to cool as the reform process got underway and possibly as the outline of his own candidacy for the 1972 presidential nomination began to take shape in his mind. This change was particularly noticeable during the enforcement period. The year before the 1972 convention Humphrey was warning that "you can't make quantum jumps overnight." Many state party leaders agreed. Glass and Cottin, "Democratic Reform Drive Falters," pp. 1293–1304.

12. Nelson to Brown, 23 May 1969. The Nelson rejoinder was circulated to the same mailing list as Brown's letter.

13. Robert Walters, "Democratic Reformers Head for Showdown with Regulars," *Washington Star,* 2 June 1969, p. 7. See also the AP dispatch of 4 June 1969. On the hearing itself see the *New Orleans Times-Picayune,* 20 June 1969, p. 1.

14. Vernon A. Guidry, Jr. "Brown Asks '72 Rules Ignored," AP Report in commission files. Copies of each article cited in this chapter can also be found in the commission files.

15. *Shreveport* (La.) *Times,* 13 November 1970, p. 1.

16. "National Democrats Dictatorial," *Monroe* (La.) *World,* 17 November 1970, editorial page.

17. Guidry, "Brown Asks '72 Rules Ignored."

18. Glass and Cottin, "Democratic Reform Drive Falters," pp. 1293–1304.

19. *New York Times,* 4 June 1972, p. E-4. Of the forty-four delegates, nineteen were black. Only three were Wallace supporters; the percentages indicate that this group and the party regulars suffered the severest underrepresentation on the state delegation.

20. On behalf of the AFL-CIO Meaney declared the federation "neutral" in the McGovern-Nixon contest, contributed no financial or organizational support to McGovern (a severe blow to his presidential hopes), and concentrated on congressional races. Labor, of course, was not united in its opposition. The U.A.W. (United Auto Workers) supported the reform movement, and one of its organizational leaders, William Dodds, served with distinction on the McGovern-Fraser Commission. U.A.W. President Leonard Woodcock briefly chaired the new delegate selection committee formed after the 1972 election before resigning owing to pressing union business. The U.A.W. also contributed some funds to the McGovern-Fraser Commission budget. The U.A.W., of course, was not a member of the AFL-CIO. Other unions independent of the Meaney position in the 1972 presidential election include the Communications Workers, the International Union of Electrical Workers, the International Association of Machinists, and the American Federation of State, County, and Municipal Employees.

21. See the *St. Louis Globe-Democrat,* 24 September 1969, p. 9; the *New York*

Times, 8 December 1969, p. 40; *Providence Journal*, 30 September 1969, editorial page; and the *Spokane Spokesman-Review*, 21 September 1969, p. 18.

22. *St. Louis Globe-Democrat*, 24 September 1969, p. 9.

23. Ibid.

24. See the *St. Paul Pioneer Press*, 21 September 1969, p. 1. The story reproduces one originally appearing in the *Washington Post* and refers to a letter written five months earlier by James C. O'Brien, the AFL-CIO's political action director, which explains federated labor's policy of noncooperation with the reform commissions and ties this posture specifically to Meaney and his principal advisors. The opposition among union leaders associated with the AFL-CIO was not unanimous, but it was nonetheless effective as a sign of deference and respect to Meaney's leadership.

25. Robert Strauss, the new national chairman of the Democratic National Committee (selected in an open and competitive election, one fruit of the reform movement) chosen a month after the 1972 presidential election, quite rightly wanted no disaffections from or problems with organized labor. Strauss chose Barkan's assistant, Robert J. Keefe, as his deputy chairman for the National Committee.

26. One analysis of labor's role can be found in R. W. Apple, Jr., "Labor's Vote May Be Split at Democratic Convention," *New York Times*, 6 February 1972, pp. 1, 46.

27. Harry Bernstein, "Union Czars Threaten Not to Back McGovern in November," *Los Angeles Times*, 12 July 1972, p. 12.

28. William J. Eaton, "Dems' Quota Policies Next AFL-CIO Target," *Chicago Daily News*, 21 November 1972, p. 4.

29. Dodds commented on federated labor's unwillingness to get out early and organize for their delegates hard enough to make a difference. Apple, "Labor's Vote May Be Split."

30. Ken Bode, "Democratic Party Reform: Turning Sour," *New Republic*, 10 July 1971, pp. 19–23; and Glass and Cottin, "Democratic Reform Drive Falters, pp. 1293–1304. Bode's organization gave background assistance to those involved in achieving reform and provided a balance to the regulars who opposed change. It aggressively and systematically kept track of the progress of enforcement and informed the press, various commission members, and others sympathetic to its point of view.

31. R. W. Apple, Jr., "Reform of Democrats," *New York Times*, 27 July 1971, p. 20. The summer of 1971 proved to be a particularly difficult time for the McGovern-Fraser Commission staff. Their accomplishments as well as their objectives seemed to be constantly called into question.

32. "Status of Guidelines Issued by Commission on Party Structure and Delegate Selection," memorandum for Lawrence F. O'Brien, chairman, Democratic National Committee, from Joseph A. Califano, Jr., counsel to the Democratic National Committee, 18 May 1970.

33. The first committee was established to consider delegate apportionment and selection (the McGovern-Fraser Commission recommendations) and consisted of Geri Joseph of Minnesota, George Mitchell of Maine, Richard Stoner of Indiana, Carrin Patman of Texas, and Grant Sawyer of Nevada. The second ad hoc committee created to review convention rules and procedures (the O'Hara Commission recommendations) was composed of Edward Breathitt of Kentucky, John Powers of Massachusetts, Mary Lou Burg of Wisconsin, Mildred Jeffrey of Michigan, and Albert Rains of Alabama.

34. David Mixner, the youngest member of the McGovern-Fraser Commission, saw the action as a "direct slap" at the commission and a "blatant misuse of the democratic process." (*Washington Star*, 24 May 1970, p. 1). McGovern was more restrained. The initial responses of both commission chairmen were in fact guarded. See the communications of O'Brien to O'Hara on 25 May 1970 and McGovern on 23 May 1970, and O'Hara's response of 26 May 1970. In the McGovern letter, O'Brien stressed that the ad hoc committees were "solely for the purpose of speeding the implementation of the Report and Guidelines of the Committee on Party Structure and Delegate Selection." The Executive Committee resolution authorizing the two ad hoc committees (22 May 1970) is fairly bland, leaving their exact purpose and role to future determination.

35. *Washington Star,* 24 May 1970.

36. Glass and Cottin, "Democratic Reform Drive Falters," pp. 1293–1304.

37. McGovern then turned around and convinced O'Brien to become one in the troika organizing his divided campaign (along with Gary Hart and Frank Mankiewicz). The dealings with O'Brien that led to McGovern's endorsement of Jean Westwood for the chair of the National Committee are complicated. Apparently, McGovern had convinced O'Brien to stay on as national chairman and then yielded to staff pressures and dumped him. Party regulars were stunned, for they had looked to O'Brien to lend a stabilizing influence and a sense of professionalism to a candidate and staff they mistrusted. O'Brien's position in the presidential campaign was limited; possibly his most notable accomplishment was in openly pursuing the Watergate issue, which attracted relatively little public notice at the time.

38. The preliminary call is an interesting document. It was issued as a result of the 19 February 1971 National Committee meeting, eighteen months before the convention. Normally, the call is published in January of the presidential election year. The O'Hara Commission recommendations concerning delegation size, the allotment of convention seats to the states (as modified), and the procedure for delegating challenges constitute about three-quarters of the document. The 1968 convention resolutions are included, together with an abbreviated mention (see following paragraphs) of the McGovern-Fraser Commission rules. The guidelines not included in the original convention resolutions were not listed. Obviously, these recommendations were not of prime concern at the meeting, although the commission rightly welcomed the National Committee's actions as a milestone in the effort to achieve full compliance. When the National Committee gathered on 14 October 1971 to approve the "final" call authorizing the National Convention, they rewrote the proposal on ex-officio delegates to allow national committeemen elected during the convention year to serve as National Convention delegates, "in accordance with procedures consistent with the 'full, meaningful and timely opportunity' mandate of the 1968 Convention." This revision qualified their earlier intent to permit national committeemen to sit as delegates with full votes regardless of when elected. The action was considered a set-back to the O'Hara Commission (which had suffered additional major reverses) and to the McGovern-Fraser Commission (its first official rebuff by the National Committee). The action violated both sets of recommendations but was hardly a significant blow. The openings it created were unique and were not exploited by the state parties.

The final call is basically an instrument reflecting the full recommendations (as modified by the National Committee) of the O'Hara Commission. It again does not elaborate the guidelines of the McGovern-Fraser Commission (which had already been repeatedly disseminated). Still, their inclusion in detail would have been symbolically important and would have reemphasized their legitimacy as part of the instrument establishing the convention.

The phrases in the McGovern-Fraser Commission (not including the provisions taken from the original 1968 convention mandate) in both the February and October calls read as follows:

Notice is also given that the Democratic National Committee has adopted the following resolution with respect to the Report of the Commission On Party Structure and Delegate Selection to the Democratic National Committee (April 1970), which relates to the requirements of subparagraphs (b) and (c) of the foregoing resolution:

BE IT RESOLVED by the Democratic National Committee that:

(a) With respect to those Guidelines of the Report of the Commission On Party Structure and Delegate Selection to the Democratic National Committee (April 1970) that said Commission "requires" state Democratic Parties to adopt pursuant to the "full, meaningful and timely opportunity" mandate of the 1968 Democratic National Convention, the Democratic National Committee adopts such Guidelines as the standards that state Democratic Parties, in qualifying and certifying delegates to the 1972 Democratic National Convention, must make all efforts to comply with, and

(b) With respect to those Guidelines of said Report that the Commission On

Party Structure and Delegate Selection to the Democratic National Committee "urges" state Democratic Parties to adopt, the Democratic National Committee joins in urging the implementation of such Guidelines by state Democratic Parties in qualifying and certifying delegates to the 1972 Democratic National Convention.

39. The McGovern-Fraser Commission met again on 19 November in conjunction with the O'Hara Commission to hear presentations and discuss ideas relevant to drafting proposals for a party charter. This meeting represented the formal opening of a new area of reform. Acting together, the commissions adopted a party charter, but it did not survive the 1972 national convention.

40. An intemperate reformer, for example, referred to staff director Robert W. Nelson's assessments as "nauseating." Bruce Biossat, "Democrats' Dilemma," *Washington Daily News*, 3 August 1971. See also Glass and Cottin, "Democratic Reform Drive Falters," pp. 1293–1304.

41. The two pieces in question are Bode, "Democratic Party Reform: Turning Sour," pp. 19–23 and Donald M. Fraser, "A Communication," *New Republic*, 21 and 28 August 1971, p. 31. Personalizing the controversy is simplistic but convenient. Overall, the Center for Political Reform had a healthy influence on the reform movement. It monitored the process in each state, directed public and party attention to trouble spots, helped prepare background materials for reformers and others involved in the effort (such as persons initiating court challenges), coordinated proreform efforts, used the media skillfully to interest a larger audience in reform questions, and published a newsletter ("The Informed Delegate"), which reviewed questions of concern. Being outside the Democratic party, it was free to criticize and to engage publicly in suits denied, for example, the McGovern-Fraser Commission staff.

42. "All Feasible Efforts," Statement to the McGovern-Fraser Commission, 16 July 1971.

43. Ibid.

44. The problem was not to be so easily dismissed. Later "clarifications" followed, culminating in Fraser's statement of 29 November.

Through its staff, the McGovern-Fraser Commission did enter two Amicus briefs, one in December 1971 in a Michigan case (*Michigan Democratic State Central Committee et al.* v. *Richard H. Austin et al.*), and one in a case in May 1972 related to Mayor Daley's Chicago challenge (*Wigoda* v. *Cousins*).

45. Hughes did the best he could to counter Harris and O'Brien. One of his most articulate sponsors was Congresswoman Shirley Chisholm. Most liberals, strong reformers, and blacks voted for Hughes, and most party regulars and southern conservatives voted for Harris; some ironic coalitions resulted. O'Brien, however, clearly had the votes.

While lopsided, the battle for votes was "savage" (as one principal said). For different perspectives see Ken Bode, "O'Brien Hurts Reform," *New Democrat*, July–August 1971, p. 13; "Democrats: Round 1 to the Regulars," *Time*, 25 October 1971, p. 13; "One for O'Brien," *New Republic*, 23 October 1971, p. 9; Paul R. Wiech, "Labor's Al Barkan: Practitioneer of the Old Politics," *New Republic*, 24 March 1973, p. 14; R. W. Apple, Jr., "Mrs. Harris Wins Democratic Post," *New York Times*, 14 October 1971, p. 1; R. W. Apple, Jr., "Mrs. Harris Vows to Fight Mistrust," *New York Times*, 15 October 1971, p. 19; Verne Newton, "The Hughes Imbroglio," *New Democrat*, November 1971, p. 10; William Chapman, "Reform Democrats Lose Key Post: Hughes Blames Labor 'Savagery,'" *Washington Post*, 14 October 1971, p. 1; Rowland Evans and Robert Novak, "Advisers Trip Muskie," *Washington Post*, 15 October 1971, p. 23; and Eli Segal, "O'Brien vs. Hughes: Inside the Squeeze on Party Reform," *Washington Monthly*, November 1971, pp. 48 ff.

A review of these pieces gives some idea of how bitter the factional battle over reform could become. As it turned out, Mrs. Harris was an impartial and strict chairman of the Credentials Committee. She was open to attack neither for being a principal in the reform drive (as Hughes would have been) nor for feeling overly sympathetic to the other side (she had been supported for the position by O'Brien, the AFL-CIO, and the party regulars).

46. Congressman Donald M. Fraser to Lawrence F. O'Brien, Chairman, Democratic National Committee, 29 November 1971, as circulated by O'Brien to state party leaders in December 1971.

47. A-1, which theoretically had already been included in state party rules by action of the Richard Hughes Special Equal Rights Committee in 1967 (as supported by the actions of the National Committee and the 1968 National Convention), was omitted from his early compilation of adoptions. As it turned out, the belief that these provisions (A-1) had been acted upon by the states proved to be overly optimistic.

48. In New York and Pennsylvania, the state parties were unable to obtain the legislative changes they needed to comply fully. The New York Democratic party went as far as to join a law suit that attempted to amend state statutes to permit a prospective delegate's presidential candidate preference to be placed on the ballot. New York's petition requirements exceeded 1 percent in law, also a violation of the guidelines (although a less serious one). Candidates for the state committee in Pennsylvania could not indicate their presidential preference under the state statutes (again a violation of C-1).

49. For example, the work of the state-level reform committees in Michigan, North Carolina, and Ohio was outstanding.

50. The ten states in "substantial" but not full compliance were Connecticut, Florida, Georgia, Indiana, Maryland, Montana, New York, Oregon, Pennsylvania, and West Virginia. All but West Virginia were challenged before the Credentials Committee of the 1972 National Convention. See note 51.

51. The standards applied by the Credentials Committee's membership varied widely. The thinking behind the "all feasible efforts" and the debates on the issues involved were influential, although the general criteria applied were closer to "a good faith effort" attempt by the state party to comply. The principals in the disputes, the presentations by partisans on both sides, the extent to which a state party was out-of-step with its sister parties, and, of course, political gain all influenced the final decisions.

52. McGovern's frequent crediting of the reforms he had pushed as making his candidacy possible did little to endear him to party professionals or to close the gap between them and the McGovern camp. See, for example, L. Clayton Dubois, "Is He Really Serious about Being President? Yes.," *New York Times Magazine*, 2 May 1971, pp. 26 ff.

53. Statement in report to Commission, commission files.

54. Both national committees have Young Democrats or Young Republicans (or their equivalents). The organizations tend to be moribund and party-based rather than issue-oriented. They are revived each presidential election year to win support among young adults for the party's candidate, but they could in no sense be considered influential in national politics.

55. The following table tells the story.

New Voters in the Twenty Largest States

State (electoral votes)	1968 Presidential Plurality	Eligible New Voters (18–25 yrs.)	% of Electorate
Cal. (45)	223,346 (Nixon)	2,580,000	18.1
N.Y. (41)	370,538 (HHH)	2,101,000	16.5
Pa. (27)	169,388 (HHH)	1,371,000	16.9
Tex. (26)	38,960 (HHH)	1,490,000	19.6
Ill. (26)	134,960 (Nixon)	1,321,000	17.5
Ohio (25)	90,428 (Nixon)	1,313,000	18.3
Mich. (21)	222,417 (HHH)	1,127,000	19.2
N.J. (17)	61,261 (Nixon)	769,000	15.3
Fla. (17)	210,010 (Nixon)	773,000	15.2
Mass. (14)	702,374 (HHH)	725,000	18.4
Ind. (13)	261,226 (Nixon)	662,000	19.0
N.C. (13)	131,004 (Nixon)	750,000	21.5
Va. (12)	147,932 (Nixon)	645,000	20.0
Mo. (12)	20,488 (Nixon)	569,000	17.7

New Voters in the Twenty Largest States (continued)

State (electoral votes)		1968 Presidential Plurality	Eligible New Voters (18–25 yrs.)	% of Electorate
Ga.	(12)	155,439 (Wallace)	354,000	11.4
Wis.	(11)	61,193 (Nixon)	565,000	19.2
Tenn.	(10)	47,800 (Nixon)	511,000	18.9
Md.	(10)	20,315 (HHH)	478,000	17.6
Minn.	(10)	199,095 (HHH)	478,000	18.9
La.	(10)	220,685 (Nixon)	497,000	21.1

271 electoral votes—270 needed to win

SOURCE: *Congressional Report* (New York: National Committee for an Effective Congress, September 1971), p. 3.

56. For one analysis of the potency of the black vote, see the *JCPS Research Bulletin* (Washington, D.C.: The Joint Center for Political Studies, February 1972).

57. The South Carolina challenge on women as argued in the Credentials Committee and on the convention floor is a case in point. McGovern's campaign manager, Gary Hart, discusses the controversy in his *Right from the Start* (New York: Quadrangle Books, 1973).

58. The most notable being the angry shouting match in front of the podium between Congresswoman Bella Abzug and actress Shirley McLaine. Both activists, Abzug argued for support of the women's cause regardless of consequence while McLaine felt that the long-run interests were best served by supporting the most sympathetic candidate (McGovern).

59. For an examination of the Chicago challenge, see William J. Crotty, "Anatomy of a Challenge: The Chicago Delegation to the Democratic National Convention," in *Cases in American Politics*, ed. Robert L. Peabody (New York: Praeger, 1976), pp. 111–58.

60. Ibid.

61. The exact figures are as follows:

Method of Choosing Delegates

Year	Primary	Convention	Committee
1972	52.8%	45.5%	1.7%
1968	40.7	46.4	12.9
Change	+12.1%	− .9%	−11.2%

62. Commission on Party Structure and Delegate Selection, "The Party Reformed: Final Report of Commission on Party Structure and Delegate Selection," mimeographed (Washington, D.C.: Democratic National Committee, 7 July 1972).

Chapter Five

1. R. W. Apple, Jr., "McGovern Facing a Difficult Task in Unifying Party," *New York Times*, 17 July 1972, p. 1.

2. *Democrats in Convention* (Washington, D.C.: Democratic National Committee, 1972), p. 126.

3. Senators Hubert Humphrey and Edmund Muskie refused invitations to join the McGovern ticket. Humphrey was chosen to lead the new reform commission, which recommended that an additional day be set aside during the convention to select the vice-presidential nominee or that the designation be made at a meeting of the National Committee, a "miniconvention" (as had been done in 1972), after the regular convention.

4. The first session was called to order at 8:00 P.M. on 10 July and adjourned at 4:52 A.M. on 11 July; the second session convened at 7:15 P.M. on the eleventh and ceased at 6:20 A.M. on the twelfth; the third began at 8:00 P.M. and adjourned at

12:52 P.M.; and the fourth and final session came to order at 7:55 P.M. on Thursday, 13 July and concluded sine die at 3:45 A.M.

5. Labor, of course, disapproved of the reform effort. Their early distaste later turned to implacable opposition, which in turn hurt O'Hara politically (see note 6). I. W. Abel of the AFL-CIO's U.S. Steelworkers never attended a meeting of the McGovern-Fraser Commission, of which he was a member. At the 1972 convention Abel gave a speech in support of Senator Henry Jackson's candidacy (federated labor's favorite at the time) that was considered the most critical and politically divisive statement of the meeting. Abel's (and Meany's and Barkan's) comments to the press and to television reporters at the convention continued to be negative (see Harry Bernstein, "Union Czars Threaten Not to Back McGovern in November," *Los Angeles Times*, 12 July 1972, p. 12). Joseph Keenan, Secretary of the International Brotherhood of Electrical Workers, was a member of the O'Hara Commission. He did attend several meetings, but he was not overly active in the deliberations. While generally numbered among the committee's conservatives, Keenan demonstrated support for the group's work by his presence and participation.

The attitude of labor is illustrated by a (probably apocryphal) story that made the rounds in 1972. Al Barkan and George Meany were considered to be among the most vehement and unforgiving opponents of reform. Barkan reputedly called O'Brien and told him that labor would need 300 delegates at the upcoming (1972) convention. O'Brien supposedly replied, "You're going to have to earn them this year." Whether true or not, the story sheds light on organized labor's (more specifically, the AFL-CIO leadership's) views. Barkan's perhaps humorous characterization of the New York delegation as "two labor union leaders and seven fags" suggests how offensive Meany and Barkan found the reforms and how pointedly they took exception to them. The reference is found in Paul R. Weick's profile "Labor's Al Barkan: Practitioneer of the Old Politics," *New Republic*, 24 March 1973, pp. 13 ff.

6. O'Hara paid a political price for his leadership in this area of the reform movement and for his later role at the 1972 convention. His ties with the AFL-CIO leadership became badly strained. In 1972, he barely won reelection (by a scant 51 percent–49 percent margin of the vote) in the white, lower-income, working-class district that he had served since 1958 and that he had carried by at least 70 percent of the vote in the two previous elections. By no means did O'Hara's work on reform determine the outcome (the paramount issue was busing, the code word for school integration), but the congressman's association with changes that were considered anti-labor and his difficult relations with the AFL-CIO did not facilitate his reelection.

Furthermore, O'Hara, long considered a potential leader of promise in the House, ran unsuccessfully for the majority leader's position. During the life of the Commission on Rules, the post was opened by the retirement of Speaker John McCormick and the elevation of Carl Albert. O'Hara was expected to be a strong contender, but he did poorly, finishing near the bottom in a five-man field.

In the post-1972 period, O'Hara became a leader in the Coalition for a Democratic Majority, a group formed by Democratic politicians and academicians to fight the reforms. The association of centrist to conservative Democrats argued for a return to a basically New Deal coalition for the Democrats, emphasized the role of labor and of party professionals in party councils, and called for a heavy defense commitment. Most of its energies were directed toward reversing or modifying the delegate selection changes by bringing pressure on the national chairman, National Committee, the Mikulski Commission (New Delegate Selection), and the Sanford Commission (Party Charter).

7. Donald Peterson's warm endorsement of O'Hara's leadership given at the commission meeting of 30 July 1971 should be viewed in this light. Peterson's comments accurately reflected the views of virtually all members of the commission. Peterson and O'Hara, presuming themselves to be on opposite sides of the political fence, were initially wary of each other. At first Peterson stood to the left of most of the others and moved center (or the center moved left). He became comfortably rooted in the mainstream of commission deliberations and, in the pattern evidenced by each of the commissioners, even found himself on the conservative side of what were, in truth, ideological positions (poorly defined for the most part). "Liberal" is here taken to mean opening and democratizing convention procedures.

8. O'Hara's remarks before the Commission on Party Structure and Delegate Selection, 16 July 1971.

9. In a speech in the *Congressional Record,* introducing the rules that were finally adopted, Representative O'Hara argued that his committee's recommendations would assure "representative, open, deliberate, and fair" conventions. Post facto, these criteria are as good as any (and outside of the "deliberative" aspect they parallel the McGovern-Fraser Commission's objectives), but they were not held explicitly before the commission as goals the members would try to meet.

The entire drafting process was more mechanical than that in the McGovern-Fraser Commission and evolved principally in line with a piecemeal schedule put before the group periodically by the chairman. A parallel to the commission's deliberations can be found in the detailed consideration given by a legislative drafting committee (which the commission came to resemble) to each section of a pending bill. The principles underlying the legislation are the last concern at this technical stage.

10. When someone finally raised the point that the commission was regressing, that its proposals (or lack of them) were less progressive even than extant party law, feeble as that may have been, many members were shocked or bemused. Others were less committed to returning to the status quo ante. Labor representative Keenan opposed an explicit reference to female equality on convention committees, primarily on the grounds that it was not needed. It took a concerted effort by the women on the committee, led by Liv Bjorlie and Congresswoman Patsy Mink (like Keenan, an infrequent contributor to group deliberations) to return the commission to a position of requiring equal female representation on all convention committees. Due to an oversight on the part of the staff, the arguments had to be made without recourse to staff information, precedents, or the numbers of women affected prior to the original adoption of the rule (although Bode's Center for Political Reform had supplied Bjorlie and Mink with enough facts to make an intelligent argument). See table 5.1, footnote c for a fuller treatment of the incident.

11. Professor Paul T. David of the University of Virginia, the most knowledgeable political scientist on national convention operations, did serve as a permanent consultant to the Commission. David attended the committee meetings and provided a badly needed perspective, but he did not have authority to direct staff work or structure the agenda for discussion.

12. The criticisms advanced by Dennis O'Toole near the end of the Commission on Rules deliberations are relevant here. O'Toole argued that the role and the *rights* of the individual delegate had never been given serious consideration. The point can be elaborated and focuses on a basic weakness in the committee's approach. No one raised such issues as what a delegate was supposed to do, whom he represented, what right he had to information, what accountability he should expect from convention officials or national committee party leaders, how much access he should have to supporting materials and staff, and to what extent he was protected under party law in seeking his rights (once these had been established). In many respects, the delegate was the forgotten man in the commission's deliberations. His concerns did not fit comfortably into deliberations focused on institutional forms.

13. The practice of the commission was to meet for one- or two-day sessions to review various topical areas (logistics, convention committees, convention size, seating arrangements, etc.) and to discuss and dispose of other commission business. At the height of its activity, it was meeting as often as every three or four weeks in Washington, D.C. Each meeting was structured by written proposals on the topic under discussion, which set the limits of debate. (The tendency was to postpone major controversies to an indefinite future date.) All proposals were read and discussed (or at least acquiesced in) a minimum of two times. All meetings were open to the public and the press, although few chose to sit in. The session on the proposals dealing with the media drew the largest turnout. Correspondents were briefed on events by the commission chairman (usually at the lunch recess), and most newsmen attended only this session.

14. *Proceedings of the January 14, 1969, Meeting of the Democratic National Committee,* chapter 1.

15. Rules Commission meeting, 17 May 1969.

16. These were Professor Paul T. David of the University of Virginia, the com-

mission consultant; Professor Carl Auerbach of the University of Minnesota Law School, a commission member; Professor Alexander Bickel of the Yale University Law School, a consultant to the McGovern-Fraser Commission; and Professor Robert G. Dixon, Jr., of the George Washington University Law School, an expert on apportionment and later an assistant attorney-general in the Nixon administration.

17. These reports are *Issues and Alternatives* (Washington, D.C.: Commission on Rules, October 1969); *Supplement to Issues and Alternatives* (Washington, D.C.: Commission on Rules, October 1970); and *Call To Order* (Washington, D.C.: Commission on Rules, 14 June 1972). The commission also published and distributed its draft rules after each working session and its complete set of rules after its meeting on 30 July 1971.

18. The decision on the public hearings and even their regional dispersion was influenced by the successful McGovern-Fraser hearings in progress at the time the Commission on Rules met.

19. O'Hara acted with restraint on this question. He gave party leaders the opportunity to vent their frustrations while delaying any decisions on convention-related media problems until tempers had cooled. His concern was to conduct an orderly convention rather than to inhibit or penalize the networks. The July 1969 meeting gave representatives of the media, who were feeling beleaguered after the official reaction to the 1968 convention coverage, an opportunity to express themselves. Eleven witnesses were at the hearing: three academicians (two with special expertise on the media) and eight representatives of the press, including AP and UPI spokesmen, the congressional press, photographers, and radio, television, and periodical personnel. The role of the media is difficult to define realistically. On occasion, reference would be made to the "entertainment values" of conventions—a red flag to most practicing politicians, who view conventions in a serious light. A juxtaposition of the 1968 Democratic convention, in which the images transmitted by newsmen angered the Democrats, and the 1972 Republican Convention, in which the party totally controlled and programmed the formal proceedings, indicate the extremes as well as the seriousness of the problem. Television is particularly vulnerable to official displeasure because of supervision by the politically controlled Federal Communications Commission. The FCC can influence programming, and it rewards or denies license applications, a power the Nixon administration exploited. As 1968 receded from memory, the Democrats, concerned with the free television exposure continually given the Republican administration, demanded equal time. An accumulation of grievances led to the Commission on Rules hearings in December 1971, called at the insistence of Congressman Hale Boggs, then Democratic House Majority Leader. The hearings focused on the media had more to do with congressional politics than commission problems.

20. *Call To Order*, p. 10.

21. See "Preliminary Codification, Rules of the Democratic National Convention, Now in Force" (Washington, D.C.: The Commission on Rules, 17 May 1969), the nine pages deal with rules since 1956; "Document II: Rules of the House of Representatives" (as applicable to the Democratic National Convention) (Washington, D.C.: The Commission on Rules, 17 May 1969); and "Up-dating of the Rules of the House" (Washington, D.C.: 17 May 1969).

22. Remarks of O'Hara at 17 May 1969 Commission on Rules meeting.

23. The O'Hara Commission did not put out a press release in each city they were to visit that specifically outlined the subjects in which they were interested. They used advance men to make the necessary arrangements, contacted local politicians to notify them of the event, and distributed copies of *Issues and Alternatives* to politicians and newsmen.

24. The steady contributors to the working sessions of the Commission on Rules were O'Hara, Auerbach, Bjorlie, Breathitt, Brown, Crangle, Kaler, McDiarmid, O'Toole, Peterson, Powers, Sylvester, Shapiro, and Franklin.

25. Much was made of the fact by the National Committee at the 19 February meeting that "your" Executive Committee had acted in "your" best interests in devising the new formula. Actually, the Executive Committee had adopted the formula proposed by the Ad Hoc Committee, which had been established by O'Brien and was sensitive to his wishes. The entire controversy could have been avoided. In the strenu-

ous debate that followed, a number of angry National Committee members wanted to know why the Executive Committee would substitute its judgment for that of the O'Hara Commission, the group chosen to do the job. It was a fair question. The victory of the National Committee was a costly one—and a seemingly unnecessary symbolic exercise in favor of the smaller states and at the expense of the national party's credibility and the Rules Commission's legitimacy.

26. National Chairman Lawrence F. O'Brien, presiding at the National Committee meeting, refused to admit under repeated questioning that the changes had been proposed by the Ad Hoc Committee; perhaps he feared that its legitimacy would be contested or that the responsibility for the revisions might be traced directly to him.

27. *Congressional Quarterly* (Washington, D.C.: Congressional Quarterly, 12 February 1971), p. 382.

28. It was apparent that many members did not know a vote was in progress and others did not know what was being voted on. Immediately after the vote had been taken these points were made by a member who asked the chair what the issues in question had been. The point was raised again by Maine's National Committeeman George Mitchell at the end of the session, after the apportionment decision had been disposed of. Several speakers argued that the Powers Motion undercut the entire principle of reform, but on a roll call a reconsideration motion was defeated, 57 to 31. *Proceedings of the Democratic National Committee* (Washington, D.C.: Democratic National Committee, 19 February 1971).

29. *Congressional Quarterly*, 19 February 1971, p. 417.

30. UPI wire service, 17 February 1971.

31. Ibid.

32. Tim O'Brien, "Democratic Party Reform: Now It Has to Be Put into Practice," *Washington Post*, 8 August 1971, p. 2.

33. Evans and Novak, "Fourth-Party Guerilla Wars," *Washington Post*, 23 July 1971, p. 23. See also Tim O'Brien, "Democrats Finish Efforts on Reform," *Washington Post*, 31 July 1971, p. 4.

34. R. W. Apple, Jr., "Reform of Democrats," *New York Times*, 27 July 1971, p. 20.

Chapter Six

1. Alabama Democratic State Chairman Robert Vance at the Salt Lake City Hearing of the Commission on Rules, 17 April 1970.

2. Ibid.

3. Congresswoman Shirley Chisholm at the New York City Hearing of the Commission on Rules, 14 August 1970.

4. The witness in question was L. Goldstein at the Washington, D.C., Hearing of the Commission on Rules, 11 September 1970.

The Eisenhower criticisms and remedies (which are considerably more authoritarian than anything the O'Hara Commission proposed) can be found in "Our National Nominating Conventions Are a Disgrace," *Reader's Digest*, July, 1966, p. 77.

5. The comments of Elizabeth Vance, who had attended eight national conventions as a delegate or alternate.

6. Statement of Olive Brooks to Commission on Rules, Boston Hearing, 15 May 1970.

7. Statement of Mrs. Paddy O. McLaughlin to Commission on Rules, Washington, D.C., Hearing, 11 September 1970.

8. Statement of Eugene H. Nickerson, Nassau County Executive, to Commission on Rules, New York City Hearing, 14 August 1970.

9. Statement of Mrs. Nathan Bullard to Commission on Rules, 24 March 1970.

10. Statement of Pat Derian to Commission on Rules, *Atlanta Hearing*, 20 February 1970.

11. Statement of Paul O'Dwyer to Commission on Rules, New York City Hearing, 14 August 1970.

12. Derian Statement.

13. Chicago, for example, offered $750,000 in cash and $116,240 worth of services as incentives to the Democrats to hold their 1968 national convention in that city. Local business leaders estimated that a national party convention is worth $4.5 to $10 million in new income. See the statement of Dr. Herbert Alexander, Director, Citizens' Research Foundation to the Commission on Rules, Washington, D.C., Hearing, 26 July 1969.

14. A journal of the convention proceedings was published within eighteen months, an unusually short time for either party.

15. The Rules Committee of the 1972 convention passed the following resolution on the subject:

> . . . beginning with its next fiscal year and thereafter, the Democratic National Committee shall maintain in a separate account monies to be used solely and explicitly to defray the reasonable and necessary expenses of those delegates and Standing Committee members to subsequent Democratic Conventions who could not otherwise attend such Conventions, and would therefore be denied their rights of full Democratic participation.
>
> The Democratic National Committee shall cause to be deposited each year in such account at least 8 per cent of its gross annual income.

In order to help delegates of modest means, the same committee investigated the feasibility of holding the 1976 convention at a large university with dormitory and cafeteria facilities available at modest cost. The O'Hara Commission had discussed this option on several occasions but took no action. Committee on Rules of the 1972 Democratic National Convention, . . . *by the people* (Washington, D.C.: Democratic National Committee, 27 July 1972), pp. 21–22.

16. Stephen Reinhardt in his testimony before the Commission on Rules in Salt Lake City on 3 April 1970. Anne Wexler made a similar point in her testimony to the commission in Washington, D.C., on 11 September 1970.

17. See Richard C. Bain and Judith H. Parris, *Convention Decisions and Voting Records*, 2d ed. (Washington, D.C.: The Brookings Institution, 1960), pp. 14–19.

18. Ibid., pp. 259–60.

19. Bonus votes were first introduced into the Republican party's allocation scheme in 1916 to reward nonsouthern states that supported the party's national ticket. The change followed the climatic fight in the 1912 Republican National Convention between the Taft and Roosevelt forces over the seating of Republican delegates from southern states that had few if any Republican voters. The bonus concept has even prospered in the Republican party, as a review of their 1972 call to the convention will indicate.

20. To be explicit, in the National Committee resolution of 13 October 1971, which established the Standing Committees, a provision was included that authorized the DNC chairman to name the acting chairman of the two committees subject to ratification by the Executive Committee of the DNC.

21. Commission on Rules, *Call to Order* (Washington, D.C.: Democratic National Committee, 1972), p. 70.

22. The 150 seats on each of the three convention committees were allocated among the state delegations as follows: California and New York, 10; Pennsylvania, 7; Ohio and Illinois, 6; Michigan and Texas, 5; Florida, Massachusetts, and New Jersey, 4; Connecticut, Georgia, Indiana, Maryland, Minnesota, Missouri, North Carolina, Virginia, Washington, and Wisconsin, 3; Alabama, Arizona, Arkansas, Colorado, Hawaii, Idaho, Iowa, Kansas, Kentucky, Louisiana, Maine, Mississippi, Montana, Nebraska, New Hampshire, New Mexico, Oklahoma, Oregon, Rhode Island, South Carolina, South Dakota, Tennessee, Utah, and West Virginia, 2; and the remainder, 1.

23. Statement of Faye Broderick, Democratic National Committeewoman from Maine and chairwoman, Committee on Permanent Organization, 1968 Democratic National Convention, before the Commission on Rules, Washington, D.C., Hearing, 19 September 1969.

24. Ibid.

25. The manual took its name from the late United States Representative Clarence Cannon of Missouri, the reigning expert in his day on House parliamentary procedure,

who compiled the brief booklet. Cannon served as the convention's parliamentarian until his death and was its (and the House's) unquestioned authority on the subject. The reference for 1968 is *Democratic Manual for the Democratic National Convention of 1968*, originally prepared by Clarence Cannon (Washington, D.C.: Democratic National Committee, 1964 [*sic*]).

26. *Call To Order*, p. 77.

27. The most thorough account of the "loyalty oath" battles can be found in Abraham Holtzman, "The Loyalty Pledge Controversy in the Democratic Party," in *Cases on Party Organization*, ed. Paul Tillett (New York: McGraw-Hill, 1963), pp. 124–54.

The problem as encountered by the O'Hara Commission had come full circle. The "loyalty oath" the party leaders were talking about at this point in time was one intended to bind liberal delegates to support convention nominees whom the delegates might feel were unsatisfactory (McCarthy supporters were the specific object of the pledge). Furthermore, the party wanted to dissuade those who felt most strongly from forming a fourth party, since it would draw support from the Democrats. The language finally adopted is more explicit than in previous years but is not dissimilar: the delegate who participates in a convention "expressly agrees that he will not publicly support or campaign for any candidate for President or Vice President other than the nominees of the Convention" and that he will do "all within his power to assure that voters of his state will have the opportunity to cast their election ballots for the Presidential and Vice Presidential nominees selected by the convention."

The historically troubled term "loyalty" was replaced by the more innocuous term "responsibility" at one of the last commission meetings. At this meeting the committee also rejected a motion put forth by Donald O. Peterson that had an interesting assumption behind it. Peterson argued that if the rank and file was to be loyal to the office seekers, then the office seekers should be loyal and accountable to the people nominating them. This sense of duty could best be demonstrated by having the nominees, and particularly the United States Senate and House candidates, pledge their willingness to implement the party platform, the new national statement of doctrine, once they had been elected. Peterson's motion offered a new departure, but it was defeated. The Peterson Motion read:

> The acceptance of the nominations for President and Vice President also carries a concomitant responsibility to support the Platform of the National Convention and a pledge to wholeheartedly work for its implementation.
>
> Congressmen and Senators of the Democratic Party must also recognize their responsibility to implement the Platform of the National Convention. Failure to actively support its implementation should be grounds for fellow Congressmen and Senators to discipline uncooperative members.

28. When he realized the volume of business his Credentials Committee would be asked to handle, Chairman Richard Hughes drew together rules of procedures that anticipated some of the O'Hara Commission regulations in less elaborate form. These he circulated to all interested or challenged delegates and to prospective challengers.

29. Statement of James V. Johnson to the Commission on Rules, Atlanta Hearing, 20 February 1970.

30. This apparently fair-minded and innocuous provision caused one bitter encounter during the Chicago convention of 1972. After an acrimonious meeting, party regulars rejected the first hearing officer sent by the Credentials Committee chairwoman on the grounds that the officer's firm and the firm that employed the challenger's lawyers had clients in common. The incident is treated in William J. Crotty, "Anatomy of a Challenge: The Chicago Delegation to the Democratic National Convention," in *Cases in American Politics*, ed. Robert L. Peabody (New York: Praeger, 1976), pp. 124–31.

31. Of the three "national" candidates, McGovern was the favorite and, as events showed, had the votes to win. Humphrey and Muskie withdrew in the few days preceding the nominations.

32. Congressional Quarterly, *The Presidential Nominating Conventions 1968* (Washington, D.C.: Congressional Quarterly, 1968), p. 202.

33. *Norman* (Okla.) *Transcript*, 29 September 1969. Quoted in William R. Brown,

"Television and the Democratic National Convention of 1968," *Quarterly Journal of Speech* 55 no. 3 (October 1969): 237–46. The Brown article and Thomas Whiteside, "Corridor of Mirrors: The Television Editorial Process, Chicago," *Columbia Journalism Review* 7, no. 4 (Winter 1968/69): 35–54) are good reviews of the impact of television on the perceptions of the convention.

34. Theodore H. White, *The Making of the President 1968* (New York: Atheneum, 1969), pp. 376–78.

35. A second commission meeting on the media was held in December 1969 at the request of United States Representative Hale Boggs. The sessions dealt more with congressional anger directed toward the networks than with any business of the O'Hara Commission.

Chapter Seven

1. Democratic Charter Commission, *Proceedings of Charter Commission Meeting* (Washington, D.C., April 1973).

2. *Proceedings of Charter Commission Meeting*. See also Linda Charlton, "McGovern Urges Better Reforms," *New York Times*, 11 April 1973, p. 15; William Chapman "McGovern Abandons Two Reforms," *Washington Post*, 11 April 1973, p. 1; Paul Hope, "McGovern Cools Reformers," *Washington Star and Daily News*, 11 April 1973, p. 18; and Charlton, "Humphrey Urges Democratic Party Unity," *New York Times*, 12 April 1973, p. 25.

McGovern had begun to turn his attention to retaining his seat in the United States Senate; the South Dakota seat would fall open in 1974 and was then in seeming jeopardy. He withdrew from any active involvement in the reform movement at this point.

3. *Proceedings of Charter Commission Meeting*. If anything, National Chairman Strauss was prepared to go to extreme and unorthodox ends to repudiate the newly instituted reform rules of 1972. Requested by a party regular, the Wyoming Democratic state chairman, Strauss unilaterally sought a ruling on the legal status of the Mikulski Commission from Chicago lawyer Newton N. Minow, apparently chosen because he would give a sympathetic ruling and because he was not involved with immediate events. Minow decreed that the 1972 convention rules "have no continuing status" as precedents for the 1976 guidelines and that all provisions adopted by the Mikulski Commission were "subject to review and adoption by the Democratic National Committee." Of course the National Committee's regular legal counsel, Sheldon S. Cohen, concurred in a ruling that would insure that the DNC had full and final authority over all Mikulski Commission proposals and all standards affecting 1976.

Predictably, the regulars were delighted and the reformers infuriated. In a brief set of remarks to the commission intended to defuse the storm that broke, Strauss declared that he felt that the people before him were in "85 per cent accord" and then, in an offhand manner, agreed to submit the dispute to former Supreme Court Justice Arthur Goldberg for adjudication (a concession that effectively undercut the ruling he had acquired). Goldberg at first agreed to issue a decision but then withdrew from the embroglio. The issue, like many that arose, was left unresolved despite its enormous importance. Some reformers threatened Strauss with a law suit if his initial stand held. Strauss sent National Committee representatives the Minow opinion with the notation that it "represented the National Committee's legal position on this matter." Mikulski countered with an opposing declaration, rendered by her chief staff assistant and legal counsel, Gerald S. J. Cassidy, which was distributed to the Democratic National Committee's membership. The principals then downplayed the conflict, Mikulski asserting that she and Strauss "agreed that if we all work together to formulate guidelines based on equity and the best interests of the Democratic Party, there would be no need to be concerned about legal opinions." True. And there would have been no dispute to begin with. Leaving such fundamental points unresolved was unwise, both for the short-run interests of the delegate selection committee and for the long-run interests of reform bodies mandated by the national convention. During a period (1972–74) of general disrespect for party rules and procedures, this controversy illustrated the extent to which matters had deteriorated.

Concerning the above, see David S. Broder, "Democrats End Dispute over Convention Rules," *Chicago Sun-Times*, 29 September 1973, p. 10; Broder, "Democratic Reformists Show Strength in Party Rules Fight," *Chicago Sun-Times*, 22 September 1973, p. 7; Christopher Lydon, "Strauss Disputed Rift over Reform," *New York Times*, 23 September 1973, p. 25; and Broder, "Goldberg Now Unwilling to Settle Democrats' Fight," *Chicago Sun-Times*, 23 September 1973, p. 16.

4. Actually, its name was identical to that of the late McGovern-Fraser Commission, i.e., the Commission on Party Structure and Delegate Selection. To clarify further, it will be referred to as the New Delegate Selection Commission, or the Mikulski Commission.

5. Paul K. Wieck, "Chairman Strauss' Hot Seat," *New Republic* (20 April 1974): 17. After the tempestuous August meeting of the Charter Commission, in which the AFL-CIO leadership played a significant role, the U.A.W.'s political coordinator in Washington and a member of the commission, Bill Dodds, put the events in perspective. "I've always felt," Dodds said, "that the Democratic party would never solve its problems until the labor movement started solving its own. Perhaps we're at the beginning of a transition period." R. W. Apple, Jr., "Democrats' Outlook Is Hurt by Wounds of '68 and '72," *New York Times*, 2 September 1974, p. 8.

6. Richard M. Scammon and Ben J. Wattenberg, *The Real Majority* (New York: Coward, McCann & Geohegan, Inc., 1970, 1971).

7. See Coalition for a Democratic Majority, Task Force on Democratic Party Rules, *Toward Fairness and Unity for '76* (Washington, D.C.: The Coalition for a Democratic Majority, n.d.). The coalition was roughly balanced by other proreform groups on the other side. The A.D.A. (Americans for Democratic Action) consistently favored a strong reform posture, and in fact Congressman Donald Fraser (also on the Charter Commission) served as its president in 1974. A much smaller operation, the Democratic Planning Group, under the conscientious direction of Alan Baron, monitored the reform process and attempted to coordinate proreform activity. In this pursuit, Baron published at irregular intervals a newsletter that was the best single source of information on the new reform activity.

8. Richard M. Scammon and Ben J. Wattenberg, "The Middle Road Leads to the White House," *Washington Post*, 25 July 1971, p. B-1.

9. Ibid.

10. Ibid.

11. Ibid.

12. The quotations in the following commentary on the CDM are taken from the coalition's *Toward Fairness and Unity for '76*.

13. Ibid.

14. Ibid.

15. David S. Broder, "Chicagoan Focus of Hectic Democratic Power Squabble," *Chicago Sun-Times*, 25 August 1973, p. 6; William J. Eaton, "Democrats May Clash over Delegate Policies," *Chicago Daily News*, 28 August 1973, p. 11; "Walker Took Seith's $1,000 Campaign Gift," *Chicago Sun-Times*, 26 August 1973, p. 3; and Fletcher Wilson, "Walker Opposes Seith for Delegate Selection Post," *Chicago Sun-Times*, 24 August 1973, p. 10.

Strauss actively intervened in the commission's affairs. This is but one incident. More than likely, Strauss did not have the authority to do this, but it was up to the commission's leadership to protect its prerogatives as McGovern and Fraser had been forced to do earlier. To assume a passive attitude and trust to the goodwill of the national chairman was to invite difficulties, as the experience of the O'Hara Commission should have foretold.

16. The drafting subcommittee was seen as being 10 to 7 or 11 to 6—depending on the observer—in favor of a pro-reform stance. On this phase of the commission's activities, see: William J. Eaton, "Democrats Set Up Panel to Draft Rules for '76," *Chicago Daily News*, 21 September 1973, p. 12; "Democratic Party Drafting Unit O.K.s New Rule: Quotas Junked," *Chicago Sun-Times*, 8 October p. 14; "Democrats O.K. Change in Rules for '76 Race," *Chicago Sun-Times*, 30 September 1973, p. 46; "Democrats Delay Decision on Quotas Issue," *Chicago Sun-Times*, 1 October 1973, p. 27; "Democratic Unit Bars Minority Quotas for '76," *Chicago Sun-Times*, 7 October

1973, p. 102; "Democrats Cite Optimism on Pact," *New York Times*, 7 October 1973, p. 34; "Democratic Unit Drops Quota Rule," *Chicago Sun-Times*, 28 October 1973, p. 10; "Using Rules to Make Ends Meet," *New York Times*, 4 November 1973, p. E-3; Jon Margolis, "Democrats Adopt Rules on Delegates," *Chicago Tribune*, 28 October 1973, p. 25; and Alex R. Seith, "How Democrats Forged Delegate Compromise," *Chicago Sun-Times*, 3 December 1973, p. 46.

17. This concern, however, was not what led to its creation. See the discussion that follows and the treatment of the way in which the Charter Commission handled the issue.

18. Commission on Delegate Selection and Party Structure (Mikulski Commission), *Democrats All* (Washington, D.C.: Democratic National Committee, 6 December 1973), pp. 11–12.

19. See the Democratic Planning Group's *Newsletter*, ed. Alan Baron, no. 17 (15 January 1974).

20. Under the agreement and in addition to the five nominees, each proposed by Mikulski and Strauss, positions were allotted to Mikulski herself, Hatcher, Seith, (the officers of the Commission), and one each to the Democratic governors, United States senators, United States representatives, and the state chairmen.

21. A good review can be found in Jonathan Cottin, "Optimistic Democrats Solving Leftover Disputes, Predict 1974 Gains," *National Journal*, 5 January 1974, pp. 7 ff.

22. The exact provision can be found in *Democrats All*, with relevant commentaries in ibid., and in the Democratic Planning Group's newsletters, especially no. 16 (16 November 1974).

23. *Draft Charter*, p. 3.

24. Ibid.

25. Ibid.

26. Wieck, "Chairman Strauss' Hot Seat," pp. 18–19.

27. See Joseph L. Rauh, Jr., "Applying the Rule of Law to Politics," *Washington Post*, 11 October 1973, editorial page.

28. Strauss strongly believed that federated labor (in particular the AFL-CIO leadership) had to be brought back into active cooperation with the Democratic party to attain a winning and united party. To this end, he supported as many of the Barkan-Meany positions as he could. He also hired a former Barkan lieutenant, Bob Keefe, as deputy chairman of the DNC. Secondly, Strauss felt that elected public officials (and others, like AFL-CIO officials) who represented organized political constituencies should predominate in party councils. Toward this goal, he appointed such representatives to party committees and sided with them on party disputes. The Fort Collins, Colorado, meeting in the summer of 1973 voted to exclude issues from the 1974 midterm convention by the slim margin of 52 to 50. The 26 October 1973 meeting of the Democratic National Committee voted, in something of a reconsideration (at least the door was left open), to hold the midterm conference from 6 to 8 December 1974, to consider the party charter and "such other matters as may be authorized by the Democratic National Committee." The DNC's authority in this regard is debatable, but it had assumed powers throughout this phase of reform. New York State Chairman Joseph Crangle had pushed for the broader wording, and Strauss and the DNC had acquiesced.

29. The Charter Commission had also held the mandatory public hearings—this time eighteen—nationwide. The Kansas City meeting (6 to 8 December 1974) included 2,509 members (2,035 delegates and 474 alternates), a truly extraordinary meeting unprecedented in the party's history.

The references to the charter that follow in the text, including the majority and minority reports, can be found in Democratic Charter Commission, *Draft Charter* (Washington, D.C.: Democratic National Committee, n.d. [1974]). See also the *Proceedings of the Charter Commission*, August 1974.

30. Ibid.

31. For a case study dealing with this issue, see William J. Crotty, "Anatomy of a Challenge: The Chicago Delegation to the Democratic National Convention," in *Cases in American Politics*, ed. Robert L. Peabody (New York: Praeger, 1976), pp. 111–58.

32. The opposition of the Coalition for a Democratic Majority to the following

provisions of the charter gives a fair indication of the conservatives' stand: (1) the authorization for a midterm convention; (2) the Judicial Convention, preferring a return to the old credentials committee procedure; (3) the expansion of affirmative action programs to "all party affairs"; and (4) the mandating of proportional representation.

33. At this stage, O'Hara, who now served as cochairman of the Coalition for a Democratic Majority, was a supporter of and prominent spokesman for federated labor's position.

34. See the Democratic Planning Group's *Newsletter*, no. 23, (1 September 1974), p. 2.

35. Ibid.

36. Labor, however, was not unified in its objectives, for the Meany-Barkan AFL-CIO leadership on these issues was opposed by unions whose positions were more pro-reform. Among these dissenting unions were the United Auto Workers, the American Federation of State, County and Municipal Employees, the Communications Workers, and the Machinists.

37. See the Democratic Charter Commission, *Draft Charter*, and the *Proceedings of the Charter Commission*, August 1974.

38. By any reckoning, the incident was bizarre. Not only was the substitute delegate the wife of an AFL-CIO staff member, but she had been an original staff member of the Mikulski Commission and had been fired by Mikulski. After a bitter series of exchanges among Barkan, Strauss, and Mikulski, she was rehired with full back-pay, one of the less pleasant incidents in the commission's stormy history. The woman next appeared as a last minute delegate to the Charter Commission gathering.

39. See David S. Broder, "Rift Ends Charter Session," *Washington Post*, 19 August 1974; Broder, "Discord among Democrats," *Washington Post*, 21 August 1974; the Democratic Charter Commission, *Draft Charter*; and the *Proceedings of the Charter Commission*, August 1974.

40. For another overview of the party charter, see William J. Crotty, *Political Reform and the American Experiment* (New York: Thomas Y. Crowell, 1977), pp. 247–55.

Chapter Eight

1. See William J. Crotty, *Political Reform and the American Experiment* (New York: Thomas Y. Crowell, 1977), pp. 103–90; and Herbert E. Alexander, *Financing Politics* (Washington, D.C.: Congressional Quarterly, 1976).

2. The challenge is discussed at length in William J. Crotty, "Anatomy of a Challenge: The Chicago Delegation to the Democratic National Convention," in *Cases in American Politics*, ed. Robert L. Peabody (New York: Praeger, 1976), pp. 111–58.

3. Ibid.

4. Ibid.

5. Cases Adjudged in the Supreme Court at October Term, 1974 (beginning of term), *United States Reports*, vol. 419, 9 October 1974 through 22 January 1975. Henry Putzel, Jr., Reporter of Decisions. (Washington, D.C.: U.S. Government Printing Office, 1976), pp. 481–82.

6. Ibid., pp. 482–83.

7. Ibid., p. 487.

8. Ibid., p. 489.

9. Ibid.

10. Ibid., p. 490.

11. As an example, see the Coalition for a Democratic Majority's *Toward Fairness and Unity for '76* (Washington, D.C.: Coalition for a Democratic Majority, n.d.).

12. All states with a Democratic governor and legislature would be required to comply with the new rules, even if this meant changes in the state law. States with Republican governors and legislatures—and New Hampshire specifically qualified here—would not be required to enact the new rules if they demanded statutory modifications (as, of course, a change in the New Hampshire primary would).

13. See Judith A. Center, "1972 Democratic Convention Reforms and Party Democracy," *Political Science Quarterly* 89 (June 1974): 325–50; for examples of the conventional rejoinders and, in answer to her article, Jeffrey L. Pressman and Denis G. Sullivan, "Convention Reform and Conventional Wisdom: An Empirical Assessment of Democratic Party Reforms," *Political Science Quarterly* 89 (Fall 1974): 539–62. For other critical assessments of the reforms, see Coalition for a Democratic Majority (CDM), *Toward Fairness and Unity for '76*; Penn Kemble and Josh Muravchik, "The New Politics and the Democrats," *Commentary* 54, no. 6 (December 1972): 78–84; CDM, *Unity Out of Diversity* (Washington, D.C.: Coalition for a Democratic Majority, n.d.); CDM, *Political Observer* and *CDM Notes*, newsletters published on an irregular basis by the Coalition for a Democratic Majority, in Washington, D.C.; Josh Muravchik, "Looking to '76: The Democrats Divided," *The New Leader* 57, no. 18 (1974): 6–9; Penn Kemble and Josh Muravchik, "Quarrels Over Quotas: 'Balancing' the Democrats," *The New Leader* 58, no. 2 (1975): 7–10; Richard M. Scammon and Ben J. Wattenberg, *The Real Majority* (New York: Coward-McCann, 1970); and Jeane Kirkpatrick, "Representation in the American National Conventions: The Case of 1972," *British Journal of Political Science*, July 1975, pp. 265–322 (also distributed by The Coalition for a Democratic Majority).

The most systematic and penetrating critiques of the reform efforts are provided by Austin Ranney in a series of writings: *Curbing the Mischiefs of Faction* (Berkeley and Los Angeles: University of California Press, 1975); "The Democratic Party's Delegate Selection Reforms, 1968–1976," in *America in the Seventies: Problems, Policies, and Politics*, ed. Allan P. Sindler (Boston: Little, Brown, 1977), pp. 159–206; "Changing the Rules of the Nominating Game," in *Choosing the President*, ed. James David Barber (Englewood Cliffs, N.J.: Prentice-Hall, 1974), pp. 71–93; and *Participation in American Presidential Nominations, 1976* (Washington, D.C.: American Enterprise Institute for Public Policy Research, 1977).

14. Ranney's work probably contains the best statement of this theme. See, in particular, "Democratic Party's Delegate Selection Reforms," pp. 159–206.

15. Hannah F. Pitkin, *The Concept of Representation* (Berkeley and Los Angeles: University of California Press, 1972), p. 214.

The Johns Hopkins University Press

This book was composed in Linotype Times Roman text and Standard bold condensed display type by Maryland Linotype Composition Co., Inc. It was printed on 50-lb. Publishers Eggshell Wove paper and bound in Holliston Roxite cloth by Universal Lithographers, Inc.